T0135286

Springer Series on Cultural Computing

More information about this series at http://www.springer.com/series/10481

Vladimir Geroimenko

Editor

Augmented Reality in Education

A New Technology for Teaching and Learning

 Springer

Editor
Vladimir Geroimenko
Faculty of Informatics
and Computer Science
British University in Egypt (BUE)
Cairo, Egypt

ISSN 2195-9056 ISSN 2195-9064 (electronic)
Springer Series on Cultural Computing
ISBN 978-3-030-42158-8 ISBN 978-3-030-42156-4 (eBook)
https://doi.org/10.1007/978-3-030-42156-4

This Springer imprint is published by the registered company Springer Nature Switzerland AG
The registered company address is: Gewerbestrasse 11, 6330 Cham, Switzerland

This pioneering research monograph is dedicated to future generations of educators.

With sincere gratitude to the British University in Egypt (BUE), a great place to work and write books.

Preface

This book is the first comprehensive monograph to provide thorough and multi-faceted research into the educational use of Augmented Reality (AR), exploring both the conceptual foundations and practical use of the novel teaching and learning technology. It investigates the state of the art in educational Augmented Reality and its usage in a wide variety of particular areas, such as medical education and training, English language education, chemistry learning, environmental and special education, dental training, mining engineering teaching, historical and fine art education. The book aims to provide an essential reading not only for educators of all types and levels, educational researchers and technology developers, but also for students and anyone else who is interested in the educational use of emerging Augmented Reality technology.

It has been written by a virtual team of 58 leading researchers, practitioners and artists, who are pioneering the use of Augmented Reality as a new teaching and learning technology and tool. The book's co-authors—distinguished by their specialist expertise, significant publications and ongoing projects—have been chosen from 15 countries all around the world: Austria, Canada, China, Egypt, Germany, Indonesia, New Zealand, Romania, Serbia, Slovenia, Spain, Sweden, United Arab Emirates, the United Kingdom and the United States.

This book can also be considered as part of a series of the following four pioneering monographs published by Springer on the same subject of Augmented Reality and with the same book editor:

- Augmented Reality Art: From an Emerging Technology to a Novel Creative Medium. Geroimenko, V. (Ed.), 1st Edition: Springer, 2014—314 pp; 2nd Edition, Revised and Updated, Springer, 2018—384 pp.
- Augmented Reality Games I: Understanding the Phenomenon of Pokémon GO. Geroimenko, V. (Ed.), Springer, 2019—256 pp.
- Augmented Reality Games II: The Gamification of Education, Medicine and Art. Geroimenko, V. (Ed.), Springer, 2019—306 pp.
- Augmented Reality in Education: A New Technology for Teaching and Learning. Geroimenko, V. (Ed.), Springer, 2020—ca. 400 pp.

The book's 20 chapters, which can be read in sequence or randomly, are arranged in four parts as follows.

Part I "General Aspects of Educational Augmented Reality" includes six chapters (Chaps. 1–6).

Chapter 1 "Augmented Reality in Education: Current Status and Advancement of the Field" begins with a statement that despite the substantial body of work and positive reported outcomes of Augmented Reality usage for education, researchers claim that compared to other digital technologies such as multimedia and web services for teaching and learning, research in Augmented Reality is still at an early stage, with the majority of studies being short-term one-time experiments with high variability in the effect size. Augmented Reality based applications targeting the educational sector are becoming ever more available, with even low-cost smartphones supporting visualization of Augmented Reality content. Regardless of the fact that the number of downloads of these applications exceeds millions and assuming they are used in the educational settings, we still lack longitudinal reports on how Augmented Reality affects learning outcomes (compared to other technologies). This chapter looks at the current status of Augmented Reality in education from different points of view: widely available technologies, types of Augmented Reality learning experiences for education, capabilities for authoring Augmented Reality, suitable audiences and topics and the status of research on Augmented Reality in education. The chapter summarizes each of these points of view and looks at the possibilities to advance the field.

Chapter 2 "Designing Augmented Reality Applications as Learning Activity" examines the conceptual design of Augmented Reality applications as learning activity with low technical requirements. With the help of the learning activity, the principles of Augmented Reality and of the subject area can be conveyed, and the learners' engagement with the learning content should be stimulated. In this study, bachelor students of civil engineering ($N = 71$) have been assigned the task of designing an Augmented Reality application for the subject domain of technical infrastructures, such as traffic management or energy supply. The students describe the design of the Augmented Reality application with their own photo shot of the technical infrastructure with the augmentation of the photo and an explanatory text of 100–200 words. Combined, these three elements serve as an illustration, which is made available to fellow students in an online gallery for peer review by means of a questionnaire. The peer review is intended both to examine the quality of the contributions—and thus possible learning outcomes among the submitters—and to stimulate the reviewers to engage with Augmented Reality and the subject domain. A subsequent survey evaluates the students' assessment of learning success. Although the study only suggests actual learning outcomes of the learning activity, it demonstrates how complex technologies, such as Augmented Reality, can be integrated into learning contexts with low technical requirements.

Chapter 3 "An Online Platform for Enhancing Learning Experiences with Web-Based Augmented Reality and Pictorial Bar Code" reveals that lack of the teaching materials is one of the common problems of the education system, especially in developing countries. The teachers attempt to give as much theoretical knowledge as possible to students while forgetting to train them with practical activities and ways of self-thinking. Augmented Reality provides the capability to overlay virtual information onto educational textbooks, which makes them more attractive and, hence, motivates students to learn. In this chapter, the authors present an online Augmented Reality study platform that is capable of running on an everyday handset without requiring any software installation. It could provide a stress-free, low-cost, portable and promising solution to use within the educational environment. In addition, they introduce a new transparent Augmented Reality marker concept that could combine the advantages of the original template markers and barcode markers.

Chapter 4 "The Concept of 'Bringing Your Own Device' in Scaffolded and Augmented Education" considers location-based games that provide new opportunities for augmenting the traditional learning space. In a time when most students have their own smartphones, the concept of bringing your own device (BYOD) also seems promising in educational settings. However, playing at random in Augmented Reality environments will not automatically bring curriculum-aligned learning outcomes. This chapter analyzes and discusses how the combination of BYOD and Augmented Reality gaming might be scaffolded to support collaborative curriculum-aligned learning. The overall research strategy was a case study approach with Affordance theory, Social Constructivism and BYOD as theoretical assumptions for deductive analysis. The case units were two outdoor sessions for middle school students with curriculum-aligned assignments in Mathematics and Social Science, solved by playing the Augmented Reality game Pokémon GO. Data have been collected by video recordings of the outdoor sessions with spy glasses and a handheld camera. Results indicate that the Augmented Reality environment stimulates active learning, but that (as with traditional learning) there is a need for scaffolding to achieve the stated learning outcomes.

Chapter 5 "The FeDiNAR Project: Using Augmented Reality to Turn Mistakes into Learning Opportunities" describes FeDiNAR (German acronym for Didactical Use of Errors with the Help of Augmented Reality)—an ongoing project, which focuses on errors as a highly beneficial learning opportunity. The aim of the project is the development and evaluation of an Augmented Reality based learning system with associated learning scenarios in order to make the most efficient use of learners' mistakes for individual competence acquisition. The chapter begins with an introduction of the main educational idea in combination with a selection of didactical theories, schemes and intervention levels. These are used to define the error term for the project. The chapter then illustrates the general setup of the proposed learning system and the technologies involved and continue with its first implementation. The prototype, which includes a range of actuators and sensors, offers many possibilities to define scenarios in which the presented system will be applied. The underlying technological foundation is based on Digital Twins, enabling the use of Augmented Reality for the presented didactical concept. The authors conclude the chapter with the findings available after the first project phase.

In Chap. 6 "Choral Konsult: Augmented Reality for Electrate Learning", the authors revisit 'Miami Virtue: Choragraphy of the Virtual City', the project initiating their collaboration in the Florida Research Ensemble, as a point of departure for updating their project to invent education native to electracy (the digital apparatus). Historically, electracy as an epoch is also characterized as the Anthropocene, identifying a causal force of reality as humanity itself (supplementing previous causalities of God and Nature). Digital technology institutionalized in entertainment corporations threatens total commodification of human visceral appetite (The Matrix). Against this disaster, Konsult as a genre for electrate learning is invented by analogy with the invention of the Dialogue in the Athenian Academies. The Greeks configured a 'stack' based on Aristotle's topical logic (Topos), correlating a systematic relationship among physical places, alphabetic writing technology, the archive of recorded culture, new rhetorical practices and the living memory of students. Benjamin Bratton described the new technological stack (Earth, Cloud, City, Address, Interface, User) of electracy. Choral Konsult reconfigures this stack with an alternative concept of space, chora, also of Greek origin, reanimated in post-structural philosophy. Theorizing the visceral imagination as chora, correlated with the inventions of avant-garde modernist arts as a logic of appetites, choragraphy proposes an Augmented Reality pedagogy to do for human passions what topical logics did for a reason.

Part II "Augmented Reality in Teaching Medicine and Science" comprises of four chapters (Chaps. 7–10).

Chapter 7 "Augmented Reality in Medical Education and Training: From Physicians to Patients" discusses the intersection of Augmented Reality and the education of medical students, physicians, surgeons and patients. For medical students tasked with absorbing a large body of medical knowledge in a short period of time, Augmented Reality technology can help them learn anatomy, view interactions with patients from new perspectives and observe novel procedures alongside their mentors. Physicians and surgeons can continue using the Augmented Reality technology that helped them through medical school as well, particularly for laparoscopic procedures, neurosurgery and cardiology. Augmented Reality technology has also been utilized to guide patients through treatments when they lack access to medical professionals, inform patients about medical procedures and allow patients to educate themselves about their conditions. As Augmented Reality is still in its infancy, this chapter explores its current capabilities as well as potential future applications in medical training and education with respect to both health practitioners and patients.

Chapter 8 "The Usage of Augmented Reality in Dental Education" highlights the issue that dental students must achieve an acceptable level of competence beforehand, since most procedures on teeth are irreversible and therefore learning these skills solely on patients is not acceptable. Simulation allows students to repeat procedures until they demonstrate required levels of skills, without putting actual patients at risk and yet acquiring procedural competence. In line with advances in technology, dental simulations are being developed to support the acquisition of necessary psychomotor skills before actual clinical applications. This chapter considers the use of Augmented Reality as one of the most sophisticated methods of simulation.

Chapter 9 "The Development of Augmented Reality Applications for Chemistry Learning" studies the use of Augmented Reality technology in chemistry education. It begins with the definition and analysis of components, working principles and steps in making Augmented Reality media and supporting applications for the chemistry teaching and learning process. The proposed Augmented Reality system consists of three parts: computers, head-mounted displays and markers. The chapter explores the use of Augmented Reality technology in the field of chemistry teaching and learning, including the concepts of crystal structure, molecular geometry, molecular chirality and molecular hybridization.

Chapter 10 "Mixed Reality Books: Applying Augmented and Virtual Reality in Mining Engineering Education" deals with the integration of Augmented and Virtual Reality (AR/VR) elements into academic mining education. The focus lies on the didactical approach within the EU-funded MiReBooks (Mixed Reality Books) project. The project aims to develop a series of AR- and VR-based interactive mining manuals as a new digital standard for higher education across European engineering education. By combining AR and VR technologies, it is possible to address current challenges in mining education in an innovative way. These virtual applications should make otherwise impossible and dangerous situations accessible to students. Classical paper-based teaching materials are enriched with Augmented Reality content and translated into pedagogically and didactically coherent manuals for integrative use in the classroom. The authors explore how AR and VR instruments can be effectively integrated into teaching. The results of a broad evaluation of AR/VR-based lectures are presented and discussed in the chapter. The experiences and findings are summarized in a decision matrix for the use of AR/VR-based technologies in teaching.

Part III "Educational Augmented Reality in Humanities and Art" consists of six chapters (Chaps. 11–16).

Chapter 11 "Beyond Historical Books, Names and Dates: Leveraging Augmented Reality to Promote Knowledge, Reasoning, and Emotional Engagement" points out that despite the relative popularity of history amongst mobile Augmented Reality apps, there is a lack of theory-driven empirical research and instructional design. The chapter describes a program of research that contributes to addressing these gaps by examining the ability of a location-aware mobile app and accompanying tour guide protocols to foster historical knowledge, historical reasoning and emotional engagement. The authors briefly introduce mobile location-aware apps before describing the theoretical frameworks that informed their instructional design, methodological decisions and interpretations of findings. Next, they describe the mobile Augmented Reality app used in their research in two empirical studies. The chapter ends with implications for future research, including connections with current and additional research carried out with different mobile Augmented Reality apps: DiscoverUofU and the Edmonton Queer History App.

Chapter 12 "Design and Implementation of Augmented Reality for English Language Education" shows a major gap in previous research on mobile Augmented Reality. As previous studies relied on the case study approach to verify the effectiveness of various mobile technologies and Augmented Reality products, they were often lacking a strong theoretical support, such as frameworks and models. Against this backdrop, this chapter first reviews mainstream language learning theories, and then examine recent studies of Augmented Reality in English language education. Then, it introduces three existing Augmented Reality design frameworks in the mobile learning context, aiming to offer theoretical insights into designing and learning technology-enhanced language learning tasks. The chapter concludes with design and learning principles for language teachers so as to promote the integration of the novel Augmented Reality technology into English language education.

Chapter 13 "Iberian Cultures and Augmented Reality: Studies in Elementary School Education and Initial Teacher Training" explores the opportunities of integrating Augmented Reality applications into elementary school education in Spain. The proposed approach was centred on the exploration of figures through Augmented Reality devices—the group work was focused on pre-Roman artworks trying to identify their characteristics. The authors have also applied this approach to higher education, namely to the initial teacher training in Castilla-La Mancha University, Spain. They concluded that the approach brings curiosity and satisfaction to the students, and also enhance their motivation because of its active and collaborative nature.

Chapter 14 "The Educational Use of the 'Harry Potter: Wizards Unite' Augmented Reality Application" focuses on a new location-based Augmented Reality game inspired by J. K. Rowling's wizarding world and the Harry Potter franchise. Players are able to actively explore real-world surroundings to unravel a global mystery, cast spells and encounter fantastic beasts and iconic characters along the way. But how could 'Harry Potter: Wizards Unite' be applied in the educational system? In this chapter, the authors address the possible impact of the creation of Augmented Reality on those players within the educational framework, as well as some practical proposals for its adaptation and possibilities as a didactical tool.

Chapter 15 "Making Inside the Augment: Augmented Reality and Art/Design Education" investigates the developing genre of Augmented Reality Design from architecture to fine arts. Although a great deal of literature exists in this area within the architectural field, this chapter seeks to delve into more holistic approaches to the use of Augmented Reality in art and design. This engages the HCI-based issues of handheld devices compared to headset (HoloLens, Magic Leap) technologies in terms of the author's theory of immersive gesture. Differences between these platforms, as well as Augmented Reality's distinctions from other immersive media, offer insights into the development of pedagogical models in the creative disciplines. Of particular interest is the use of Augmented Reality in Design Education, allowing future possibilities for hybrid models of creative expression, like augmented overlays on physical models/artworks, to the use of Augmented Reality as a tool in material work. The chapter aims to look at the current literature, draw inferences through analyzing case studies on how educational models are being constructed through the theory of gesture and consider models for the use of these technologies in improving the creative disciplines.

Chapter 16 "The Romantic App: Augmented Reality in Fine Art Education" presents 'The Romantic App'—an ongoing project in the School of the Art Institute of Chicago. It is a custom application for smartphones or tablets made especially for the nineteenth and twentieth-century paintings of the European Painting and Sculpture wing in the Art Institute of Chicago. Art Institute students designed and executed The Romantic App in the Fall semester of 2015, with a second iteration produced in Spring 2019. It is intended both as a teaching vehicle but also as artwork, allowing young people to engage collaboratively with mentors from another time and period. Augmented Reality was chosen as a medium for this project because it functions in parallel to the grand painting tradition of the nineteenth century—that moment when photography had its first dizzying impact on Parisian culture. Like so many of the optical viewing devices of that époque, The Romantic App also reveals illusions and phantasmagoria hidden beneath the surface of the visible world. When the app is open, one can glimpse visions and optical illusions through the interface of a device, integrated into a curated selection of paintings scattered throughout the Museum. Using one's phone as a kind of magical mirror or optical lens, users are encouraged to examine individual paintings, to see hidden animations, enactments and other kinds of moving pictures subtly mixed into their surfaces.

Part IV "Augmented Reality in Environmental and Special Education" contains four chapters (Chaps. 17–20).

Chapter 17 "Augmented Reality for Outdoor Environmental Education" indicates that designing technologically-enhanced learning activities for environmental education is particularly challenging because they often take place in informal settings and outdoors, for example, through field trips or visits to parks. The chapter discusses the potential of Augmented Reality for outdoor environmental education. It provides a brief overview of learning theories that promote learning in context, describes a number of illustrative examples of Augmented Reality mobile apps for environmental education, and analyzes the purpose and forms of digital augmentations in the context of environmental education.

Chapter 18 "Augmented Reality in Environmental Humanities Education" introduces environmental humanities—an emerging multidisciplinary field of research focused on identifying the impact of modern human (including cultural) activities on the environment, as well as of environmentally-friendly solutions. Environmental damage can have serious consequences for the present, as well as for the past, as in the case of archaeological sites, whose investigation becomes difficult and whose process of decay is accelerated. As these issues have not yet been addressed through effective and systematic educational solutions, this chapter proposes (as part of the environmental humanities strategy) digital humanities educational solution centred on the technology of Augmented Reality. The IT application proposed aims to identify the areas of ecological risk and provide detailed information on the destruction processes, as well as the ability to connect with networks of specialists. The authors' aims are to stimulate critical thinking focused on environmental issues provide a solution for continuous learning for both specialists and the public, thus contributing to the protection of the environment and of archaeological subjects, and to further the development of sustainable activities through education and awareness.

Chapter 19 "Interacting Across Contexts: Augmented Reality Applications for Developing the Understanding of the Anthropocene" starts with a statement that Augmented Reality provides new ways that humans can engage with the world. The affordance of Augmented Reality to mediate human–environment relationships addresses some major challenges people face in understanding the idea of the Anthropocene, which refers to the current geological stage of our planet, where human impact is the dominant force. This is important because being aware of how human activities change the planet is constructive to building the human–environment relation that is sustainable for the future. As a result, with the growing popularity of mobile Augmented Reality applications, pioneering designs in the last decade attempt to integrate Augmented Reality with the Anthropocene. The chapter presents a systematic review of these Augmented Reality applications guided by qualitative content analysis methods. Results indicate that Augmented Reality creates multiple learning opportunities across contexts for understanding the Anthropocene based on particular forms of interaction. Implied in these interactions are two major approaches (exploration and creation) that the designers adopted to engage users with the theme context of the Anthropocene. The findings of the review can inform the future design of Augmented Reality applications that mediate more meaningful interactions with the Anthropocene.

Chapter 20 "Alaskan Timeosaurs and Interplanetary Human Spaghetti: A Regional Look at Augmented Reality in Special Classrooms" looks at how Augmented Reality has been used as an enrichment activity in special education and other classrooms in Alaska, with a regional focus, including the integrating of Indigenous knowledge. Examples of integrated Augmented Reality enrichments and Indigenized replacement curriculum for special education with a critical examination of the way that third party educational programs are permeating the educational system, creating less regional diversity, in lieu of standardization. Examples of differentiated education in Augmented Reality artist Nathan Shafer's Peer Art program, part of the Structured Learning Classroom (a classroom for students on the autism spectrum) at Wendler Middle School in Anchorage, Alaska, are anecdotally examined, with an emphasis on ways to use Indigenous thinking over top of special education programs such as Social-Emotional Learning, Social Stories and Social Thinking. Specific analysis of the Dena'ina Athabascan notion of 'evil' in their storytelling traditions is overlaid on the way Structured Learning classrooms develop routines to help students on the autism spectrum negotiate their school days.

Finally, we hope that the reader will not judge us (the book's editor and co-authors) too harshly. We have accepted the challenge of being the first, and we have done our best to bring out this pioneering work on the use of Augmented Reality in Education. Please just go ahead and read the monograph. We hope sincerely that you will enjoy it.

Cairo, Egypt   Vladimir Geroimenko

Contents

Contributors

Anas Abdelrazeq Institute of Information Management in Mechanical Engineering (IMA), RWTH Aachen University, Aachen, Germany

Alexander Atanasyan Institute for Man-Machine Interaction, RWTH Aachen University, Aachen, Germany

Jannicke Baalsrud Hauge BIBA—Bremer Institut für Produktion und Logistik GmbH, Bremen, Germany;
Royal Institute of Technology, Södertälje, Sweden

Christine A. Campisi Division of Developmental and Behavioral Pediatrics, Steven and Alexandra Cohen Children's Medical Center of New York, New York, USA

Torben Cichon Institute for Man-Machine Interaction, RWTH Aachen University, Aachen, Germany

McKay Colleni Department of Mechanical and Aerospace Engineering, Utah State University, Logan, UT, USA

Klen Čopič Pucihar Faculty of Mathematics, Natural Sciences and Information Technologies, University of Primorska, Koper, Slovenia;
Faculty of Information Studies (FIŠ), Novo Mesto, Slovenia

Ramon Cozar-Gutierrez Faculty of Education, Universidad de Castilla-La Mancha, Albacete, Spain

John Craig Freeman Emerson College, Boston, USA

Lea Daling Institute of Information Management in Mechanical Engineering (IMA), RWTH Aachen University, Aachen, Germany

Julie Ducasse Faculty of Mathematics, Natural Sciences and Information Technologies, University of Primorska, Koper, Slovenia

Markus Ebner Educational Technology, Graz University of Technology, Graz, Austria

Martin Ebner Educational Technology, Graz University of Technology, Graz, Austria

Sofia Eriksson Bergström Department of Education, Mid Sweden University, Sundsvall, Sweden

Ida Farida Department of Chemistry Education, UIN Sunan Gunung Djati, Bandung, Indonesia

Vladimir Geroimenko Faculty of Informatics and Computer Science, The British University in Egypt, Cairo, Egypt

Dragoş Gheorghiu Doctoral School, National University of Arts, Bucharest, Romania;
Earth and Memory Institute (ITM), Quaternary and Prehistory Group of the Geosciences Centre, Coimbra, Portugal

Marvin Goppold Institute of Industrial Engineering and Ergonomics, RWTH Aachen University, Aachen, Germany

Chayse Haldane Department of Educational Psychology, University of Alberta, Edmonton, Alberta, Canada

Jason M. Harley Department of Surgery, McGill University, Montreal, Quebec, Canada;
Research Institute of the McGill University Health Centre (RI-MUHC), Montreal, Quebec, Canada;
Department of Educational Psychology, University of Alberta, Edmonton, Alberta, Canada;
Institute for Health Sciences Education, McGill University, Montreal, Quebec, Canada;
Department of Educational and Counselling Psychology, McGill University, Montreal, Quebec, Canada

Claudia Hart Department of Film, Video, New Media and Animation, School of the Art Institute of Chicago, Chicago, IL, USA

Ferli Septi Irwansyah Department of Chemistry Education, UIN Sunan Gunung Djati, Bandung, Indonesia

Jimmy Jaldemark Department of Education, Mid Sweden University, Sundsvall, Sweden

David E. Jimenez Division of Developmental and Behavioral Pediatrics, Steven and Alexandra Cohen Children's Medical Center of New York, New York, USA

Matjaž Kljun Faculty of Mathematics, Natural Sciences and Information Technologies, University of Primorska, Koper, Slovenia;
Faculty of Information Studies (FIŠ), Novo Mesto, Slovenia

Dennis Kobelt Laboratory for Industrial Engineering, University of Applied Sciences and Arts Ostwestfalen-Lippe, Lemgo, Germany

Christopher Kommetter Educational Technology, Graz University of Technology, Graz, Austria

Susanne P. Lajoie Institute for Health Sciences Education, McGill University, Montreal, Quebec, Canada;
Department of Educational and Counselling Psychology, McGill University, Montreal, Quebec, Canada

Huy Le School of Engineering, Computer & Mathematical Sciences, Auckland University of Technology, Auckland, New Zealand

Elizabeth H. Li Division of Developmental and Behavioral Pediatrics, Steven and Alexandra Cohen Children's Medical Center of New York, New York, USA

Patrick Lichty College of Arts and Creative Enterprises, Zayed University, Dubai, United Arab Emirates

Breanne K. Litts Department of Instructional Technology and Learning Sciences, Utah State University, Logan, UT, USA

Sebastián López-Serrano Faculty of Humanities and Educational Sciences, Group HUM-943: Physical Activity Applied to Education and Health, University of Jaen, Jaen, Spain

Emilio J. Martínez-López Faculty of Humanities and Educational Sciences, Group HUM-943: Physical Activity Applied to Education and Health, University of Jaen, Jaen, Spain

Dian Sa'adillah Maylawati Department of Informatics, UIN Sunan Gunung Djati, Bandung, Indonesia

Brea McLaughlin Department of Educational Psychology, University of Alberta, Edmonton, Alberta, Canada

Ruth L. Milanaik Division of Developmental and Behavioral Pediatrics, Steven and Alexandra Cohen Children's Medical Center of New York, New York, USA

Rasa Mladenovic Faculty of Medicine, Department for Dentistry, University of Pristina, Kosovska Mitrovica, Serbia

Mihaela Moțăianu National University of Arts, Bucharest, Romania

Peter Mozelius Department of Computer and System Science, Mid Sweden University, Östersund, Sweden

Minh Nguyen School of Engineering, Computer & Mathematical Sciences, Auckland University of Technology, Auckland, New Zealand

Efa Nur Asyiah Department of Chemistry Education, UIN Sunan Gunung Djati, Bandung, Indonesia

Eric G. Poitras Department of Educational Psychology, University of Utah, Salt Lake, Utah, USA

Muhammad Ali Ramdhani Department of Informatics, UIN Sunan Gunung Djati, Bandung, Indonesia

Alberto Ruiz-Ariza Faculty of Humanities and Educational Sciences, Group HUM-943: Physical Activity Applied to Education and Health, University of Jaen, Jaen, Spain

Jose-Manuel Saez-Lopez Faculty of Education, UNED, Spanish National University of Distance Education, Madrid, Spain

Michael Schluse Institute for Man-Machine Interaction, RWTH Aachen University, Aachen, Germany

Nathan Shafer Structured Learning Classrooms, Anchorage School District, Anchorage, Alaska, USA;
Wintermoot Shared Universe, Anchorage, Alaska, USA

Heinrich Söbke Bauhaus-Institute for Infrastructure Solutions (b.is), Bauhaus-Universität Weimar, Weimar, Germany

Livia Ştefan Bucharest, Romania

Sara Suárez-Manzano Faculty of Humanities and Educational Sciences, Group HUM-943: Physical Activity Applied to Education and Health, University of Jaen, Jaen, Spain

Marcus Sundgren Department of Education, Mid Sweden University, Sundsvall, Sweden

Gregory L. Ulmer University of Florida, Gainesville, USA

Minjuan Wang Learning Design and Technology, San Diego State University, San Diego, USA

Mario Wolf Bauhaus-Institute for Infrastructure Solutions (b.is), Bauhaus-Universität Weimar, Weimar, Germany

Junjie Gavin Wu Department of English, City University of Hong Kong, Hong Kong, China

Lili Yan Department of Instructional Technology and Learning Sciences, Utah State University, Logan, UT, USA

Danyang Zhang Faculty of Education, University of Cambridge, Cambridge, UK; School of Foreign Languages, Shenzhen University, Shenzhen, China

Part I
General Aspects of Educational Augmented Reality

Chapter 1
Augmented Reality in Education: Current Status and Advancement of the Field

Matjaž Kljun, Vladimir Geroimenko and Klen Čopič Pucihar

Abstract Despite the substantial body of work and positive reported outcomes of AR (Augmented Reality) usage for education, researchers claim that compared to other digital technologies such as multimedia and web services for teaching and learning, research in AR is still at an early stage, with the majority of studies being short-term, one-time experiments with high variability in the effect size. AR-based applications targeting the educational sector are becoming ever more available with even low-cost smartphones supporting visualization of AR content. Regardless of the fact that the number of downloads of these applications exceeds millions, and assuming they are used in educational settings, we still lack longitudinal reports on how AR affects learning outcomes (compared to other technologies). This chapter looks at the current status of AR in education from different points of view: widely available technologies, types of AR learning experiences for education, capabilities for authoring AR, suitable audiences and topics, and the status of research of AR in education. The chapter summarizes each of these points of view and looks at the possibilities to advance the field.

M. Kljun (✉) · K. Čopič Pucihar
Faculty of Mathematics, Natural Sciences and Information Technologies,
University of Primorska, Koper, Slovenia
e-mail: matjaz.kljun@upr.si

K. Čopič Pucihar
e-mail: klen.copic@famnit.upr.si

Faculty of Information Studies (FIŠ), Novo Mesto, Slovenia

V. Geroimenko
Faculty of Informatics and Computer Science, The British University in Egypt, Cairo, Egypt
e-mail: vladimir.geroimenko@bue.edu.eg

© Springer Nature Switzerland AG 2020
V. Geroimenko (ed.), *Augmented Reality in Education*,
Springer Series on Cultural Computing,
https://doi.org/10.1007/978-3-030-42156-4_1

3

1.1 Introduction

Asking educators across the globe to develop an Augmented Reality Learning Experience (ARLE) might still illicit a questioning expression on their faces (Tinti-Kane and Vahey 2018). This despite the fact that these technologies have already been vastly explored and analyzed in the contexts of teaching and learning (Bacca et al. 2014; Koutromanos et al. 2015; Lee 2012; Muñoz 2017; Santos et al. 2013a; Weerasinghe et al. 2019; Wu et al. 2013) and a simple Google Scholar search sprung up more than half a million results for the term 'education augmented reality'.

Through AR, students can develop important practices and literacies that cannot (or are hard to) be developed and enacted in other technology-enhanced learning environments (Squire and Jan 2007). The body of work in this area has revealed several advantages (Santos et al. 2013a) such as (i) availability of desirable naive physics provided by AR affordances (Hornecker 2012), (ii) positive impacts on cognitive load and motivation (Cheng 2017) as well as on spatial abilities (Martín-Gutiérrez et al. 2010), (iii) positive effects on the collaborative experience (Alhumaidan et al. 2018; Gomez 2003) (iv) ease in visualizing complex spatial relationships and abstract concepts (Arvanitis et al. 2009), (v) the possibility to experience phenomena that are hard or not possible to experience in the real world (Klopfer and Squire 2008) and (vi) positive effects on learning outcomes (Weng et al. 2019).

Regardless of the substantial body of work and reported positive outcomes, some researchers maintain that 'compared to studies of other more mature technologies in education (e.g. multimedia and web-based platforms), research of AR applications in education is in an early stage, and evidence of the effects of AR on teaching and learning appears to be shallow' (Wu et al. 2013). Other researchers supported this by revealing a high variability of the effect size between different studies (Santos et al. 2013a). The individual studies of AR systems in academic literature also appear to be just one-time, short experiments (Prieto et al. 2014). Muñoz argues that the research community needs to collaborate with educators in order to progress the field (Muñoz 2017, p. 32) and move from these short-term to longitudinal in-the-wild studies that would measure the effects in the long run.

We also have no official data as to how many schools, educators or institutions are using AR as an addition to their lessons or training. One way to infer this might be from the number of downloads of AR-based educational applications in digital distribution platforms such as the Apple App Store and Google Play. Google Expedition, which is one of the most widespread and affordable AR and VR educational applications, providing hundreds of AR 3D models, currently exceeds one million installs in Google Play[1] alone. There are several others and even if not focused on the education they might still be used for teaching and learning (see e.g. Bertrand et al. 2018) for the use of mobile applications demonstrating war-affected places for learning empathy).

---

[1]Google Play store: Google Expeditions. https://play.google.com/store/apps/details?id=com.goog le.vr.expeditions&hl=en.

In order to move away from 'shallow' evidence, to study the effects of AR on education in the long run and advance the body of research in the field we need to (i) better understand the needs of the research community on one side and educators on the other, (ii) bring these two communities together and consequently (iii) support longitudinal in-the-wild studies. To better understand the current state of affairs and outline a possible future direction we are going to explore the current status and direction of the developments by looking at the available data from academic literature, advancements in technology and anecdotal evidence.

In the next section, we will first look at the available off-the-shelf technologies, followed by the section about AR Learning Experiences (ARLE). Section four discusses the authoring of AR content, section five looks at suitable audiences and topics, and section six covers research aims and the theoretical basis of ARLE. The chapter will finish with a summary of how all described concepts fit together to advance knowledge in the field.

1.2 Technologies

The AR Software Development Kits (SDK) have been evolving rapidly in the past two decades and have been available to a wider community since the ARtoolkit was released in 1999[2] (Kato and Billinghurst 1999). Among others, both major players in the mobile platform's market, Apple and Google, have recently released their AR SDKs (ARKit[3] and ARCore[4] respectively) and paved the way for a plethora of AR applications in their digital distribution platforms.

AR for education has also experienced recent investments from the corporate world. For example, in 2017 Google released the AR Expeditions[5] application offering a low-cost AR classroom experience with currently over 100 different study materials. All students need is a phone that supports either ARCore or ARKit and the application installed on their phones (see Fig. 1.1). However, it is also possible to run non-native AR in a web browser, be it on a smartphone, tablet or personal computer with WebAR technologies.[6] All Android-based phones from version 6 (currently 74%[7] of all Android devices) and all iOS from version 11 (currently over 91%[8] of iPhones) support WebAR, which covers a vast array of devices.

With evermore phones supporting AR SDKs to run native AR applications and phones supporting WebAR in all price range the use of AR in education might

---

[2]Wikipedia. ARToolKit. https://en.wikipedia.org/wiki/ARToolKit.

[3]Apple ARKit. https://developer.apple.com/augmented-reality/arkit/.

[4]Google ARCore. https://developers.google.com/ar/.

[5]Google. Bring your lessons to life with Expeditions. https://edu.google.com/products/vr-ar/expeditions/.

[6]Create WebXR. Augmented reality on the web. https://www.createwebxr.com/webAR.html.

[7]Android developers. Distribution dashboard. https://developer.android.com/about/dashboards.

[8]Apple store. Support: Apple Developer. https://developer.apple.com/support/app-store/.

Fig. 1.1 An example of Google AR Expeditions AR learning content—The Roman Colosseum

become more widespread. The availability of SDKs, WebAR and the omnipresence of smartphones makes them the current AR platform of choice. This is also supported by the literature—the majority of AR applications surveyed in the last decade have been implemented on smartphones (Muñoz 2017, p. 28; Koutromanos et al. 2015; Krevelen and Van Poelman 2010; Pucihar and Kljun 2018; Weerasinghe et al. 2019).

In 2015 Google started testing their VR headsets and Expeditions application in several schools across six U.S. states (California, Illinois, New York, New Jersey, Connecticut, Texas) and later in Brazil, Australia, New Zealand and the UK as a part of the Expeditions Pioneer Program (Protalinski 2015; Pierce 2016). It was estimated that they reached more than two million pupils over a period of two years. Regardless, a 2016 survey by Samsung USA found that among 1000 K-12 educators in the USA only 2% used VR in their classrooms and a 2018 survey of 115 educators revealed that the adoption of VR and AR technologies is hindered by the lack of resources to buy appropriate hardware and software and the lack of training (Tinti-Kane and Vahey 2018). The schools might dive into AR either by providing their own devices (e.g. mobile phones or a projector) or by allowing students to use their own devices (e.g. if a 'bring your own device' (BYOD) policy is in place).[9]

However, phones are just one of the devices capable of delivering AR content. Other off-the-shelf devices that experienced considerable investments from the corporate sector include head-mounted AR displays such as MicrosoftHoloLens[10] and

---

[9]Whether bringing the devices to school is acceptable or not and the discussion about possible consequences related to the (prolonged) use of smartphones (either at home or at school) by younger children and teenagers is beyond the scope of this chapter.

[10]Microsoft HoloLens. https://www.microsoft.com/en-us/hololens/.

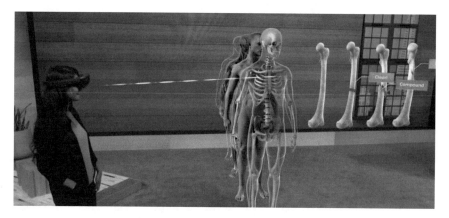

Fig. 1.2 The human anatomy viewed through HoloLens (CWRU 2017)

Magic Leap.[11] Education-wise, these head-mounted displays are targeting the professional market and tertiary students in various fields such as healthcare learners with immersive simulation-based training in ultrasound and anatomy (Healthcare IT Today 2017), medical students (see Fig. 1.2) with an interactive digital human anatomy curriculum (Vassallo et al. 2017), or astronomy enthusiasts with an educational application about the Milky Way (Microsoft 2018). The price range of these is currently tenfold that of the cheapest smartphones supporting AR SDKs. However, it is expected that these technological solutions will become more affordable in the future.

1.3 AR Learning Experience

In order to frame Augmented Reality Learning Experiences (ARLE) we can look at the related fields of e-learning and m-learning. One of the fundamental concepts in these fields is a learning object (LO) (Friesen 2005). Although definitions of learning objects vary greatly, the understanding in this work is that they are any digital resource that can be (re)used to support learning (Wiley 2000). They can have several components such as content, learning activities and elements of context (Williams 2004; Laverde et al. 2007). Willey (2000) taxonomy divides them into five different groups based on their characteristics:

- Fundamental: an uncombined individual digital resource (content only).
- Combined-Closed: a small number of combined but not individually accessible digital resources.
- Combined-Open: a larger number of combined but also directly accessible digital resources.

---

[11]Magic Leap. https://www.magicleap.com/.

- Generative-Presentation: fundamental and combined digital resources coupled with logic and structure.
- Generative-Instructional: generative-presentation digital resources coupled with evaluating interactions, created to support the instantiation of abstract instructional strategies (content, context, learning activities and evaluation).

AR content is just a digital resource that can be a part of a learning object also called ARLO (Santos et al. 2013b). In addition to the above taxonomy, we can take into account how ARLOs engage users, which spans from passive consumption of AR content to active creation of AR content represented on the user engagement continuum (Kljun et al. 2019).

An example of a fundamental ARLO is the aforementioned Colosseum example from Fig. 1.1, which is a stand-alone AR model to be explored and manipulated. The Google Expeditions application provides various AR (animated) 3D models that educators can incorporate into their lessons but does not provide any additional content, context, guidance or didactical approaches that could be used with a particular content. A more complex example is AR books that provide individual 3D AR models of the content that is available in the 2D form on pages (Billinghurst 2002; Kljun et al. 2019)—these models are interlinked with the content of the book and cannot be considered purely as fundamental ARLOs. All such AR models usually allow only passive consumption.

An example of a combined ARLO is a guided tour of a city that includes a collection of ordered or unordered (AR and non-AR) resources (Lochrie et al. 2013) one can explore when on a city tour. When we start to incorporate a variety of activities, assessments, services, game elements (such as challenges, points, badges, leader-boards, performance graphs, signs of progress, meaningful stories, avatars, teammates, role-playing, etc.) we move to the generative side of the ARLOs spectrum.

The generative ARLOs representing an activity or lesson are the ones that are usually explored in academic literature (Nilsson et al. 2012). There are also various classifications of generative ARLOs such as the one from Wu and her colleagues (Wu et al. 2013) who divided AR educational applications into role-based (Squire and Jan 2007; Dunleavy et al. 2009; Viinikkala et al. 2014), location-based (Lochrie et al. 2013; Rosenbaum et al. 2007) and task-based (Laine and Suk 2016; Rogers et al. 2015), increasing engagement, contextualization and authenticity respectively. These categories are not exclusive and they often overlap.

The level of complexity of the design and implementation of AR applications rises when we move from fundamental (stand-alone content only) to generative-instructional full-blown ARLOs as shown in Fig. 1.3. The complexity depends on what an ARLO includes such as the complexity of the structure, logic and evaluating elements, the complexity and size of the problem environment (e.g. difficulty of tasks to be solved, the amount of tasks), the amount of fundamental and combined AR resources, the amount of game elements (roles, tasks, badges, scores, etc.), the inclusion of collaboration with co-located students, the amount of location-based elements, the amount of active involvement in the creation of new content, etc.

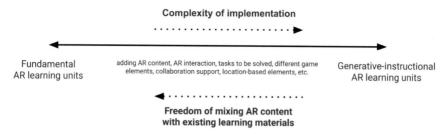

Fig. 1.3 The continuum on which the complexity of application implementation rises from fundamental to generative AR learning objects while the freedom of incorporating AR content into existing lessons drops

There are advantages and disadvantages of fundamental versus generative AR learning objects when it comes to integrating them into a wider context of the curriculum (see Table 1.1). One of the differences between them is how much freedom is left to educators to build a lesson around an AR learning object since the fundamental content can be easily mixed with the existing teaching materials. Opposite to the level of complexity, the level of freedom drops when we move from fundamental to generative-instructional ARLOs as seen in Fig. 1.3.

The advantage of generative AR learning objects is that educators can take them and use them on their own to cover a specific learning objective. These objects take students more time to finish and cover more content but they also give less freedom to educators to implement one's changes into the activity or lesson(s). As we will discuss later, the complexity of ARLOs requires software development skills (Bacca et al. 2014) in order to implement changes (if code is even available and open source).

Several AR games are location-based and need to be played at a particular location such as Astrid's steps (Nilsson et al. 2012) that is played in the Astrid Lindgren's World theme park in Sweden, which makes it impractical for much of the world. Similar are the majority of outdoor-based AR applications in Weerasinghe et al.

Table 1.1 Advantages and disadvantages of fundamental versus generative AR learning objects

	Advantages	Disadvantages
Fundamental AR object	– Freedom to incorporate it into existing lessons and mix it with existing materials – Easy to design, create and implement (e.g. photogrammetry)	– Hard to link AR objects into the wider context of user's surroundings
Generative AR object	– Ready to be used on its own with the whole activity or lesson covered – Cover more content	– Less freedom to mix it with existing materials – Location-based AR objects are not portable – Hard to design and implement – Hard to implement changes

(2019) and Muñoz (2017, p. 187), and applications in the chapter 'Augmented Reality for outdoor environmental education'.

Another matter is how to link AR content to the user's surroundings. Most of the fundamental AR objects can be viewed anywhere. For example, the Expeditions application allows users to display an animation of an atom over a desk and there is no connection between the atom and the surroundings; the atom is shown on its own and no other object in the surroundings relates to it (similar to the Colosseum in Fig. 1.1). As such the object loses two of the three advantages of AR—contextual visualization and real-world annotation, while it retains vision-haptic visualization (Santos et al. 2013a). If users were capable of linking various AR objects in space that would start to interact (e.g. each user has their own atom shown in AR and they are able to join them into a molecule) then this would give them a context in space (similar to how they might do it with physical models of atoms). An ARLO that takes advantage of users' location has the potential to be linked into the surroundings such as showing certain AR content only at a certain location that is relevant to it; however, this is also more difficult to the author.

1.4 Authoring AR Content

Based on all the available off-the-shelf technologies presented above, one would assume that authoring AR content is easy. This is currently true for simple fundamental AR content.

To envision the near future of authoring AR content we can take a look at the current state of authoring VR content as AR will likely follow a similar path. After the release of Expeditions in 2015, Google started to build a community around it and invited educators to contribute their own VR (Virtual Reality) learning materials.[12] They made readily available different tools such as applications to create photo spheres or 360 panoramas with smartphones[13] and Google Poly platform[14] that allows users to easily create, share and access panoramas with added multimedia. Educators can, for example, create virtual journeys with multiple linked photospheres and in each of the photospheres, students are able to read additional text explanations and open photos or play videos placed within. There are currently over 900 such readily available VR journeys,[15] which could be described as generative-presentation learning objects. However, the Poly platform lacks the capability to incorporate additional learning activities (e.g. questionnaires) and game design elements (e.g. collecting points). It is nevertheless possible to expand Poly journeys if

---

[12] See for example TES Global. https://www.tes.com/resources/search/?q=%23Googleexpeditions.

[13] The panoramas can be viewed with a low cost VR headset Google Cardboard viewer. https://arvr.google.com/cardboard/.

[14] Google Poly platform to upload, manage and distribute 3D content. https://poly.google.com/.

[15] Google's list of VR Expeditions. https://docs.google.com/spreadsheets/d/1uwWvAzAiQDueKXkxvqF6rS84oae2AU7eD8bhxzJ9SdY/edit#gid=0.

Fig. 1.4 An example of a gamified Google Poly VR journey. Top left is a map of the trail with all locations of the VR journey; the top centre is the current question, the answer to which is hidden in the panoramic image below; top right is the badges that users collect by answering the questions correctly. Users move from one location to another and try to explore the panorama, answer questions and collect badges

one has software development skills as was for example done for the Škocjan caves educational trail[16] visible in Fig. 1.4 (Jesenko et al. 2019).

Google recently started to add AR content into their Poly platform and encourages the teaching community to build up the materials as they did with the VR. One way to create fundamental AR is stereophotogrammetry that allows reconstruction of real objects from multiple 2D photos (see Fig. 1.5). This can be achieved with several apps available for smartphones (e.g. SCANN3D[17] for Android or Scandy Pro 3D Scanner[18] for iOS) as well as with special sensors (e.g. Structure IO[19] or MS Kinect) coupled with desktop software (e.g. Skanect).[20] The research community is also exploring different ways to support users in this process (e.g. Andersen et al. 2019 or see Bot and Irschick 2019 for a more detailed description of the available software and techniques). Besides Google Poly, other online platforms support uploading, sharing

---

[16]Virtual tour of the Škocjan caves educational trail. https://skocjan.hicuplab.com/. YouTube video: https://youtu.be/ExoGTohXvt8.

[17]SCANN3D application for Android. https://play.google.com/store/apps/details?id=com.smartmobilevision.scann3d&hl=en.

[18]Scandy Pro 3D Scanner application for iOS. https://apps.apple.com/us/app/scandy-pro/id138028223?ls=1.

[19]Structure IO sensor. https://structure.io/.

[20]Skanect 3D scanning software from Windows and macOS. https://skanect.occipital.com/.

Fig. 1.5 Left: a 3D model of a real thatched barn created with stereophotogrammetry. Right: the barn used to create a 3D model

and viewing of 3D models such as Sketchfab.[21] These 3D models can be converted into fundamental AR experiences by using one of several WebAR platforms that allow users to experience AR right from the web browser.

It is thus relatively easy to create simple fundamental AR content. However, the development and implementation of more complex generative ARLOs are still in the domain of software developers Bacca et al. (2014), which is also confirmed by the recent study where the majority of surveyed AR educational applications are 'exclusively engineered by low-level programmers/designers' (Muñoz 2017, p. 32). This is not to say that there have been no attempts to formalize the authoring of ARLOs (Santos et al. 2013b) and attempts to create authoring tools for AR learning experiences (Medlock-Walton 2012; Wojciechowski and Cellary 2013; Camba and Contero 2015; Park 2011). Muñoz (2017, p. 34) surveyed over 20 AR authoring applications proposed and observed by the research community. However, the degrees of ease-of-use, accessibility, effectiveness and efficiency vary a lot (Muñoz 2017, p. 34).

Tools to create generative AR learning objects are likely to evolve into more usable products for a wider community. However, the community needs to work towards formalization and standardization of AR learning objects in order to increase discoverability, reusability and interoperability. Since we took a stance that ARLOs are learning objects containing AR content, the community can base their authoring tools on already existing standards developed by the e-learning community (Del Blanco et al. 2013). For example, thexAPI (or Experience API) standard, the successor of SCORM,[22] covers novel learning experiences including mobile learning, serious games, simulations and blended learning experiences mixing digital and real objects, and is already used for authoring ARLOs (Rodrigues et al. 2017).

It is worth mentioning that with more user-friendly ARLO-authoring software the inverse relationship between freedom of mixing AR content with existing learning materials and complexity of implementation might disappear. With user-friendly

---

[21] Sketchfab online library of AR and VR content. https://sketchfab.com/.

[22] SCORM Explained 201: A deeper dive into SCORM. https://scorm.com/scorm-explained/.

authoring tools supporting xAPI, educators should be capable of adapting existing ARLOs to a variety of subjects and contexts and tailor them to their needs.

1.5   The Audience and Topics

The research of AR in education most often focuses on formal education that includes pre-school, primary, secondary and tertiary levels. Weerasinghe and her colleagues revealed that the majority of 30 studies surveyed were conducted with primary school students (56.6%), followed by high school students (20%) and undergraduate students (6.7%), while one game targeted special education (Weerasinghe et al. 2019). The review made by Muñoz (2017) also revealed that the majority of the applications support primary (26%), followed by lower secondary (13%) and upper secondary education (10%). Interestingly, 20% of surveyed applications were studied with master's students, while only 5% with undergraduate students and 5% with doctoral students.

The results are very similar to the age groups targeted by the TES community,[23] which is currently the biggest open repository of lesson plans for primary and secondary education. Only 3% of the plans that include the Expeditions application are designed for pre-school education, while 10% are targeting early primary, 24% late primary, 29% lower secondary and 22% upper secondary students. The remaining 11% are designed for 16+ students. Muñoz argues that AR's didactic and experimental nature makes it easier to introduce in elementary education rather than higher education (Muñoz 2017, p. 31).

However, in the survey of 32 studies completed by Bacca et al. (2014) the majority of AR educational apps were targeting undergraduate students (34%) followed by primary school (19%) and lower secondary school students (18%); while none were listed in pre-school, master's and doctoral categories. This shows how different sets of surveyed AR studies (e.g. focusing on AR games or augmented paper only) produce different results. Nevertheless, all these studies of various ARLOs show that AR is suitable for all age groups in formal education.

Some surveyed applications do not target any particular age group or the age group is not mentioned. For example, the majority of the AR applications used by museums and tourist sites to inform users about art and natural and cultural heritage do not target any specific age group (Pucihar and Kljun 2018). These applications belong to the category of informal learning.

In professional settings, the practicality of AR assistance for industrial maintenance has long been advocated (Lee 2012). In sectors such as military, manufacturing and other industries 'AR competitively thrives and expands the scope of the technology itself' (Lee 2012). For example, in a study (Henderson and Feiner 2009) focusing on the military sector, the military mechanical staff could conduct their

---

[23]Tes lesson plans including the use of Expeditions application. https://www.tes.com/resources/se arch/?q=%23Googleexpeditions.

routine maintenance tasks more safely and conveniently with the assistance of AR. In manufacturing, BMW is known to have been investing in AR and VR for over a decade now. A recent report revealed that they currently use Google Glass Enterprise Edition[24] in their Production academy in training sessions for engine assembly units (Green car report 2019). Interestingly, the reports about evaluations of participants' learning success have shown that there are no differences in quality compared to conventional training courses. Moreover, the company developed their own authoring tool and is claiming that setting up new training programmes for other screw joint processes should be quick and easy, which additionally confirms that such authoring tools will also become available for other areas. AR for professional training has also been explored for example in Hořejší (2015), Boulanger (2004), Besbes et al. (2012). However, the majority of AR usage in industry is used as a means to support staff in their complex and technical work environments and not for training—see Fraga-Lamas et al. (2018) and Rankohi and Waugh (2013) for a review and Kothari (2017) for a general overview of Glass usage in the industry.

As with a vast variety of audiences, surveys have also identified a variety of topics that AR learning objects have covered so far. Science was reported as mostly investigated by all the reviews (Bacca et al. 2014; Koutromanos et al. 2015; Muñoz 2017, p. 31; Santos et al. 2013a; Sommerauer and Müller 2018; Weerasinghe et al. 2019) including subjects such as biology, chemistry and physics. Other topics include mathematics, history, language learning, psychology, humanities and arts, agriculture, health, engineering and so on.

1.6   The Status of ARLE Research

Studies of individual AR applications as well as reviews try to classify them into various teaching and learning paradigms, theories, models and activities. Weerasinghe et al. (2019) classified 30 educational AR games and found that they were designed based on several learning models: 43% as challenge-based learning, followed by situated learning (20%) and experiential learning (17%). In addition to these models, educational AR games are also designed upon scaffolding (7%), problem-based (7%), collaborative (3%) and contextual (3%) learning models. A chapter 'Augmented Reality for outdoor environmental education' in this book also categorized AR applications for outdoor learning based on whether they support situated learning, place-based learning or experiential learning. In addition, the author emphasizes the prevalence of inquiry-based approach in place-based learning. The results also coincide with a survey of 36 AR applications (Sommerauer and Müller 2018) that classified 78% of these under the constructivism learning paradigm (situated learning, game-based learning and simulations, experiential learning, etc.) followed by 19% classified under the cognitivism (cognitive theory of multimedia learning, embodied cognitive dissonance theory, etc.). Learning theories were also used to explain

---

[24]Google Glass Enterprise Edition: https://www.google.com/glass/start/.

the effectiveness of AR, in particular multimedia, experiential learning and animate vision learning theory (Muñoz 2017, p. 32).

Fundamental AR Learning Objects (ARLOs) hardly support learning theories on their own. As mentioned in previous sections, with fundamental ARLOs educators have all the freedom to mix ARLOs with other materials and thus have the freedom to base their teaching on a variety of paradigms, theories, models and activities, while for the AR content that already takes part in the application, such as educational games (Klopfer 2008), the models are already predefined.

In Weerasinghe et al. (2019) the authors argue that the reason why challenge-based learning is mostly used in educational AR games may be related to the compensations of gamification and game-based learning. Their results also show that possible game genres for situated learning can be a simulation or role-playing games. And these game genres relate to the practice, immersion and imitation of learning activities. At the same time, it shows that the possible game genres for experiential learning can be adventure or treasure hunt games that relate to the practice and interaction learning activities. Similar results can be found in Rapeepisarn et al. (2008) on the relationship between learning techniques, learning activities and possible game genres, as well as in the already mentioned classification of AR learning software into role-, location- and task-based Wu et al. (2013). The later classification does not focus on games only, but it is clear that the AR software exhibiting role-, location- and task-based activities rely on game elements as well.

Despite the fact that surveyed AR educational applications were based on various extents of learning paradigms and models, the majority of them were exclusively developed by software engineers (Muñoz 2017, p. 32; Bacca et al. 2014). Only in 18% of 30 surveyed applications did the development teams include educators, while none of the applications were exclusively authored by educators (Muñoz 2017, p. 32). The situation is the same for AR applications that are used for informal learning. The survey of 86 AR applications on art and cultural heritage exposed that several of them are just fact giving, do not allow communication and personalization and have poor support for analytical and sensual activities (Pucihar and Kljun 2018). It is safe to conclude that educators have not been involved in the development of these AR experiences.

Notwithstanding the fact that the majority of AR applications have been studied and positive outcomes reported, current evidence appears to be 'shallow' (Wu et al. 2013). This claim is also supported by Prieto et al. (2014) that revealed 'that comparatively few studies provide evidence about the learning effects of system usage, or perform evaluations in authentic setting conditions. The analysis [...] also highlights the need for further longitudinal, in-the-wild studies and the existence of design tensions that make the conception, implementation and appropriation of this kind of systems still challenging'. The importance of the inclusion of educators in the design and implementation of AR technologies for learning has been stressed numerous times. For example, Prieto and colleagues argued that inclusion can foster the appropriation in in-the-wild scenarios and allow for longitudinal studies to be carried out (Prieto et al. 2014).

Appropriating ARLOs in educational practice requires an interdisciplinary approach that considers learning theory, pedagogy and instructional design (Santos et al. 2013b). Appropriation of ARLOs by educators is also important since authoring ARLOs needs time and effort, and similarly to other digital and non-digital learning objects, there is only a later advantage of becoming a permanent and re-usable learning resource (Yuen et al. 2011). An interdisciplinary approach is also needed if we would like to produce more in-depth knowledge into the effects of AR on teaching and learning. The research community, including AR researchers as well as researchers in the field of educational research, should work with educators and help in setting up and supporting ARLO environments that could be used for longitudinal studies. For example, simply helping educators to include fundamental ARLOs (e.g. using the Expeditions application or authoring AR content with photogrammetry) into their lessons, would allow the community to study the long-term effects of AR on teaching and learning.

1.7 Conclusion

In order to advance the body of knowledge of long-term AR effects on educational outcomes, the research community should consider the concepts described in this chapter. For each, we tried to look at the current trends, what is available off-the-shelf to educators and what is discussed by the research community. We will summarise each of these below.

Technologies: When planning to design an Augmented Reality Learning Object (ARLO), researchers together with educators need to take into consideration how the content will be presented to students based on what technology is available at hand or what can be procured. Mobile AR on phones has become very accessible in past years with both major mobile OS players investing in their own AR SDKs. Even more, smartphones support WebAR, which enables a plethora of devices to run AR in a browser. However, the adoption of AR technologies relies also on training educators to use these technologies. The research community needs to step in and support educators in familiarizing themselves with the technologies and revealing the possibilities besides discussing possible research plans.

AR learning experiences: The complexity of these spans from simple fundamental objects to be viewed and manipulated on their own to generative-instructional learning objects containing different types of interactions, various game elements (Weerasinghe et al. 2019), the number of tasks to be solved, collaborative interaction, location-based elements, contextually visualized AR content with the surroundings (Santos et al. 2013a), passive or active engagement (Kljun et al. 2018), etc. The complexity of development rises when we move from fundamental to more complex generative ARLEs, while the freedom of using existing learning materials and the ease of adapting the ARLE drops in the same direction. For the appropriation of ARLE by educators, researchers need to discuss their needs and requirements and the desired complexity of ARLE in relation to the existing learning materials and practices. This is especially needed if we would like to study long-term effects immediately. In the long run, we need authoring tools as described below.

Authoring AR content: Simple fundamental AR Learning Objects (ARLOs) are available in various applications for smartphones. It is also easy to create simple 3D models of real objects based on photogrammetry. Developing more complex AR learning experiences requires software development skills (Bacca et al. 2014). The easy-to-use authoring tools are still not available although there have been some attempts in this direction. In order to increase discoverability, reusability and interoperability of ARLOs, the authoring tools should take standardization into account and one possible candidate is Experience API (xAPI). With easy-to-use authoring tools educators will have complete freedom to adapt ARLEs and appropriation is more likely to materialize. Collaboration between researchers, developers and educators is also needed to create usable authoring ARLOs tools based on the previously mentioned needs, requirements and current practices as well as the available resources (programmers, time, money).

The audience and topics: The overview of several reviews have shown that AR has been studied in educational settings on all levels of formal education for all sorts of topics (Bacca et al. 2014; Muñoz 2017; Weerasinghe et al. 2019). AR has also been used in informal education, for example by museums, galleries and tourist sites (Pucihar and Kljun 2018). AR is thus suitable for all types of learning and all age groups, which makes it easy to decide on based on educators' needs and requirements.

ARLO research: AR is well situated in and explained by learning theories and models. However, the evidence about the learning effects seems to be shallow (Wu et al. 2013). The majority of ARLEs studied by the research community did not have educators involved in the planning and designing process (Muñoz 2017). There is a clear need for researchers developing AR learning experiences to start collaborative research activities with researchers in educational sciences as well as educators in order to support their needs and requirements, which will encourage them to appropriate ARLOs in their lessons.

The importance of collaboration between communities has been stressed by several researchers. Wu and her colleagues also emphasized that 'the educational value of AR is not solely based on the use of technologies but closely related to how AR is designed, implemented and integrated into formal and informal learning settings' (Wu et al. 2013). Without the collaboration, the design step might not be optimal and without support, the integration and implementation into the lessons might not happen. Collaboratively discussing all the above-described concepts needs to take place in order to create meaningful ARLEs for all stakeholders involved in the process from the design, development and implementation to longitudinal research. Only if ARLEs are meaningful to educators by supporting their needs, requirements and available technologies will they use them in the long run. Consequently, this will help researchers set research goals and enable them to conduct longitudinal in-depth studies that will give concrete evidence of the effects of AR on teaching and learning.

If we draw the comparison with recent past developments with VR research, there is anecdotal evidence that the Google VR Expeditions was prototyped and tested extensively with teachers and students in schools around the world (Waismann

2016). It is also currently being studied long term in several U.S. primary schools by researchers[25] (Cheng et al. 2018). It is safe to assume that AR technologies will follow if we take the right steps.

Acknowledgements The authors acknowledge the European Commission for funding the InnoRenew CoE project (Grant Agreement 739574) under the Horizon 2020 Widespread-Teaming program and the Republic of Slovenia (Investment funding of the Republic of Slovenia and the European Union of the European Regional Development Fund). The research was also supported by the Slovenian research agency ARRS (P1–0383 and J1–9186).

References

Alhumaidan H, Lo KPY, Selby A (2018) Co-designing with children a collaborative augmented reality book based on a primary school textbook. Int J Child-Comput Interact 15:24–36

Andersen D, Villano P, Popescu V (2019) AR HMD Guidance for Controlled Hand-Held 3D Acquisition. IEEE Trans Visual Comput Graph 25(11):3073–3082

Arvanitis TN, Petrou A, Knight JF, Savas S, Sotiriou S, Gargalakos M, Gialouri E (2009) Human factors and qualitative pedagogical evaluation of a mobile augmented reality system for science education used by learners with physical disabilities. Pers Ubiquit Comput 13(3):243–250

Bacca J, Baldiris S, Fabregat R, Graf S (2014) Augmented reality trends in education: a systematic review of research and applications. Educ Technol Soc 17(4):133–149

Bertrand P, Guegan J, Robieux L, McCall CA, Zenasni F (2018) Learning empathy through virtual reality: multiple strategies for training empathy-related abilities using body ownership illusions in embodied virtual reality. Front Robot AI 5:26

Besbes B, Collette SN, Tamaazousti M, Bourgeois S, Gay-Bellile V (2012) An interactive augmented reality system: a prototype for industrial maintenance training applications. In 2012 IEEE international symposium on mixed and augmented reality (ISMAR), 2012, November. IEEE, pp 269–270

Billinghurst M (2002) Augmented reality in education. New Horiz Learn 12(5):1–5

Bot JA, Irschick DJ (2019) Using 3D photogrammetry to create open-access models of live animals: 2D and 3D software solutions. In: The academic library: emerging practices and trends, p 54

Boulanger P (2004) Application of augmented reality to industrial tele-training. In: 2004 Proceedings of first Canadian conference on computer and robot vision. IEEE, pp 320–328

Camba JD, Contero M (2015) From reality to augmented reality: rapid strategies for developing marker-based AR content using image capturing and authoring tools. In: 2015 IEEE frontiers in education conference (FIE). IEEE, pp 1–6

Cheng BH, D'Angelo C, Zaner S, Kam M, Hamada RA (2018) Teaching and learning using virtual reality: identifying and examining two design principles of effective instruction. Int Soc Learn Sci [ISLS]

Cheng KH (2017) Reading an augmented reality book: An exploration of learners' cognitive load, motivation, and attitudes. Australas J Educ Technol 33(4)

CWRU Case Western Reserve University (2017) CWRU takes the stage at Microsoft's Build conference to show how HoloLens can transform learning. https://case.edu/hololens/. Retrieved 6 Nov 2019

Del Blanco Á, Marchiori EJ, Torrente J, Martínez-Ortiz I, Fernández-Manjón B (2013) Using e-learning standards in educational video games. Comput Stand Interf 36(1):178–187

---

[25]CIRCL. Virtual Reality in Educational Settings. https://circlcenter.org/events/cyberlearning-2017/expertise-exchanges/vr/.

Dunleavy M, Dede C, Mitchell R (2009) Affordances and limitations of immersive participatory augmented reality simulations for teaching and learning. J Sci Educ Technol 18(1):7–22

Fraga-Lamas P, Fernández-Caramés TM, Blanco-Novoa Ó, Vilar-Montesinos MA (2018) A review on industrial augmented reality systems for the industry 4.0 shipyard. IEEE Access 6:13358–13375

Friesen N (2005) Interoperability and learning objects: An overview of e-learning standardization. Interdiscip J E-Learn Learn Objects 1(1):23–31

Gomez H (2003) Parent and child reading, designing for an interactive, dimensional reading experience. In: Proceedings of technology for interactive digital storytelling and entertainment

Green Car Congress (2019) BMW Group production leveraging virtual reality and augmented reality applications, 12 April 2019, BioAge Group. https://www.greencarcongress.com/2019/04/20190412-bmwarvr.html. Retrieved 6 Nov 2019

Healthcare IT Today (2017) CAE Healthcare announces first mixed reality ultrasound simulation solution with Microsoft HoloLens, January 27, 2017 https://www.healthcareittoday.com/2017/01/27/cae-healthcare-announces-first-mixed-reality-ultrasound-simulation-solution-with-microsoft-hololens/. Retrieved 6 Nov 2019

Henderson SJ, Feiner S (2009) Evaluating the benefits of augmented reality for task localization in maintenance of an armored personnel carrier turret. In 2009 8th IEEE international symposium on mixed and augmented reality. IEEE, pp 135–144

Hořejší P (2015) Augmented reality system for virtual training of parts assembly. Proc Eng 100:699–706

Hornecker E (2012) Beyond affordance: tangibles' hybrid nature. In: Proceedings of the sixth international conference on tangible, embedded and embodied interaction. ACM, pp 175–182

Jesenko T, Čopic Pucihar K, Kljun M (2019) Gamification of the virtual tour to the Skocjan Caves Educational Trail using mobile technologies and photospheres. In: Proceedings of the human-computer interaction in information society HCI-IS 2019, Ljubljana, Slovenia

Kato H, Billinghurst M (1999) Marker tracking and HMD calibration for a video-based augmented reality conferencing system. In: Proceedings 2nd IEEE and ACM international workshop on augmented reality (IWAR'99). IEEE, pp 85–94

Kljun M, Pucihar KČ, Coulton P (2018) User engagement continuum: art engagement and exploration with augmented reality. In: Augmented reality art. Springer, Cham, pp 329–342

Kljun M, Pucihar KČ, Alexander J, Weerasinghe M, Campos C, Ducasse J, Čelar M (2019) Augmentation not duplication: considerations for the design of digitally-augmented comic books. In: Proceedings of the 2019 CHI conference on human factors in computing systems. ACM, p 103

Klopfer E (2008) Augmented learning: research and design of mobile educational games. MIT Press

Klopfer E, Squire K (2008) Environmental detectives—the development of an augmented reality platform for environmental simulations. Educ Technol Res Dev 56(2):203–228

Kothari J (2017) A new chapter for glass. Medium, The Team at X, 2017, July 18. https://blog.x.company/a-new-chapter-for-glass-c7875d40bf24

Koutromanos G, Sofos A, Avraamidou L (2015) The use of augmented reality games in education: a review of the literature. Educ Media Int 52(4):253–271

Laine TH, Suk HJ (2016) Designing mobile augmented reality exergames. Games Cult 11(5):548–580

Laverde AC, Cifuentes YS, Rodriguez HYR (2007) Toward an instructional design model based on learning objects. Educ Tech Res Dev 55(6):671–681

Lee K (2012) Augmented reality in education and training. TechTrends 56(2):13–21

Lochrie M, Čopič Pucihar K, Gradinar A, Coulton P (2013) Time-wARpXplorer: creating a playful experience in an urban time warp. Phys Digital Games Play

Martín-Gutiérrez J, Saorín JL, Contero M, Alcañiz M, Pérez-López DC, Ortega M (2010) Design and validation of an augmented book for spatial abilities development in engineering students. Comput Graph 34(1):77–91

Medlock-Walton MP (2012) TaleBlazer: a platform for creating multiplayer location-based games (Doctoral dissertation, Massachusetts Institute of Technology)

Microsoft (2018) Galaxy explorer: you shared your ideas. We're sharing the code. https://docs.mic rosoft.com/en-us/windows/mixed-reality/galaxy-explorer. Accessed 6 Nov 2019

Muñoz T (2017) Supporting technology for augmented reality game-based learning (Doctoral dissertation, Universitat de Girona, Departament d'Arquitectura i Tecnologia de Computadors)

Nilsson S, Arvola M, Szczepanski A, Bång M (2012) Exploring place and direction: mobile augmented reality in the Astrid Lindgren landscape. In: Proceedings of the 24th Australian computer-human interaction conference. ACM, pp 411–419

Park JS (2011) AR-Room: a rapid prototyping framework for augmented reality applications. Multimedia Tools Appl 55(3):725–746

Pierce D (2016) 3D technologies add another dimension to learning. J Transform Educ Technol 43(1):9–10

Prieto LP, Wen Y, Caballero D, Dillenbourg P (2014) Review of augmented paper systems in education: an orchestration perspective. J Educ Technol Soc 17(4):169–185

Protalinski, E (2015) 100,000 students and counting: Google brings VR kits to schools in 15 more cities. VB Venture Beat. https://venturebeat.com/2015/11/09/100000-students-and-counting-go ogle-brings-vr-kits-to-schools-in-15-more-cities/. Accessed 10 Nov 2019

Pucihar KČ, Kljun M (2018) ART for art: augmented reality taxonomy for art and cultural heritage. In: Augmented reality art. Springer, Cham, pp 73–94

Rankohi S, Waugh L (2013) Review and analysis of augmented reality literature for construction industry. Vis Eng 1(1):9

Rapeepisarn K, Wong KW, Fung CC, Khine MS (2008) The relationship between game gen-res, learning techniques and learning styles in educational computer games. In: International conference on technologies for E-learning and digital entertainment, pp 497–508. Springer, Berlin

Rogers K, Frommel J, Breier L, Celik S, Kramer H, Kreidel S, Schrader C (2015) Mobile augmented reality as an orientation aid: a scavenger hunt prototype. In: 2015 International conference on intelligent environments. IEEE, pp 172–175

Rodrigues AB, Dias DRC, Martins VF, Bressan PA, de Paiva Guimarães M (2017) WebAR: a web-augmented reality-based authoring tool with experience API support for educational applications. In: International conference on universal access in human-computer interaction. Springer, Cham, pp 118–128

Rosenbaum E, Klopfer E, Perry J (2007) On location learning: Authentic applied science with networked augmented realities. J Sci Educ Technol 16(1):31–45

Santos MEC, Chen A, Taketomi T, Yamamoto G, Miyazaki J, Kato H (2013a) Augmented reality learning experiences: Survey of prototype design and evaluation. IEEE Trans Learn Technol 7(1):38–56

Santos MEC, Yamamoto G, Taketomi T, Miyazaki J, Kato H (2013b) Authoring augmented reality learning experiences as learning objects. In 2013 IEEE 13th international conference on advanced learning technologies. IEEE, pp 506–507

Sommerauer P, Müller O (2018) Augmented reality for teaching and learning-a literature review on theoretical and empirical foundations. In: ECIS

Squire KD, Jan M (2007) Mad City Mystery: developing scientific argumentation skills with a place-based augmented reality game on handheld computers. J Sci Educ Technol 16(1):5–29

Tinti-Kane H, Vahey P (2018) xR in EDU Survey 2018: Benchmarking Adoption Trends in K12 and Higher Education. Report series, EdTech Times

Van Krevelen DWF, Poelman R (2010) A survey of augmented reality technologies, applications and limitations. Int J Virtual Reality 9(2):1–20

Viinikkala L, Heimo OI, Korkalainen T, Mäkilä T, Helle S, Pönni V, Lehtonen T (2014) The Luostarinmäki adventure–an augmented reality game in an open-air museum. Engaging SpacES 231

Waismann C (2016) Virtual Reality promise: a contemporary version of "The Emperor's new clothes"? EdTech Mindset: your must-have educational guide to the future. https://www.min dcet.org/

Weerasinghe M, Quigley A, Ducasse J, Pucihar K Č, Kljun M (2019) Educational augmented reality games. In: Augmented reality games II. Springer, Cham, pp 3–32

Weng C, Rathinasabapathi A, Weng A, Zagita C (2019) Mixed reality in science education as a learning support: a revitalized science book. J Educ Comput Res 57(3):777–807

Wiley DA (2000) Connecting learning objects to instructional design theory: A definition, a metaphor, and a taxonomy. Instr Use Learn Objects 2830(435):1–35

Williams R (2004) Context, content and commodities: e-learning objects. Electron J e-Learn 2(2):305–312

Wojciechowski R, Cellary W (2013) Evaluation of learners' attitude toward learning in ARIES augmented reality environments. Comput Educ 68:570–585

Wu HK, Lee SWY, Chang HY, Liang JC (2013) Current status, opportunities and challenges of augmented reality in education. Comput Educ 62:41–49

Yuen SC, Yaoyuneyong G, Johnson E (2011) Augmented reality: an overview and five directions for AR in education. J Educ Technol Dev Exch 4(1)

Chapter 2
Designing Augmented Reality Applications as Learning Activity

Mario Wolf, Heinrich Söbke and Jannicke Baalsrud Hauge

Abstract This chapter examines the conceptual design of AR applications as a learning activity with low technical requirements. With the help of the learning activity, the principles of AR and of the subject area can be conveyed, and the learners' engagement with the learning content should be stimulated. In this study, Bachelor students of civil engineering ($N = 71$) have been assigned the task of designing an AR application for the subject domain of technical infrastructures, such as traffic management or energy supply. The students describe the design of the AR application with an own photo shot of the technical infrastructure with the augmentation on the photo and an explanatory text of 100–200 words. Combined these three elements serve as an illustration, which is made available to fellow students in an online gallery for peer review by means of a questionnaire. The peer review is intended both to examine the quality of the contributions—and thus possible learning outcomes among the submitters—and to stimulate the reviewers to engage with AR and the subject domain. A subsequent survey evaluates the students' assessment of learning success. Although the study only suggests actual learning outcomes of the learning activity, it demonstrates how complex technologies, such as AR, can be integrated into learning contexts with low technical requirements.

M. Wolf (✉) · H. Söbke
Bauhaus-Institute for Infrastructure Solutions (b.is), Bauhaus-Universität Weimar, Weimar, Germany
e-mail: ulrich.mario.wolf@uni-weimar.de

H. Söbke
e-mail: heinrich.soebke@uni-weimar.de

J. Baalsrud Hauge
BIBA—Bremer Institut für Produktion und Logistik GmbH, Bremen, Germany
e-mail: baa@biba.uni-bremen.de; jmbh@kth.se

Royal Institute of Technology, Södertälje, Sweden

© Springer Nature Switzerland AG 2020
V. Geroimenko (ed.), *Augmented Reality in Education*,
Springer Series on Cultural Computing,
https://doi.org/10.1007/978-3-030-42156-4_2

2.1 Introduction

In light of the fast technological development in the past years, Augmented Reality (AR) has become a mature technology for the exchange of information and communication (Ludwid and Reiman 2005; Rauschnabel et al. 2019; Schmalstieg and Höllerer 2016). The central idea is, that an environment experienced by users is sensory enriched by additional information (Azuma 1997). In Milgram's Reality-Virtuality Continuum spanning from real to completely virtual environment, AR is positioned in the middle of the spectrum since it is not replacing but instead broadening the real environment (Milgram et al. 1994). According to Azuma (1997), AR is defined by three characteristics: the combination of real and virtual objects; the appearance of images interactively and in real time; and the registering (aligning) of real and virtual objects with each other. Originally used for military, industrial and medical applications, AR can be found in entertainment, architecture, tourism, marketing and more today (Aukstakalnis 2016; Schart and Tschanz 2015; Schmalstieg and Höllerer 2016). Among others, Furth (2011) points to education being a field of application for AR. The range reaches from early childhood education and primary education (Castellanos and Pérez 2017) via secondary to higher education (Burkhard and Schmitt 2009). Although further research is required, studies indicate the advantages of AR applications in educational settings. For example, studies suggest that learners remember impressions and experiences longer from AR-based settings than from settings using conventional educational media, such as presentations (Sommerauer and Müller 2014), therefore AR might improve cognitive abilities (Telefónica 2011). AR might increase the motivation of students in learning situations resulting in improved academic results (Di Serio et al. 2013; Wei et al. 2015). A systematic analysis of the advantages of AR is presented by Akçayır and Akçayır (2017) and categorizes the advantages of AR in educational settings in learner outcomes, pedagogical contributions, interactions and others. Further, in his meta-study, Radu (2014) points at increased content understanding, long-term memory retention, improved physical task performance, improved collaboration and increased student motivation as major advantages. Further meta-studies (Hantono et al. 2018; Karakus et al. 2019; Khoshnevisan and Le 2018; Petrovich et al. 2018; Sommerauer and Müller 2018; Wen and Looi 2019), empirical studies (Dorribo-Camba and Contero 2013; Söbke et al. 2018; Vafa 2018) and theoretical studies (Tomara and Gouscos 2014) underline the relevance of AR in education.

Despite the advantages, AR can hardly be considered as an established learning tool in educational settings. This is related to the number of disadvantages and challenges, including the design, implementation and operation of AR applications hampering integration into learning environments (Akçayır and Akçayır 2017; Radu 2014; Zender et al. 2018). Thus, if students are assigned the task of designing AR applications, students might be capable of conceptualizing scenarios in their field but might miss sufficient knowledge on computer science limiting the creativity and the creation process. Another barrier is related to the link between technical requirements and design: Users need to have access to appropriate mobile devices such as smartphones, tablets or head-mounted display and the educational institutions need to provide the necessary IT infrastructure including mobile internet and data servers, which can be quite costly and time-consuming. In addition, the design and implementation of AR applications requires high interdisciplinary efforts.

Starting from the notion that the implementation and operation of AR applications require advanced technical skills and complex technical infrastructure and are a barrier to the use of AR applications in educational settings, this study examines to what extent the design of AR applications can be used as a learning activity.

The process of learning is subject to various theories, that can amongst others be distinguished into instructivist and constructivist approaches (Huitt 2013). While instructivist approaches such as behaviourism state that learning is determined by analyzing and reinforcing behaviour comprising repetitions and provided feedback (Skinner 1976), constructivist approaches base on Piaget's work on cognitive development (1964) and focus on explorative and interactive approaches. Related to Piaget's constructivism is the learning theory of constructionism (Ackermann 2001; Papert and Harel 1991); describe constructionism as actively 'building knowledge structures' and learning to learn. Papert (1987) states: "The word constructionism is a mnemonic for two aspects of the theory of science education underlying this project. From constructivist theories of psychology, we take a view of learning as a reconstruction rather than as a transmission of knowledge. Then we extend the idea of manipulative materials to the idea that learning is most effective when part of an activity the learner experiences as constructing a meaningful product." Following, the main traits of constructionist models are, that students might learn by making tangible or experienceable objects coordinated by a guided collaborative process that also incorporates peer feedback (Roffey et al. 2016).

In the past years, constructivist and constructionist traits imposed the development of maker education. As a kind of constructionism (Katterfeldt et al. 2015), maker education is based on the maker movement, which represents a growing group of hobbyists, tinkerers, engineers, hackers and artists focusing on the creation of objects for constructive and creative purposes (Martin 2015). Amongst others, González-González and Arias (2018) refer to the following characteristics of the maker movement: 'a culture based on technology and doing things yourself' resulting from the need to create and innovate related to real problems, supporting innovation by making prototypes. The maker movement is not driven economically but by passion for collaborative work and sharing ideas, further it 'promotes learning in less structured environments'. Embedding these ideas, maker education aims at fostering maker skills, such as creativity, imagination, engineering and problem solving, among learners through making in educational settings (Stager 2014). Due to the promising advantages for learners, approaches to integrate maker education in formal educational settings are increasingly welcomed (Taylor 2016). In such settings, maker education is seen as an approach transforming the way of thinking about pedagogy and learning (Kafai 1996; Kafai and Burke 2015; Kurti et al. 2014).

This study explores the potentials of a maker-based approach in a conceptual learning activity in order not to limit design reflections by technical constraints. The aim is to understand, to what extent a theoretical, non-technical and conceptual but nevertheless, active maker-related activity carried out by students using AR can lead to learning among students at the university level. By focusing on the analogous creation and not on the actual usage of an AR application, the study particularly refers to the challenges of design. In order to not hamper the creativity of students, the study is based on low technical requirements on the side of students as well as the educational institution and does not require any specific knowledge in the field of computer science. Furthermore, it incorporates the central ideas of the maker movement. The learning activity in the study is initiated by three educational elements: (a) an idea contest encouraging students to critically analyze the existing infrastructures regarding its functionality, current challenges as well as common work routines and procedures of engineers, (b) creating an entry point to AR that needs to be independently worked on meeting certain formal standards, and (c) reviewing submissions supporting students to conduct structural evaluations. Therefore, the study can be understood as a learning activity with low technical entry hurdles to create learning opportunities for students in the field of infrastructure development using the medium of AR.

The remainder of the chapter is structured as follows: in the next section, the scope and design of the study conducted are depicted. In section three, the results of the study are presented and in section four discussed. Finally, conclusions are drawn.

2.2   Scope, Study Design and Experimental Set-Up

The study has been conducted evaluating the introductory course *Infrastructure Development—Waste, Energy,* Transportation *and Water Management* at Bauhaus-Universität Weimar during the summer term 2019. The course objectives are to achieve a general understanding of technical infrastructure systems as well as to foster interest. Lectures introduce topics like transportation, water supply, wastewater disposal, energy supply and waste disposal and treatment. The course is compulsory for students of the Bachelor's program *Civil Engineering (Construction, Environment, Building Materials)* and the Bachelor's program *Management (Building, Real Estate, Infrastructure).* The students participating ($N = 71$) were mainly in their 4th semester of the regular three years of undergraduate programs. The students possess basic theoretical knowledge about infrastructural development, however, only a few could rely on practical experience gained through training, internships or similar activities. The learning activity to be examined must be successfully completed by each student for being admitted to the final examination. Admission to the final examination requires the submission of an augmented and commented photo and participation in the peer review. These rather formal hurdles have been successfully met by all participants who submitted a photo. For four participants, however, a second attempt was necessary, as the picture submitted first did not fulfill the formal requirements, e.g. not addressing AR and was rejected by the lecturers. To prevent students from relying on the possibility of a second attempt, the second attempt is coupled with an increased degree of participation in the peer review: Students, who need a second attempt are required to review ten submissions instead of two submissions.

The learning activity comprised of three sub-activities, which are given as follows:

Creation of an augmented photo Students were asked to create a photo depicting a self-chosen technical infrastructure system or specific elements of it. Assuming the photo was a live-picture on a mobile device, such as smartphone or tablet, students had to add supplementing, in the real-world invisible information in form of augmentation, having in mind the goal of supporting engineering tasks. Subterranean infrastructures such as pipes for water supply or wastewater disposal, measured values for fine dust, energy consumption and indicators for traffic density served as examples for such information. Students were instructed not to let their ideas be restricted by the current technical state of the art. Also, students could select a tool of their preference for editing the photo, such as a business presentation program. Furthermore, it was required to write a text of 100–200 words explaining the setting, the role of augmentation and how far it supports engineers in fulfilling their tasks. In this way, the photo together with the text can be regarded as a conceptual prototype of an AR application. Two examples of the submissions created are shown in Figs. 2.1 and 2.2.

Rating To foster the engagement and to encourage students to submit appealing augmented photos, a competitive element was introduced: the photos submitted were presented to a jury of 17 lecturers and scientific associates belonging to the participating chairs. Based on the rating of the augmentation as well as the textual explanation, the best entry was honoured with the 'Jury Award' in a public ceremony following a one-week lasting exhibition in the main building of the university's library. For the rating procedure, the web-based open-source photo gallery software Piwigo (2019) was used. Piwigo allows a single-dimensional assessment procedure, in which submissions can be rated with one (bad) up to five stars (very good) (Fig. 2.3). The ratings do not require any further explanations. In another step, the online gallery was also opened to the students, enabling them to rate the submissions. The 'Audience Award' was given based on the students' ratings. The following didactic intentions

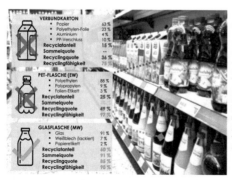

In Germany approximately six million tons of plastic waste are produced annually. According to the Federal Ministry for the Environment, only 45 per cent of the plastic waste are recycled, the remaining garbage is incinerated or landfilled. Furthermore, half of the waste collected for recycling is exported to other countries for further processing resulting in negative consequences for climate, environment and people. The challenges of waste recycling and recyclable material processing as elements of technical infrastructure do not only include the waste disposal. Instead, they are located at the beginning of the chain at the producers of waste - industry and consumers. Therefore, the aim of the illustrated AR application is to sensitize consumers on material cycles in order to reduce the amount of environmentally harmful waste in the long term and promote the use of efficiently recyclable materials.

Fig. 2.1 Submission: Example 1, visualization of waste-related information (S. Fingerle)

Technical infrastructure does not only include the development and construction of roads, energy supply systems or industrial buildings, but also refers to their protection in the event of a disaster. In case of emergency response or disaster control, fire brigades are an essential unit.

In order to make their operations more effective and safer, it would be possible to enter additional information of the object into the windscreen of the vehicles. If more information than "Attention electricity" is needed then it is possible to touch this symbol and detailed recommendations for action open up. These instructions are only visible from the position of the group leader (co-pilot). The machine operator (driver) can see other information such as installation areas or distances to obstacles.

Fig. 2.2 Submission: Example 2, operational support for fire brigades (L.-L. Simon)

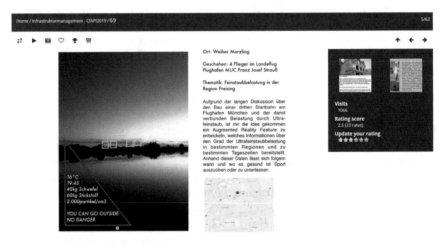

Fig. 2.3 Screenshot of the online gallery showing an example of a submission: the augmented picture (left), description (middle) and rating information (right)

underlie the activity of rating: The awards again serve to promote the engagement of the students probably leading to learning. Further, students are intended to get an overview of the technical infrastructure and their fellow students' perception of technical infrastructure. Furthermore, rating demands mental engagement with the subjects' AR and infrastructure.

Review In a third task, students had to review at least two submissions. The review— conducted via questionnaire—comprised of a quantitative and qualitative part. In the quantitative part, the students were asked to categorize the submissions regarding a few criteria on the one hand and evaluate them according to several criteria on a Likert scale on the other (see Sect. 2.3.1), while in the qualitative part the students had to make a statement about the augmented photo (see Sect. 2.3.2). Again, the

Table 2.1 Study sizes (N)

Size	N	Description
Participants	71	All participants handing in a photo
General feedback	71	All participants filled the feedback questionnaire
Review	190	Participants had to provide at least two reviews, some participants have been demanded to provide more (up to ten reviews) as substitute tasks for the submission not completed in time
Photos exhibited	65	Submission had to meet quality requirements to be admitted to the online gallery and the exhibition. Six submissions were assessed by the lecturers as sufficient for granting admission to the final examination, but not sufficient for exhibition participation

review sub-activity should foster a mental engagement with the subjects' AR and infrastructure.

Feedback Following the learning activity, students were asked to complete a questionnaire on their individual perception of the learning activity and understanding of AR in an educational setting. Thanks to great efforts in targeting the students, every student completed the questionnaire as a voluntary activity. Nevertheless, in the course of the study, varying study sizes occurred. Table 2.1 describes the various study sizes.

2.3   Results

2.3.1   Quantitative Evaluation of the Reviews

As part of the review, students were asked to categorize the photos according to a set of criteria. In the following, the categorizations are discussed and compared with the definitive categories of the infrastructures depicted in the photos to obtain a measure of the carefulness of the students' reviews. The definitive categorization was determined by two experts. The questions and categories are presented in the following subsections.

2.3.1.1   Preference for Infrastructure System Types

The students were free in their choice of the type of infrastructure system they wanted to investigate and work on. To understand the preferences of the infrastructure system type chosen, the fellow students were asked to categorize the photo they had to review. The initially given categories were: '*Water supply/waste water treatment*', '*Communication*', '*Energy supply*', '*Transportation*' *and* '*Resource cycles*'. Barely

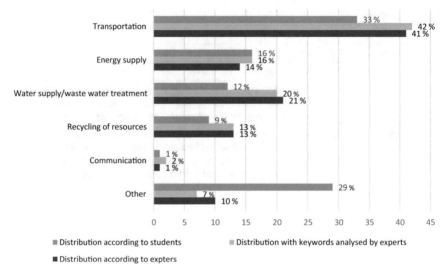

Fig. 2.4 Preferences for infrastructure system types ($N = 190$)

anyone chose '*Communication*' *as category*. In case none of these categories seemed interesting, the students could also choose 'Other', but had then to deliver a brief statement describing the technical field they associated with the augmented photo.

Focusing on the specific infrastructure system, the peer review revealed that the majority of augmented photos depicted the system of 'Transportation' (32%), followed by 'Energy supply' (16%) and 'Water supply/waste water treatment' (12%) as shown by Fig. 2.4. Although major infrastructure system types were offered as categories, a large part of reviewed photos was categorized as 'Other' (29%), A recategorization by the two experts lowered the actual percentage of 'Other' to 10%. In fact, the analysis of this category revealed that the majority was depicting particular aspects or elements of the suggested systems such as emergency management for rail-bound vehicles or pipes for water management. As reasons for the shortcoming of defining specific infrastructure systems lack of attention by students fulfilling the tasks or a limited ability to create the mental connection between the level of abstraction and the offered infrastructure systems are assumed. Further, the experts noticed that 10% of the photos relate to different kinds of processes, such as surface analyses or awareness-raising for environmental issues, implying not all students were aware of definitions of technical infrastructures.

2.3.1.2 Source of Augmented Information

AR applications are based on five essential components and actions: recording of the real environment, tracking of the visual focus of the user at each moment, integration of virtual elements into the real and by user seen environment, rendering of virtual objects and displaying the merged situations (Broll 2013; Schmalstieg and Höllerer 2016). The integration, rendering and displaying of augmenting information as virtual objects must occur in real time (Jung and Vitzthum 2013; Pangilinan et al. 2019). This requirement is one of the reasons to ask students for an assessment of the data source needed. Furthermore, this question was supposed to ascertain whether the students are aware of the complexity of the required data source and its generation processes. The following categories were presented: '*In mobile devices integrated sensors*', '*General sensors*', '*Web-based data*' and '*Other*'.

Figure 2.5 shows most of the answers (46%) assuming that the augmenting information would have its source in sensors that are integrated into the AR devices, such as tablets or smartphones, even if reviewers had no objective measure on this assumption. In addition, the reviewers could not rely on the current technical state of the art, since the submissions were to be designed regardless of limitations imposed by technical feasibility. Only in few cases (5%) the category 'Other' was chosen. Revising the cases in which students could not define a specific category (e.g. the filling level of public refuse containers) led to slightly higher results among the category of stationary sensors and web-based data. To understand how far the student's assumptions were correct, two experts analyzed the submissions as the last step. The results revealed that most of the depicted information in the photos must be web-based data (71%). With stationary sensors only 23% and integrated sensors only 6% of the information could be measured.

Discovering that in most cases a specific category for the source of the augmented information was chosen implies that most of the students reflected the source intensively. However, as the remaining 5% of the photos could be easily matched with a specific category by experts, it is assumed that students were not able to create the technical understanding based on the given level of abstraction. Although it can be assumed that students may have developed a general technical understanding about sources of augmented information by fulfilling the task, the review of all submissions demonstrated gaps in more detailed knowledge. The technical capabilities of

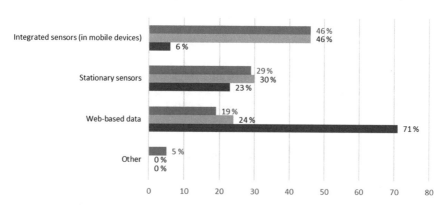

Fig. 2.5 Source of augmented information ($N = 190$)

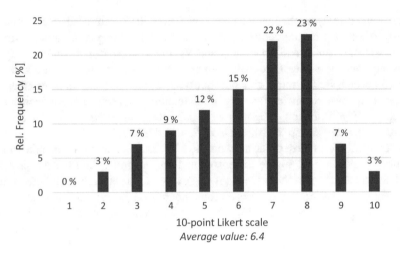

Fig. 2.6 Benefit of AR application ($N = 190$)

integrated sensors were overestimated—possibly due to the instruction not to consider technical feasibility as restrictive, while the potential of incorporating stationary sensors and web-based data for AR appeared to be perceived less relevant.

2.3.1.3 Benefit of the AR Application Within Engineering Environments

In order to understand if the created augmentation can fulfill a useful purpose, students were asked to evaluate the benefit of the augmentation if it would be used in engineering environments. For that, a 10-point Likert scale was offered (see Fig. 2.6). The value 1 was defined as 'the application is a gimmick with no engineering purpose', the value 10 stated, 'the application would revolutionize the work of engineers'.

The results show that the majority of submissions were evaluated as useful for engineering environments. 70% of the submissions were evaluated in the value range of 6–10 with a focus of 45% on the values of 7–8. While 3% were defined as having the potential to revolutionize the work of engineers, none was seen as meaningless. Overall, with an average value of 6.4, the answers suggested the submissions being helpful that students were putting effort in conceptualizing the augmentation.

2.3.1.4 Effort Estimated for the Implementation of the Application

Aiming to foster critical reflection processes of technical aspects, in addition to the Likert scale previously used, students had to provide an estimation regarding the technical effort in terms of innovation that is required to implement the application (see Fig. 2.7). On the 10-point Likert scale the value 1 referred to 'the application

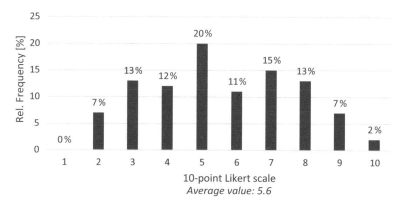

Fig. 2.7 Effort estimated in the reviews for implementation of the proposed AR application ($N =$ 190)

exists already', value 10 was defined as 'the implementation of the application will not be possible within the next 20 years'.

In general, a wide distribution among the values is observed. Most of the submissions (84%) are ranked between the values 3–8, showing that students believe in the implementation of the augmentation. The highest single percentage shows value 5 with 20%, indicating a general trust in technical innovation and the availability of the augmentation in the close future. The general average value of 5.6 reflects this perception. None of the submissions was defined as already existing on the free market. However, 2% of the students believed that technological innovation is required over a time span exceeding 20 years in order to create the app.

2.3.1.5 Effort Incurred for the Submission

Furthermore, students were asked to evaluate the creative and technical efforts that were spent creating the submission (see Fig. 2.8). This question aimed at understanding how far students had invested time and skills in the process of creation. The effort invested is considered as important as the actual occupation with the subject should be an important prerequisite for learning. Thus, on a 10-point Likert scale the value 1 referred to 'the submission has been created carelessly'. The other pole with the value 10 stated, 'the augmentation was created with a high level of diligence and could be subject to a Bachelor's thesis'.

According to the reviewing students, the vast majority of the submission (85%) meet the values 4–8 meaning that they were created with medium to high effort. In total, 47% were created with a value above the average value of 6.2. From those, a few (3%) were even rated as comparable to a Bachelor's degree indicating a high motivation of the students.

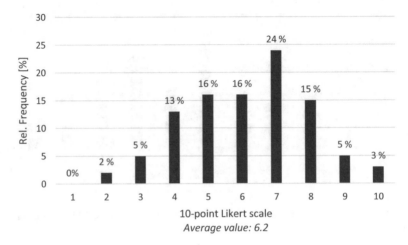

Fig. 2.8 Effort incurred for the submission ($N = 190$)

2.3.1.6   Relevance for AR

To receive an appraisal in how far the submissions met the principles of AR, students had to provide information if the submission under review is 'not related to AR at all' (value 1 on a 10-point Likert scale) or if the submission can be seen as 'a best example of AR' (value 10).

Figure 2.9 shows that most of a submission received a positive value stating that the principles of AR were at least partially met. The majority (59%) of the submissions are ranked within the value of 6–9, with a significant peak (35%) at

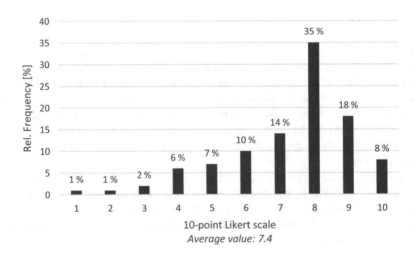

Fig. 2.9 Relevance of application proposed for AR ($N = 190$)

value 8. Some of the submissions (8) were evaluated as best examples for AR, while only a few (4%) experienced low values. Due to this composition, a high average value (7.3) was reached, indicating that most students understood the principle of AR. Students internalized possibilities and opportunities that can be achieved through such applications and could transfer the knowledge gained through applications that were presented as examples by the lecturers and apply it to the design of own concepts of AR applications.

2.3.2   Qualitative Evaluation of the Reviews

In the final step of the review process, students were asked to express their opinion on the submission reviewed in one sentence. The textual feedback was voluntary, so in total 32 students gave 67 comments. One of the goals of this task was, again, to foster mental processes through the required abstracting considerations of the submissions. Since the task was optional, this goal was only partially achieved, in consequence, this task has to become obligatory in future. For evaluating the feedback, a qualitative content analysis (QCA) was conducted. Based on the QCA the individual comments were coded and in total six categories were defined (see Fig. 2.10). The categories identified are 'Idea and concept appreciation', 'Realisation challenge', 'Usability and usefulness apprehension', 'Design appreciation', 'Suggestions for improvements' and 'Other'. Each of these categories suggests that the reviewers generally reflected on the content of the submissions, which is an indicator of learning. The first category, 'Idea and concept appreciation', could also suggest the surprise of reviewers about the ideas, which is also a good prerequisite for learning. For the submitters, the reviewer's acknowledgement of a good idea can also be understood as a mental engagement with the subject of AR and infrastructure.

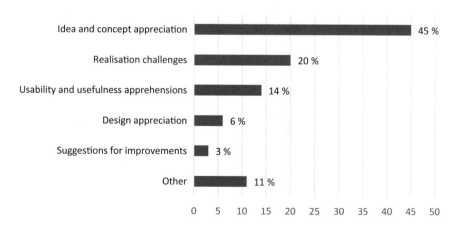

Fig. 2.10   Categorized comments ($N = 190$)

   The first and largest category (45%) includes statements expressing positive feed-back of the reviewed photo. Statements are valuing the presented ideas and concepts defining it as innovative or useful approaches by stating e.g. '*great idea, many people could benefit*' and '*good idea and definitely useful*'. 20% of the students used that comment option to express thoughts referring to general aspects that might hamper or support the creation of the application or raised specific questions such as where the required data should come from. Examples are '*the realisation would not demand a lot of effort*' or '*the required technical features are not developed yet*'. 14% of the comments express concerns about the feasibility of the idea under review and point out that the objective of the application is not in line with their concept. Also, it was mentioned, that some submissions appeared to be not useful since the target audience might not be interested in the provided information. Statements included '*the photo could be useful, if the purpose is amplified*' and '*the intention is good, but it is questionable how the depicted application can support engineers in accomplishing their tasks*'. Further, the design of augmentations was in parts well-received (e.g. '*the integrated legend makes the photo very understandable*') (6%) and specific suggestions for improvements were made, such as '*I think the perspective must be changed in order to work with the presented data*' (3%). 11% of the comments were not categorized due to the wide spectrum of themes, such as describing challenges of or infrastructure systems itself.

   In total, most students expressed their appreciation regarding the work of their fellow students and even provided specific ideas of how the application designed can be improved. The high amount of comments referring to the aspects of realization showed that the students critically analyzed the augmentations and were able to reflect its potential development process. The stated apprehensions indicate that the students elaborated on the usage of the applications as well and were able to evaluate how far they are needed indeed.

2.3.3   The Learning Activity from the Students' Perspective

2.3.3.1   Self-perception of the Learning Activity

Regarding the perceptions of the learning activity, the students were asked to assess various statements on a 7-point Likert scale (see Table 2.2). Statement 3 was intended to evaluate the students' interest in the subject. The value of 5.5 is to be valued as a high level of interest in the subject, which should also lead to a high level of motivation conducting the learning activity. That the learning activity was indeed regarded as meaningful in achieving learning objectives, might be concluded from Statement 7, which received little approval (2.1). The learning activity was more fun than comparable learning activities (Statement 4–4.9) and is also preferred to other learning activities (Statement 5–2.8). At the same time, students confirm that the learning activity has improved their knowledge of AR (Statement 1) and technical infrastructure (Statement 2). In general, students confirm that there is good potential

Table 2.2 Students approval of statements on their perception of the learning activity (7-point Likert scale: 1: false–7: true)

	Statement	Mean
1	The task has improved my theoretical knowledge about AR	4.9
2	The task has improved my knowledge in at least one of the disciplines of technical infrastructure	4.8
3	It is for me important to have a working knowledge about technical infrastructure	5.5
4	I enjoyed the task more compared to other learning activities during my studies	4.9
5	Instead of the task, I prefer a learning activity such as writing an essay elaboration or a calculation task—if the effort would be the same	2.8
6	The task was meaningless for me. I just had to do it	2.1
7	The task leads to good learning outcomes compared to other learning activities	4.5

for learning with the learning activity (Statement 7–4.5). Overall, the self-assessment of the students can be regarded as very positive: they prefer the learning activity to other activities, confirm the learning potential and actual learning outcomes.

2.3.3.2 Textual Comments

In addition to the previous question using a Likert scale, the questionnaire allowed the students to provide a textual comment on the learning activity. 28 of the students (39%) made a comment. The comments were categorized by two experts. Table 2.3 shows the criteria under which an assignment was made and the number of actual assignments of a comment to a category. The requirements for an assignment had to be strictly met, e.g. all comments assigned to the category 'Fun' explicitly included the word 'Fun'. Multiple categories could be assigned to a comment.

The majority (23 out of 28) of the comments are explicitly positive. There is no negative comment. On the other hand, six students took the opportunity to suggest improvements (C11). These include recommendations to describe the task clearer, to link the competition with credits for the final examination and to introduce the basics better, such as discussing the technical requirements for determining the position of the AR device. Further, three comments mark the learning activity as fun (C4). The creativity fostered by the learning activity (C5) is positively mentioned out of eight comments. The learning activity is characterized as diverse in three comments (C6). Six times the students positively mention the possibility of having their own product at their own initiative in the learning activity (C7). Furthermore, six times it is mentioned that the learning activity differs strongly from the learning activities offered so far in the study program and is to be regarded as unique in its form (C8). From a didactic point of view, noteworthy are six comments confirming the learning activity prompting the students to familiarize themselves with a topic not yet known (C9)—one of the important non-technical learning objectives of a course of study in higher education. One student praises the overall outcome of the learning activity

Table 2.3 Categories of the comments, absolute frequency and assignment criteria ($N = 71$)

	Category	f_i	Assignment criteria
C1	Positive	23	The student comments positively on the competition
C2	Negative	0	The student comments negatively on the competition
C3	Competition	4	The student names the competition or the exhibition as a positive part of the learning activity
C4	Fun	3	The student characterizes the learning activity as fun generating
C5	Creative	8	The student characterizes the learning activity as fostering creativity
C6	Diversified	3	The student describes the learning activity as diversified
C7	Own artefact	6	The student explains that the learning activity enables him to create his own artefact
C8	Unique learning activity	6	The student regards the learning activity as exceptional regarding its structure in comparison to the other learning activities of the study program
C9	Topic exploration	6	The student indicates that the learning activity was an occasion to delve deeper into a topic
C10	Good results of the course	1	The student appreciates the results of the learning activity as good
C11	Suggestions	6	The student requests for future improvement of the learning activity

(C10). In addition, one of the students, who has participated in the same learning activity in the past year, reports an actual implementation by a company following the idea submitted last year.

A selection of comments and their assignments:

– "*I enjoyed dealing with the subject area of infrastructure in this way and also making my own project out of it.*" (C1, C4, C7, C9)
– "*That was a varied task, which also stimulated creativity a little bit and differed from the other tasks of the degree course, but in a positive sense.*" (C1, C4, C6, C8)
– "*I enjoyed [the learning activity] because I was able to design the technical aspects of the infrastructure and there were no limits to my creativity. It's also nice that many contributions are exhibited in the library.*" (C1, C3, C4, C5).

In sum, the learning activity in the comments freely written is assessed as very positive and described as creative and very diverse. The uniqueness of such a learning activity is emphasized. In particular, the possibility of independently advancing a project at one's own discretion was praised. This self-reliance of the students is just as much an educational goal as the promotion of self-learning. Overall, the comments also draw a very positive picture of the learning activity.

2.4 Discussion

As a starting point for the discussion, it can be stated that the learning activity presented is very well received by a larger faction of the students as it enables the students to work creatively and self-determined work on products that students can themselves identify with. However, although the students indicate subjectively learning processes, an evaluation of the learning outcome is still missing. In a field study like the one at hand, however, such an evaluation is difficult to achieve, as learning effects of parallel learning activities such as lectures must be isolated.

Structurally, variations of the presented learning activity are conceivable. For example, some students complained that their submissions were not available in the online gallery and the exhibition. These submissions had previously been sorted out by the lecturers, as the submissions formally complied with the guidelines but were obviously produced without much effort. Removal aimed at not giving a less good example to the other students that would lower the level in the subsequent learning activity of the next year, because students would assume that submissions will be accepted regardless of the effort spent on producing the submissions. A change in the learning activity, which could solve this problem, would be using a peer review procedure, as it also occurs in the academic context: the student submissions are reviewed by other students and may have to be revised until being accepted or being finally rejected approved by the lecturer. The introduction of such a more genuine peer review would also remedy a weakness of the presented peer review method: The reviewing students did not receive any feedback, e.g. by improving the submission reviewed or by the option to compare their review with the reviews of fellow students to the same submission—nor were the submitters exposed to the reviews of their submissions.

The reviews asked for an estimation of the effort required to produce the submission. The average of 6.2 indicates reasonable effort. However, this measure could become more meaningful if the technical skills of the submitting and reviewing students were surveyed beforehand. This would make it easier to correlate the efforts made and the technical understanding of the reviewers with the review results. For example, a submission may seem trivial due to low technical skills, even though a lot of effort was put into the preparation. This question highlights, in particular, the need for awareness about the baseline for all work and assessments. In general, however, also for the classification of the other assessments, for example, the question of the submission's AR relevance, the information about a baseline for each student would allow more accurate classification of the answers.

The approach presented is intended to reduce the technical and organizational capabilities required for the use of AR applications in teaching. It should not be forgotten, however, that effort is also necessary here: the online gallery must be installed, the submissions must be uploaded, and the exhibition must be equipped. If a peer review process is carried out, appropriate software must also be installed and managed. All in all, however, this effort is seen as easier to be accomplished, as keeping various AR applications demonstrating the concepts of AR functionable.

2.5 Conclusions

AR technology is becoming more and more widespread and should therefore also be incorporated into the curriculum supporting contemporary learning activities. The actual integration of current AR-based tools into educational contexts, however, requires high technical and organizational efforts and skills both on the part of the students and the lecturers. As an alternative with less technical and organizational effort, this article describes a learning activity that includes the conceptual design of an AR application for use in the area of technical infrastructure. In terms of learning, it is based on the principles of maker education. The learning activity comprises the taking of photos of technical infrastructure systems, the designing of a concept for the augmentation of the photo and the visualization as well as the writing of an explanatory text. These activities should lead to a deeper understanding of the topic of technical infrastructure as well as the peer review that will take place subsequently. The evaluation of the learning activity with the help of a questionnaire and an analysis of the reviews shows that the students perceive the learning activity as meaningful, fun generating and creative. Learning processes take place as students assess themselves. Further work includes the evaluation of the actual learning outcomes achieved through the learning activity and the integration of a real peer review. Despite the still missing validation of the learning outcomes, the presented learning activity seems to be a good alternative to convey the principles of AR in technical infrastructure systems with only minor technical and organizational efforts. The learning activity might be transferred to other disciplines—besides technical infrastructure systems—in which AR might be of use.

References

Ackermann E (2001) Piaget's constructivism, Papert's constructionism: what's the difference. Future of Learning Group Publication 5(3):438

Akçayır M, Akçayır G (2017) Advantages and challenges associated with augmented reality for education: a systematic review of the literature. Educ Res Rev 20. https://doi.org/10.1016/j.edurev.2016.11.002

Aukstakalnis S (2016) Practical augmented reality: a guide to the technologies, applications, and human factors for AR and VR: Addison-Wesley Professional, New York

Azuma R (1997) A survey of augmented reality. Presence Teleoper Virtual Environ 6:355–385. https://doi.org/10.1.1.30.4999

Broll W (2013) Augmentierte Realität. In: Dörner R, Broll W, Grimm P, Jung B (eds) Virual und augmented reality. Springer, Berlin, pp 241–294

Burkhard R, Schmitt G (2009) Visualising future cities in the ETH value lab: new methods for education and learning. In: Wang X, Schnabel M (eds) Mixed reality in architecture design and construction. Springer, Dordrecht, pp 205–218

Castellanos A, Pérez C (2017) New challenge in education: enhancing student's knowledge through augmented reality. In: Ariso J (ed) Augmented reality: reflections on its contribution to knowledge formation. De Gruyter, Berlin, pp 273–293

Di Serio Á, Ibáñez B, Kloos D (2013) Impact of an augmented reality system on students' motivation for a visual art course. Comput Educ 68:586–596. https://doi.org/10.1016/j.compedu.2012.03.002

Dorribo-Camba J, Contero M (2013) Incorporating augmented reality content in engineering design graphics materials. In: Proceedings of the frontiers in education (FIE) conference, Oklahoma City, 23–26 October 2013

Furth B (ed) (2011) Handbook of augemented reality. Springer, New York

González-González C, Arias L (2018) Maker movement in education: maker mindset and makerspaces maker movement in education: maker mindset and makerspaces. In: Proceedings of the 2018 IV Jornadas de Interacción Humano-Computador (HCI), Popayan, 23–27 April 2018

Hantono B, Nugroho L, Santosa P (2018) Meta-review of augmented reality in education. In: Proceedings of 10th international conference on information technology and electrical engineering (ICITEE), Universitas Gadjah Mada, Bali, 24–26 Juni 2018

Huitt W (2013) Summary of theories relating to learning and development. https://www.edpsycinteractive.org/topics/summary/lrndev.html. Accessed 12 Sep 2019

Jung B, Vitzthum A (2013) Virtuelle Welten. In: Dörner R, Broll W, Grimm P, Jung B (eds) Virual und augmented reality. Springer, pp 65–96

Kafai Y (1996) Learning design by making games: children's development of design strategies in the creation of a complex computational artifact. In: Kafai Y, Resnick M (eds) Constructionism in practice: designing, thinking, and learning in a digital world. Lawrence Erlbaum Associates, Mahwah, pp 71–96

Kafai Y, Burke Q (2015) Constructionist gaming: understanding the benefits of making games for learning. Educ Psychol 50:313–334. https://doi.org/10.1080/00461520.2015.1124022

Karakus M, Ersozlu A, Clark A. (2019) Augmented reality research in education: a bibliometric study. EURASIA J Math Sci Technol Educ. https://doi.org/10.29333/ejmste/103904

Katterfeldt E, Dittert N, Schelhowe H (2015) Designing digital fabrication learning environments for Bildung: IMPLICATIONS from ten years of physical computing workshops. Int J Child-Comp Interact 5:3–10. https://doi.org/10.1016/j.ijcci.2015.08.001

Khoshnevisan B, Le N (2018) Augmented reality in language education: a systematic literature review. In: Proceedings of the global conference on education and research (GLOCER) conference, University of Nevada Las Vegas, 17–20 April 2018

Kurti S, Kurti L, Fleming L (2014) The philosophy of educational makerspaces, part 1 of making an educational makerspace. Teacher Librarian 41:8–11

Ludwid C, Reiman C (2005) Augmented reality: information im fokus. C-Lab Report. https://www.c-lab.de/fileadmin/clab/C-LAB_Reports/1_C-LAB-TR-2005-1-Augmented_Reality_Information_im_Fokus.pdf. Accessed 12 Sept 2019

Martin L (2015) The promise of the maker movement for education. J Pre-College Eng Educ Res 5:30–39. https://doi.org/10.7771/2157-9288.1099

Milgram P, Takemura H, Utsumi A et al (1994) Mixed reality (MR) reality-virtuality (RV) continuum. Telemanipulator Telepresence Technol 2351:282–292. https://doi.org/10.1.1.83.6861

Pangilinan E, Lukas S, Mohan V (2019) Creating augmented and virtual realities: theory and practice for next-generation spatial computing. O'Reilly Media, Beijing

Papert S (1987) Constructionism: new opportunity for elementary science education. NSF Grant Application. https://nsf.gov/awardsearch/showAward?AWD_ID=8751190. Accessed 12 September 2019

Papert S, Harel I (1991) Constructionism. Ablex Publishing, Norwood

Petrovich M, Shah M, Foster A (2018) Augmented reality experiences in informal education. In: Proceeding of 2018 IEEE international conference on teaching, assessment, and learning for engineering (TALE), Institute of Electrical and Electronic Engineers (IEEE), Wollongong, 4–7 December 2018

Piaget J (1964) Part I: cognitive development in children: Piaget development and learning. J Res Sci Teach 2:176–186

Piwigo (2019) Piwigo.org. https://piwigo.org/. Accessed 12 June 2019

Radu I (2014) Augmented reality in education: a meta-review and cross-media analysis. Pers Ubiquit Comput 18:1533–1543. https://doi.org/10.1007/s00779-013-0747-y

Rauschnabel P, Felix R, Hinsch C (2019) Augmented reality marketing: How mobile AR-apps can improve brands through inspiration. J Retail Consum Serv 49:43–53. https://doi.org/10.1016/j.jretconser.2019.03.004

Roffey T, Sverko C, Therien J (2016) The making of a makerspace: pedagogical and physical transformations of teaching and learning, curruculum guide (ETEC 510). https://www.makerspaceforeducation.com/uploads/4/1/6/4/41640463/makerspace_for_education_curriculum_guide.pdf. Accessed 12 Sept 2019

Schart D, Tschanz N (2015) Augmented reality. Praxishandbuch, UKV Verlangsgesellschaft, Konstanz

Schmalstieg D, Höllerer T (2016) Augmented reality: principles and practice. Addison-Wesley Professional, Boston

Skinner B (1976) About behaviorism. Vintage, New York

Söbke H, Zander S, Londong J (2018) Augmented reality als lernmedium: potenziale und implikationen. In: Proceedings of interact conference, Technische Universität Chemnitz, Chemnitz, 28–29 June 2018

Sommerauer P, Müller O (2014) Augmented reality in informal learning environments: a field experiment in a mathematics exhibition. Comput Educ 79:59–68. https://doi.org/10.1016/j.compedu.2014.07.013

Sommerauer P, Müller O (2018) Augmented reality for teaching and learning—a literature review on theoretical and empirical foundations. In: Proceedings of 26th European conference on information systems (ECIS 2018). University of Portsmouth Portsmouth, 23–28 June 2018

Stager G (2014) What's the maker movement and why should i care? https://www.scholastic.com/browse/article.jsp?id=3758336. Accessed 17 July 2019

Taylor B (2016) Evaluating the benefit of the maker movement in K-12 STEM education. Electron Int J Educ Arts Sci. https://www.eijeas.com/index.php/EIJEAS/article/view/72. Accessed 17 Feb 2019

Telefónica F (2011) Realidad aumentada: unanueva lenteparaver el mundo. Fundación Telefónica, Madrid

Tomara M, Gouscos D (2014) Using augmented reality for science education: issues and prospects. ELearning Papers. https://doi.org/10.13140/RG.2.1.1907.1207

Vafa S (2018) Using augmented reality to increase interaction in online courses. Int J Educ Technol Learn 3:65–68. https://doi.org/10.20448/2003.32.65.68

Wei X, Weng D, Liu Y et al (2015) Teaching based on augmented reality for a technical creative design course. Comput Educ 81:221–234. https://doi.org/10.1016/j.compedu.2014.10.017

Wen Y, Looi C-K (2019) Review of augmented reality in education: situated learning with digital and non-digital resources. In: Díaz P, Ioannou A, Bhagat K, Spector J (eds) Learning in a digital world. Springer, Singapore, pp 179–193

Zender R, Weise M, Heyde M et al (2018) Lehren und Lernen mit VR und AR—was wird erwartet? Was funktioniert? In: Schiffner D (ed.) Proceedings der pre-conference-workshops der 16. E-learning fachtagung informatik co-located with 16th e-learning conference of the German Computer Society (DeLFI 2018), Frankfurt

Chapter 3
An Online Platform for Enhancing Learning Experiences with Web-Based Augmented Reality and Pictorial Bar Code

Huy Le and Minh Nguyen

Abstract Lacking the teaching materials is one of the common problems of the education system, especially in developing countries. The teachers attempt to give as much theoretical knowledge as possible to students while forgetting to train them with practical activities and ways of self-thinking. Augmented Reality (AR) provides the capability to overlay virtual information onto educational textbooks which makes them more attractive; hence, motivates students to learn. In this chapter, we present an online AR study platform which is capable of running on an everyday handset without requiring any software installation. It could provide a stress-free, low-cost, portable and promising solutio to use within the educational environment. In addition, they introduce a new transparent AR marker concept that could combine the advantages of the original template markers and barcode markers.

3.1 Introduction

3.1.1 E-Learning and Traditional Learning Methods

Nowadays, online learning materials have become extremely popular, as tons of different companies and organisation are offering courses online. However, traditional training (classroom) is still playing as a significant role in education preferred delivery method. The effectiveness of both methods usually becomes the debate topic see Fig. 3.1 (Zhang et al. 2004). For some people, the traditional classroom is unreplaceable training method while for others e-learning is more efficient. The place to learn is one of the significant advantages of e-learning over traditional learning

H. Le (✉) · M. Nguyen
School of Engineering, Computer & Mathematical Sciences, Auckland University of Technology, Auckland, New Zealand
e-mail: huy.le@aut.ac.nz

M. Nguyen
e-mail: minh.nguyen@aut.ac.nz

© Springer Nature Switzerland AG 2020
V. Geroimenko (ed.), *Augmented Reality in Education*,
Springer Series on Cultural Computing,
https://doi.org/10.1007/978-3-030-42156-4_3

Fig. 3.1 The e-learning versus traditional classroom environments are the on-going debate topic

method. In the setting of a traditional classroom, there is always one physical room. Unlikely in e-learning environment (Downes 2005) where students can choose to study anytime at wherever the internet connection is available. The material reviewing and replaying is another downside of the traditional classroom. The information replay/reviewability helps the students understand the issues better. It does not mean that it would be impossible in traditional learning, but not as quickly. The students tend to forget the learning content easily due to dishonestly reviewed them after class. The e-learning method gives the student the ability to review the information at the moment of need. It allows them to refresh themselves on the learning contents that would fade away immediately after a traditional class. Hence, this further improves the quality of the learning process and reduces mistakes.

The social interaction tends to be the significant advantages of the traditional learning method. The classroom environment allows students to personally interact with the instructors and other students in real life, whereas we have to depend on the virtual media to interact with the learning material in e-learning. Another highlight of studying in the physical classroom is that there is always someone to motivate and guide the students. The research (Ivanova 2009) states that there are more than 30% of students could not live without having their eyes out of the smartphone screen and below 20% of them are willing to study by reading hard copy learning material. Hence, the students are required to be self-driven and very quickly to get distracted by the unrelated contents from the online network. However, the e-learning methods generate a higher amount of participation and substantive discussion (Karayan 1997; Smith 2000) due to the effect of personalisation level. In reality, there are not many students willing to ask questions in class rather than posting their difficulties on the online discussion forums. In the classroom, the learning problems are usually solved by one to one or one to many; whereas they could be done privately with

Table 3.1 Comparison of social interaction between e-learning and traditional learning methods

	E-learning	Traditional classroom
Communication style	Communication could be either verbal or text Could be structured, dense and permanent	Verbal communication often is a standard model, but impermanent
Focus-ability	Less sense of instructor control More comfortable for students to ignore the instructor	The instructor controls the environment Not so easy to ignore instructor
Feedback	Feedback on each individual's piece of work very detailed and focused, Textual feedback only, and it could be private or shared in public	Less likely to cover as much detail, often more general discussion Verbal, textual feedback and often public shared

the e-learning method. The research (Elkjær 2001) has pointed out a few critical differences related to social interaction between two learning methods and adapted in Table 3.1.

A typical e-learning course could take 70% study less time than a traditional course. However, it does not mean that the adopted contents are reduced. The students tend to break the learning content into smaller parts and spends smaller amounts of time over more days. It is believed to be another way to improve the quality of the learning and the cost benefits. In general, people save about 50–70% on training cost with e-learning due to reduced or eliminated travel and other service costs.

Furthermore, the e-learning courses could be quickly developed in about 3–4 weeks of time; whereas months for traditional learning courses. It shows that people are still adopting e-learning and traditional learning methods due to their unique advantages over each other. For the solutions of those issues, the blended learning which combines both learning methods tends to be the top choice on the list (Oliver and Trigwell 2005).

3.1.2 Augmented Reality and Motivation

Augmented Reality (AR), also sometimes known as mixed reality, is a different beast than Virtual Reality (VR). AR primary purpose is not to cut out the real world and transport the users to another world but rather is to be an enhancement of the real world with a set of virtual objects in it (Carmigniani 2011; Azuma 1997). The term AR attributed to a former Boeing researcher Tom Caudell in 1990 (Caudell 1990) and word augment is from the Latin word "Augere" which means to increase or to add. Hence, AR technology is adding to the existing reality. When a person's real environment is supplemented or augmented with computer-generated images, usually motion tracked then that is AR. Many people say that AR is the revolutionary,

(a) Word firt AR prototype   (b) Heads-up display on fighter jets

Fig. 3.2 Examples of real-world AR application

but the technology started in 1962 when cinematographer Morton Heilig created the sensorama (Heilig 1962) a simulator with visuals sound vibration and smell. At the same period, a group of MIT research lead by Sutherland also introduced another AR workable prototypes in the late-1960s (Sutherland 1965) as seen in Fig. 3.2a. However, the AR first real-world application was the heads-up display (HUD) in fighter jets (Caudell 1992). The symbols projected onto a transparent glass screen which takes away the distraction of looking at gauges and allows pilots to aim their weapons better. Nowadays, AR is getting more and more common around us. For instance, the primitive forms of AR could be seen while we are playing Pokemon go or having the snap chat lens face filters (Rios 2018). Currently, AR technology is showing promise with tons of different investments and research efforts in both software and hardware supported equipment (Heather Bellini 2016). AR is believed to ease activities such as travel and shopping and could be a significant change to education.

3.1.3   Proposed Method

There are different tools such as tracking and virtual information registration required for generating a practical AR experience. These tools could be implemented quickly with nowadays technologies. However, most of them come up with different system requirements and required to have a physical application installed. In order to solve this issue, we introduce an online learning system which is powered by web-based AR. The web-based platform considered for this system; because it is portable, easy to re-implement and does not have the high demand for required resources. The user

Fig. 3.3   AR markers with embedded transparent QR code

could easily access the system using any electronic devices with internet connection. Low memory storage of the 3D models or other virtual information is no longer on the concern list as there is no offline installation required. Our system aims to present a sufficient AR experience and believed to have some advantages over the previous AR solutions:

- The system does not require the installation of software.
- The system works instantly as long as the device connected to the internet (Wi-Fi or 3/4G).
- The marker is a transparent quick-response (QR) code (Fig. 3.3); hence, most the important information on the figure on the textbook preserved.

3.2   Transparent QR Code on Colour Figures

3.2.1   QR Code Structure Overview

The quick-response (QR) codes have become more and more popular as one of the significant tracking methods used in transport, manufacturing and many other different industries. Nowadays, many mobile devices equipped with the QR code scan capability (Liu 2008). QR code is also used as of the augmented reality (AR) marker due to its high storage capacity and speed of decoding. The structure of the QR code usually includes three different regions, as shown in Fig. 3.4. The message encoded into the squared black and white boxes called as modules.

1. **Required patterns region** includes three different sub-regions: position (also known as finder), alignment and timing. The position patterns are presented as

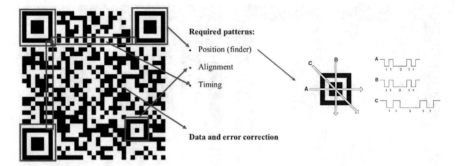

Fig. 3.4 The QR code required patterns highlighted in red and its data/error correction region

three large black and white equal-sized modules and arranged at three corners of the QR code. These modules help to detect the boundary of the QR code to allow high-speed reading capability. They are designed to be readable horizontally, vertically and diagonally (A, B and C) with the same of black and white pixels is 1:1:3:1:1. Hence, this algorithm allows reading the QR code from any orientation forms, which significantly improves work efficiency. The alignment pattern ensures the QR code can be decrypted when there is the modules shifted due to lighting distortion. The timing pattern lies horizontally and vertically between the three-position patterns and allows to identify the individual QR data cells when the code is partially damaged easier.

2. **Data encoded region** is the encoded data region that is delimited by the position patterns. This region divided into consisting of blocks of 8 QR modules. These codewords blocks then could be decoded by using the Reed Solomon code.

3. **Error correction region** has one of four different levels of error correction, define as low (L), medium (M), quartile (Q) and high (H) (Kubo 2019) support 7%, 15%, 25% and 30% error recoveries respectively. The error correction level also defines the version of the QR code, which determines the code size. The error correction usually implemented with the Reed Solomon error correction algorithm (Reed and Solomon 1960).

3.2.2   QR Code Decoding Algorithm

Today, the QR code easily decoded with any built-in smartphone app; however, the principle of the decoding algorithm is remaining unchanged. Typically, the decoding process involves the use of digital cameras to capture the QR code image and then to use the image processing techniques to locate the black and white modules. Those modules then will be transformed into the decode-able matrix for future subsequently decryption using the decoding algorithm (Ohbuchi 2004). The decoding process then continues with three typical steps: binarisation, detection and recognition.

3.2.2.1   Binarisation

The binarisation transforms the RGB input texture into the binary one, which generally consists of two different steps. Firstly, the coloured texture needs to be converted to single-channel colour or grayscale, using the following equation:

$$Y_x = \alpha R_x + \beta G_x + \gamma B_x$$

where $\alpha = 0.299$, $\beta = 0.587$, $\gamma = 0.114$ is the output grayscale value at the pixel x. R_x, G_x, B_x are the respectively red, green and blue channels of the colour texture at pixel x. Then the grayscale output is converted into the binary one by using the threshold method. However, choosing the suitable threshold method is the key to the performance of QR code detection. ZXing is one of the most popular open-source libraries which uses the hybrid method to calculate the average luminance value in a group of square blocks. This is also called a mean block binarisation method which firstly divides the captured image into non-overlapping 8-by-8 blocks $\beta_{x,y}$. Then, the luminance average of 5-by-5 overlapping sub-window blocks calculated as the final threshold by using the below equation:

$$A_{x,y} = \sum_{x-2}^{x+2} \sum_{y-2}^{y+2} \frac{1}{25 \times 64}$$

where $A_{x,y}$ is the average for each block $\beta_{x,y}$.

3.2.2.2   Detection

The main task of the detection step is to locate the QR code position and orientation from the binary image in 3D spaces. The finder patterns are playing as a vital role in determining the QR position by using the pattern matching technique. As described above, the three QR code position patterns designed as large squares located on three corners. They respectively formed by 7-by-7 black modules, 5-by-5 white modules and 3-by-3 black modules. The black-white-black-white-black patterns of the QR code with corresponding ratios of 1:1:3:1:1 are the same size in an either horizontal, vertical, or diagonal direction. During the detection process, these patterns would be matched in order to identify the boundary of a QR code. At that point, according to the relative positions of the three-position patterns, the exact position and orientation of the QR code are confirmed.

3.2.2.3   Recognition

Once the QR code boundary and orientation obtained, the encoded information extracted by grid estimated sampling. The sampling first refers to estimate the size of the modules, then obtaining the number of the modules. The central pixel sampled in order to estimate the information of the whole module (whether it is black or white); finally, a matrix with all modules formed.

3.3 Design and Implementation

3.3.1 The Design and Running Process

We have implemented a Python script called "myQR.py" which automatically build a run-able HTML webpage after all the required parameters provided. The sample command could be "*myQR.py air-plane airplane.jpg model.gltf 1.0*". After executing this line, many new files are generated in folder "air-plane" as seen in Fig. 3.5. There are only four input parameters as listed below:

1. **folderURL** is a folder with that name will be created, and the QR code will be related to that folder name.
2. **imageName** is any RGB image stored inside that folder, which will be used to generate the AR marker.
3. **modelName** is the 3D model of objects; at this moment, we support GLTF and OBJ formats. Models (e.g. model.gltf) could be downloaded from the repository website such as https://sketchfab.com.
4. **modelScale** is optional. This parameter allows us to re-scale it to fit the screen and marker best.

After a successful run, four other files are generated:

1. **arImgTagBlackBorder.png** is the printable AR marker, and the 3D model will be rendered on top of it.

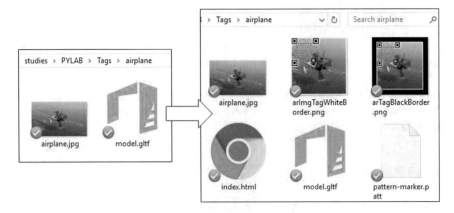

Fig. 3.5 "myQR.py" automatically builds a run-able html webpage

2. **pattern-marker.patt** is the pattern file which is used to recognise the AR card.
3. **index.html** is the index webpage which initiates the camera and displays the 3D model (model.gltf) on the card.

This folder then can be uploaded to a public web host. At later stages, all the processing will be pushed online, so that all the setup could be done on a web browser.

3.3.2   Transparent QR Code on Colour Images

The position, alignment and timing patterns remain unchanged. However, other encoded modules are minimised into 20% of their original sizes, and other empty spaces are coloured as transparent as seen in Fig. 3.6. This transparent marker is designed to be printed an adhesive plastic paper using either Inkjet or Laser printer. However, most of the printers do not provide the white colour of ink (as it is the neutral paper colour); hence, the yellow colour is used to override the white modules, and we keep the same colour for the dark modules. We believed that the use of this transparent QR marker could be beneficial. For instance, the transparent marker does not fully cover the texture content, and the users are free to locate it anywhere for the best readability.

Fig. 3.6 Transparent QR marker example

3.3.3   AR.js for Augmented Reality for the Web

The AR.js (Etienne 2017) is an excellent open-source AR framework made by Jerome Etienne and other contributors on Github.[1] This web-based javascript platform is portable, lightweight, free-to-run and not resource-demanding (e.g. It is a simple web solution, so no installation required. It can be run efficiently on low-cost mobile devices with WebGL and WebRTC). Low memory storage would no longer be a significant issue. This method is believed to make a significant advantage in term of financial due to non-inexpensive AR supported equipment for essential commercial use. Our demonstration website could quickly detect and decode the hidden information on the client's sample marker (either print out or displayed on their phone). The system will render the virtual objects such as 3D models or a video frame on top of the AR marker. The main drawback of AR.js framework is the lack of documentation as it is still under development. However, the framework has strong community support and outstanding results for a prototype demonstration. The code snippet and documentation bellow show a simple way to create a scene that we can use for our AR environment.

In the <body> tag, we need to disable scroll pane for better user experience since the camera viewport is larger than the screen. It would be uncomfortable for user scrolling to see the video content. We set body CSS styling "overflow" to hidden. If the "overflow" does not set to hidden, it will clip out some of the video content, but this is the most optimal solution than zoom out all video content to fit the screen size. The setup for caption in AR Scene in HTML is:

```
< a-scene embedded stats; arjs="sourceType: webcam; debugUIEnabled: false;
patternRatio: 0.5; trackingMethod: best; maxDetectionRate: 30">
```

Inside "A-scene" tag of the *index.html* file, we modified "a-marker" attributes so it can recognise new marker. The main drawback of AR.js, so far, is the ability to detect any marker, it can only detect markers that we trained. Commonly, we have to manually add a new HTML tag if we want to add a new marker:

```
< a-marker type="pattern" url="bar.patt" id= "foo" >
    < a-gltf-model src="model\_name.gltf" >
    </a-gltf-model >
</a-marker >
```

The code snippet above shows how to train AR.js to detect a new marker. There are some new attributes:

- **"preset"**: We are using our custom marker. So we do not need to include this attribute. The default value is set to empty.
- **"type"**: There are three types of markers which are 'pattern', 'barcode' and 'unknown'. For the best visual experience, we chose to use 'pattern' value as our marker type.
- **"url"**: The attribute is used to tell the camera to recognise a new pattern file. It is an essential attribute that needs to be set in order to make custom marker detectable.

---

[1] https://github.com/jeromeetienne/AR.js.

- **"id"**: Unique indicator of the marker.

After setting the "url" attribute and "type" attribute, AR.js will be able to recognise a new pattern. To add a new pattern, the developer needs to add a new HTML tag with different URL value. Inside "a-marker" tag, you can use other 3D entity such as image or video. However, for the best visual demonstration, we used a 3D model.

3.3.4 Adding Interactive with 3D Model

The main drawbacks of the previous demonstration are the lack of ability to use gesture to rotate or move the object around. The lack of finger gesture manipulation forces the user to move the camera around the marker to see all side of the object. To solve this problem, we used a touch gesture library written in Javascript called Hammer.js.[2] This library has several touch-actions that will enhance interaction with the 3D model. All we need to do is register the new component from the official documentation of Aframe (Diego Marcos 2015)—a framework used in AR.js. When a developer registers for a new component, it is essential to initialise Hammer object. There are some other objects that the developer needs to add in Hammer object to enable zoom in and zoom out. The developer needs to add "Pinch" object which extended from Hammer object. After initialising Hammer object, we called a method named "on" to start listening to the event. "On" method is a call back function which will save memory and fast execution time. Since the different application will define different gesture that the user can use, so the gesture will be defined by the developer who wants to alter our demonstration site.

3.4 Results and Conclusion

At this stage, the base of this application has been achieved. The results appear promising, as seen in Fig. 3.7. This Figure displays two other more complicated 3D models with more vertices, textures and faces. The current deployment works with all iOS and Android devices that run the latest version of Google Chrome. On iOS, the performance is slower to render a 3D model and user will expect some delay between marker detection and rendering 3D object. Overall, both platforms when tested on a different device all have impressive performance around 60 fps.

In any field, not only education, "A picture is worth a thousand words"; and a moving picture or a 3D model is probably worth much more. Education enhancement is where AR found useful. In this chapter, we have proposed a web-based system that allows for enhancing the Augmented Reality (AR) experiences in the educational environment. The system is designed to be user-friendly, portable and lightweight.

---

[2]https://hammerjs.github.io/.

Fig. 3.7 Two AR views of 3D models overlaid on top of two proposed AR markers

We also introduced the concept of transparent AR marker which allows the flexibility of using the AR marker on any physical hard copy materials. At the future stage, we believe that our proposed concept could be dynamically applied to other activities such as movie entertainments or video games.

References

Azuma T (1997) A survey of augmented reality. Presence Teleoperators Virtual Environ 6: 355–385. MIT Press
Carmigniani J, Furht B (2011) Augmented reality: an overview. 3–46. Springer
Caudell P, Mizell W (1992) Augmented reality: an application of heads-up display technology to manual manufacturing processes, pp 659–669. IEEE

Caudell T (1990) AR at Boeing. 2002–07–10 [2014–11–02]. https://www.idemployee.id.tue.nl/gwmrauterberg/presentations/hci-history/sld096.htm

Diego Marcos, Kevin Ngo, Don McCurdy (2015) Writing a component. https://aframe.io/docs/0.8.0/introduction/writing-a-component.html

Downes S (2005) E-learning 2.0. Elearn magazine 1

Elkjær B (2001) Implementing computer supported cooperative learning. Manag Learn (Sage Publications Ltd.) 32:280

Etienne J(2017) Creating augmented reality with AR.js and A-Frame. July. https://aframe.io/blog/arjs/#add-augmented-reality-in-your-a-frame-project.

Heather B, Wei C, Masaru S, Marcus S, Shateel A, Daiki T (2016) Profiles in innovation virtual and augmented reality. https://www.goldmansachs.com/our-thinking/pages/technology-driving-innovation-folder/virtual-and-augmented-reality/report.pdf.

Heilig ML (1962) Sensorama simulator. Google Patents, August 28

Ivanova A, Ivanova G (2009) Net-generation learning style: a challenge for higher education. In: Proceedings of the international conference on computer systems and technologies and workshop for PhD students in computing, vol 72. ACM

Karayan SS, Crowe JA (1997) Student perceptions of electronic discussion groups. J 69–71

Kubo Y, Eguchi K, Aoki R, Kondo S, Azuma S, Indo T (2019) FabAuth: printed objects identification using resonant properties of their inner structures. In Extended abstracts of the 2019 CHI conference on human factors in computing systems, LBW2215. ACM

Liu Y, Yang J, Liu M (2008) Recognition of QR code with mobile phones. In: 2008 Control and decision conference, CCDC 2008, Chinese, pp 203–206. IEEE

Ohbuchi E, Hanaizumi H, Hock LA (2004) Barcode readers using the camera device in mobile phones. In 2004 International conference on cyberworlds, pp 260–265. IEEE.

Oliver M, Trigwell K (2005) Can 'blended learning' be redeemed? E-learn Digital Media (SAGE Publications) 2:17–26

Reed IS, Solomon G (1960) Polynomial codes over certain finite fields. J Soc Indus Appl Math (SIAM) 8:300–304

Rios JS, Ketterer DJ, Wohn DY (2018) How users choose a face lens on Snapchat. In: Companion of the 2018 ACM conference on computer supported cooperative work and social computing (ACM), pp 321–324

Smith D, Hardaker G (2000) E-learning innovation through the implementation of an internet supported learning environment. J Educ Technol Soc (JSTOR) 3:422–432

Sutherland IE (1965) The ultimate display. From Wagner to virtual reality, Multimedia

Zhang D, Zhao JL, Zhou L, Jr Jay NF (2004) Can e-learning replace classroom learning? Commun ACM (ACM) 47:75–79s

Chapter 4
The Concept of 'Bringing Your Own Device' in Scaffolded and Augmented Education

Peter Mozelius, Jimmy Jaldemark, Sofia Eriksson Bergström
and Marcus Sundgren

Abstract Location-based games have enabled new opportunities for augmenting the traditional learning space. In a time when most students have their own smartphones, the concept of bringing your own device (BYOD) also seems promising in educational settings. However, playing at random in augmented reality environments will not automatically bring curriculum-aligned learning outcomes. This chapter analyses and discusses how the combination of BYOD and augmented reality gaming might be scaffolded to support collaborative curriculum-aligned learning. The overall research strategy was a case-study approach with Affordance theory, Social Constructivism and BYOD as theoretical assumptions for deductive analysis. The case units were two outdoor sessions for middle school students with curriculum-aligned assignments in Mathematics and Social Science solved by playing the augmented reality game Pokémon GO. Data have been collected by video recordings of the outdoor sessions with spy glasses and a handheld camera. Results indicate that the augmented reality environment stimulates active learning, but that there like in traditional learning, is a need for scaffolding to achieve the stated learning outcomes.

4.1 Introduction

The combination of location-based augmented reality games and mobile devices has opened up new opportunities for augmenting the traditional orchestration of teaching and learning activities (Akçayır and Akçayır 2017; Chen 2017). A frequently used augmented reality game in educational settings is Niantic's Pokémon GO, but there are other augmented reality games to consider as well, where one example is the recently released Wizards Unite. To build on a popular game seems like a wise

P. Mozelius (✉)
Department of Computer and System Science, Mid Sweden University, Östersund, Sweden
e-mail: peter.mozelius@miun.se

J. Jaldemark · S. Eriksson Bergström · M. Sundgren
Department of Education, Mid Sweden University, Sundsvall, Sweden
e-mail: jimmy.jaldemark@miun.se

© Springer Nature Switzerland AG 2020
V. Geroimenko (ed.), *Augmented Reality in Education*,
Springer Series on Cultural Computing,
https://doi.org/10.1007/978-3-030-42156-4_4

choice, but the critical factor for positive learning outcomes is how the game is used and scaffolded (Ruiz-Ariza et al. 2019; Mozelius et al. 2019).

In many countries today, a majority of students have their own mobile devices and an interesting idea is that students utilise their personally-owned technology devices in school activities. There are several research studies reporting on successful examples of students bringing their own devices to teaching and learning sessions (Song 2014; Song and Wen 2018). However, to implement the concept of bringing your own device (BYOD) in educational settings also raises new questions such as security challenges, teacher acceptance and parental acceptance (McLean 2016; Kiger and Herro 2015).

BYOD in education has often been presented as a one-to-one concept, with the problem of possible exclusion of students from certain socio-economic groups (Bathon 2013; McLean 2016). On the contrary, students sharing mobile devices might be a way to orchestrate collaborative learning (Mozelius et al. 2017).

There are several studies on how location-based games can be combined with the BYOD concept in education (Herro et al. 2013; Xanthopoulos and Xinogalos 2018). Less has been studied about the affordances that emerge in the interplay between students and applied BYOD sessions with augmented reality games. This study had a focus on affordances that might support collaborative learning in primary school learning activities.

The aim of our study was to analyse and describe the interplay between aspects of students, mobile devices, augmented reality applications and the design of collaborative educational settings. The research question was as follows: 'Which affordances emerge in the interplay of BYOD and augmented reality in scaffolded and collaborative middle school educational settings?'.

4.2 Theoretical Assumptions

In this study, the theoretical assumptions for a deductive analysis and discussion have been the BYOD concept, Social Constructivism and the Affordance theory.

4.2.1 Bring Your Own Device

Traditionally, companies and organisations have provided the necessary information technology, but this is a changing phenomenon (Caldwell 2012). The idea of bringing your own device (BYOD) got a breakthrough in 2009 when the world-wide IT-company Intel encouraged their employees to bring their own laptops, tablets and mobile phones to work (Govinfo-Security n.d.). BYOD started in the IT-industry and is still mostly used at companies, but the trend has also reached the educational sector with the use of BYOD both in higher education (Afreen 2014), as well as in primary school (Song 2014).

New BYOD could be defined as 'the practice of people bringing their own laptops, tablets, smartphones, or other mobile devices with them to learning or work environments' (Johnson et al. 2016, p. 36). The role of BYOD in education is much the same, and according to a survey conducted in the UK and the US 85% of the answering institutes allowed staff and students to access the school network. However, the percentage of BYOD in primary school settings was lower (Afreen 2014). Another challenge for primary school is how to involve parents and as suggested by Kiger and Herro (2015), create concrete parental guidelines.

The concept of BYOD has often been presented as a one-to-one technology design with one device per student (Cardoza and Tunks 2014; McLean 2016). There are also studies discussing if the use of BYOD might aggravate the digital divide between different socio-economic and geographical groups (Motlik 2008; Siani 2017), but as found in the study by Adhikari et al. (2016), access to mobile devices do not necessarily have to be a critical barrier. A one-to-one design would certainly have a strong potential to transform the traditional classroom and extending learning from school only into other environments. To blur the boundaries between formal and informal learning spaces is an interesting challenge (Liu et al. 2014), but another essential and well-discussed idea is to support collaborative learning (Falloon 2015). Might the concept of students sharing a mobile device stimulate interplay and collaborative learning?

4.2.2 Social Perspectives and Collaborative Learning

Collaborative learning has its roots in social theories of learning dating back to among other the sociocultural ideas developed by Vygotsky and the ideas of pragmatist philosophers such as Dewey in the early twentieth century. Nevertheless, its impact was minor until it received wider attention in the 1980s. An emergence that coincided with the deemphasizing of cognitive perspectives of learning in the research of educational technologies. Collaborative learning builds on the idea that learning fundamentally is a social phenomenon. Such learning includes human beings' interplay with the surrounding world and other humans. This interplay involves the purposeful application of technologies. Such purposeful application of technologies turns them into tools for learning.

This interdependent relationship between humans and tools 'provide the link or bridge between the concrete actions carried out by individuals and groups, on the one hand, and cultural, institutional and historical settings, on the other hand'. Human application of tools also transforms the settings in which they are applied. This means that collaborative learning is an emerging phenomenon that depends on tools and cultural, ecological, historical and social aspects of settings in the surrounding world. Therefore, mobile technologies, such as location-based augmented reality games and mobile devices, act as tools that mediate the process of collaborative learning. Such world view and conceptualisation of learning suits well with human beings perceiving of affordances in the surrounding environment. The next section goes deeper into affordance theory.

4.2.3 The Concept of Affordance

The concept of affordance was coined by Gibson (1979/1986) and concerns a relationship 'that refers to both the environment and the animal' (Gibson 1979/1986, p. 127). This conceptualisation is emphasised as a complementarity, a holistic non-dualistic world view. Such view emphasises affordances as a inseparable relationship between humans and the surrounding environment. The affordance supports and limits human actions in the surrounding environment and are relative to the individual. Nevertheless, the 'affordance is neither an objective property nor a subjective property; or it is both' (Gibson 1979/1986, p. 129). It is 'properties taken with reference to the observer' (Gibson 1979/1986, p. 143).

Moreover, it is both related to the environment and the behaviour of an individual, including being both physical and psychical. In the concept, Gibson emphasised a world view, where aspects of culture and nature are linked to the environment. Meaning that it is not possible to divide human actions in the world into different environments. In practice, an affordance assists the human being in their perceiving of the world by simultaneously co-perceive themselves. Human beings learn to perceive affordances of things for both themselves and other persons. This process leads to socialisation into the surrounding society. In other words, the students' actions while playing location-based games are emphasised as being inseparable from the surrounding environment.

The concept of affordance is related to the ability of the observer to perceive the surrounding environment (Rietveld and Kiverstein 2014). While Shaw et al. (1982) apply the concept of effectivity, Snow (1992) use the concept of aptitude to discuss this relationship. However, Greeno's (1994) concept of ability is chosen in the conceptualisation of affordance in this chapter. He discussed the inseparable relationship between affordances and abilities and highlighted that affordances relate attributes of things in the surrounding environment, to the activities of agents with various abilities. Moreover, he also claims that ability relates attributes of agents to an activity 'with something in the environment that has some affordance' (Greeno 1994, p. 338). By this, he meant that affordances and abilities co-define each other.

Rietveld and Kiverstein (2014) emphasises that affordances could be discussed as a sociocultural phenomenon embedded in human activities. Such a link emphasises the link between abilities as affordances emerging through human participation in sociocultural practices. The consequence for understanding the playing of location-based games is the need to understand such activity from a sociocultural perspective, including an emphasis on various abilities to perceive affordances.

4.3   Method and Data Collection

The used research strategy was the case-study approach, with the two outdoor learning sessions using BYOD and augmented reality games as the case units. Main participants in the mobile outdoor activities were students and teachers from a fifth-grade class and a sixth-grade class. Furthermore, researchers from the Mid Sweden University participated as observers in the teaching and learning sessions. The location-based augmented reality game that was used on students' smartphones in the outdoor activities was Pokémon GO. Students played the game and solved assignments in small groups of three to four students with one smartphone per group.

Both learning sessions, one in mathematics and one in social science, were orchestrated as walks that used existing PokéStops in the local environments. When a student group passed one of the stops, the teacher tried to attract the students' attention. Students had been instructed beforehand to prepare for specific tasks that all were related to either social science or mathematics. An example is that they had to make calculations related to both Pokémon GO and real-world objects in the vicinity. One group counted the number of cars during the walk. In addition to the pre-planned assignments, the gaming sessions also included more spontaneous discussions. After completing the orchestrated activities, teachers and students met in their classrooms for follow-up activities. In the follow-up lessons, teachers brought up various issues that arose during the walks and gaming sessions.

To answer the research questions data were collected by video recordings of the activities in the outdoor sessions. During the activities, teachers and researchers wore spy glasses to capture collaborations and communications from the various wearers' perspectives. One of the researchers recorded the group activities with a handheld video camera to get a more complete overall picture of the various perspectives collected with the spy glasses. The analysis of the recorded video material has also been compared to the finding from an earlier analysis of the same sessions (Mozelius et al. 2017).

4.4   Findings and Discussions

The data analysis had a focus on affordances that emerge while applying BYOD in scaffolded, collaborative and augmented educational settings and which affordances that emerge in the interplay of BYOD and augmented reality. Results have been divided into four various categories of affordance: *task-ability*, *social-ability*, *teach-ability* and *knowledge-ability*. These affordances were found both by teachers and by students in the recordings from spy glasses and the handheld camera. How this might lead to a deeper understanding of collaborative learning in primary school activities is described and problematised in the categories below.

4.4.1 Task-Ability

Video recordings from the spy glasses show how students often shift focus in their mobile phones, zapping between the game and other apps. Initially, the main attention is on the game, but later this change to things such as maps and social media. In the videos from the spy glasses, it is obvious it is also very obvious how the students shift focus from the 'mobile space' to the real world. In the students' interplay, there are moments of competition with comparisons of numbers of caught Pokémon monsters, numbers of thrown balls and achieved levels in the Pokémon GO game.

//They jointly walk forward on the sidewalk.

Gustav - oh look look look, a pokémon / he starts to run.

Gustav - Yeahhhh, I caught it !!!

Robert- but hey listen, don't show the car their number. (he means by the camera in the spy glasses).

Gustav - yeah I caught a pokemon !!!! I got 100 Xp and three candies and a hundred pokemon go.

//They stop.

Thomas - I see a 'Sikhir'.

Chris - but who doesn't have a Sikhir? (goes next to Samson, who holds the mobile phone).

Gustav - Yes! Gotcha!!!!

Furthermore, the gaming had several breakdowns due to failing connections, discharged batteries and non-functioning GPS signals. The latter issue leads to the problem of PokéStops that are out of reach. This negative aspect of affordances that resulting in limitations rather than possibilities was also recognised both by teachers and students.

4.4.2 Social-Ability

This category is closely aligned to the task-ability category that is described above. An example of when these affordances overlap is when the students identify opportunities that consider the game itself and want to share their results and compare with others. As a result of walking in small groups sharing a mobile, discussions arise about other topics than the content in the lesson. The sharing of a mobile device also led to agreements where everyone in the group should be involved in the catching of Pokémon monsters. In the thesis by Walldén Hillström (2014) the discussions around a shared mobile device are compared to the discussions around a campfire.

By sharing a mobile, students identify each other as social affordances and the benefits of collaboration. The videos not only show student collaboration for successful gaming but also students collaborating to answer the questions from the teacher:

Teacher - What's the name of this PokéStop? //beside the Bertil Malmberg statue (Fig. 4.1)

Fig. 4.1 The statue of Bertil Malmberg as seen in the Pokémon GO app (GPS coordinates: 62.6310, 17.9459)

Victor, Roger and Thomas gathers around the mobile that Samson carries searching for the name of the PokéStop.

Victor - Click on it now!

Roger Yes, I know.

And Roger answers the teacher - Bertil Malmberg!

The sharing of a device seems to create social affordances that probably would not have occurred in a one-to-one orchestration. At the same time, the BYOD sharing initiates somehow peripheral discussions where students lose their immediate focus on the learning activity. However, discussions and collaboration are seldom completely focused, and peripheral discussions can be an important part of learning.

4.4.3   Knowledge-Ability

During the walking sessions, the students and the teacher passes a series of knowledge affordances that are associated with the PokéStops. This can be identified in the videos as dialogues where the teacher asks questions to the students to catch their attention on the emerging affordances. Students perceive, as seen in the excerpt below, that mobile phones offer knowledge-seeking that could answer the questions that are asked by the teacher.

Teacher - What's the name of the PokéStop then? Do you know the name?

Victor reading on the mobile screen, exclaims, - The Franzén monument! (See Fig. 4.2).

There are also questions and dialogues about things in the real-world surroundings that are not mapped to the game world. It seems that the walking lesson structure makes students identify affordances of the knowledge-ability category when the teacher perceives the surroundings as a knowledge affordance.

Teacher – What do you say, what kind of house has this been earlier? Anyone that knows that?

Gustav – A fire station.

These affordances in the knowledge-ability category are mostly perceived by the teacher, and that the teacher later tries to communicate this to the students. However,

Fig. 4.2 The statue of Frans Mikael Franzén and his muses as seen in the Pokémon GO app (GPS coordinates: 62.6303, 17.9470)

the video clips show some knowledge affordances that are directly perceived by the students. Through the gameplay, students need to keep track of how the game world corresponds to the virtual, otherwise, they would not find the virtual PokéStops that are mapped to real-world objects.

4.4.4   Teach-Ability

During the walking lesson, the teacher finds interesting affordances in the mobile. The teacher also uses the game content as teaching content by asking questions to the students. An example of a Pokémom GO related question is the one about how long it would take to hatch a five km egg at a certain walking speed. In this situation, the teacher uses a teaching affordance in the game to enhance students' understanding of a specific phenomenon. This is a way of creating interplay between the game and the teacher's teacha-bility, which is different from Pokémon GO gaming during students' spare time.

> Victor - /…/Oh, you got a five kilometer egg!
> Teacher – Then you have to walk five kilometers. How long would that take?

4.4.5   General Discussion

These different types of affordances co-exist in various ways and are at different occasions super- respectively subordinated each other. The focus for this chapter has been to analyse and describe the affordances that support collaborative learning in middle school educational settings emerging from the interplay between augmented reality and the concept of BYOD. These emerging affordances are the ones that have been perceived by the participants in the walking sessions, based on the conducted video analysis where the choice of these aspects has been a deliberate perspective. The aspects can be seen as categories, but affordances are defined individually with a student and a teacher perspective.

The perceiving of affordances aligned to knowledge-ability was understood in the analysis as the teacher perceiving affordances that later were mediated to the students. This was often mediated by questions from the teacher to the students, for affordances that appeared and were perceived in the Pokémon GO game. For the type of affordances related to the game, gaming success or gaming failure categorised as task-ability it was, on the other hand, the students that perceived the affordances and mediated them to the teacher. This constructs an image of a teaching and learning session where the teacher's knowledge authority sometimes is on the same level as the students', a phenomenon that seems to inspire the students to challenge the teacher's leadership.

Furthermore, the video analysis identified a change or development of task-ability aspects towards knowledge-ability in the sequences where students could find answers to teacher questions in the game. Affordances that in the analysis have been categorised as teach-ability were perceived by the teacher, and that these affordances emerge from the didactic resources that the teacher uses to enhance the students' understanding of a phenomenon. The analysis also identified several aspects of social-ability that emerge when students perceiving of task-ability affordances creates a social space for interplay. The same goes for affordances of knowledge-ability that creates social interplay where students talk and discuss with each other. The collaborative aspect lays in the fact that individuals perceived affordance shares affordance.

A walking session is characterised by transitions between different spaces and different subjects. During a traditional activity in a classroom, transitions are often something that is disturbing. In newly built modern schools, walls are often replaced by large transparent glass sections as well as doors with large glass windows (de Laval et al. 2019). In these flexible solutions, the transitions between lessons have become such a big problem that has led to a reconstruction of more closed traditional classrooms. Compared with this study, where the teaching and learning activities are located in a local open environment, there are no findings that indicate any problematic transitions. Transitions between individual and collaborative activities, as well as transitions between different subjects such as Mathematics, History and Swedish, seem to have run smoothly. Furthermore, the idea of BYOD as a mobile phone to play an augmented reality game was perceived as a supporting affordance by both the teacher and by the students.

It can be claimed that the results from this study exemplify how a learning activity is situated in an augmented educational context, outside the traditional school premises. The boundless flexibility that this implies might provide too wide and unfocused affordances for the students. However, through the augmented reality and the mobile game world, there is attention directed towards the interplay between students and the teacher. The perceived affordances reinforce collaborative learning in this augmented educational setting. An important condition for the perceiving of such affordances is the interplay between the student, the teacher and the mobile and the surroundings in both the augmented and the real world.

Without the teacher in the previous study, there is a completely different interplay, and likewise without the students or without the mobile. The primary contribution of this study is a counterimage to the perception of technology replacing the teacher. Authors claim that involving the concepts of BYOD and augmented reality in middle school outdoor activities rather would increase the importance of the teacher. At the same time, the students' interplay in an augmented reality stimulates and encourages the idea of collaborative learning.

4.5 Conclusion

One of the more positive findings in this study was that this mobile, game-based, augmented reality setting seemed to stimulate students to engage in collaborative activities. The categories of affordance that the analysis resulted in show that interplay is of crucial importance. Knowledge-ability requires interplay between students and teachers in order for students to perceive opportunities for the knowledge-based affordances. Furthermore, teaching-ability requires students to be present to interact with the teacher, otherwise, the teacher does not perceive the opportunities to teach. It is clear that affordance can be understood and discussed as a sociocultural phenomenon embedded in human activities (Rietveld and Kiverstein 2014).

The analysis of the video clips also confirms the idea that several students sharing a device can support interplay, discussions and collaborative learning. In some orchestrations of BYOD for education, a one-to-one setup might be important, but this must not be seen as a condition for teaching and learning activities. As discussed by Kernutt (2018), one-to-one arrangements can sometimes tend to replace human interplay with technology and disturb the 'campfire talk' that spontaneously occurs when a group of students gathers around a shared device.

References

Adhikari J, Mathrani A, Scogings C (2016) Bring your own devices classroom: exploring the issue of digital divide in the teaching and learning contexts. Interact Technol Smart Educ 13(4):323–343

Akçayır M, Akçayır G (2017) Advantages and challenges associated with augmented reality for education: a systematic review of the literature. Educ Res Rev 20:1–11

Afreen R (2014) Bring your own device (BYOD) in higher education: opportunities and challenges. Int J Emerg Trends Technol in Comput Sci 3(1):233–236

Bathon J (2013) One student, one device, and a thousand laws: a thicket of legal issues has sprung up in response to modern 1-to-1 and BYOD programs. in every rollout, schools have some tough choices to make. THE J (Technological Horizons In Education) 40(8):24

Caldwell C, Zeltmann S, Griffin K (2012) BYOD (bring your own device). In: Competition forum, vol 10, no 2. American Society for Competitiveness, p 117

Cardoza Y, Tunks J (2014) The bring your own technology initiative: an examination of teachers' adoption. Comput Sch 31(4):293–315

Chen P, Liu X, Cheng W, Huang R (2017) A review of using augmented reality in education from 2011 to 2016. In: Innovations in smart learning. Springer, Singapore, pp 13–18

de Laval S, Frelin A, Grannäs J (2019) Skolmiljöer: utvärdering och erfarenhetsåterföring i fysisk skolmiljö. Ifous, Stockholm

Falloon G (2015) What's the difference? learning collaboratively using iPads in conventional classrooms. Comput Educ 84:62–77. https://doi.org/10.1016/j.compedu.2015.01.010

Gibson JJ (1979/1986) The ecological approach to visual perception. Erlbaum, Hillsdale, NJ

Govinfo-Security (n.d) Mobile: learn from intel's CISO on securing employee-owned devices. https://www.govinfosecurity.com/webinars/mobile-learn-from-intels-ciso-on-securing-employee-owned-devices-w-264, Accessed 28 June 2019

Greeno JG (1994) Gibson's affordances. Psychol Rev 101(2):336–342

Herro D, Kiger D, Owens C (2013) Mobile technology: case-based suggestions for classroom integration and teacher educators. J Digit Learn Teach Educ 30(1):30–40

Johnson L, Adams Becker S, Cummins M, Estrada V, Freeman A, Hall C (2016) NMC Horizon Report: 2016 Higher, Education. The New Media Consortium, Austin, TX

Kernutt C (2018) Changing the conversation. https://www.chriskernutt.com/creativity-and-collaboration, Accessed 23 Aug 2019

Kiger D, Herro D (2015) Bring your own device: parental guidance (PG) suggested. TechTrends 59(5):51–61

Liu M, Scordino R, Geurtz R, Navarrete C, Ko Y, Lim M (2014) A look at research on mobile learning in K-12 education from 2007 to the present. J Res Technol Educ 46(4):325–372

McLean KJ (2016) The implementation of bring your own device (BYOD) in primary [elementary] schools. Front Psychol 7:1739

Motlik S (2008) Mobile Learning in Developing Nations. Int Rev Res Open Distance Learn 9(2):1–7

Mozelius P, Eriksson Bergström S, Jaldemark J (2017) Learning by walking—pokémon go and mobile technology in formal education. In: proceedings of 10th international conference of education, research and innovation, Seville, Spain

Mozelius P, Jaldemark J, Eriksson Bergström S, Sundgren M (2019) Augmented education: location-based games for real-world teaching and learning sessions. In: Augmented reality games I. Springer, Cham, pp 217–235

Rietveld E, Kiverstein J (2014) A rich landscape of affordances. Ecol Psychol 26(4):325–352

Ruiz-Ariza, A, López-Serrano S, Manuel J, Martínez-López EJ (2019) A theoretical-practical framework for the educational uses of pokémon GO in children and adolescents. In: Augmented reality games I. Springer, Cham, pp 191–202

Shaw R, Turvey M, Mace W (1982) Ecological psychology: the consequence of a commitment to realism. In: Weimer W, Palermo D (eds) Cognition and the symbolic processes, vol 2. Erlbaum, Hillsdale, NJ, pp 159–226

Siani A (2017) BYOD strategies in higher education: current knowledge, students' perspectives, and challenges. New Directions Teach Phys Sci (12)

Snow RE (1992) Aptitude theory: yesterday, today, and tomorrow. Educ Psychol 27(1):5–32

Song Y (2014) "Bring Your Own Device (BYOD)" for seamless science inquiry in a primary school. Comput Educ 74:50–60

Song Y, Wen Y (2018) Integrating various apps on BYOD (Bring Your Own Device) into seamless inquiry-based learning to enhance primary students' science learning. J Sci Educ Technol 27(2):165–176

Walldén Hillström K (2014) I samspel med surfplattor: om barns digitala kompetenser och tillträde till digitala aktiviteter i förskolan / Interacting with tablet computers: Preschool children's digital competencies and everyday access to digital activities, Doctoral dissertation, Institution for pedagogy, didactics and educational studies, Uppsala University

Xanthopoulos S, Xinogalos S (2018) Opportunities and challenges of mobile location-based games in education: exploring the integration of authoring and analytics tools. In: 2018 IEEE global engineering education conference (EDUCON). IEEE, pp 1797–1805

Chapter 5
The FeDiNAR Project: Using Augmented Reality to Turn Mistakes into Learning Opportunities

Alexander Atanasyan, Dennis Kobelt, Marvin Goppold, Torben Cichon, and Michael Schluse

Abstract This chapter describes FeDiNAR (German acronym for Didactical Use of Errors with the Help of Augmented Reality)—an ongoing project, which focuses on errors as a highly beneficial learning opportunity. The aim of the project is the development and evaluation of an Augmented Reality (AR) based learning system with associated learning scenarios in order to make the most efficient use of a learner's mistakes for individual competence acquisition. The chapter begins with an introduction of the education-based main idea in combination with a selection of didactical theories, schemes and intervention levels. Next, the authors define the error term for the project and illustrate the setup of the proposed learning system in general and the technologies involved. They then present their prototype, which includes a range of actuators and sensors, offering many possibilities to define scenarios in which the presented system will apply. The chapter continues with the underlying technological foundation based on digital twins enabling to use augmented reality for the presented didactical concept and concludes with the findings after the first project phase.

A. Atanasyan (✉) · T. Cichon · M. Schluse
Institute for Man-Machine Interaction, RWTH Aachen University, Aachen, Germany
e-mail: atanasyan@mmi.rwth-aachen.de

T. Cichon
e-mail: cichon@mmi.rwth-aachen.de

M. Schluse
e-mail: schluse@mmi.rwth-aachen.de

D. Kobelt
Laboratory for Industrial Engineering, University of Applied Sciences and Arts
Ostwestfalen-Lippe, Lemgo, Germany
e-mail: dennis.kobelt@th-owl.de

M. Goppold
Institute of Industrial Engineering and Ergonomics, RWTH Aachen University, Aachen, Germany
e-mail: m.goppold@iaw.rwth-aachen.de

© Springer Nature Switzerland AG 2020
V. Geroimenko (ed.), *Augmented Reality in Education*,
Springer Series on Cultural Computing,
https://doi.org/10.1007/978-3-030-42156-4_5

71

5.1   The FeDiNAR Idea

When investigating the state of the art of technical vocational education and training in craftsmanship and industry in Germany, it is evident that many concepts exist, which aim at the integration of modern technology into learning processes (Bundesministerium für Bildung und Forschung 2019; e.g. Fehling 2017). All of them contribute to the simplification of learning and support of competence fostering. Most approaches have in common that they use technology to illustrate and demonstrate the functionality and causality of technical systems in vocational education situations. In addition to the explicit knowledge requirements, many other factors contribute to designing a work process. In literature, some authors summarise them to tacit knowledge (Eraut 2000; Polanyi and Sen 2009), situational constraints (Klafki 2000) and further constructs. Overall, there does not exist one correct solution when considering all these facts in a decision-making problem, which leads to a compromise that cannot satisfy all requirements of stakeholders and objective requirements in a perfect way (cf. Rauner 2013; Atkinson 1999).

Therefore, future skilled workers, who take part in an apprenticeship program in the German dual education system, need to address decision-making and argumentation. On top of that, they should learn from wrong decisions, the corresponding analysis and planning mistakes and subsequent action errors (Weingardt 2004). Currently, few concepts for learning from errors exist in the German apprenticeship dual education system, especially in technical occupational fields.

In fact, teachers and apprenticeship supervisors explicitly try to prevent apprentices from making mistakes in order to avoid negative consequences for safety, business or environment (Cannon and Edmondson 2005; Janis and Mann 1977).

In contrast to that, work-based learning processes offer excellent conditions to learn from errors. Experience by learning from errors in work-based learning enables to foster a substantial understanding of the work process and the topics related to it. Work processes provide an opportunity to illustrate the drastic consequences of human errors for all stakeholders and the environment.

In summary, this opportunity is the motivation of FeDiNAR to visualise dangerous consequences of errors in work processes with the help of augmented reality (see Fig. 5.1).

Senge (1990) already stated that learning from experience is only powerful when humans see the consequences of their actions and get a chance to choose alternatives

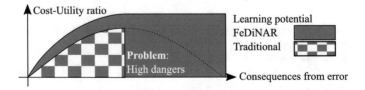

Fig. 5.1 Advantages of FeDiNAR compared to conventional vocational training behaviour

afterwards. Observing consequences instantly after actions is difficult, but technology might help to solve this issue. Augmented reality (AR) is quickly reaching maturity and will be state of the art in a few years in professional contexts such as production in industry and craftsmanship (Gartner 2017). This offers an opportunity to research and develop a didactic concept incorporating augmented reality systems for effectively learning from errors. AR technology presents a solution for direct feedback of erroneous actions as Rausch (2012) described for work-based learning scenarios in vocational education and training. FeDiNAR uses empirically proven learning effects of errors (Bauer and Harteis 2012; Kapur 2015) in order to provide the opportunity of making dangerous errors in work-based learning processes in a safe way. The positive mindset towards errors (cf. Tulis et al. 2017) will lead to the learning system design. Didactics can enforce error triggers by tweaks in the learning situation conditions. All of these tweaks have to be part of the didactic concept and the didactic reasoning process. Furthermore, FeDiNAR will develop or select a learning theory (cf. Oser and Spychiger 2005) in its didactic concept.

Due to the technical constraints of the selected process representation approach, the FeDiNAR system can only perceive discrete states of action. Because of that, in a first attempt, the FeDiNAR system is only capable of detecting phenomenological errors (cf. Sträter 2000). It needs additional information to facilitate a causal error perspective, which is the main interest of all educational research questions (cf. Sträter 2000). Mehl (1993) verifies a methodological issue when detecting errors from observed action outcomes. Observations of actions alone cannot be the basis for an interpretation of error causes. Therefore, FeDiNAR uses an approach similar to the learning concepts of Kapur (2015, 2016). FeDiNAR includes a debriefing or feedback phase after system usage by apprentices. Although there is no guarantee nor desire for the occurrence of errors in the work-based learning situations, debriefing is always a productive learning phase, even in cases of perfect solutions (e.g. Ellis and Davidi 2005). The system does not eliminate the need for sophisticated vocational education personnel, as, among other tasks, they are necessary to supervise the debriefing and feedback including interpretations of the actions taken and inferring possible error causes. Furthermore, Ellis and Kruglanski (1992) show that the higher the perceived competence difference of participants and reviewers, the more positive performance effects exist.

FeDiNAR's goal goes along with scenarios for future vocational education and training in Germany (cf. Frenz et al. 2015) because the learning system supplies a concept to foster problem-solving skills of apprentices as, for example, Abele (2018) suggests. Multiple states of the FeDiNAR system help apprentices to not only learn work-based problem-solving but also to reflect their solutions with respect to different social, ethical, legal, individual and technical issues (Rauner 2013).

5.2 Definition of the Error Term in the Project

The project team derived their error term definition within an interdisciplinary work-shop. In it, experts in human factors, human systems integration, education and technical vocational apprenticeship supervisors from the industry took part. All participants have a focus on human errors, which result from human interaction with technical systems. As such, there are two alternatives for error term definition. On the one hand, there is a human-centred approach rooted in education and human factors, which comes with a deterministic technology perspective. On the other hand, there is a system approach, which rests on reliability theory and incorporates humans as one source for reliability weakness (e.g. Dhillon and Misra 1984) based on a stochastic technology perspective.

A group discussion arrived at the consensus to choose the human-centred approach over the reliability-driven approach due to the didactic focus of the project. Consequently, all errors are assumed to root in human tasks, which are parts of work processes and induce error propagation into all involved technical systems. Moreover, all stochastic technical elements are simplified to deterministic models to fit the chosen approach. As a consequence, faults (ISO/IEC/IEEE 2010) and failures (ISO/IEC 2005) are not part of the further investigation due to their stochastic nature. In summary, all errors considered in the project are human errors.

This definition is in line with common interdisciplinary error research results such as Senders and Morray (1991). They state that errors are human actions, which contradict intentions, expectations as well as implicit or explicit standards.

Therefore, human actions cause errors when their outcome deviates from intended goals. Moreover, the deviation from the intended goal must not be part of a random cause. This view on errors has parallels with the IEEE Standard Classification for Software Anomalies on errors (IEEE STD 2010) or mistakes (cf. ISO/IEC/IEEE 2017).

As mentioned above, standards help to classify human actions into correct and erroneous actions (e.g. EN ISO 9000:2005). Thus, all human actions in work processes require defined standards to enable error detection using a discrete event system. In concordance with the last mentioned definition, the project will establish a methodology to set up a requirement list for action outcomes in order to identify errors by comparison. When considering constructivist didactics, there exist many feasible solutions to a work-based problem rather than a singular correct one. For this reason, the requirement list needs to define a solution space that distinguishes between several tiered outcomes. These can trigger different sequences that may both be correct or involve error propagation. Referring to Senders and Morray (1991), the FeDiNAR system needs to operationalise a continuous work process by setting up standards for technologically observable events and actions that allow discrete descriptions.

While the project investigates a contemporary technical solution, it serves the realisation of the pedagogical intention of FeDiNAR, which itself is in the focus of research. Especially in the light of past research efforts in this discipline, the

FeDiNAR error term definition has to align with these results. Considering the first milestone of pedagogical research of learning from failure, the definition falls into the second category of Weimer (1929), which corresponds to human actions. In contrast to this historical point of view (cf. Weimer 1940), FeDiNAR assumes a possibility of errors even if human has proven skills, knowledge, motivation and attention for a work task. Fundamental research outcomes prove this understanding (e.g. Schwarz 1927; Reason 1984).

Taking the presented intentions of FeDiNAR into account, the next section introduces the structure of the system's realisation and briefly outlines its necessary components. In the section after, the formalism of process representation allowing error consideration is introduced together with the first instance of an actual demonstrator. The succeeding section details the technological and architectural means realising the FeDiNAR principles while the final one summarises the current state of the project and the acquired insights.

5.3 Technical System

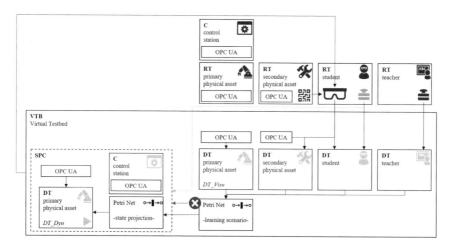

Fig. 5.2 Technical implementation perspective of the structure of the FeDiNAR system in action: All real components (RTs) have their digital counterpart (DT) connected either via standardised IoT interfaces like OPC UA or using the HoloLens for data processing (tracking of the user, of secondary technical assets via AR markers and more). The state of the learning scenario Petri net represents the current state of the system at any given moment. The representation serves as a starting point when the State Projection Component (SPC) simulates the digital twin's state progression into the future. The output of the virtual testbed is the visualisation on the HoloLens worn by the student. Two additional buttons are currently used to either manually trigger the SPC by the student or to confirm a completed action of the student by the teacher

Figure 5.2 schematically presents the overall technical and logical structure implementing the FeDiNAR system in action. Some omissions are made, since data logging and storage, database and cloud integration, as well as additional gamification aspects, are not a focus of this chapter.

The student (or, depending on the context, learner, apprentice, subject or user of the system), around whom the learning system is centred, constitutes its main component. As the system focuses on technical vocational education, the typical work processes further involve a primary physical asset (often some type of machine). As was mentioned previously, only processes with *observable changes* of the overall system can be reliably registered and, with this, only phenomenological errors can be tracked. Such processes can be maintenance, overhaul or general usage (like milling or turning) and involve tools or additional materials aside from the primary physical asset. Augmentation of the learning process, especially the visualisation of error consequences to the student, is achieved by means of a semi-transparent head-mounted display (HMD), which in the case of FeDiNAR is the Microsoft HoloLens (HL). The sensors included in this device provide information about the user's actions and additional information about the system and process state. This state is aggregated in a central node (denoted 'VTB' for *virtual testbed* in Fig. 5.2), which can also receive data from the 'smart' (read 'connected') primary physical asset and 'smart' tools or other secondary assets involved in the process the student is acquiring. The core interface enabling this communication can be a native interface available with the asset or be provided by an additional device translating necessary data into a standardised format. In Fig. 5.2 such a device is denoted 'OPC UA', which by itself is a modern and standardised machine-to-machine communication protocol (M2M).

With this, the central node's task is *communication*: Firstly, receiving data from the main physical asset, sensor data from the HMD and additional data from secondary assets. Secondly, sending visualisation data to the HMD based on the digital twin of the primary asset as well as the learning system's state representation. Additionally, the VTB is used as an interface for auxiliary AI-driven services that are required for system state recognition and tracking. It, hence, also serves as the primary source for further evaluation with the teaching personnel, as it stores the complete information of ideal and actual execution of the task.

Aside from the main online system for live task execution tracking, consequence visualisation and subsequent evaluation, the FeDiNAR system introduces a holistic infrastructure for its didactic approach. This infrastructure provides a database with cloud access as central storage for common tasks, from which different institutions using the same types of assets and tasks can benefit. As, further, the FeDiNAR system is laid out as a learning *platform* and different performance measures can be captured with the system, the FeDiNAR cloud allows the implementation of gamification aspects, leading to further positive learning effects.

5.4 Prototypical Implementation of the FeDiNAR Concept (Demonstrator)

The formal description of the dynamic behaviour of the FeDiNAR system is done using time-extended Petri nets (Petri 1962). Petri nets offer a visual modelling language with a mathematical foundation for describing a priori known states of a system. They have a formal syntax and semantics from which a graphical representation, as well as a formal description of temporally varying system states, can be derived. This makes Petri nets suitable to describe sequential, mutually exclusive as well as concurrent states based on defined events. Petri nets are directed graphs consisting of alternating places and transitions, which represent descriptions of permissible states and events respectively. When the preconditions for a specific event are fulfilled, transitions 'fire' and lead to a change of state of the system such that the dynamic behaviour to be described emerges. The system state at a specific point in time is given by the assignment of tokens (also called 'marks') to the places of the Petri net. When an event occurs, the temporally following state is indicated by a discrete generation and destruction of tokens according to the a priori defined system behaviour—resulting from the switching rules of the transitions. For a more detailed introduction to Petri net theory, see Peterson (1981).

According to the understanding of errors as introduced at the beginning of the chapter, the total number of possible states of the learning system in a specific learning scenario follows from the potential actions of the learner. The actions must be detectable by the FeDiNAR system in order to derive a chronological order of possible events and system states. If a known intention is pursued by means of a specific action (represented by a particular system state of the Petri net) and not reached, then, based on the prior actions, a new a priori known state is assigned to the system. According to Senders and Morray (1991), this state resulting from the action represents the error. Such an unintended state can be known or unknown to the learner.

The knowledge about the process allows designing a Petri net that expresses the totality of the a priori known results of action. These results are either error-free or contain errors. The switching rules of the network and the data from the real world then determine the occurrence of a concrete result, which is represented by a defined state of the Petri net. Information about the real world is acquired by means of the sensors included in the AR HMD (Microsoft HoloLens) or is made available by sensors of the respective primary or secondary physical assets.

The project team selected the 'fischertechnik Computing Robo TXT' modular construction system (MCS, cf. Fig. 5.3) as a first demonstrator for concept development and validation. It has a strong analogy to the components and functions of equipment used for vocational education in real enterprises. Furthermore, it offers flexible access to its components via the TXT control unit.

Learners interact with a real demonstrator, which is directly connected to its corresponding digital twin.

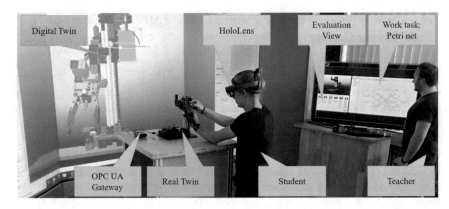

Fig. 5.3 A prototypical implementation of the FeDiNAR learning system using a modular construction system demonstrator, the fischertechnik modular construction system (FT MCS)

The current state is the initial state for simulations on the digital twin (cf. Cichon and Rossmann 2018). Simulations can be visualised directly in AR as an overlay or next to the real system. Teachers follow the progress of the learner via their own interface, confirm the completion of individual learning steps, support the learner directly and proceed with the reflection phase with the learner after learning task completion.

As part of a first scenario, a designated motor has to be replaced by a learner. During the execution, different types of errors can occur, which need to be represented in the Petri net. The learner might, e.g. ignore the *turn off voltage* or the *disconnect motor cabling* operation, which would both be possible omission errors.

Figure 5.4 shows the Petri net excerpt that can represent all possible states for these exemplarily selected two actions. A token is placed in support place 1 (initial state), which activates the transitions t_1 and t_3. This adds one token to each of the places p_1 and p_2, which represents the currently performed action of the learner. The FeDiNAR system detects the completion of an action and the system status based on input from the sensors (system is voltage-free: {yes, no}). Depending on the actual state of the robot, one token is placed in each of the places h_1 and z_1 (={"action 1 has been performed"} and {"system measures a nonzero voltage"}) when the action is completed and an omission error occurs. With an error-free execution, a placement occurs in places h_2 and z_2. This activates either transition t_2 or t_4, respectively, and leads to its immediate switching. This causes the placement of a token in support place 2, which corresponds to the completion of the first action. Furthermore, the switching process of the transition adds an attribute to the token regarding the action result (activity "Disable voltage" | omission error {yes, no}). At the same time, it is the start trigger for the subsequent activity 'Disconnect wiring', which can also contain an omission error.

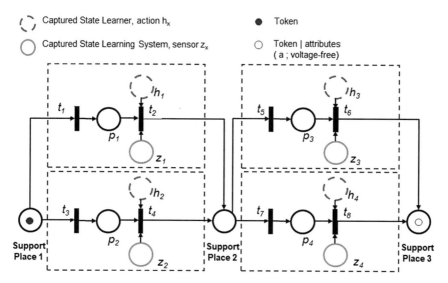

Fig. 5.4 Section of a Petri net representing actions and errors

5.5 Technical Implementation and Connection of the Digital Twin

The core element of the FeDiNAR system implementation are digital twins (DTs) of the technical asset, of the humans interacting with the asset and of all tools involved in the process. In this described case (cf. Figs. 5.2 and 5.3), the asset is the demonstrator in the form of a modular construction system (MCS) and the interacting human is the system operator (student). Digital twins are representations of physical assets (Bundesministerium für Wirtschaft und Energie). Within the VTB these DTs become experimentable (thus, also called Experimentable Digital Twins (EDTs)). These DT allow evaluating the behaviour of the asset and consequences of interactions with them without using their real counterparts. This possibility enables the realisation of a system like FeDiNAR, where consequences of mistakes can be observed on the digital twin of machines and people rather than on the real ones, preventing damage, harm and losses.

5.5.1 Virtual Testbeds

DTs reside within virtual testbeds (VTBs; Rossmann and Sommer 2008), i.e. software frameworks integrating animations, pre-defined action and various modalities of simulation and interaction. Some of the basic components of a VTB are Support for CAD data to include geometric representations of the RTs, an active database keeping track of their dynamic properties and a graphics engine to visualise the

DTs accompanied by additional information not only on flat displays but also or in virtual or augmented reality (VR or AR). To enable experimentability, the VTB also requires a physics simulation component, as well as frameworks for modelling cause-and-effect relationships between the various involved entities, e.g. a scripting language. Additionally, components allowing to interface the real assets of the DTs and the VR and AR hardware are required. In FeDiNAR, the role of the VTB is assumed by VEROSIM, a modular and flexible simulation system fulfilling the listed requirements.

5.5.2 Hardware Setup

Being the primary physical asset, the previously introduced MCS is the central component within the task and requires a comprehensive DT. The real twin (RT) connects with the DT by means of the MCS's native TXT controller. A Raspberry Pi ('Pi') acts as a bridge between the RT and its DT. On the one hand, it uses a Python API to interface the TXT and gather state information of the motors (like current position or rpm) and sensors (button pressed states) and to send motor commands. On the other hand, the Pi maps this interface, also using Python, onto an OPC UA (OPC Unified Architecture) structure representing the MCS's current state. OPC UA is a machine-to-machine (M2M) network protocol that is especially suited for IoT (Internet of Things) applications and smart devices and is supported in VEROSIM. This allows establishing a semantic representation of the MCS within the simulation system. Together with a visual and structural rigid body model of the building blocks, this constitutes the MCS's DT.

The system tracks passive secondary physical assets (those without included sensors), like tools, using fiducial markers in conjunction with the HoloLens's forward-facing camera. Another way to interpret the user's interaction with physical assets is their defined placement within the user's workspace. This way, tracking the user's hand allows the detection of, e.g. confusion errors ('usage of the wrong tool') even when there is no possibility of otherwise tracking the tool itself. Since the Microsoft HoloLens relies on tracking a precise environment-related 6-dof pose of its wearer's head, this datum is the primary input for the DT of the learner. As mentioned above, the position of the wearer's hands can also be tracked and serves as another important input for the user DT and hence the overall system.

One additional benefit of using the VTB approach is that we can create purely virtual scenarios using the same database, the same simulations and especially the same DTs. In this case of purely virtual scenarios with no RT present, a VR HMD together with the associated controllers serves the same tracking purpose as the HoloLens in the AR setup.

5.5.3 Implementation of the Process Description

As described earlier, in FeDiNAR time-extended Petri nets describe learning scenarios. The tasks are observed in real contemporary work processes in companies, reflected against a didactic background and the dedicated work process for learning is created in the didactic concept. It is then used to derive a more formal description via extended Event-driven Process Chain (eEPC, cf. Keller et al. 1992). Using eEPCs can be seen as the intermediate step between the method of didactically describing human actions and the associated learn process towards the formal Petri net descriptions, which are normally used in purely technical contexts. This eEPC is then converted to a Petri net, for which the Platform-Independent Petri net Editor (PIPE2, cf. Dingle et al. 2009; Bonet et al. 2007) proved to be a suitable tool. It saves Petri nets in a human-readable XML format with places, transitions and arcs as the main components. VEROSIM natively uses Petri nets to automate and control the flow of simulations. There, the nets are described via the proprietary state-oriented modelling language (SOML++, cf. Schluse 2002). Naturally, its structure is similar to the format of PIPE XML files, allowing a straightforward conversion process to acquire the general structure of a SOML Petri net. The descriptions of the states and transitions, however, require additional attention. While the names of places and transitions describe the action phenomenologically prior to the conversion to SOML, the final SOML script contains precise instructions for the simulation system. This implies, for example, parts of the DT (sensors and actuators) to have defined names or identifiers. Moreover, actions need to have measurable characteristics, e.g. force or angle thresholds for tool usage, timings, or relative positions of objects. The procedure of deriving precise scenario descriptions from the initial process descriptions is not automatable. Either the initial Petri net structure must contain additional information for the final implementation (e.g. in the form of comments to places and transitions) or the structure is filled manually based on the process information given in the previous stages—the task description, eEPC and graphical Petri net.

5.5.4 AR Interaction and Error Detection

In summary of the above paragraphs, the detection methods of the current state of the FeDiNAR system, using the HoloLens (HL), the Raspberry Pi (Pi) and computer vision methods (CV), are as follows:

1. Determining that the student is located in a wrong position (HL)
2. Determining that the student's hands are placed wrongly (grabbing wrong tools of materials, placing them at a wrong position) (HL)
3. Reading data from current machine state to deduce wrongly performed actions (Pi)
4. Determining the presence and poses of secondary assets furnished with AR markers (HL, CV)

Additionally, the following aspects can be realised based on the developed VTB concept using further computer vision libraries and/or additional cameras (Cam) or hardware sensors (Sens) in the overall system:

5. Determining the presence of secondary assets by extensive data processing using elaborated computer vision methods (e.g. image recognition, object detection, pose estimation) (HL, Cam, CV)
6. Acquire further machine or process data using additional sensors (Sens).

The last two points are not in the focus of the project as one of its goals is keeping the cost of a resulting system low to allow maximally broad acceptance and to keep the programming efforts within a reasonable scope, as computer vision problems are particularly time-intensive to set up and implement.

The listed methods allow detecting a variety of erroneous actions. It is, e.g. possible to detect that students are using wrong parts of a machine or are located near the wrong tool cabinet (method 1, error mode object (Hollnagel 1993)) or are grabbing or trying to grab the incorrect tools or materials (method 2, error type: error mode object, e.g. random object). It can also be detected that they are pressing wrong buttons, turning wrong knobs (or by a wrong amount), connecting wrong cables (or to wrong ports) or selecting incorrect settings (method 3, error mode object/direction) or are, e.g. tightening the wrong nut or having grabbed the wrong tool (method 4, error mode object, e.g. neighbour).

5.6 Evaluation of the Learning Concept

At this point, the components to evaluate the main idea of the FeDiNAR project—using errors to foster competence acquisition—have been defined and undergone initial implementation using an MCS as a demonstrator. The task of assembling a part and attaching it to the body of the MCS allows visualising different consequences from which the student can gain experience.

During the definition and prototype implementation phase, the authors identified different questions on levels from conceptual to hardware-related:

- Subtypes of errors exist, that cannot easily be detected, even though they belong to the family of execution errors—the type of errors which the project focuses on due to them being potentially observable. Complex wiring scenarios are an example: Without additional sensors, it is nearly impossible to perform automated checks whether wires are connecting the correct ports. As a consequence, such errors require dedicated modelling or have to be circumvented at the preparation stage of a learning scenario.
- Even when the hardware can determine and communicate its state, the data can be too limited for some applications. Some of the motors of the FT MCS are not equipped with encoders, such that their current position can only be estimated, and even with installed encoders, the precision is below 4°. This implies that the

predicted state in case of error visualisation may not coincide with what would actually happen with the asset. Cases that are more critical include failures to detect errors due to insufficient precision in the estimation of the current state. Consequently, no validated system that prevents 100% of errors can be designed without introducing modifications.

- Formative evaluation has also revealed other hardware-related limitations and indicated that they make it necessary to break down system components into a subsystem structure to make domain-specific problems discussible interdisciplinarily. An example for this is the HoloLens's API and VTB integration, which at the time of writing prohibited to use the stream of the front-facing camera for data processing and to provide the user's view to external observers simultaneously. A division of, e.g. the device into its capabilities and their limitations allows each discipline to efficiently pursue its specific goals while facilitating inter-domain communication. This also holds for the example in the previous point.
- A key question tied to the visualisation of error consequences holds for the presented demonstrator. Should the system show the consequence to the student immediately after the mistake is made or only on request or before a critical action would lead to damage?

The didactic side of the project needs to work with the latter point. The adaptable concept has to develop solutions that ensure learning in other ways if a particular scenario does not allow a definitive answer.

A difficulty for the technical side arises from the former option of the question— the consequence space 'explodes': In case of a task with n subtasks and only binary decisions (*correct* or *incorrect*) 2^n paths of execution exist. Here, not all paths might make sense logically and need to be considered and simulated during the preparation of the learning scenario. However, the question, which future actions should be assumed if the consequences of the mistake are presented based on the result of the entire task, remains open. In the context of the development of a didactic concept, all involved disciplines need to participate in the elaboration of a possible answer. This can furthermore not be achieved without external expertise, which in the FeDiNAR project is provided by industry partners.

5.7 Summary and Future Work

In the initial quarter of the project's duration, the project team successfully devised and implemented the first demonstrator. In the next project phase, it will serve as a means to address the recognised questions to allow identifying optimal intervention points and visualisation methods to maximise the positive impact on the quality of the learning outcome. After the initial stage of implementation, the demonstrator will receive additional components, allowing the reproduction of a larger amount of error types. In a third phase, the system will be applied to a use case that is part of a specific real vocational education scenario. Evaluation of the system with respect to the project's didactic concept and the refinement of definitions is ongoing and serves, under mutual influence of the pedagogic and the technical sides, as the primary guidance of the technical FeDiNAR system implementation.

Acknowledgement The writing of this chapter was enabled within the context of the project 'FeDiNAR—Didactical Use of Errors with the Help of Augmented Reality'. It is funded by the Federal Ministry of Education and Research (BMBF) as part of the 'Digital Media in Vocational Education and Training' programme and is supported by the German Aerospace Center (DLR) under the funding codes 01PV18005A and 01PV18005C.

References

Abele S (2018) Diagnostic problem-solving process in professional contexts: theory and empirical investigation in the context of car mechatronics using computer-generated log-files. Vocat Learn 11:133–159

Atkinson R (1999) Project management: cost, time and quality, two best guesses and a phenomenon, its time to accept other success criteria. Int J Proj Manag 17:337–342

Bauer J, Harteis C (2012) The ambiguity of errors for work and learning. In: Bauer J, Harteis C (eds) Human fallibility: the ambiguity of errors for work and learning. Springer, Netherlands, Dordrecht, pp 1–17

Bonet P, Lladó CM, Puijaner R, Knottenbelt WJ (2007) PIPE v2. 5: a Petri net tool for performance modelling. In: Proceedings of the 23rd Latin American conference on informatics (CLEI 2007)

Bundesministerium für Wirtschaft und Energie Glossary of the Platform Industry 4.0, Accessed 15 Octo 2019

Cannon MD, Edmondson AC (2005) Failing to learn and learning to fail (intelligently). Long Range Plan 38:299–319. https://doi.org/10.1016/j.lrp.2005.04.005

Cichon T, Rossmann J (2018) Digital twins: assisting and supporting cooperation in human-robot teams. In: 2018 15th international conference on control, automation, robotics and vision (ICARCV). IEEE, Piscataway, NJ, pp 486–491

Dhillon SB, Misra RB (1984) Reliability evaluation of systems with critical human error. Microelectron Reliab 743–759

Dingle NJ, Knottenbelt WJ, Suto T (2009) PIPE2. SIGMETRICS Perform Eval Rev 36:34. https://doi.org/10.1145/1530873.1530881

Ellis S, Davidi I (2005) After-event reviews: drawing lessons from successful and failed experience. J Appl Psychol 90:857–871. https://doi.org/10.1037/0021-9010.90.5.857

Ellis S, Kruglanski AW (1992) Self as an epistemic authority: effects on experiential and instructional learning. Soc Cogn 10:357–375. https://doi.org/10.1521/soco.1992.10.4.357

EN ISO 9000:2005 (2005) Qualitätsmanagementsysteme—Grundlagen und Begriffe. DIN Deutsches Institut für Normung e. V., Berlin

Eraut M (2000) Non-formal learning and tacit knowledge in professional work. Br J Educ Psychol 70:113–136. https://doi.org/10.1348/000709900158001

Fehling CD (2017) Neue Lehr- und Lernformen in der Ausbildung 4.0: social augmented learning in der Druckindustrie. Berufsbildung in Wissenschaft und Praxis - BWP 46:30–33

Frenz M, Schlick CM, Heinen S (2015) Industrie 4.0 Anforderungen an Fachkräfte in der Produktionstechnik. Berufsbildung in Wissenschaft und Praxis – BWP, 12–16

Gartner (2017) Top trends in the gartner hype cycle for emerging technologies. https://www.gartner.com/smarterwithgartner/top-trends-in-the-gartner-hype-cycle-for-emerging-technologies-2017/

Hollnagel E (1993) The phenotype of erroneous actions. Int J Man-Mach Stud 39:1–32

IEEE STD (2010) IEEE STD 1044-2009. IEEE Computer Society

ISO/IEC (2005) ISO/IEC 25000:2005. International Organization for Standardization

ISO/IEC/IEEE (2010) ISO/IEC/IEEE 24765–2010(E). International Organization for Standardization

ISO/IEC/IEEE (2017) ISO/IEC/IEEE 24765:2017. International Organization for Standardization

Janis IL, Mann L (1977) Decision making: a psychological analysis of conflict, choice, and commitment, 1. Free Press paperback ed. Free Press, New York, NY

Kapur M (2015) Learning from productive failure. Learn: Res Pract 1:51–65. DOI: https://doi.org/10.1080/23735082.2015.1002195

Kapur M (2016) Examining productive failure, productive success, unproductive failure, and unproductive success in learning. Educ Psychol 51:289–299. https://doi.org/10.1080/00461520.2016.1155457

Keller G, Nüttgens M, Scheer A-W (1992) Semantische Prozeßmodellierung auf der Grundlage Ereignisgesteuerter Prozeßketten (EPK). Veröffentlichungen des Instituts für Wirtschaftsinformatik

Klafki W (2000) Didaktik analysis as the core of preparation of instruction. In: Westbury I (ed) Teaching as a reflective practice: the German Didaktik tradition. Erlbaum, Mahwah, NJ

Mehl K (1993) Über einen funktionalen Aspekt von Handlungsfehlern - was lernt man wie aus Fehlern. Zugl.: Bremen, Univ., Diss., 1993. Fortschritte der Psychologie, vol 8. LIT-Verl., Münster, Hamburg

Oser F, Spychiger M (2005) Lernen ist schmerzhaft: Zur Theorie des negativen Wissens und zur Praxis der Fehlerkultur. Beltz-Pädagogik, Beltz, Weinheim

Peterson JL (1981) Petri net theory and the modeling of systems. Prentice-Hall, Englewood Cliffs, N.J

Petri CA (1962) Kommunikation mit Automaten. Dissertation, Technische Hochschule Darmstadt

Polanyi M, Sen A (2009) The tacit dimension, [Nachdr.]. University of Chicago Press, Chicago, Ill

Rauner F (2013) Competence development and assessment in TVET (COMET): theoretical framework and empirical results. In: Technical and vocational education and training, vol 16. Springer, Dordrecht

Rausch A (2012) Errors, emotions, and learning in the workplace—findings from a diary study within VET. In: Wuttke E, Seifried J (eds) Learning from errors at school and at work. Budrich, Opladen, pp 111–126

Reason J (1984) Little slips and big disasters. Interdisc Sci Rev 9:179–189. https://doi.org/10.1179/isr.1984.9.2.179

Rossmann J, Sommer B (2008) The virtual testbed: Latest virtual reality technologies for space robotic applications. In: CDROM-Proceedings of 9th international symposium on artificial intelligence, robotics and automation in space (i-SAIRAS 2008), p 78

Schwarz G (1927) Untersuchungen zur Handlungs-und Affektpsychologie. Psychologisches Institut Berlin, Berlin

Schluse M (2002) Zustandsorientierte Modellierung in virtueller Realität und Kollisionsvermeidung, Als Ms. gedr. Fortschrittberichte VDI : Reihe 8, Meß-, Steuerungs- und Regelungstechnik, Nr. 968. VDI-Verl., Düsseldorf

Senders JW, Morray N (eds) (1991) Human error: Cause, prediction, and reduction ; analysis and synthesis ; [papers presented at the Second Conference on the Nature and Source of Human Error, held 1983, at Bellagio, Italy. Series in applied psychology. Lawrence Erlbaum, Hillsdale, NJ

Senge PM (1990) The fifth discipline: The art and practice of the learning organization, 1. Currency paperback ed. Currency Doubleday, New York, NY

Sträter O (2000) Evaluation of Human Reliability on the Basis of Operational Experience. Dissertation, TU München

Tulis M, Steuer G, Dresel M (2017) Positive beliefs about errors as an important element of adaptive individual dealing with errors during academic learning. Educ Psychol 38:139–158. https://doi.org/10.1080/01443410.2017.1384536

Weimer H (1929) Psychologie der Fehler, 2., verbesserte Auflage. Schriften zur Fehlerkunde, vol 1. Klinghardt, Leipzig

Weimer H (1940) Zur Theorie und Praxis des Fehlerproblems. Zeitschrift für Psychologie:282–305

Weingardt M (2004) Fehler zeichnen uns aus: Transdisziplinare Grundlagen zur Theorie und Produktivitat des Fehlers in Schule und Arbeitswelt. Julius Klinkhardt, Bad Heilbrunn

Chapter 6
Choral Konsult: Augmented Reality for Electrate Learning

John Craig Freeman and Gregory L. Ulmer

Abstract The authors revisit *Miami Virtue: Choragraphy of the Virtual City*, the project initiating their collaboration in the Florida Research Ensemble, as a point of departure for updating their project to invent education native to electracy (the digital apparatus). Historically, electracy as an epoch is also characterized as the Anthropocene, identifying a causal force of reality as humanity itself (supplementing previous causalities of God and Nature). Digital technology institutionalized in entertainment corporations threatens total commodification of human visceral appetite (*The Matrix*). Against this disaster, Konsult as a genre for electrate learning is invented by analogy with the invention of the Dialogue in the Athenian Academies. The Greeks configured a "stack" based on Aristotle's topical logic (Topos), correlating a systematic relationship among physical places, alphabetic writing technology, the archive of recorded culture, new rhetorical practices, and the living memory of students. Benjamin Bratton described the new technological stack (Earth, Cloud, City, Address, Interface, User) of electracy. Choral Konsult reconfigures this stack with an alternative concept of space, Chora, also of Greek origin, reanimated in poststructural philosophy. Theorizing the visceral imagination as Chora, correlated with the inventions of avant-garde modernist arts as a logic of appetites, Choragraphy proposes an augmented reality pedagogy to do for human passions what topical logics did for a reason.

J. Craig Freeman (✉)
Emerson College, Boston, USA
e-mail: john_craig_freeman@emerson.edu

G. L. Ulmer
University of Florida, Gainesville, USA
e-mail: gregorylelandulmer@gmail.com

© Springer Nature Switzerland AG 2020
V. Geroimenko (ed.), *Augmented Reality in Education*,
Springer Series on Cultural Computing,
https://doi.org/10.1007/978-3-030-42156-4_6

6.1 Border Konsult

Education is undergoing an apparatus transition, from alphabetic writing (literacy) to digital design (electracy), a transition involving every institution of society, concerning not just technology but metaphysics (what counts as reality). Augmented reality (AR), in this context, may be understood as augmented metaphysics (AM), through which learners experience the space–time-cause of their emergent reality. Augmented reality within the electrate genre of konsult asks the question: which reality is to be augmented? Although Ulmer defined the theory and practice of konsult in several books (Ulmer 2005, 2019a, b), its invention remains a process inviting collective collaboration. Freeman's augmented reality project, *Virtual U.S./Mexico Border*, is a prototype that serves as a paradigmatic experiment in Konsult.

Freeman received a call (an emotional summons) from the U.S./Mexico border. This is how konsult begins. All narratives begin with an interruption that disturbs everyday existence. There is a disaster (there are too many to count; one chooses you). Any disaster that stings (punctum) alerts egents (electrate agents) to what matters, to care (concern, worry, anxiety) relative to their own being in the world (Dasein), placing them within a particular potential story. 9/11 provides a shorthand survey gathering the four apparatus (apparatuses) of civilizational history into one confrontation: On 9/11 Religion (Orality) used Science (Literacy) to attack Corporations (Electracy), killing members of thousands of Families (Paleolithic). This emblematic calamity displays the entanglement of four different realities, four institutions, four incommensurable yet interdependent accounts of space–time-cause, cumulatively evolving through conflict and fundamental antagonism. Every irremediable disaster testifies to this condition, posing a challenge to konsult, to learn what Maurice Blanchot called the writing of the disaster—what the disaster itself gives as pharmakon (gift and poison), ultimately to further well-being, human thriving, life against death. *Virtual U.S./Mexico Border* is ontology.

6.2 The Zone

Virtual U.S./Mexico Border is an augmented reality public art project, which allows people to immerse themselves in virtual experiences, documenting key locations along the U.S./Mexico border, including the people and the stories of exile, migration, and environmental displacement found there. Starting with work produced on location in the border zone between San Ysidro and Tijuana in July 2017 (see Fig. 6.1), the project is now being expanded to include work from the Rio Grande River Valley and across the continent.

In the context of this chapter, *Virtual U.S./Mexico Border* constitutes a prototype Choral konsult for electrate learning, with its constituent elements, the zone, the disaster, and the denizens. In this prototype work, the border region constitutes the defining physical boundary of investigation or Chora.

Fig. 6.1 Imagery © 2019 Google, Imagery © 2019 Maxar Technologies, U.S. Geological Survey USDA Farm Service Agency, Map data © 2019 INEGI

Konsult is a genre introduced to support apparatus transition, organizing a curriculum and pedagogy of digital schooling based on its own invention (epochal creativity). The pedagogy is heuristics—the logic of invention, guided by a motto taken from the poet Basho, not to follow in the footsteps of the masters, but to seek what they sought. The master of literacy is Plato, who founded the Academy, the first school in the Western tradition, opening a place for alphabetic invention in the oral civilization of Classical Greece. This metaphysical opening of an apparatus is called Chora—Greek term meaning "space" or "region," as distinct from "place" (topos) or "void" (kenosis). Plato appropriated the term Chora from everyday parlance for Philosophy in his dialogue, *Timaeus*, to address the question of how Being and Becoming (Form and Matter) relate and interact, given that Form is universal eternal and Matter is material ephemeral. Chora is the third order of generation (life) that is not an entity itself but a relational interface.

Each apparatus opens Chora in its own way; each constructs an interface to augment the space–time-cause reality of its metaphysics. Paleolithic had its magic caves, orality its transcendent churches, literacy its utilitarian schools, electracy its entertaining theme parks. Another shorthand emblem may suggest the radical difference distinguishing the reality of each apparatus. The emblem is that of the four cuts, each one configuring life–death: Paleolithic: the sharpened stone arrow tips for hunting (physical survival); Orality: The knife consecrated for sacrifice, as in the Biblical story of Abraham and Isaac (God's determination of Right and Wrong); Literacy: the scalpel used for knowledge, as in Leonardo da Vinci's anatomical studies (True and False); Electracy: the fantasmatic cut of castration, defining the split subject of the unconscious, figured in *An Andalusian Dog*, the silent film by Luis Buñuel and Salvador Dali, the scene juxtaposing the cloud crossing the moon and the razor slicing the eyeball (Attraction–Repulsion): hunt, worship, know, dream. Individuals are capable of doing all four without contradiction, unlike civilizations. Literacy educated individuals; electracy must educate collectivities. Conventional consulting is a form of collective pedagogy, hence its value as a metaphor mediating egent introduction to electracy.

6.3   The Disaster

During the 2016 presidential campaign, Donald Trump was quoted as saying:

> When Mexico sends its people, they're not sending their best. They're not sending you. They're not sending you. They're sending people that have lots of problems, and they're bringing those problems with us. They're bringing drugs. They're bringing crime. They're rapists. And some, I assume, are good people. Donald Trump, June 16, 2015. (Ye Hee Lee 2015)

This border has always generated intense political and philosophical passions. Since the 2016 presidential election, however, tensions around the movement of people from the south have hardened and the issue has been used as a political cudgel. The rhetoric has led to the dehumanization of refugee families fleeing violence in their home countries, and migrants in search of work and a better life. The most powerful hedge against this kind of abusive statecraft tactic, are the stories of the individuals who have been caught up in this dynamic, told in their own voices. This work will test the hypothesis of whether new forms of virtual and augmented reality can evoke empathy in its users (see Fig. 6.2).

The Choral interface constitutes a "stack" or set of correspondences among dimensions of existence, articulated by means of allegory for purposes of education in every epoch, mapping the relation of microcosm to macrocosm, so that individuals know their position relative to the whole, the totality of what is real. This is Existential Positioning (EPS), augmenting individual proprioception, which is much more than just GPS. Here is a symptom of the inadequacy of literate education to the condition of electracy, which clarifies the task of konsult. The interface Chora between Being (the totality of what is) and Becoming (individual phenomenological experience) requires updating. Fredric Jameson identified the problem in terms of the alienation of citizens from their own agency in conditions of the modern city created by the Industrial Revolution (which is to say: electracy). A symptom of this alienation is the fact that Donald Trump, a conspiracy theorist who denies climate science, was elected President of the United States. Electracy begins with the Industrial Revolution in the later eighteenth century, which also marks the beginning of the Anthropocene when human productivity (techne) and evolutionary nature (phusis) merge or align. Jameson noted that in these conditions if an individual experience is authentic it cannot be true; and if a scientific model of the same content is true then it escapes individual experience. Jameson blamed the totality created by the rise of global capitalism for this loss of EPS. Multinational corporations (the institutional formation of electracy)

Fig. 6.2 Border fence mural, south side of the United States border with Mexico. Photo courtesy of the artist, © John Craig Freeman, 2017

constitute a hyperobject that exceeds individual phenomenology. Jacques Lacan had a similar assessment of human disorientation and displacement, characterized as the unconscious. The unconscious is to individual phenomenology what global capital is to totality. Descartes's famous Cogito (I think, therefore I am), is replaced in Psychoanalysis with Desidero (I Desire), I think where I am not; and am not where I think. Both Jameson and Lacan refer to modern ontology in which objects no longer are understood in terms of substance and essence characterized by attributes or features, but as relational fields characterized by statistical probabilities (a shift in ontology from substance to process).

6.4   The Denizens

There is nothing particularly new about politicians demonizing immigrants from Mexico and other parts of Latin America, however, since Donald Trump's campaign and subsequent election to the Presidency of the United States, and his relentless attempts to build a wall, tensions have increased and the border has become a symbol of division and intolerance. Yes, there is a crisis at the border, but only acts of humility and humanity can solve it. *Virtual U.S./Mexico Border* is intended to transport users, virtually, to this important border, and to act as a foil to the political vitriol. (See Fig. 6.3 for examples of four denizens of the Virtual U.S./Mexico Border zone).

Fig. 6.3 Artist's renderings of four of the denizens from *Virtual U.S./Mexico Border*, © John Craig Freeman, 2019

I wish they gave them a different opportunity to talk to their relatives, not with a fence in between. This is almost like a prison for them. I wish that the ones that are trying to solve their situation had better conditions of talking and being closer to their relatives. They don't mean to do any harm to anyone. Because it's not possible for us to stay like this, divided. Luis (2017).

The implications of collapsed EPS for a literate classroom are apparent in this loss of position, considering that the fundamental project of a written essay is to take a position on a given topic: Thesis is the Greek word for position. Topos is Greek for the location of an individual entity. Aristotle preferred it to the more holistic Chora, used by his mentor Plato in *Timaeus*. Aristotle invented the topical logic that organized all education through the manuscript era and still is taught today for argumentative writing. The allegorical stack he proposed serves us as a template as well, to be translated into digital equivalents. The stack includes three orders of "topic"—physical, mental, textual. These relationships must be entirely reorganized in digital conditions of real time, light speed global information technology that urbanist philosopher Paul Virilio warned has collapsed dimensionality itself, eliminating any positional here and reducing temporality to now. Virilio notes the possibility of a general accident happening everywhere simultaneously, considering that every invention includes its own form of accident, leading him to speculate on what might be an Internet Accident. We have experienced it already, perhaps, in the 2016 election in the United States, and Brexit, for starters. A related crisis, as these accidents indicate, is that the institutional and identity forms developed within literacy (the democratic state and the individual self) are not adequate politically to the threat of global disaster, requiring policy decisions by a world community.

Fig. 6.4 Border Field Park on the north side of the United States border with Mexico including the secondary security fence and buffer zone, © John Craig Freeman, 2017

Konsult as genre is not literate, meaning it leaves topical theses to the essay form, in order to create a new support for human capabilities that Ulmer calls theopraxesis, forming a portmanteau word from the three intellectual virtues—Theoria, Praxis, Poiesis—identified by the Classical Greeks, that have organized all Western (and world) culture. Confronted by the Anthropocene in conditions of real time, egents (electrate agents) no longer have the luxury of the rivalry, hierarchy, and hostility that separated and set these virtues against one another as recorded in the philosophy, history, and arts of world culture. Theopraxesis is thinking–willing–imagining integrated into a unified intelligence, necessarily possible only within a digital apparatus. What theopraxesis might be in practice has been modeled in the appropriation of Zen Mushin (No-Mind) aesthetics by American Beat poets. Konsult is the genre supporting theopraxesis in a digital medium. (Fig. 6.4 represents the site of Konsult).

People are on the move around the world. With *Virtual U.S./Mexico Border*, movement through space becomes an act of reasoning. The project not only represents the manifestations of global statecraft, but it also represents the border between our physical experience and our virtual experience. Increasingly, we all interact with a new virtual public space, every time we try to get a better cellular signal to send a text, every time we connect to a Wi-Fi network or navigate with GPS. By juxtaposing the U.S./Mexico border in arbitrary locations around the world using augmented reality technology, this work is intended to give this new virtual public space form and meaning.

Jameson undertook a project to invent a new cognitive mapping, EPS designed to reconnect digital microcosm and macrocosm, a hybrid practice appropriated from features of Kevin Lynch's study of mental maps citizens use to navigate their cities, Louis Althusser's *Ideological State Apparatus* (ISA), and Dante's Medieval four-fold allegorical form structuring *The Divine Comedy.* Cognitive mapping is one source of Choragraphy that Ulmer and Freeman (with the Florida Research Ensemble) tested in a proto-konsult on the Miami River (Miami, Florida)—*Miami Virtue* (Ulmer et al. 2012). Given that literacy begins with the Greek discovery of nature (phusis), electracy emerging with the Anthropocene must engage with a reality of Second Phusis. *Virtual U.S./Mexico Border* applies Choragraphy to undertake an encounter with the Anthropocene.

6.5   The Anaximander Model

Electracy, in general, and konsult in particular, are invented by means of grammatology, the history and theory of writing, whose scholars introduced apparatus theory. Much is known about how literacy emerged from orality, as described for example in Walter Ong's *Orality and Literacy; The Technologizing of the Word* (Ong 1982). Ong identified another epochal shift underway in electronic culture, which he did not name but described as "secondary orality." Ulmer introduced the term "electracy" (hybrid combining "electricity" with Jacques Derrida's "trace") to supply the name, considered necessary in order to clarify that the new era is not simply "digital literacy," any more than literacy was simply "alphabetic orality," but rather involved a completely new metaphysics created not only in technology but also institution formation and identity behaviors. The basic insight of this history is that apparatus is a social or desiring machine, determined as much by ideology as by technology. To repeat our theme: each apparatus is invented to augment its own reality, constructing the cause of the world and human thriving against disaster. What is possible in *Virtual U.S./Mexico Border's* augmented reality encounter with Second Phusis may be appreciated by means of an analogy with one of the founding events of literacy, the invention of Philosophy by the Presocratic Greeks in Miletus, Ionia. Thales was the first Ionian philosopher, but the oldest surviving written document of this beginning is a fragment by a contemporary of Thales, Anaximander (b. 610 BCE).

   The first iteration, or episode, of *Virtual U.S./Mexico Border* was produced on location where the border fence terminates into the Pacific Ocean, the project focuses on a small parcel of land on the bluffs above the ocean extending a few hundred meters south into Mexico at Playas de Tijuana, and north into the United States at Border Field State Park. Dedicated as Friendship Park by First Lady Pat Nixon in August 1971, the space was originally intended to be a shared place where families and loved ones from both countries could meet and spend time together.

   Although it is now separated by a tall rusty fence, Friendship Park is centered on a historic obelisk boundary marker monument (see Fig. 6.5). The monument commemorates the Treaty of Guadalupe Hidalgo, which ended the war between the United States and Mexico on February 2, 1848, when Mexico conceded California, Arizona, New Mexico, and Texas along with what is now the entire Southwest United States. The agreement provided that an international border between the two countries would be established by the joint United States and Mexican boundary survey. The

Fig. 6.5 Obelisk boundary marker monument from the south side of the United States border with Mexico. Photo courtesy of the artist, © John Craig Freeman, 2017

commission began its survey work at Border Field at the very point where the obelisk is placed.

> I am here in Tijuana, because it is a battlefield, it is a human rights battlefield, and they need allot of help, and I decided that I would come here to help. Here in Tijuana we have four different fronts of immigration, you have forced migration of the Mexicans, deported Mexicans. And there is the forced migration of Central American citizens trying to get to the United States. And there is the forced migration of the Haitians who are looking for refugee status and asylum. And also, the forced migration of Mexicans who have been displaced by the narco-traffic and the narco-wars. And that's why I am here, and since 2002, I have been fighting for the rights of migrants. Castro (2017).

This fragment of just a few words, from a book called *On Nature*, is of immense interest (discussed in Ulmer's *Konsult: Theopraxesis*), but the relevant point, for now, is to learn from Anaximander's example a strategy of invention to extrapolate to the emergent reality of Second Phusis. Anaximander's encounter with phusis occurred on the site of the building of one of the early Greek temples, such as the one at Ephesus, or Samos, the temple dedicated to Hera, wife of Zeus. One of the important elements of the plan concerned the orientation of the temple to the sacrificial altar central to the rituals of worship (the slaughter of oxen). The temple of Hera at Samos is a monument of orality, manifesting a metaphysics in which divine beings, gods, are the cause of reality. The creative intelligence of civilization in this metaphysics was devoted to negotiations with gods. Here is the fundamental point, promoting the pedagogical value of comparative apparatus, to understand that everything in an apparatus is invented, but invented relative to a metaphysics (an apparatus is the ultimate augmented reality). Augmented reality in Paleolithic is a cave painting; in Orality a ritual sacrifice; in Literacy a laboratory experiment. And in electracy?

Anaximander shifted his attention away from the metaphysical function of the temple to its physical construction. This redirection of attention away from the obvious is the gesture to emulate. He was impressed not by the religious purpose of the construction, but the engineering feat of stacking drum sections of quarried stone to construct columns opening an area between floor and roof, creating sacred space (Chora). Each drum was fitted to the next resulting in a seamless column. Photographs of the ruins of these temples often show these drums fallen and scattered on the site. Credited with composing the first prose text, Anaximander was appropriating practices of the architects, who wrote their notes in prose. He titled his work *Historia Peri Phuseos* (phusis, cognate of "to grow," is natura in Latin), a generic title, to pose a question, and even entertain a thesis: the material world in its present state, how did it come to be from its origin to the present? This is a metaphysical question. The tradition records that Philosophy begins with a sense of wonder, and our history specifies this wonder as Anaximander contemplating the construction of Hera's temple. The new cause that he received and recognized was not that of divine beings nor human laws or customs (nomos), but a material force coming out of itself, expressed in the construction of the fitted column drums, informing the craft of the architects. What was the secret of that craft? Anaximander experienced a revelation, epiphany, insight with the aid of the temple. Sacred space was an effect of columns revealing a region (a Chora) whose causal power was communicated through mathematics. This opening is the key: quarried marble; precise cut of the drums; mathematical ratio; proportional geometry. The pivot term registering in history is fit, jointure, justice. Justice disclosed through nature. Such is the "topic" of Historia Peri Phuseos: Justice, jointure, what is fitting in every sense: an orientation that initiated a new direction for civilization.

By 1973, all that separated the two countries at this location was a simple barbed wire cattle fence. Subsequent years brought an ever-escalating fortification and militarization, reflecting the changing tone of U.S. border politics from friendship to distrusted adversary. However, families still come here to meet and spend time together (see Figs. 6.6 and 6.7).

> I am waiting here today for my son-in-law and granddaughter. My granddaughter, the smaller one, was seven years old when they went, and today she is twenty-one, and I am expecting them to come here today. I don't come here often because it is far and I have to do some planning to come here. But then when we hear news from them, we make plans to come here. My son-in-law's sister is sick with cancer on this side in Mexico, and he wants to get some news about his sister. Romana Suárez (2017).

Today, the obelisk at Friendship Park is an epicenter of the U.S. migration policy. Every Saturday and Sunday, from 10:00 am to 2:00 pm, the U.S. Border Patrol allows 25 people at a time to enter a small monitored area in the buffer zone between the main fence and the secondary fence, which was added after 9/11. Families and friends, some who have traveled from all over both countries, meet and have intimate exchanges beneath ten meters of hardened steel mesh.

What is the metaphysical discovery? How did truth appear (literacy shifts from oral religion right and wrong to scientific true and false)? It is Plato's question, received from the Presocratics, concerning the relation between form and matter:

Fig. 6.6   Friendship Park, Tijuana, © John Craig Freeman, 2019

Fig. 6.7   Friendship Park, San Ysidro, © John Craig Freeman, 2019

matter is *Dunamis* (potential); form is *Energeia* (actuality). For Anaximander, life shows itself in a mathematical ratio. Being (life vitality) comes into appearance in the way that mathematical ratios function in material (the mystery of the Fibonacci sequence). Pythagoras's *music of the spheres* is the emblem. In practical terms, when the spacing of oarlocks on a boat embodies the fitting ratio, the boat comes alive in the water when rowed, but otherwise is dead weight. The truth is the ratio. A temple is an ideal interface between totality and phenomenology, but not (only) for the reason assumed within orality. Rather, the temple disclosed an alternative working principle of life, a power not divine but material—nature—which has its own rules, "comes out of itself," caused not by God or man. Anaximander not only introduced a concept—the Boundless—to identify this new cosmology, but also made the first 3D model of the world, the first map, and the first gnomon (a sundial configured horizontally to track the angle of the sun). The information derived from his gnomon enabled him to calculate an accurate measure of the size of the earth (a history of which Columbus, unfortunately, was not aware).

A lesson for us is that Anaximander *modeled his cosmology in the very form of the temple itself.* His 3D model was, in fact, a column drum, and his map was on its surface. The physical temple was appropriated as allegory or analogon, transport from one metaphysics to the other, from orality to literacy. This modeling or visualization of concepts is a common practice in science up to the present. Think of J. J. Thomson and Lord Kelvin, their early attempts to visualize the atom, which they described as negative electrons embedded in a sphere of positive charge, *like raisins in a Christmas pudding.* Niels Bohr offered a competing model, saying that the atom was structured in the same way as our solar system. When Quantum Physics was introduced nature disappeared for a time, resisting all intuitive visualizations (a scientific version of alienation) until Richard Feynman devised his famous diagrams. These diagrams, showing *the attraction and repulsion* between elementary particles, moving toward one another up to a certain distance, then away while exchanging a photon (energy charge), serve as an emblem for *Desidero* in electracy (the photon models Lacan's object cause of desire, object @).

6.6   Screen City Biennial, Stavanger Norway

Virtual U.S./Mexico Border was originally commissioned in 2017 by the Screen City Biennial, in downtown Stavanger Norway (see Fig. 6.8).

Curated by Tanya Toft and Daniela Arriado, Screen City Biennial was produced in partnership with the Stavanger Maritime Museum. The theme of the Biennial, Migrating Stories, reflected topics of migration and post-colonialism, new geographies and ecology, real and virtual voyages, storytelling and narratives traveling through time.

In July of 2017, in response to the theme of the biennial, and in reaction to the degrading political rhetoric surrounding immigration in the United States, Freeman traveled to the border to create a full-scale three-dimensional virtual representation of the experience of being there. (See Figs. 6.9 and 6.10 for screenshots of the Virtual U.S./Mexico Border augmented reality app in Boston Common).

The completed scene was then placed across the Vågen Harbor in Stavanger, invoking Norway's own history of migration. Stavanger was an important point of departure for people migrating from Scandinavia to the United States during the nineteenth and twentieth centuries. (Semmingsen 2000–2016).

Fig. 6.8 Viewing *Virtual US/Mexico Border*, geo-located augmented reality, Screen City Biennial, Stavanger Norway, © John Craig Freeman, 2017

Fig. 6.9 *Virtual U.S./Mexico Border*, geo-located augmented reality public art, screenshots made on location in Boston Common, © John Craig Freeman, 2017

With the rich history of its port of entry and departure, Stavanger is indeed a border of a different name. In July 1825, during a time of particularly fierce religious strife in Norway, a group of six religiously repressed families, set sail from Stavanger in an undersized sloop, the Rest-au-ration-en. The ship landed in New York City, where it was at first, impounded for exceeding its passenger limit. After an intervention from

Fig. 6.10 *Virtual U.S./Mexico Border*, geo-located augmented reality public art, screenshots made on location in Boston Common, © John Craig Freeman, 2017

President John Quincy Adams, local Quakers helped the destitute emigrants, who eventually established a community in upstate New York. Today, their descendants are still known as "sloopers."

> The U.S. government should stop persecuting migrants because migrants are people of God, like any other people of God in the community. Because Jesus was also a refugee. Perez (2017).

The Presocratic paradigm shift from mythology to mathematics became the fundamental principle of the first school, Plato's Academy, set up in a grove of trees outside Athens (387 BCE), with an inscription on the gate saying let no one ignorant of geometry enter here, thus instantiating the new Chora within which to invent literacy. Aristotle followed Plato with his own school, the Lyceum, continuing the heuretic project. We see how each metaphysics has its own understanding of time and space, but our focus is on the cause. If the gods are not the causal force of reality, what is? Aristotle (following from Plato's Demiurge in *Timaeus*), adopted Anaximander's model in his book *Metaphysics*. The cosmos according to Aristotle, setting the terms for the Western tradition, is created as if a kind of architecture. The causes (of anything) are four, as modeled by a temple: Material (marble); Efficient (the designer); Formal (geometry); Final (purpose: worship). Meanwhile, alphabetic writing of an Indo-European language enabled the discovery of grammar, subject–predicate constructions organized into propositions: declarative statements expressed in neutral modality could be determined true or false, a feature Aristotle codified in his syllogisms organized in truth tables. These truth tables, combined in historical development of science with Leibniz's binary numbers and Tesla's logic gate, ultimately were put into a machine—the computer.

Konsult is haunted by Anaximander (hauntology). Freeman's tour of the border exposed him to an experience of Second Phusis, intuiting a new metaphysics that may be glimpsed or otherwise derived from the writing of this disaster. His experience is not that of wonder, recorded at the origin of Philosophy, but emergency, as Walter Benjamin recommended. Our reality comes to us today, not from nature but history, to which we should attend (Benjamin said) as if to a fire alarm ringing for 60 s each minute. History gives Second Phusis, documenting our discovery that God and nature are us. Heuretics as method dictates that we suspend (phenomenological epoché) the reality of the border presented according to the three extant apparatus. What is the cause of which the disaster writes? Paleo says Family (life–death); Orality says God (right–wrong); Literacy says Nature (true–false). These answers have their own validity and already set the terms of policy debate. And yet the continuing irreducible disaster associated with borders globally signals that there is still some further cause (even if "cause" as such is inherently ideological, or a Kantian transcendental category, an illusion of human perception).

6.7 Instead of Conclusion: Background and Context

Freeman has been an exhibiting artist since the mid-1980s. He grew up and went to art school in San Diego just twenty minutes from the San Ysidro Port of Entry, the busiest international border crossing in the world. In the decades since, he has made work and exhibited all over the world. But the one topic, and place, he returns to time and time again is the U.S./Mexico Border. Border Panorama from 1986 is an early example of Freeman's attempts to immerse the viewer in the experience using panoramic techniques (see Fig. 6.11).

Virtual U.S./Mexico Border opens mobile Chora, constructing an interface supporting electrate ontology, in which the inchoate cause may appear and become accessible to theopraxesis. Freeman does not follow in the footsteps of Anaximander, but seeks what he sought—the other cause, the other scene (unconscious). A stack begins to take shape, an allegory giving access to the border as event (a correlation of lived and represented experience in real time). The allegory design opens a gap, poros, abyss (mise-en-abyme) between the physical place and its simulacrum. The resultant reality effect does not declare (it is not a proposition) but indicates, winks, gestures (as Heraclitus said of the Oracle at Delphi), evoking a dimension that

Fig. 6.11 Border Panorama, acrylic on gessoed paper nine panels, 216″ × 36″, © John Craig Freeman, 1986

is itself not representable, unspeakable. The lesson from Anaximander is: accept the work site as zone, including its structures and the associated individual and collective behavior, but suspend (reduce) the explicit rationale (the accepted metaphysics), in order to receive from the scene what it may give in its own terms. The suspended zone of the U.S./Mexico border models electrate cause. The project of *Virtual U.S./Mexico Border* is to design this model.

The purpose of this brief essay is not to answer all the questions it raises, nor to explain the history and theory of its rationale, which we defer to our larger collaborative experiment in progress. We offer konsult as a relay for teaching the reading and writing of augmented reality. A pedagogy of augmented metaphysics introduces the Anaximander relay to motivate reality design. The theory outlines what to expect: an experience of the other border emerging as causality in electrate metaphysics: Desidero—the border in me, in us, registering libidinal drive, the forces of attraction and repulsion ruling our quantum appetite. Apparatus theory argues this insight at length: cause today is human appetite, libidinal drive whose institutional prosthesis is the corporation (commodity-form) that functions to feed the drive. This institution is structured not by life–death, right–wrong, true–false, but attraction–repulsion.

Freeman's first experience working at the obelisk boundary marker monument was in the *Imaging the U.S./Mexico Border* project, an early form of place-based virtual reality developed in collaboration with Ulmer and the Florida Research Ensemble following the *Miami Virtue* project in the late 1990s (see Fig. 6.12).

Freeman evokes in *Virtual U.S./Mexico Border* the force of this appetite, entangling love and hate (passion). The design to date engages with this force or power (virtue, capability) through migrant bodies, allegorical personifications of Being (life) encountering Wall (death) in a way that recalls those video clips of green plants pushing up through invisible cracks in a paved surface.

Perhaps enough has been said for pedagogical purposes. Our point is not to claim electrate cause is fully understood (it is not). Apparatus theory suggests a likely place to begin addressing our alienation (see Fig. 6.13). The framing macrocosm discloses the extimate quality of reality, familiar to poets and artists composing epiphanies, analyzed in contemporary theory, and now emerging in the operating practices of electracy: the external totality and interior intuition are mutually constructed in every apparatus. Basho's poetics again reveals a method. Exploiting a pun in Japanese (but English has a similar pun), he explained one learns about pining from the pine tree. Between the experience and the image of a pine tree emerges yugen (a mode of aesthetic knowing).

Virtual U.S./Mexico Border learns bordering from the border. The cause of division is primordial, necessary and accidental at once (automaton and tuché Aristotle said, noting how determinism creates opportunity) as the resource of identity at every level of stack. There are (il y a) borders.

Whereas the public square was once the quintessential place to air grievances, display solidarity, express difference, celebrate similarity, remember, mourn, and reinforce shared values of right and wrong, it is no longer the only anchor for art in the public realm. That geography has been relocated to a novel terrain, one that encourages exploration of mobile location-based public art.

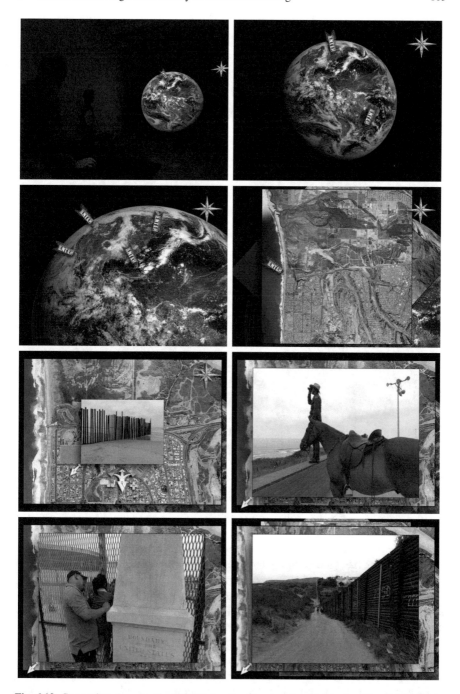

Fig. 6.12 Screenshot, *Imaging the U.S./Mexico Border*, place-based virtual reality, © John Craig Freeman, 2005

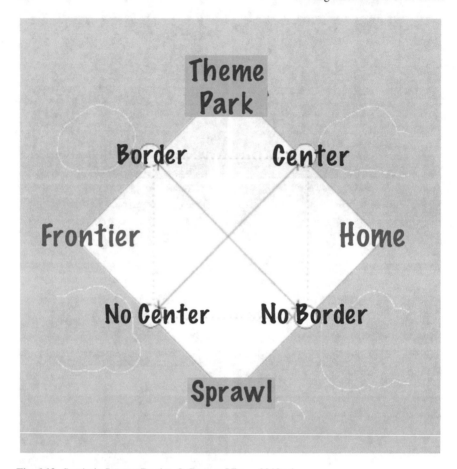

Fig. 6.13 Semiotic Square: Border, © Gregory Ulmer, 2019a, b

In the early 1990s, we witnessed the migration of the public sphere from the physical realm, the town square, and its print augmentation, to the virtual realm, the placelessness, the everywhere-but-nowhere of the Internet. In effect, the global digital network has facilitated the emergence of a new virtual public space, which corresponds to the physical geography around us.

Geo-located augmented reality does not require permission. Moreover, public space is now truly open, as artworks can be placed anywhere in the world, without approval from curators, museum directors, civic authorities, nor government officials, with profound implications for art in the public sphere and the discourse that surrounds it.

The public sphere is now reconnecting to place in the form of location aware mobile technology. Native to this reconnection, geo-located virtual and augmented reality has the potential to activate the meaning of place without losing the distributed character of networked communications or the connections to the vast resources of

Fig. 6.14 Border Memorial: Frontera de los Muertos, Lukeville border crossing, Arizona, © John Craig Freeman, 2012

the Internet. The public sphere is now crashing back down to place in the form of place-based virtual and augmented reality.

The most important augmented reality project leading up to *Virtual U.S./Mexico Border* was *Border Memorial: Frontera de los Muertos*, an augmented reality public art project and memorial, dedicated to the thousands of migrant workers who have died along the U.S./Mexico border in recent years trying to cross the desert southwest in search of work and a better life (see Fig. 6.14).

Built for smartphone mobile devices, this project allows people to visualize the scope of the loss of life by marking each location where human remains have been recovered with a virtual object or augmentation. The public can simply download and launch a mobile application and aim their devices' cameras at the landscape along the border and the surrounding desert. The application uses geolocation software to superimpose individual augments at the precise GPS coordinates of each recorded death, enabling the public to see the objects integrated into the physical location as if they existed in the real world. Imagine now, the entire mobile Internet, and its physical manifestations of place, as a worldwide public square.

There is a barrier or abjection separating one metaphysics from the other, something that makes one world view repellant to the other, as emblematized in the trial of Galileo (the unacceptability of literacy to orality). The challenge of konsult is to undertake this passage from literacy to electracy. Given that the entertainment corporation is the paradigm expressing the guiding principle of electracy—enjoyment (usufruct)—with Disneyland as prototype, konsult confronts the apparent disjointure or differend between theme park and disaster. Walt Disney wanted his theme parks to be the happiest places on earth. The U.S./Mexico border is one of the saddest places on earth. Here is the reality whose metaphysics must be received and constructed, acknowledging this dynamic continuum relating joy–sadness (Spinoza), pleasure–pain (Kant), attraction–repulsion (Freud). Applying Aristotle's causes, we might say that this sublime affect has been the final cause of every apparatus, but that electracy is the first to address it directly, in its own terms.

Virtual U.S./Mexico Border makes use of state-of-the-art augmented reality technology and research, coupled with emerging photogrammetry asset generation. Virtual reality is a computer-generated 3D environment that is presented to the user in such a way that she suspends disbelief and accepts it as real (see Fig. 6.15). It is typically assumed that the user is isolated from the surrounding world by some sort of headset viewing system or projected enclosure. The experience most often simulates imaginary worlds. Even if rendered in photorealistic detail, it remains a simulation.

Geo-located augmented reality, on the other hand, engages users with the surroundings by allowing people to experience alternative realities at site-specific locations, through the camera of a mobile device.

Photogrammetry is a technology used to create 3D models from the real world, (see Fig. 6.16). Models can be produced by taking hundreds of photographs at slightly different angles with a conventional camera, or by scanning with a laser scanner. Freeman has developed a unique workflow to create world-scale virtual scenes.

Fig. 6.15 *Frontera Virtual*, virtual reality "Borders: Us and Them," New York University Shanghai Art Gallery, © John Craig Freeman, 2017

Fig. 6.16 Artist's rendering of the U.S. side of the border with border patrol agent, © John Craig Freeman, 2019

This technology represents an important evolution in the history of photography, allowing the photographic image to be immersive and explorable. Photogrammetry can be used on location to create 3D models of the world and represents real people, real places and real experiences, bringing the real to virtual reality. As an experienced visual and media artist, Freeman has chosen photogrammetry for its ability to move the viewer closer to virtual representation of the experience itself and allows for the exploration of the liminal space between representation and simulation.

The affirmative point is that border is a plasmatic line (first discovered or invented in the Paleolithic cave), renewed in modern animated cartoons, such as Disney's Steamboat Willie (1928) praised by Sergei Eisenstein (one of the inventors of cinematic montage) as a work of genius. What Eisenstein admired in Disney's animated line was that it is not bound by actuality whether physical or cultural: its plasticity is directed by imagination, fiction, fancy, fantasy. Any line (in principle) is writable fantasmatically in a fictional aesthetic dimension, a Chora opened in the real in response to the loss of here and now, there and then. Electracy opens fiction to metaphysics, which is to say that in our digital apparatus fictions are power. This dimension has been imagined as cyberspace. The border is a line. The augmenting of this plasmatic reality, in order to make it culturally imaginable, scriptable, malleable, serving well-being, is underway in *Virtual U.S./Mexico Border*.

References

Castro H (2017) A quote from human rights activist, included in Virtual U.S./Mexico Border virtual reality experience, transcribed from recording made on location at Playas de Tijuana

Luis J (2017) A quote from migrant, deported after forty years of work in San Diego, included in Virtual U.S./Mexico Border virtual reality experience, transcribed from recording made on location at Playas de Tijuana

Ong W (1982) Orality and literacy. the technologizing of the word, Routledge, London and New York

Perez A (2017) A quote from migrant, included in Virtual U.S./Mexico Border virtual reality experience, transcribed from recording made on location at Playas de Tijuana

Semmingsen I (2000–2016) Haugeans, Rappites, and the Emigration of 1825, trans C.A. Clausen. Norwegian-American Historical Association 29:3

Suárez R (2017) A quote from resident of Tijuana, included in Virtual U.S./Mexico Border virtual reality experience, transcribed from recording made on location at Playas de Tijuana

Ulmer GL (2005) Electronic monuments. University of Minnesota Press, Minneapolis, Minnesota

Ulmer GL (2019a) Konsult scenario: genre for electrate learning, in Kate Hanzalik and Nathalie Virgintino, Eds. Exquisite Corpse: Studio Art-Based Writing in the Academy. Parlor Press, Anderson, South Carolina

Ulmer GL (2019b) Konsult: Theopraxesis. Parlor Press, Anderson, South Carolina

Ulmer GL, Freeman JC, Revelle BJ, Tilson W (2012) Miami virtue: Choragraphy of the virtual city. Small Cities Imprint, vol 2(2). Kamloops, BC, Canada

Ye Hee Lee M (2015) A quote from. Donald Trump's false comments connecting Mexican immigrants and crime, Washington Post, July, p 8

Part II
Augmented Reality in Teaching Medicine and Science

Chapter 7
Augmented Reality in Medical Education and Training: From Physicians to Patients

Christine A. Campisi, Elizabeth H. Li, David E. Jimenez, and Ruth L. Milanaik

Abstract This chapter discusses the intersection of Augmented reality (AR) and the education of medical students, physicians, surgeons, and patients. For medical students tasked with absorbing a large body of medical knowledge in a short period of time, AR technology can help them learn anatomy, view interactions with patients from new perspectives, and observe novel procedures alongside their mentors. Physicians and surgeons can continue using the AR technology that helped them through medical school as well, particularly for laparoscopic procedures, neurosurgery, and cardiology. Augmented reality technology has also been utilized to guide patients through treatments when they lack access to medical professionals, inform patients on medical procedures, and allow patients to educate themselves about their conditions. As AR is still in its infancy, this chapter will explore AR's current capabilities as well as potential future applications in medical training and education with respect to both health practitioners and patients.

7.1 Introduction

Research studies of preliminary Augmented reality (AR) prototypes reveal that AR has potential as a unique educational tool, especially in medicine. AR applications may not only enhance medical education at each stage of training but may also help patients become more involved and informed in their medical decision-making. For

C. A. Campisi (✉) · E. H. Li · D. E. Jimenez · R. L. Milanaik
Division of Developmental and Behavioral Pediatrics, Steven and Alexandra Cohen Children's Medical Center of New York, New York, USA
e-mail: cacampisi22@gmail.com

E. H. Li
e-mail: li.elizabeth.h@gmail.com

D. E. Jimenez
e-mail: dejimenez77@gmail.com

R. L. Milanaik
e-mail: rmilanai@northwell.edu

© Springer Nature Switzerland AG 2020
V. Geroimenko (ed.), *Augmented Reality in Education*,
Springer Series on Cultural Computing,
https://doi.org/10.1007/978-3-030-42156-4_7

instance, in medical school, students are required to mentally convert 2D textbook images of human anatomy to 3D models that they can later apply in a clinical setting. With AR technology, medical students will be able to more accurately and swiftly detect malformations, educate patients, and understand anatomy. In the surgical field, AR simulations may provide a risk-free environment for residents to practice without increasing patient risk and may also be used to deliver additional information to surgeons intraoperatively. Lastly, physicians may turn to AR applications to help patients better understand their treatments, thus empowering patients to take an active role in their medical treatment plan and participate in medical decision-making.

To better understand the value of AR in medical education, it is first important to understand how it differs from its closely related, and more well-known sister technology—Virtual reality (VR). VR refers to the generation of an entirely artificial, computer-simulated 3D image or environment with which users can interact in real-time (Khor et al. 2016). Everything the user sees during a VR experience is computer-generated. However, AR involves overlaying an interactive, digital layer of information on top of the physical environment (Barsom et al. 2016). For instance, AccuVein superimposes a map of vasculature on the surface of a patient's skin to help medical professionals find veins before drawing blood or inserting an intravenous line (Fig. 7.1) (Khor et al. 2016). Thus, AR modifies or enhances the user's real-life experience, while VR places the user in a completely simulated environment.

As technology advances, applications and simulations involving AR are becoming increasingly incorporated into various aspects of the medical field. Although AR technology is still in its infancy, this chapter discusses the beginnings of AR in medicine and its current and potential future applications in the field of medical education.

Fig. 7.1 A medical professional using AccuVein to visualize veins before drawing blood (AccuVein Inc., NY, USA)

7.2   Augmented Reality in Medical School

Medical students are tasked with becoming experts in human anatomy, adept at diagnosing disease, proficient in creating beneficial treatment plans, and effective at guiding and comforting their future patients throughout their medical journey. While medical school only lasts four years, learning is a career-long process for physicians, especially since the body of medical knowledge is growing exponentially. One study examining the challenges facing medical education estimates that by 2020, the current body of medical knowledge will double every 73 days (Densen 2011). Thus, medical professionals are lifelong learners, constantly working to remain knowledgeable about the latest medical breakthroughs and discoveries.

Augmented reality shows great potential in facilitating medical students' learning, whether by aiding in studying for anatomy exams by providing intuitive 3D models, improving fine motor skills, or helping students see interactions from a patient's perspective. Augmented reality can make learning faster, more efficient, and more engaging. Thus, it gives medical students new ways to fully understand the complex structures described in their textbooks and apply that learning in realistic settings. However, it has also been argued that AR, though efficient and engaging, cannot replace interactions with real patients and can even act as a distraction that hinders, rather than aids, a medical student's education. As advancements are made in the medical field, it is important to keep the patient at the forefront of a medical student's education and ensure new technology does not create a barrier between the patient and physician. If used carefully, AR has great potential to better connect medical students to the material they are learning and to the patients they serve.

7.2.1   Augmented Reality and Anatomy

For medical students—who are learning a high volume of information about the human body, often for the first time—any innovation that makes learning more efficient is welcome. Medical students reported that learning with mobile AR technology, specifically 3D video animations, 3D human anatomy models, and diagrams on their phones, requires less cognitive effort than textbook learning. Mobile AR technology (Fig. 7.2) also allows them to access materials whenever they want, giving them flexibility in their studying. These mobile AR applications, or "apps" integrate virtual learning objects into the real world and allow students to interact directly with the environment (Kucuk et al. 2016). Medical students who studied anatomy using a mobile app with AR technology were able to learn more items in an allotted time period than students who studied using textbooks alone (Albrecht et al. 2013). In addition to increasing efficiency, AR technology gives students a better understanding of spatial relationships, better captures their attention, and reduces failure rate once a student is actually applying what they learned (Zhu et al. 2014). Thus, AR gives students a comprehensive introduction to the human body before they work

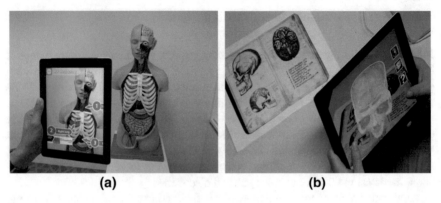

(a)   **(b)**

Fig. 7.2 a AR Anatomy app used to help medical students memorize organs. *Photo courtesy of Zed Interactive.* **b** AR Anatomy app used to help medical students with spatial orientation and learning parts of the skull. *Photo courtesy of Wikimedia Commons. No changes were made. The license for this photo may be found at* https://creativecommons.org/share-your-work/licensing-considerations/compatible-licenses

directly with patients or cadavers, making the transition from textbook pictures to real structures easier (Kugelmann et al. 2018).

AR provides real-time feedback that captures medical students' attention and immerses them in the learning experience (Kamphuis et al. 2014). When compared to students who studied anatomy using Virtual reality (VR) and tablet-based learning, students who used AR scored similarly on anatomy tests but had increased engagement and learner immersion without the adverse effects of VR, such as dizziness or nausea (Moro et al. 2017). The employment of AR technology such as a "Magic Mirror" (Fig. 7.3), which uses a computed tomography, or CT dataset to allow a student to view the anatomical structures in their own body, and "Gunner Goggles,"[1] which add links, videos, and 2D images to a traditional textbook, further advances this engagement in learning anatomy. A vast majority of medical students felt the "Magic Mirror" had educational value (Ma et al. 2015) as did the "Gunner Goggles," and found AR to be a viable, and sometimes better alternative to previous exam review methods (Wang et al. 2016).

By providing medical students with an immersive experience, AR allows them to practice patient care in a realistic setting without putting any patients in the care of inexperienced students. Augmented reality that superimposes images from anatomical datasets onto simulated patients allows medical students to visualize anatomical structures and interact directly with anatomy in a way that they can easily apply to a clinical setting (Fig. 7.4).

This can also be replicated using radiological images to give students a view of spatial anatomy or ultrasound images to visualize blood flow. Augmented reality can also be combined with haptic technology to give students tactile feedback, allowing

---

[1]For more information about "Gunner Goggles," please visit: https://www.us.elsevierhealth.com/gunnergoggles.

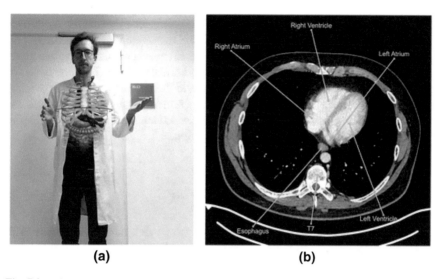

Fig. 7.3 **a** A man using the "Magic Mirror" to view his ribcage and organs. **b** The CT dataset corresponding to the red circle in image **a** (Bork et al. 2019)

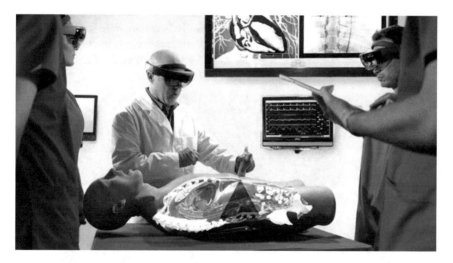

Fig. 7.4 Using AR technology to project anatomical dataset onto a simulated patient. *Photo courtesy of CAE Healthcare*

them to feel the difference between tissues without touching a patient before they are experienced enough to do so (Khor et al. 2016). The applicability of AR to anatomy education extends even further, with studies showing students using AR to visualize patient-specific idiosyncrasies and deformations in the lungs (Kamphuis et al. 2014) or accurately measure a patient's kidney in preparation for an ultrasound (Ebner et al. 2019).

This technology can be used to aid students in observing procedures for the first time, providing them with patient-specific diagrams of anatomy for learning purposes. For example, students working with the same cadaver regularly have the opportunity to really get to know that particular body's normal anatomy. However, with AR goggles or mobile AR technology, students could then view that anatomy overlaid with various abnormal pathologies that can teach them about various diseases and how they present. Thus, AR technology provides students with early opportunities to learn about patient-specific disease presentation.

7.2.2 Augmented Reality and Mentoring

AR fosters interactions between medical students and their mentors in remote locations, allowing students to virtually experience procedures they are not yet skilled enough to perform themselves. In recent years, AR has developed to the point that a remote surgeon could superimpose their hands onto another surgeon performing a procedure with an AR headset. Similarly, Microsoft Hololens[2] (Fig. 7.5) employs AR technology to project a hologram of someone in a different location, which allows surgeons worldwide to work in the same operating space with holographic projections of each other. These technologies could similarly be employed to train medical students in their clinical years and help them become more comfortable performing new procedures alongside their mentors and peers (Khor et al. 2016).

Fig. 7.5 A man wearing Microsoft Hololens. *Photo courtesy of Tyler Ferguson—Creation Media. No changes were made*

---

[2]For more information about "Microsoft Hololens," please visit: https://www.microsoft.com/en-us/hololens.

7.2.3   Augmented Reality and Clinical Skills

AR also has the potential to help medical students improve their clinical skills and better interact with patients. Typically, medical students assess their clinical skills by working with simulated patients and watching the interaction afterward from a "bird's eye view" camera in the corner of the room. Students have expressed that this bird's eye view does not always allow them to properly assess their ability to make eye contact or adjust their facial expressions throughout the conversation.

To remedy this, Google Glass,[3] AR technology on glasses that can record from the point of view of the wearer, was used to help medical students improve their interactions with patients (Fig. 7.6). One study allowed medical students to perform a clinical simulation while watching a video of a simulated patient in respiratory distress through Google Glass. In another study, students were recorded giving a terminal cancer diagnosis to a standardized patient who wore Google Glass to record the interaction. A majority of medical students felt the Google Glass would be valuable to the clinical skills training program, though some students found it distracting or felt self-conscious because of it (Tully et al. 2015). Overall, students felt positively about the simulation and felt it was realistic, though some cited technical difficulties such as difficulty connecting to a wireless network, short battery life, and overheating equipment as a challenge (Chaballout et al. 2016).

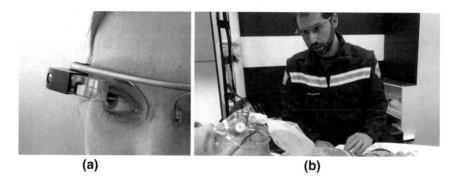

(a)   (b)

Fig. 7.6   a A woman wearing Google Glass. *Photo courtesy of Antonio Zugaldia. No changes were made*. The license for this photo may be found at https://creativecommons.org/licenses/by/2.0/. **b** A man using Google Glass to perform a clinical simulation in an ambulatory setting. *Photo courtesy of Institut Informatique de Gestion. No changes were made. The license for this photo may be found at* https://creativecommons.org/licenses/by-sa/4.0/deed.en

---

[3]For more information about "Google Glass," please visit: https://www.google.com/glass/start/.

7.2.4 Limitations of Augmented Reality for Medical School

Despite its many benefits to medical students, AR still has its limitations, and medical schools are still determining the best way to implement this new technology. Though engaging, AR places a larger extraneous cognitive load on students because it forces them to orient physical models in their minds. A study done in 2019 shows that students studying neuroanatomy who worked with physical cross sections of the brain showed significantly more improvement in test scores than students who worked with AR (Henssen et al. 2019). Thus, the classical method of learning with a physical model may sometimes be superior to AR learning methods, as a classical model incorporates a tactile component into learning and allows students to rotate a model physically. It has been argued that though AR can bring students valuable immersive experience, it still can never compare to the tactile learning that results from working with a cadaver (Kamphuis et al. 2014). However, medical students in these studies expressed a compromise: AR could be used to prepare students for the learning they will do in a dissection room and supplement, rather than replace, that tactile learning with cadavers that is so important in medical education. Augmented reality allows students to see not just what normal looks like, but also abnormal, which may be difficult to observe using only cadavers. Thus, this new technology may be the key to exposing more medical students to abnormal pathologies earlier in their medical education.

AR is still finding its place in medical education, engaging students with a holistic view of anatomy and a patient's view of their clinical skills. As these students progress in skill, graduate medical school, and become residents, we will begin to see the impact of AR on these students' abilities. Until then, we will continue to discover ways that AR can have a place in their learning.

7.3 Augmented Reality for Residents and Attendings

Augmented reality applications have attracted public and scientific interest due to their gradual incorporation into medical practices. Medical professionals have already begun using AR to enhance global collaboration, aid patients in rehabilitation, and improve surgical training and outcomes (Khor et al. 2016).

A review of approximately 2500 published studies revealed that AR applications have helped healthcare providers better understand spatial relationships, strengthen cognitive-psychomotor abilities, and prolong concept retention (Zhu et al. 2014). They have also proven especially useful for training surgical residents: while current surgical curricula heavily emphasize the acquisition and perfection of technical skills, there is a dearth of situational awareness training for residents (Barsom et al. 2016). As no two patients are the same, attention to detail and an ability to adapt to unexpected variations are crucial for residents to avoid making errors during surgery

(Graafland et al. 2014). To better prepare residents for rare cases or unexpected complications, AR applications are a promising way to more optimally and realistically train residents (Barsom et al. 2016). Increasing student engagement and situational immersion during training also helps enhance conceptual understanding, knowledge retention, and automatic skills (Birt et al. 2018).

The incorporation of AR in medicine also has the potential to revolutionize the world of surgery beyond training. On an individual level, surgeons would no longer need to break scrub to check test results or consult patient scans, as the information can be virtually delivered to them, thus increasing efficiency and reducing the risk of infection (Fig. 7.7) (Khor et al. 2016). On a global scale, AR technology has the ability to connect physicians on opposite sides of the globe and make international surgical collaborations easier. For instance, Virtual Interactive Presence and Augmented Reality (VIPAR) is an AR application that allows surgeons to project their hands into the displays of other remote surgeons wearing headsets (Fig. 7.8). Other platforms like Proximie have also enhanced the global dissemination of surgical experience, as surgeons in developing countries can watch experts in other parts of the world perform operations (Khor et al. 2016).

Due to its ability to effectively fill the gap between virtual and physical reality, AR has quickly risen as a promising technology to be integrated into the medical field. The following sections examine three common surgical areas that have already begun to utilize AR in more detail.

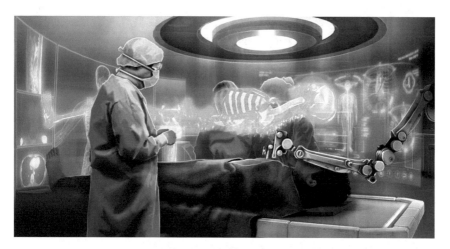

Fig. 7.7 With AR technology, patient data could be delivered directly to the surgeon's field of view without requiring the surgeon to break scrub. *Photo courtesy of Brother UK. No changes were made. The license for this photo may be found at* https://creativecommons.org/licenses/by/2.0/

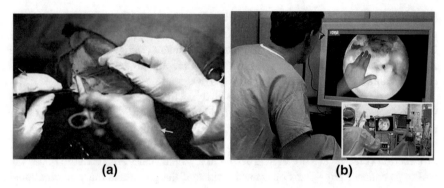

(a)   **(b)**

Fig. 7.8 **a** The remote surgeon's hand (yellow arrow) can be seen in the center while the operating surgeon's hand is on the left and right (red arrows). **b** A remote surgeon's hand is projected into the surgical field of view to guide the operating resident (Baker et al. 2015). *Photo courtesy of The Orthopedic Journal of Harvard Medical School*

7.3.1 Laparoscopic Surgery

7.3.1.1 Challenges of the Field

Laparoscopic surgery, which involves the insertion of a miniature camera into a patient's abdomen to perform a procedure, has several benefits, including reduced scar size, low postoperative morbidity, and a shorter recovery time (Nicolau et al. 2011). While open surgeries put patients at greater risk compared to minimally invasive ones, endoscopic procedures are more challenging for surgeons due to reduced depth perception, a limited field of view, and an altered sense of touch transmitted through an instrument—known as the fulcrum effect (Fig. 7.9) (Kamphuis et al. 2014). Augmented reality can help physicians overcome these challenges in part by increasing their intraoperative vision, or how much they can see during a procedure. More specifically, AR applications can help surgeons see into a patient prior to laparoscope insertion and provide additional information about hidden structures during the surgery after the instrument has been inserted. However, to achieve the seamless integration of virtual learning experiences and real-life physical context, several systems must first be developed and synchronized.

7.3.1.2 How Augmented Reality Applications Work

In order for an AR application to be routinely incorporated into laparoscopic surgeries, four systems must work in unison to deliver the final, desired blend of virtual and real data: a 3D visualization system, a display system, a tracking system, and a registration system (Nicolau et al. 2011).

First, preoperative data must be converted into intraoperative information. Patient-specific data gathered from CT and magnetic resonance imaging (MRI) scans is used

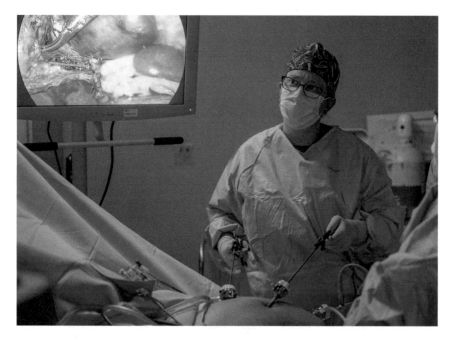

Fig. 7.9 A surgeon uses laparoscopes to perform a minimally invasive laparoscopic surgery. *Photo courtesy of Seaman Jordan Bair. No changes were made. This photograph is considered public domain and has been cleared for release*

to generate 3D models of patients either through direct volume rendering or surface rendering. Direct volume rendering is best for visualizing malformations detected through contrast imaging but less useful for procedures involving the removal of all or part of an organ, as image volume cannot be computed. On the other hand, surface rendering is useful for planning resections and preoperative simulations but often takes longer and is more difficult (Nicolau et al. 2011).

After creating a virtual model of the patient, there are several ways to display AR data, each with its own benefits and drawbacks. See-through displays place a semi-transparent mirror in front of a surgeon's gaze: while still being able to see their patient through the mirror, surgeons are also able to see AR data displayed on a screen and reflected by the mirror into the surgeon's eye. Although this method allows surgeons to combine the quality of human sight—something that cameras cannot replicate—with virtual information, this system is expensive and requires real-time, accurate tracking of pupil positions. Projection-based display systems are another option, where AR information is directly projected onto the patient's skin. Even though this technique provides one of the most real feelings of patient transparency, it is also one of the most inaccurate because of significant perception errors. The location of a surgeon's head and the patient's skin must be tracked, and even then, this technique would still only be accurate for structures that lie directly under the skin. Video-based displays work by superimposing preoperative patient data onto the live video

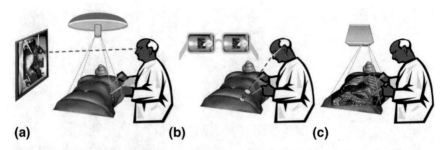

(a)   (b)   (c)

Fig. 7.10 Systems for displaying AR data. **a** In a video-based display, preoperative data is super-imposed on a live video stream. **b** In a see-through display, data is reflected in the surgeon's eyes. **c** In a projection-based display, AR data is projected directly onto the patient (Nicolau et al. 2011). (Reprinted from Surgical Oncology, 20, Nicolau S, Soler L, Mutter D, Marescaux J, 189–201, (2011), with permission from Elsevier.)

stream. In other words, AR information is directly displayed on the endoscopic image (Fig. 7.10). Thus far, this method seems most appropriate for laparoscopic surgeons (Nicolau et al. 2011).

To maximize the efficiency and accuracy of AR applications, a tracking system is also needed to monitor both the endoscopic instrument and the location and direction of the surgeon's head. Current techniques use optical infrared tracking, normal calibrated cameras, or electromagnetic tracking. Such devices are necessary for the real-time tracking of position and orientation (Nicolau et al. 2011).

Lastly, a registration system is responsible for superimposing the intraoperative information at the correct physical position. It is of utmost importance that this system be as accurate as possible, as any errors can result in the incorrect guidance of a surgeon and dangerous surgical movement. The two most common methods are interactive registration AR and automatic registration AR. Interactive Augmented Reality (IAR) requires users to manually identify anatomical landmarks on both the real patient and the 3D patient model while automatic AR (AAR), as the name suggests, is a fully automated process to register anatomical landmarks. To date, researchers have had more success with IAR. Projector-based IAR has been reported to improve port placement in laparoscopic gastric surgery and reduce operative time and X-ray exposure in kidney stone removals. Camera-based IAR has also helped surgeons resect tumors on the adrenal gland, liver, pancreas, and parathyroid (Nicolau et al. 2011). Although more applications currently use IAR, these systems not only require additional medical personnel but also heavily depend on the skill of the user, thus limiting its clinical feasibility. Researchers will eventually need to overcome the challenges posed by AAR in order to create AR applications that can realistically be incorporated into medical practice.

For laparoscopic surgeons, AR information would ideally be displayed directly in the endoscopic view (Fig. 7.11). But before this can be done, AR applications first must account for natural human movements, like breathing motions and heartbeats, as well as real-time changes to organs made by the surgeon during the operation. Ultimately, even though significant progress has been made on the separate systems, the

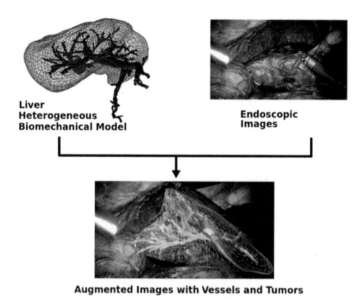

Liver
Heterogeneous
Biomechanical Model

Endoscopic
Images

Augmented Images with Vessels and Tumors

Fig. 7.11 AR technology is used to superimpose vein and tumor locations gathered from pre-operative images onto the liver during a tumor resection (Talbot et al. 2015; Haouchine et al. 2013)

different pieces of the AR puzzle have yet to be perfected and seamlessly assembled into an accurate, cost-effective, user-friendly AR application.

7.3.1.3   Uses of Augmented Reality in Laparoscopic Surgical Training

Despite the need for further technical development, AR applications still have several educational benefits that allow for experiential learning (Dalgarno and Lee 2010). For laparoscopic surgery specifically, "part-task practice" has been shown to be the most effective way to master the complex psychomotor skills required in procedures. Through "part-task practice," trainees repeatedly practice certain motions until they become ingrained in muscle memory and reach a certain level of automation (Kamphuis et al. 2014). Residents and newer surgeons can practice on mannequins that have been overlaid with anatomical AR information (Fig. 7.12). To minimize simulation dissonance, AR applications must be easy to use and have high simulation quality, design, and realism. Given the technical challenges and high costs of developing AR applications, educators must be able to decide which surgical skills are worth investing time and money into developing simulations for (Birt et al. 2018). However, it is still important to remember that simulation training should be seen as a supplement, rather than a replacement, for hands-on training.

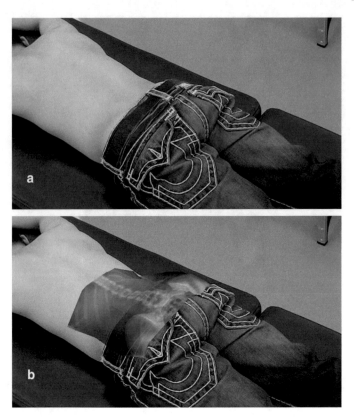

Fig. 7.12 A model without (**a**) and with (**b**) anatomical information projected onto it allows residents to study and practice techniques (Aaskov et al. 2019)

7.3.2 Neurosurgery

7.3.2.1 Challenges of the Field

Neurosurgery is the medical specialty concerned with the diagnosis and surgical treatment of illnesses associated with the human nervous system, including the brain and the spinal cord. Neurosurgery requires an enormous amount of knowledge, near-perfect technical skill, and meticulous preparation. In addition to being limited to a minuscule surgical field to maneuver in, surgeons must also avoid the fragile blood vessels and critical brain structures scattered throughout the surgical field, mere millimeters away from their surgical instruments (Pelargos et al. 2017). Even the smallest error can potentially render patients blind, deaf, or paralyzed.

Given the gravity of technical error in neurosurgery (Matthew et al. 2014), it is especially important for trainees to receive rigorous and thorough training before beginning to operate on live patients. Current education models are largely based on models created in the 1890s and focus mostly on mentorship, number of operations performed, and time spent in the hospital (Pelargos et al. 2017). However, with recent laws placing working-hour restrictions to not only improve resident working conditions but also patient safety, the neurosurgical field needs to take advantage of technological advancements to create higher quality, more time-efficient training paradigms (Matthew et al. 2014).

7.3.2.2 Uses of Augmented Reality in Neurosurgical Training

Unlike the laparoscopic surgical field that has already begun incorporating AR applications into surgeries on live patients, AR applications in neurosurgery are mostly limited to use in education, training, and preoperative rehearsals. Given the current state of AR technology, AR applications are most valued in this field for their ability to increase opportunities for residents to gain surgical experience without a corresponding increase in risk for patients. Even though AR systems in neurosurgery are still significantly underdeveloped compared to their VR counterparts, they can still be used to project anatomical information gathered from pre-scanned CT, MRI, or ultrasound data onto the surgical field, thus illuminating structures hidden intraoperatively. Lastly, they could possibly be used to develop a proper, standardized set of evaluation criteria for freshly minted trainees and experienced surgeons alike (Pelargos et al. 2017). Specific procedures that scientists and physicians have begun using AR applications for include percutaneous vertebroplasty, thoracic pedicle screw placement, percutaneous spinal needle placement, facet joint injection, and spinal needle insertion (Pfandler et al. 2017).

7.3.2.3 Limitations of Augmented Reality in Neurosurgery

A systematic review of published studies on AR applications in neurosurgery revealed that the majority of study participants gave positive feedback and commented on the realistic feel of the simulations. However, these results have not been completely validated due to major design flaws identified in the majority of the studies, including a lack of controls, validity assessments, and randomized study designs. Inconsistencies in how studies define "validity" and "reliability" also make it difficult to compare and validate one study's results with another's. In general, current studies on AR applications in neurosurgery are too different in terms of study design, quality, and outcome measures to allow for any meaningful conclusions to be made. Ultimately, more rigorous, standardized studies need to be conducted before the benefits of AR simulation in neurosurgery can be confirmed (Matthew et al. 2014).

7.3.3 Cardiology

Researchers and physicians alike have begun exploring how to apply AR applications to various areas in cardiology, including physician education, cardiac rehabilitation, pre-procedural planning, and intraoperative use. For surgeries, AR applications have the potential to help physicians visualize hidden structures in 3D, manipulate digital images in real-time, and improve control of surgical tools.

One early feasibility study evaluated the use of an AR guidance system in conjunction with Microsoft Hololens during aortic valve replacement and device placement procedures. With AR technology, physicians no longer needed to perform aortic arch angiograms–which involves injecting a dye into the patient's arteries and using X-rays to observe how it travels–and patients experienced less exposure to X-rays. Researchers optimistically concluded that AR applications are clinically feasible, reduce surgery time, and decrease patient risk (Southworth et al. 2019).

Another study looked at the use of a first-person point of view AR application meant to guide needle insertion during catheter placement. Surgeons found the AR technology realistic, easy to use, and helpful. They also thought the integration of AR into medical education would benefit future students. However, they criticized the fit of the AR goggles, the restricted allowable head movement, and the cost of implementation. Despite these limitations, outcomes indicate that AR applications have much potential: with AR guidance, experienced and non-experienced participants were equally likely to identify anatomical landmarks and insert needles correctly (Rochlen et al. 2017).

Other assessments of the effects of AR simulations on echocardiography training revealed similar sentiments (Platts et al. 2012; Weidenbach et al. 2009). In addition, a significant number of participants believed that, due to the unpredictable and imperfect nature of the clinical environment, simulation training would not be able to completely replace hands-on, clinical experience. Thus, these budding technologies may prove to be more useful during the initial training stages (Platts et al. 2012).

Ultimately, AR provides surgeons with a multitude of new ways to improve surgical outcomes, educate residents, and increase efficiency and patient safety. Though nothing can fully replace hands-on learning, AR has the potential to provide a valuable supplement to surgical experiences. With new applications continuing to be developed, AR applications can also be used to help patients better understand their medical treatments and surgical procedures. As healthcare delivery becomes increasingly patient-centered, utilizing technology to allow patients to become more active in developing their treatment plans will become essential.

7.4   Patient Education

In recent years, the medical field has begun shifting toward a more patient-centered approach instead of a more traditional, disease-centered approach. While the latter is effective when a patient has one primary illness or concern, it quickly becomes less so when a patient is experiencing multiple chronic conditions (Tinetti et al. 2016). This shift to the patient-centered approach—which focuses on identifying the patient's individual health goals and what they are willing to undertake in order to reach those goals—is timely considering the aging of the U.S. population, which will inevitably lead to an increase in the number of patients with multiple chronic conditions (Colby and Ortman 2014).

A critical factor in successfully employing this approach is an active doctor-patient relationship where the patient is able to communicate their goals and the physician is able to inform the patient about their condition(s) and potential treatments. In fact, empowering patients to become active participants in their health care has numerous benefits, such as increased patient satisfaction and trust in their physicians, decreased patient anxiety, and improved adherence to medical regimens (Vahdat et al. 2014). Due to its interactive and visual format, there is a growing belief that AR is particularly suited to engage and educate patients at various stages of their treatments, from the preoperative consultation and the inpatient experience to the recovery and rehabilitation process (Zucker et al. 2018; Courtney et al. 2015).

7.4.1   Preoperative Education

Surgery, most likely due to its immediate results and clear risks, is one area of medicine where patients are particularly motivated to have a comprehensive understanding of their options and the potential results. The preoperative consultation is the surgeon's opportunity to educate their patients and ensure they have the tools and information necessary to make informed decisions; in some fields, such as urology, physicians heavily rely on preoperative images when discussing significant procedures with their patients (Wake et al. 2019). However, learning about the complex structure of human anatomy through 2D images can be difficult, which is only exacerbated by the stress of deciding whether or not to undergo surgery (Fig. 7.13).

There has been a long-standing interest in utilizing AR to provide patients with a 3D visualization of their specific anatomy. In 2010, a team comprised of computer scientists and plastic surgeons in Germany developed a "Magic Mirror" for patients preparing for breast augmentation. Wearing a target tracker on their shoulder, patients could stand in front of a screen where their body would be virtually reconstructed and projected, illustrating the potential breast augmentation. When the team consulted with multiple surgeons regarding this software, all of the surgeons stated there was a need for more advanced teaching tools for patients, and most of the surgeons expressed interest in employing the "Magic Mirror" in their own practice, assuming

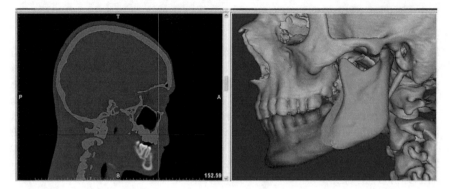

Fig. 7.13 2D image (left) versus a 3D image (right) both illustrating the outcome of jaw surgery to a patient. Photo provided courtesy of Dr. Michael Malek and Akh Linz. The top of the original photo was cropped for the purpose of this chapter. Otherwise, no changes were made. The license for this photo may be found at https://creativecommons.org/licenses/by-nc-nd/2.0/.

the visualizations were accurate (Wucherer et al. 2010). More recently, an AR tool aptly called RAD-AR was developed to assist in the various facets of radiotherapy treatments. In addition to providing physicians with more detailed 3D datasets and improving the accuracy of patient positioning during treatment, RAD-AR may also be used for educating patients on the importance of pre-treatment preparation. It is common to use 2D sketches of patients' anatomy in these educational sessions, but a 3D visualization may be more intuitive and more likely to improve patient understanding and compliance with pre-treatment procedures (Cosentino et al. 2017).

The conversation regarding AR's potential application in preoperative consultation was reignited in 2018 by a letter written by Benjamin Zucker, Dr. Paris Tekkis, and Dr. Christos Kontovounisios, which was published in a surgical medical journal. The authors argued that AR's intuitive visualization—compared to traditional 2D imaging such as a CT scan or MRI—and innate interactive nature would allow patients to gain a better understanding of surgical procedures and enable patients to direct their educational experience. However, a study conducted in 2019 comparing the effectiveness of 3D printed models, AR, and 3D computer visualizations (Fig. 7.14) in educating surgical patients found that AR may not be the optimal tool, currently, for patient education. The 3D printed model was found to be the most beneficial overall, increasing patients' understanding of their anatomy, disease, and treatment plan as well as making patients feel more comfortable with their treatment. Despite the fact that patients perceived AR to be useful, it did not seem to actually improve their understanding (Wake et al. 2019).

Although the results of this study raise doubts regarding the efficacy of AR in patient education, this is currently the only relatively large-scale study published on this topic and there is still much more research to be done. Augmented reality's optimal role may be serving as a supplementary resource, as opposed to a primary one. Furthermore, its potential will grow as AR evolves and both physicians and patients develop their proficiency in utilizing the technology.

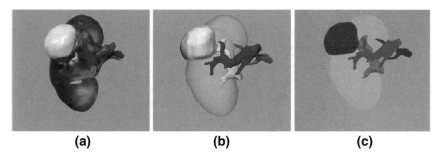

(a)   **(b)**   **(c)**

Fig. 7.14 Kidney cancer models that are **a** 3D printed, **b** 3D computer-generated, and **c** AR. The tumor is shown in white in the 3D printed and 3D computer-generated models and purple in the AR model. The artery is shown in red, the vein in blue, and the collecting system in yellow (Wake et al. 2019). *The bottom of the original figure was cropped for the purpose of this chapter. Otherwise, no changes were made. The license for this photo may be found at* https://creativecommons.org/licenses/by/4.0/

7.4.2   The Pediatric Inpatient Experience

Going to the hospital can be a stressful experience, particularly for children who are less likely to understand why they are at the hospital or why they should allow the doctor to run a test. To help alleviate children's potential fear and anxiety, some children's hospitals have begun incorporating VR and AR games into medical procedures and the inpatient visit. While the majority of these experiences utilize VR and focus mainly on entertaining and distracting the child during a procedure, some games use AR to familiarize the patient with a specific medical procedure or the inpatient visit overall.

The Alder Hey Children's Hospital in the United Kingdom recently released an application called "Alder Play" for both Android and iOS (Fig. 7.15). It can be downloaded prior to a child's visit and was designed to prepare children for their hospital stay, guide them through potentially frightening moments, and reward them for their courage (Alder Play). Users choose a virtual animal guide who leads them through the hospital, familiarizing them with the facility by using AR. They can even message with their guide who is equipped with an artificially intelligent chatbot powered by IBM's Watson. The app also supplies video tutorials on common procedures, such as blood tests, so children are less intimidated when they experience the procedure. Doctors can also award their patients in-game stickers as positive reinforcement (Jimenez et al. 2019; Debczak 2017).

Lucile Packard Children's Hospital Stanford is another hospital applying this technology through their Packard Children's Childhood Anxiety Reduction through Innovation and Technology (CHARIOT) program. The majority of their initiatives utilize VR to engross patients in virtual adventures as they undergo procedures, but they have begun using AR to allow curious patients to observe and even be an active participant in their procedures (Jimenez et al. 2019; CHARIOT Program 2018; DeTrempe 2017). For those children who may be more inquisitive than afraid, the

Fig. 7.15 The Alder Play children's guide gives a child a tour of the hospital playroom (Debczak 2017)

latter fulfills the patient's curiosity while also making it easier for medical staff to execute their procedures. Through these experiences, children are able to learn more about their hospital stay, understand their procedures, and feel more comfortable in a hospital setting.

7.4.3 Telemedical Applications

Augmented reality's potential for patient education is not restricted to the four walls of the hospital or the doctor's office. Access to health care, especially in rural areas, is an ongoing and major issue in the U.S. A study published in 2015 reported that rural communities were still facing considerable barriers to accessing healthcare, including limited health care services and public transportation, understaffing of trained physicians, and a lack of internet access (Douthit et al. 2015). Additionally, a report by the Georgetown University Health Policy Institute noted that the rural population is more likely to be older, poorer, and uninsured as well as experience higher rates of injury and suicide (Wagnerman 2019). Telemedicine, the use of technology to provide medical services to a patient in a distant location, has been a key element in the medical field's campaign to deliver health care to all in need of it. Augmented reality is now being integrated into telemedicine in order to increase both the physician's and patient's ability to interact and communicate with each other.

In 2014, two pilot studies were published regarding two telemedicine systems supported by AR and their effectiveness in training laypersons to accomplish a specific task. The first was a preliminary test for a telerehabilitation system called Ghostman. This system was designed to allow physical therapists to remotely instruct, correct, and monitor their patients' progress by placing them in their patient's point of view (Fig. 7.16). Ghostman was first tested by having an instructor guide a participant using chopsticks. Participants received either a face-to-face session with the instructor or a remote Ghostman session with the instructor. There was no difference between the groups with respect to frequency of errors or skill retention over one week, which indicated that Ghostman was as effective as the traditional in-person session (Chinthammit et al. 2014).

The second study sought to assess AR and telemedicine's potential to guide untrained persons to correctly use an electrocardiogram (ECG) device to successfully conduct an ECG on a patient. The AR application, developed using ARToolKit, an open-sourced AR library, was specifically designed to navigate the user with a combination of audio messages and visuals such as a text-box, pointers, and spots superimposed on the user's field of view (Fig. 7.17). Participants were able to successfully conduct an ECG on a real patient with an average positioning error of less than 7 mm (Bifulco et al. 2014). However, as noted in the study, these tests were conducted in an extremely controlled environment, and the system's ability to account for fluctuations in both the patient's and environment's characteristics needs to be developed before it is employed in real-life scenarios.

Dr. Brett Ponce and colleagues at the University of Alabama at Birmingham School of Medicine took the next step by examining if a telemedical system known as the virtual interactive presence (VIP) system could be used to guide patients through postoperative care when supported by AR. The postoperative period is a crucial time for healing and recovery and generally necessitates follow-ups with providers, as services such as redressing wounds and wound evaluation are commonly required. However, many people are simply unable to attend their follow-ups for logistical or

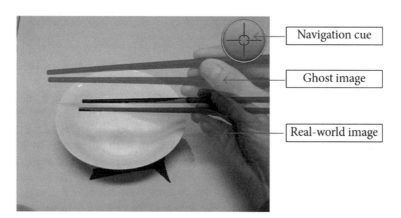

Fig. 7.16 An example of teacher instructing a student on how to use chopsticks through Ghostman (Chinthammit et al. 2014). *No changes were made. The license for this photo may be found at* https://creativecommons.org/licenses/by/3.0/

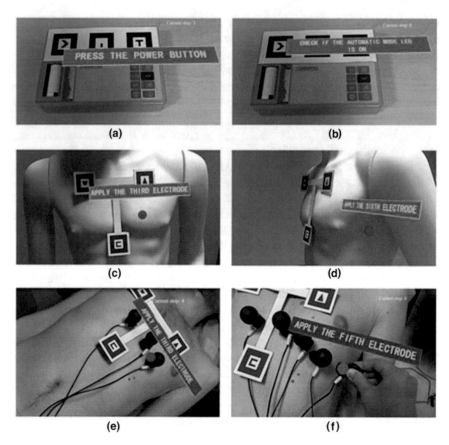

Fig. 7.17 Point of view of a user being guided by the AR application by correctly placing electrodes on a mannequin or human body to carry-out an ECG (Bifulco et al. 2014). *No changes were made. The license for this photo may be found at* https://creativecommons.org/licenses/by/4.0/

financial reasons. The VIP system, available as a free iOS mobile application, creates a hybridized feed of the patient and physician viewpoints, allowing them to virtually interact (Fig. 7.18). The study found that both patients and surgeons found the system useful for wound inspection, dressing, and medical equipment management, and felt it was superior to communication via phone, text, or email. Unfortunately, there were two instances where patient-participants attempted to contact their surgeon via the application during a medical emergency instead of seeking immediate, physical attention, but both were eventually resolved without long-term effects. Technical difficulties were another issue, as 20 of the 50 participants were unable to complete their session due to set-up troubles, poor network connections, inability to use the application, or incompatible devices (Ponce et al. 2016). As this technology develops, so will its potential applications.

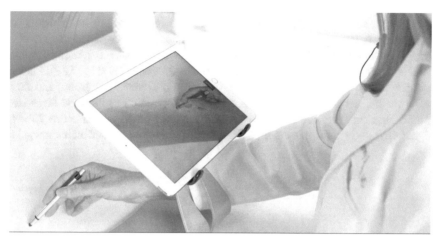

Fig. 7.18 This photo illustrates how a dermatologist may virtually interact with their patients, with the VIP system, by remotely examining a patient's arm. *Photo courtesy of Help Lightning*

While the integration of AR and telemedicine shows great promise, it currently faces several limitations. As mentioned at the beginning of this section, a considerable portion of rural areas do not have internet access (Eighth Broadband 2012). Without a reliable and adequate internet connection, this technology is rendered unusable. Additionally, these systems need to optimize inclusivity. For example, when designing them as mobile applications, they should be compatible with both iOS and Android devices. The VIP system was only compatible with iOS, excluding a considerable portion of the U.S. population. Given that Android users are 86% more likely to live in rural areas and iOS users are 27% more likely to live in urban areas, a system compatible with both Android and iOS devices is necessary to reach more of the rural population (Alexander 2019). Security is another major concern; any information transmitted during these sessions should be heavily encrypted, and the databases storing all the information must be closely monitored. Developers should be wary of using open-source libraries to develop their system as there are no requirements regarding who can contribute to the code, and mal-intentioned or poorly written code may be uploaded, potentially introducing security flaws. Given adequate attention and resources, these obstacles are manageable and can be overcome.

7.4.4 General Patient Education

In addition to facilitating physician to patient education, AR applications are also being created for individual, self-directed use. The EyeDecide App is a free mobile application for iOS devices, which allows users to examine the anatomy and structure of the eyeball at 360°. According to an online publication for medical professionals, users may be able to self-diagnose by compiling their symptoms into the application's simulation. It even provides a list of recommended, local eye-specialists (Lewis 2013; EyeDecide App). Researchers also developed an AR game for Android mobile devices to support and educate pediatric patients with diabetes (Fig. 7.19). Players advance through three levels, each focusing on a different food group, and must select the correct carbohydrate content level corresponding to the food visualized on the physical plate. To move on to the next level players must score 70% or higher. One study found that children who played the game improved their knowledge

Fig. 7.19 An outline of each of the three levels along with screenshots of the gameplay (Calle-Bustos et al. 2017). *No changes were made. The license for this photo may be found at* https://creativecommons.org/licenses/by/4.0/

surrounding the carbohydrate content of foods displayed in the game regardless of age or gender (Calle-Bustos et al. 2017).

7.5 Conclusion

Ultimately, as the field of medicine changes and evolves, incorporating new technologies to better serve patients, AR will find its place educating physicians and patients alike. It is important that medical schools take the time to understand these new technological advancements, utilizing them to improve the education of the next generation of physicians and supplement traditional learning. Though nothing can truly replace the tactile learning experience of working with cadavers or actual patients, AR technology can similarly engage and inform medical students and physicians. Tools such as the "Magic Mirror" and Google Glass can provide an immersive, holistic learning opportunity for medical students that they can carry with them throughout their training. Utilizing AR for laparoscopic surgeries, neurosurgery, and cardiac procedures have allowed physicians to perform minimally invasive, high-risk procedures in a more efficient and safe way. Augmented reality aids physicians in educating patients of any age about their anatomy, their condition, and what their options are, giving them control over their own care during an often stressful time.

Despite the many positive implications of widespread AR use in the medical field, it is not without its drawbacks. Cost and availability are still of great concern, as AR technology is expensive, requiring powerful microcomputers that are not yet widely available and specially trained instructors to implement AR technology in hospital settings (Zahiri et al. 2018). These devices must be functional, light, durable, and comfortable for the wearer performing procedures that require a high level of concentration. As AR technology is more widely implemented in medical education and the medical field, this issue of availability and cost may be reduced due to higher demand and increased comfort using AR technology among doctors. Confidentiality and data management are also important to consider, as bringing technology into the operating or exam room runs the risk of breaching HIPAA (Khor et al. 2016). However, as medical professionals have become increasingly comfortable using technology in their practice, the medical field has also improved the protection of patient privacy through technological advancements and will continue to do so with AR.

In an increasingly digitally-centered world, where even our youngest members of society are engaged with AR technology through games like Pokémon GO, AR will no doubt continue to make its way into the medical field. Though there are many avenues still left to explore, current innovations in AR have already made care more cost-effective and patient-centered. By using this new technology to more fully understand anatomy and patient interactions, medical students are able to enter residency more prepared and confident. Surgeons can not only improve outcomes for their patients long-term but also help them fully understand their procedure and condition like never before. Patient education through AR can improve compliance, stop preventable conditions before they start, and ease patients' concerns. Patients may one day even be able to communicate with providers long-distance, using AR to understand and discuss their condition. Innovations improving and implementing AR technology are greatly beneficial to doctors and patients alike, providing new perspectives that truly place the patient at the forefront of care.

References

Aaskov J, Kawchuk GN, Hamaluik KD, Boulanger P, Hartvigsen J (2019) X-ray vision: the accuracy and repeatability of a technology that allows clinicians to see spinal X-rays superimposed on a person's back. PeerJ 7:e6333. https://doi.org/10.7717/peerj.6333

Albrecht U, Folta-Schoofs K, Behrends M et al (2013) Effects of mobile augmented reality learning compared to textbook learning on medical students: randomized controlled pilot study. J Med Internet Res. https://doi.org/10.2196/jmir.2497

Alder Play. https://www.ustwo.com/work/alder-play. Accessed 15 Oct 2018

Alexander A (2019) Android users vs. iPhone users—The demographics. https://ansonalex.com/infographics/android-users-vs-iphone-users-the-demographics/#infographic. Accessed 31 Oct 2019

Baker D, Fryberger C, Ponce B (2015) The emergence of augmented reality in orthopaedic surgery and education. Orthopaedic J Harvard Med School 16:8–16

Barsom EZ, Graafland M, Schijven MP (2016) Systematic review on the effectiveness of augmented reality applications in medical training. Surg Endosc 30:4174–4183. https://doi.org/10.1007/s00464-016-4800-6

Bifulco P, Narducci F, Vertucci R et al (2014) Telemedicine supported by augmented reality: an interactive guide for untrained people in performing an ECG test. Biomed Eng Online 13(1):153

Birt J, Stromberga Z, Cowling M et al (2018) Mobile mixed reality for experiential learning and simulation in medical and health sciences education. Australas J Educ Technol. https://doi.org/10.3390/info9020031

Blendon R, Benson J, Hero J (2014). Public Trust in Physicians — U.S. Medicine in International Perspective. N Engl J Med 371(17):1570–1572. https://doi.org/10.1056/nejmp1407373

Bork F, Stratmann L, Enssle S et al (2019) The Benefits of an Augmented Reality Magic Mirror System for Integrated Radiology Teaching in Gross Anatomy. Anat Sci Educ 12(6):585–598. https://doi.org/10.1002/ase.1864

Chaballout B, Molloy M, Vaughn J et al (2016) Feasibility of Augmented Reality in Clinical Simulations: Using Google Glass with Manikins. J Med Internet Res. https://doi.org/10.2196/mededu.5159

CHARIOT Program (2018). https://www.stanfordchildrens.org/en/innovation/chariot. Accessed 17 October 2019.

Chinthammit W, Merritt T, Pedersen S et al (2014) Ghostman: Augmented Reality Application for Telerehabilitation and Remote Instruction of a Novel Motor Skill. BioMed Res Int 2014:1–7. https://doi.org/10.1155/2014/646347

Colby S, Ortman J (2014) Projections of the size and composition of the U.S. Population: 2014 to 2060. Accessed 15 Oct 2018

Cosentino F, John N, Vaarkamp J (2017) RAD-AR: RADiotherapy - Augmented Reality. An augmented reality tool for radiotherapy implemented on consumer electronics devices. https://doi.org/10.1109/CW.2017.56

Courtney K, Kuo A, Shabestari O (eds) (2015) Driving Quality in Informatics: Fulfilling the Promise. IOS Press, Amsterdam

Dalgarno B, Lee M (2010) What are the learning affordances of 3-D Virtual environments? Br J Educ Technol 40(6):10–32. https://doi.org/10.1111/j.1467-8535.2009.01038.x

Debczak M (2017). This Augmented-Reality App Makes the Hospital Experience Less Scary for Kids. https://mentalfloss.com/article/521854/augmented-reality-app-makes-hospital-experience-less-scary-kids. Accessed 15 October 2019

Densen P (2011) Challenges and opportunities facing medical education. Trans Am Clin Climatol Assoc 122:48–58

DeTrempe K (2017). Virtual reality alleviates pain, anxiety for pediatric patients. https://med.stanford.edu/news/all-news/2017/09/virtual-reality-alleviates-pain-anxiety-for-pediatric-patients.html. Accessed 17 October 2019

Douthit N, Kiv S, Dwolatzky T et al (2015) Exposing some important barriers to health care access in the rural USA. Public Health 129(6):611–620. https://doi.org/10.1016/j.puhe.2015.04.001

Ebner F, De Gregorio A, Schochter F et al (2019) Effect of an Augmented Reality Ultrasound Trainer App on the Motor Skills Needed for a Kidney Ultrasound: Prospective Trial. J Med Internet Res. https://doi.org/10.2196/12713

Eighth Broadband Progress Report. https://www.fcc.gov/reports-research/reports/broadband-progress-reports/eighth-broadband-progress-report Accessed 20 Oct 2019

EyeDecide App. https://sciencenetlinks.com/tools/eyedecide-app/. Accessed 22 Oct 2019

Graafland M, Schraagen J, Boermeester M et al (2014) Training situational awareness to reduce surgical errors in the operating room. BJS Society Ltd 102:16–23. https://doi.org/10.1002/bjs.9643

Henssen D, van den Hauvel L, De Jong G et al (2019) Neuroanatomy Learning: Augmented Reality vs. Cross-Sections. Anat Sci Educ https://doi.org/10.1002/ase.1912

Haouchine N, Dequidt J, Peterlik I, Kerrien E, Berger M et al (2013) Image-guided simulation of heterogeneous tissue deformation for augmented reality during hepatic surgery. In: ISMAR—IEEE international symposium on mixed and augmented reality 2013, Oct 2013, Adelaide, Australia

Jimenez D, Shah J, Das P, Milanaik L (2019) Health implications of augmented reality games on children and adolescents. In: Geroimenko V (ed) Augmented reality games I, 1st edn. Springer, Switzerland

Kamphuis C, Barsom E, Schijven M et al (2014) Augmented reality in medical education? Perspect Med Educ 3(4):300–311. https://doi.org/10.1007/s40037-013-0107-7

Khor WS, Baker B, Amin K et al (2016) Augmented and virtual reality in surgery—the digital surgical environment: applications, limitations and legal pitfalls. Ann Transl Med 4(23):454–463. https://doi.org/10.21037/atm.2016.12.23

Kucuk S, Kapakin S, Goktas Y (2016) Learning anatomy via mobile augmented reality: effects on achievement and cognitive load. Anat Sci Educ. https://doi.org/10.1002/ase.1603

Kugelmann D, Stratmann L, Nuhlen N et al (2018) An augmented reality magic mirror as additive teaching device for gross anatomy. Ann Anat 215:71–75

Lewis T (2013). Augmented reality and patient education, Eye Decide iPhone medical app review. https://www.imedicalapps.com/2013/07/medical-app-augmented-reality-patient-education/ Accessed 22 Oct 2019

Ma M, Fallavollita P, Seelbach I et al (2015) Personalized augmented reality for anatomy education. Anat Sci Educ. https://doi.org/10.1002/ca.22675

Matthew AK, Maria A, Angelique FA, Mark HW, Dipankar N, Nick S (2014) The use of simulation in neurosurgical education and training. J Neurosurg 121(2):228–246. https://doi.org/10.3171/2014.5.JNS131766

Moro C, Stromberga Z, Raikos A et al (2017) The effectiveness of virtual and augmented reality in health sciences and medical anatomy. Anat Sci Educ. https://doi.org/10.1002/ase.1696

Nicolau S, Soler L, Mutter D, Marescaux J (2011) Augmented reality in laparoscopic surgical oncology. 20(3):13. https://doi.org/10.1016/j.suronc.2011.07.002

Pelargos P, Nagasawa D, Lagman C et al (2017) Utilizing virtual and augmented reality for educational and clinical enhancements in neurosurgery. J Clin Neurosci. https://doi.org/10.1016/j.jocn.2016.09.002

Pfandler M, Lazarovici M, Stefan P et al (2017) Virtual reality-based simulators for spine surgery: a systematic review. Spine J 17(9):1352–1363. https://doi.org/10.1016/j.spinee.2017.05.016

Platts D, Humphries J, Burstow D et al (2012) The use of computerised simulators for training of transthoracic and transoesophageal echocardiography: the future of echocardiographic training? Heart Lung Circ 21(5):267–274. https://doi.org/10.1016/j.hlc.2012.03.012

Ponce B, Brabston E, Zu S et al (2016) Telemedicine with mobile devices and augmented reality for early postoperative care. In: 2016 38th annual international conference of the IEEE engineering in medicine and biology society (EMBC), pp 4411–4414. https://doi.org/10.1109/EMBC.2016.7591705

Rochlen L, Levine R, Tait A (2017) First-person point-of-view-augmented reality for central line insertion training: a usability and feasibility study. Simul Healthc 12(1):57–62. https://doi.org/10.1097/SIH.0000000000000185

Southworth M, Silva J, Silva J (2019) Use of extended realities in cardiology. Trends Cardiovasc Med. https://doi.org/10.1016/j.tcm.2019.04.005

Talbot H, Haouchine N, Peterlik I, Dequidt J, Duriez C et al (2015) Surgery training, planning and guidance using the SOFA framework. Eurographics, Zurich, Switzerland (2015)

Tinetti M, Naik A, Dodson J (2016) Moving from disease-centered to patient goals-directed care for patients with multiple chronic conditions: patient value-based care. JAMA Cardiol. 1(1):9–10. https://doi.org/10.1001/jamacardio.2015.0248

Tully J, Dameff C, Kaib S et al (2015) Recording medical students' encounters with standardized patients using Google Glass: providing end-of-life clinical education. Acad Med 90(3):314–316

Vahdat S, Hamzehgardeshi L, Hessam S et al (2014) Patient involvement in health care decision making: a review. Iran Red Crescent Med J. https://doi.org/10.5812/ircmj.12454

Wagnerman K (2019). Research update: health care in rural and urban America. https://ccf.georgetown.edu/2017/10/20/research-update-health-care-in-rural-and-urban-america/. Accessed 15 Oct 2019

Wake N, Rosenkrantz A, Huang R et al (2019) Patient-specific 3D printed and augmented reality kidney and prostate cancer models: impact on patient education. J 3D Printing Med 5(4):1–8. https://doi.org/10.1186/s41205-019-0041-3

Wang J, Suenaga H, Yang L et al (2016) Video see-through augmented reality for oral and maxillofacial surgery. Int J Med Robot. https://doi.org/10.1002/rcs.1754

Weidenbach M, Rázek V, Wild F et al (2009) Simulation of congenital heart defects: a novel way of training in echocardiography. Heart 95(8):636. https://doi.org/10.1136/hrt.2008.156919

Wucherer P, Bichlmeier C, Eder M et al (2010) Multimodal medical consultation for improved patient education. In Proceedings of Bildverarbeitung für die Medizin (BVM 2010), Aachen, Germany, March 2010.

Zahiri M, Nelson C, Oleynikov D et al (2018) Evaluation of augmented reality feedback in surgical training environment. Surg Educ 25(1):81–87

Zhu E, Hadadgar A, Masiello I et al (2014) Augmented reality in healthcare education: an integrative review. Peer J. https://doi.org/10.7717/peerj.469

Zucker B, Tekkis P, Kontovounisios C (2018) Is reality limiting patient understanding? A discussion of the implications of augmented reality technology to patient understanding. Surg Innov 25(2):188–189

Chapter 8
The Usage of Augmented Reality in Dental Education

Rasa Mladenovic

Abstract Dental students must achieve an acceptable level of competence, since most procedures on teeth are irreversible and therefore learning these skills solely on patients is not acceptable. Simulation allows students to repeat procedures till they demonstrate required levels of skills, without putting actual patients at risk and yet acquiring procedural competence. In line with advances in technology, dental simulations are being developed to support the acquisition of necessary psychomotor skills before actual clinical applications. This chapter considers the use of Augmented Reality as one of the most sophisticated methods of simulation.

8.1 Introduction

Simulation is defined as a situation in which a particular set of conditions is created artificially in order to study or experience something that could exist in reality (Oxford Advanced American Dictionary 2019).

Nowadays, simulation is used for a variety of purposes, including entertainment, education, training, system evaluation and research (Smith and Smith 1989). It is commonly used in areas where people need to manipulate or control complex systems, including aviation, healthcare, power plant operations, and the like (Bell and Waag 1998; Seymour et al. 2002). Some simulators are designed to be as realistic as possible and provide an experience almost identical to a real system, while others reproduce only the key features of a simulated system. Regardless of their design or complexity, the simulator is used in situations where the use of a real system is impractical due to financial constraints, unavailability of the system, ethical considerations, or life-threatening effects (Haluck 2000).

R. Mladenovic (✉)
Faculty of Medicine, Department for Dentistry, University of Pristina, Kosovska Mitrovica, Serbia
e-mail: rasa.mladenovic@med.pr.ac.rs

© Springer Nature Switzerland AG 2020   139
V. Geroimenko (ed.), *Augmented Reality in Education*,
Springer Series on Cultural Computing,
https://doi.org/10.1007/978-3-030-42156-4_8

8.2   Development of Simulation Methods in Dentistry

Simulation in dental education is quite mature and has been applied for many years (see Fig. 8.1). Dental students must achieve an acceptable level of competence, since most procedures on teeth (such as cavity preparation, endodontic therapy, and orally surgical interventions) are irreversible, and learning these skills solely on patients is not acceptable practice (Levine et al. 2009).

Simulation allows students to repeat procedures till they demonstrate required levels of skills, without putting actual patients at risk and yet acquiring procedural competence. Thus, most psychomotor skills are first taught in a simulated manner before students engage in patient management (Dutã et al. 2011).

8.2.1   Phantom Head

The use of simulation for preclinical dental education has been around for quite some time. As early as the eighteenth century, at Baltimore College in Ohio, restorative treatments were practiced using extracted teeth (Perry et al. 2015).

In 1894, Oswald Fergus introduced the first phantom head and thus laid the foundation stone for dental education. His phantom consisted of an upper and lower jaw into which the extracted teeth were embedded. Although the Fergus base has now been upgraded to a more realistic plastic manikin for training, the basic principle is still the same. In addition to the classic phantom head model, electronic training models have been applied for three decades; here, an audible signal indicates that a student has reached the right puncture site of a particular local anesthesia (Knipfer et al. 2018).

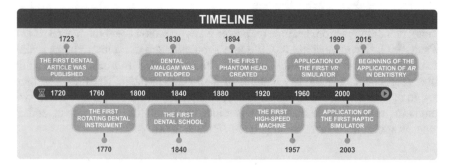

Fig. 8.1   Important dates in dentistry development (Image by the author)

8.2.2 Cadavers

Teaching anatomy without the use of cadavers is almost impossible. Obtaining sufficient cadavers locally is very difficult. In the past 30 years, a number of new fixatives have been developed that preserve some of the features of fresh tissue, such as flexibility, resilience, and coloration, allowing the development of teaching aids that could not be implemented using formalin-fixed cadavers (Balta et al. 2015). Thiels (Walter Thiel) (Thiel 1992) embalming method has been successfully used to demonstrate a number of oral surgery techniques such as local anesthesia, tooth extraction, and implants. Performing these procedures on a cadaver may enhance students' confidence prior to operating on their first patients and reduce the incidence of complications (Grohmann et al. 2013; Kühl et al. 2016).

8.2.3 Robotics

The next generation of simulation is the patient simulator robot (Hanako/Dentaroid, Nissin, Netherland) (see Tanzawa et al. 2011). This patient–robot offers elements of interaction and represents a patient with anatomical and physiological characteristics. The patient–robot is fitted with clothing, a wig, and other ornaments not only to improve her appearance, but also to consider the possibility of spillage of a drug solution or impression material on the clothing. The robot patient comprises autonomous moving parts with eight degrees of freedom (eyelids, eyeballs, jaw, tongue, and neck) and passive moving parts (shoulder, arm, elbow, waist, hip joint, knee, and ankle).

8.2.4 Application of Computers in Education

Since the development of the personal computer, numerous computer programs have complemented conventional teaching. These provided a means for students to learn at their own pace. Computer-based instruction in the health profession, also known as Computer-Aided Learning (CAL), is becoming a popular vehicle to provide information to students, patients, and practitioners alike (Rosenberg et al. 2003; Mladenovic et al. 2018).

The fact that mobile devices today play an important role in education has been confirmed by numerous scientific studies, which have noted the positive impact, as well as the advantage of these devices from a pedagogical perspective (Hwang et al. 2009; Uzunboylu et al. 2009; Mladenovic et al. 2019a, b). At present, mobile devices provide students with easy access to a wide range of educational resources.

8.2.5   Virtual Reality and Haptics

In recent years, technological advances have made it possible to incorporate Virtual Reality (VR) simulation technology into preclinical dental education. Virtual reality simulators provide the ability to integrate clinical scenarios into the operating environment and facilitate tactile skills using haptic technology (Dută et al. 2011).

Haptics is a tactile feedback technology that takes advantage of users' sense of touch by applying force, vibrations, or motion to the user. The literal meaning of haptics is to fasten onto, touch. Haptic technology is widely used in aviation, telecommunications, and medicine.

There are two types of computerized virtual reality simulators available: mannequin-based simulators on which certain dental procedures can be performed using real dental instruments (DentSim, DentX, Israel) and haptic-based simulators that employ an haptic device and virtual models as a platform to facilitate dental training (Simodont Dental trainer, Nissin, Netherland) (see LeBlanc et al. 2004; Buchanan 2001). Simodont provides a virtual environment to practice various dental skills in virtual oral and dental environment. The system also produces convincing visual and audio effects during performance to enhance the simulation experience and make it more realistic (Cutler et al. 2013).

8.2.6   Augmented Reality

Augmented Reality (AR) is a simulation of a three-dimensional environment created using hardware and software that provides the user with realistic experiences and ability to interact. The term Augmented Reality originated in the 1960s. John E. Sutherland is considered the creator of the augmented reality concept (Sutherland 1968).

Augmented Reality evolved after Virtual Reality, because it required more complex technological specifications, though it is essentially simpler to realize than Virtual Reality. The reason is that it enhances the existing environment by adding virtual elements, rather than replacing it with a completely new environment. Yet, it encounters real-world dynamics that are generally difficult to control and often unpredictable (Bugaric 2013). The key to using Augmented Reality was the development of personal computer devices that can be carried around with ease. Due to the intense development of new AR and VR devices (which began with Oculus Rift in 2012 and accelerated in 2014 with the advent of Google Cardboard), these technologies have once again become the focus of educational researchers. Most researchers agree that there are significant educational and motivational potentials for using virtual technologies in teaching and learning to promote active, individual and larger group learning (Liu et al. 2017).

The concept of AR has found wide application in the arts, gaming industry, architecture, daily life, industrial design, navigation, automotive industry, archaeology and other areas (Kerr and Lawson 2019; Riener et al. 2019). Great efforts have been made to apply AR technology in biomedical sciences, and the advancement of technology has brought augmented reality concepts to mobile devices.

The concepts of Augmented Reality and Virtual Reality are frequently confused with one another due to their similarities in their names and what they do. Therefore, it is necessary to clarify what the two terms are (see Fig. 8.2). The difference is primarily in the technology used. Virtual Reality attempts to create an artificial world that a person can experience and explore interactively, through his or her senses, whereas Augmented Reality also brings about an interactive experience, but aims to supplement the real world, rather than creating an entirely artificial environment (Höllerer and Fiener 2004).

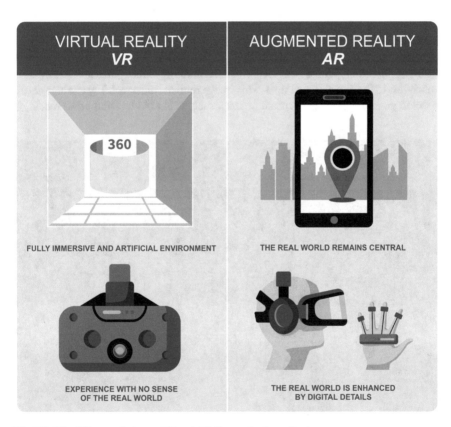

Fig. 8.2 The difference between VR and AR (Image by the author)

8.3 AR in Local Anesthesia Training

Administering local anesthesia is a critically important skill in operative dentistry. The student should understand the concepts of the procedure and develop fine motor skills to implement it. The development of technical skills is an essential component of safe clinical practice. Administration of mandibular anesthesia is one of the most common and important procedures in dentistry with widespread use in all fields, including oral surgery, endodontics, periodontology, and prosthetics.

In the study by Mladenovic et al. (2019a, b) a mobile Dental Simulator (v1.13—Campinas, Brazil) was used for anesthesia training for Inferior Alveolar Nerve Block (IANB). It is available for iOS (App Store) and Android platform (Google Play Store). The Dental Simulator application has three modes: study mode, simulation and Augmented Reality (AR) mode, and using Vuforia Engine (*PTC, Parametric Technology Corporation, Boston, USA*). Vuforia is an Augmented Reality Software Development Kit (SDK) for mobile devices that enables the creation of augmented reality applications. It uses computer vision technology to recognize and track planar images and 3D objects in real time. This image registration capability enables developers to position and orient virtual objects, such as 3D models and other media, in

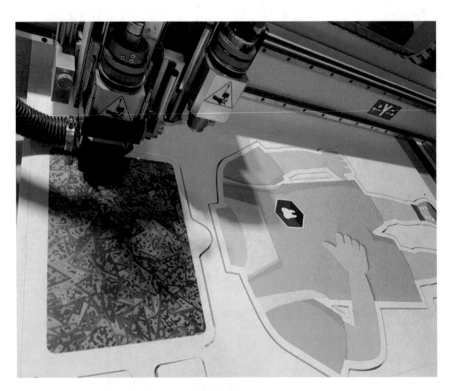

Fig. 8.3 Plastic model specially designed for exercise (Image by the author)

relation to real-world objects when they are viewed through the camera of a mobile device. The virtual object then tracks the position and orientation of the image in real time so that the viewer's perspective on the object corresponds with the perspective on the target. It thus appears that the virtual object is a part of the real-world scene. The angle between the camera and the image target does not need to be 90°; Vuforia is still able to recognize the image target at only 20°. These features make the augmented experience much more complete than when other types of markers are used. AR schemes are the basis for recognition and overall use of this technology (see Fig. 8.3). To make the simulation process as realistic as possible, special plastic models for practice in the dental office were made (see Figs. 8.4 and 8.5).

Comparing conventional training methods for mandibular anesthesia and the use of the AR mobile simulator, we concluded that students of the experimental group who received additional training with the AR simulator reported significantly shorter performance time for anesthetic procedure. The human brain operates on the principle of images and associations; the fastest and easiest way it adopts content is through images, that is, through a visual experience. In addition, the human understanding of reality is limited to a three-dimensional space, which supports the augmented reality concept used in the study.

Fig. 8.4 Students using AR system for Android devices (Image by the author)

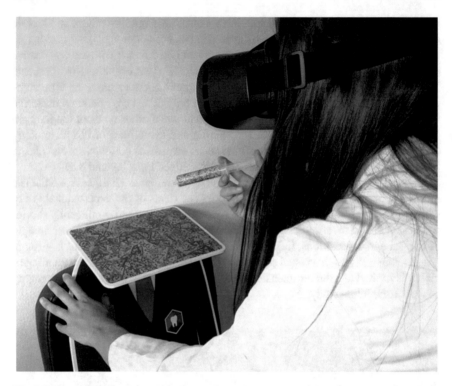

Fig. 8.5 Exercise on plastic model in augmented reality mode with virtual reality goggles (Image by the author)

Data from post-clinical questionnaires to evaluate students' knowledge and skills about local anesthesia procedures supported the augmented reality simulator. Specifically, a statistically significant value for the items "I can easily localize the puncture site" and "My movements with the hand taking the syringe are controlled", showed that the group of students who used AR had more positive responses. All this is in support of the fact that these students were better acquainted with anatomical details and reference points for the performance of mandibular anesthesia and had better control of the syringe device during the local anesthesia procedure. In practice, even with a standardized anesthesia technique, not all procedures are successful. IANB failure rates have been reported as high as 29–39% (Madan et al. 2002; Mikesell et al. 2005). The most common reason for unsuccessful IANB is mandibular foramen position. Thus despite good knowledge of anatomical reference points, one cannot accurately determine the shape of the mandible or the exact position of the mandibular opening. When it comes to anesthetic success measured by lip/tongue numbness, the students of the experimental group had a success rate of 90.2% while the control group students had a success rate of 72%. These results support AR technology. Using the augmented reality technique, anatomical structures in the oral cavity and anatomic reference points are simpler for localization and identification,

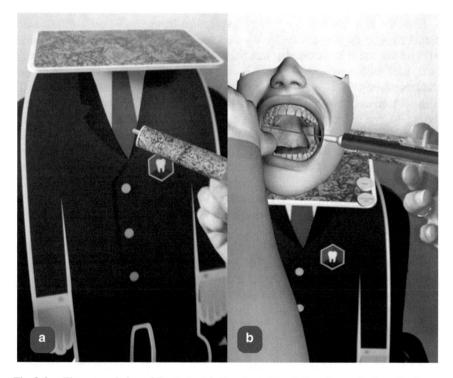

Fig. 8.6 a The external view of the student. **b** The view of the student (Image by the author).

regardless of the operator's skill, and mistakes in the positioning of the mandibular foramen are significantly reduced (see Fig. 8.6). 3D anatomical positioning of the mandibular foramen is important for the procedure. The position of the mandibular foramen should be found three-dimensionally relative to the oral anatomical structures. Using the augmented bone structures in the oral cavity as references to optimize the position of the mandibular foramen may increase the efficiency of the procedure for an inferior alveolar nerve block.

What is in the subconscious of every human being when it comes to new and unfamiliar skills, and which can also be an inhibiting factor in students' work with patients is fear. Fear of the new and the unknown can greatly limit the ability of the student himself. Anxiety in dental students is higher than in medical students due to the immediate contact with the patient. On the other hand, the greater the patient's fear, the higher the anxiety level in the student performing their first dental intervention (Nuttall et al. 2001).

It has been demonstrated that theoretical knowledge combined with step-by-step practical instructions can reduce the anxiety in both students and patients in relation to administration of anesthesia (Meechan 2005; Chandrasekaran et al. 2014). Anxiety levels can vary during different stages and procedures, which can be estimated using different anxiety scales, and the most commonly used is the Visual Analogue Scale.

Even the first researches on stress that studied its physiological characteristics reported that stress was caused by any situation that required some new adaptation, whereas increased heart rate was noted and as one of its first indicators Mladenovic et al. (2019a, b) measured heart rate values before and during administration of local anesthesia. When administering anesthesia, heart rates increased significantly with all students, which was associated with the opinion of many clinicians that the application of local anesthesia was one of the more stressful aspects of clinical practice (FIset et al. 1985; Simon et al. 1994). However, a statistical analysis showed that there was no significant difference in heart rate values between the test groups and that the AR simulator did not affect the acute stress of students performing mandibular anesthesia for the first time. The relationship between emotional and physiological states of anxiety is complex and involves the interaction of the neurohormonal axis, circadian rhythm, and individual variability in the chronotropic response to stress (Kudielka et al. 2004).

Having the syringe in the patient's line of sight and performing lengthy treatments may result in unsatisfactory analgesia, specifically in children. Using the AR technique, the anatomical structures in the oral cavity are easy and convenient to use and give a good introduction to clinical anesthesia due to user interaction.

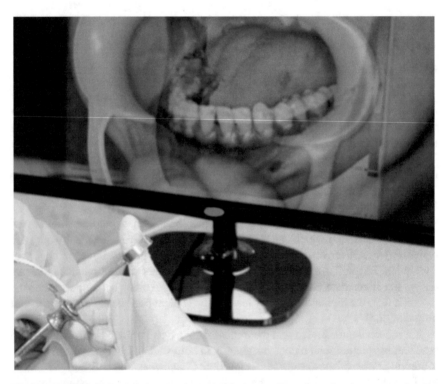

Fig. 8.7 Performing of an inferior alveolar nerve block procedure using a simple augmented reality method (Images reproduced under creative commons)—Won and Kang (2017)

A solution to better AR integration should be sought in haptic simulators and robotics (Gandaglia et al. 2016; Gettman and Rivera 2016; Moglia et al. 2016).

Thanks to CBCT and the development of computer software, Won and Kang (2017) developed a simple AR method for mandibular anesthesia training (see Fig. 8.7). AR technique provided related information for bony structures in the oral cavity that can be referred to during anesthetic injections in order to easily and accurately locate the position of the mandibular foramen. This application of AR techniques to dental treatment may lead to the development of clinically applicable AR techniques.

8.4 Application of AR in Maxillofacial Surgery

Operative dentistry is a demanding area of clinical education. The development of clinical competence requires the assimilation of large amounts of knowledge combined with the development of clinical and problem-solving skills. Therefore, Augmented Reality has found application in the field of maxillofacial surgery.

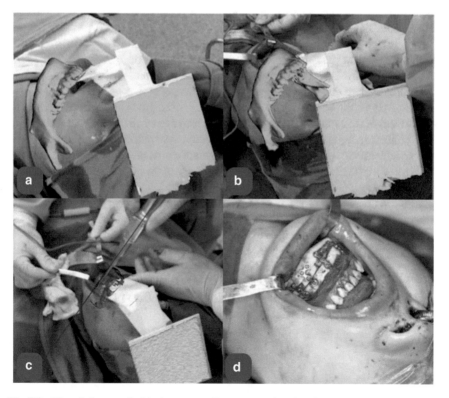

Fig. 8.8 AR technique applied during surgery (Images reproduced under creative commons)—Zhu et al. (2017)

Zhu et al. (2017) aimed to develop a novel registration and tracking technique to establish a navigation system based on Augmented Reality (see Fig. 8.8). The novel registration strategy that they created uses an occlusal splint compounded with a fiducial marker to establish a relationship between the virtual image and the real object. After the fiducial marker is recognized, the virtual image is superimposed onto the real environment, forming the "integrated image" on the semi-transparent glass.

This augmented reality system was applied in the clinic, and good surgical outcomes were obtained. The position error of this navigation system is 0.96 ± 0.51 mm. The augmented reality system established for maxillofacial surgery has the advantages of easy manipulation and high accuracy, which can improve surgical outcomes. Thus, this system exhibits significant potential in clinical applications.

8.5 Application of AR in Dental Implantology

Dental implant procedures must meet biomechanical, functional, phonetic and aesthetic requirements and as such demand precise location and the right direction of the implant (Ewers et al. 2005).

In a review of two clinical cases reported by Pellegrino et al. (2019), AR was applied in implant placement planning (see Fig. 8.9). Prior to the procedure itself, the position of the implant was virtually planned, which contributed to a dynamic navigation system that was displayed on AR glasses.

This, in turn, allowed for the use of a computer-aided procedure to occur. The deviations were of 0.50 mm and 0.46 mm. AR can prove to be an exceptional resource in dental implant surgery, due to its simple procedures and reduced operating time. This type of technology can increase the use of dynamic navigation because it solves the problem of simultaneous monitoring of the patient and the output from the navigation system display.

Ma et al. (2018) also proposed an AR navigation system for dental implant surgery. Their navigation system provides the visual field of the surgical site and the display of the overlaid scene at different depths. The results of their experimental study show that the developed AR navigation system has acceptable accuracy. The proposed system can realize in situ image guidance, which eliminates the hand–eye coordination problem.

It has been demonstrated that AR guided implant placement method possesses potential for the future of dental implant surgery.

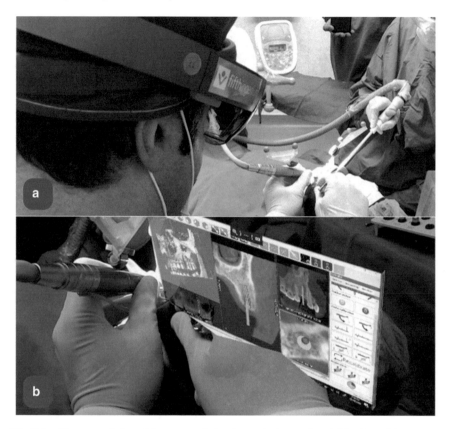

Fig. 8.9   a The external view of the surgeon during the surgical procedure. **b** The view of the surgeon during the surgery wearing HoloLens glasses (Images reproduced under creative commons)— Pellegrino et al (2019)

8.6   Application of AR in Learning Dental Morphology

Dental morphology is a branch of dentistry that deals with the study of anatomical factors of the teeth in order to know their function, exterior shape, position, size, structure, and development. In all dental specialties, it is considered essential to fully know dental morphology.

Juan et al. (2016) developed an AR system for learning dental morphology (see Fig. 8.10). Students using the AR system were extremely pleased with the ease of use and would be happy to use it as an additional tool in their daily practice.

This AR system has been effective when it comes to transmitting knowledge in the short term, and students can reinforce the knowledge acquired in the classroom with the help of a mobile device without the supervision of a professor. They also studied whether or not there were differences in the acquired knowledge regarding gender, specialization, and age. No significant differences were found. This means

Fig. 8.10 Image Target and the augmented scene with tooth number 36 (Images reproduced under creative commons)—Juan et al. (2016)

that the AR system is well suited for these factors and that it can be used without many restrictions. Therefore, it can be used equally and effectively by both men and women.

8.7   Application of AR in Aesthetic Dentistry

AR has also found application in cosmetic dentistry. IvoSmile (IvoSmile® / Kapanu, Ivoclar-Vivadent, Liechtenstein) application is available for iOS (App Store) (see Fig. 8.11). It uses AR for visualizing the possibilities for esthetic dental makeovers directly on the patient. The application turns your mobile device into a virtual mirror. Patients can see what they would look like with the prospective esthetic restoration in place, and they will find it easier to decide whether or not to commit their time and money to the process of detailed cosmetic treatment planning. The effect can be displayed in photo or video mode and in live; patients can see themselves speaking with the proposed esthetic makeover in place. Users can focus their attention on creating powerful visualizations of esthetic dental improvements without having to

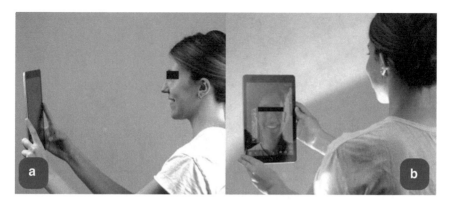

Fig. 8.11 Use of the device. **a** Participant can use the technology by maintaining the tablet at a required minimal distance as a mirror. **b** User can see himself on the screen and interact with the software (Images reproduced under creative commons)—Touati et al. (2019)

spend a long time explaining them. IvoSmile includes a Bleaching option and can be used to advise patients on the ideal degree of whiteness.

The limitation of IvoSmile® application reported by Touati et al. (2019) was the impossibility to match the smile design with the digital cast of the patient, and the addition of other face and tooth recognition markers was proposed (Zollhöfer et al. 2018; Vávra et al. 2017). Further investigations are then required to evaluate the accuracy of this innovative device and to determine the precision needed in dentistry.

8.8 Application of AR in Restorative Dentistry

Dental simulation still uses the teeth attached to artificial jaws to teach the basic skills required for restorative dentistry. The dental preclinical laboratory contains mannequin heads affixed to laboratory benches, in a manner that allows adjustment of position to allow the student to work in a seated position as he/she would in a clinical setting.

AR has also found application in restorative dentistry. In a study published by Llena et al. (2018), the application of AR technology has been used in teaching cavity preparation. The experimental group further educated with the AR method showed a significant improvement in skills related to Class I and Class II cavity preparation. It should be emphasized that cavity preparation and the understanding of different parts of cavities is strongly conditioned by spatial vision, and it is in these areas that the experimental group has shown greater success.

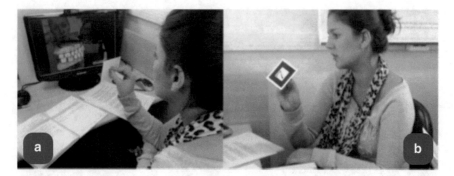

Fig. 8.12 A participant in the study using the learning object. **a** Shows user applying the Augmented Reality (AR) tool in front of the computer screen. **b** Shows user moving the AR graphic marker to magnify and better visualize details of the image (Images reproduced under creative commons)—Espejo-Trung et al. (2015)

8.9 AR in Dental Teaching and Learning

Information and Communication Technology (ICT) is a way of integrating telecommunication and computer technologies that enable users to access, store, transmit, and manipulate information. Students mostly use it to learn anatomy, find more information about medicines, or read e-books (Jamal et al. 2016; Robinson 2015).

In their study, Espejo-Trung et al. (2015) presented an AR for operative dentistry education and applied to tooth-preparation techniques for indirect restorations (see Fig. 8.12). It has several important applications because it interactively illustrates the 3D details and allows a view of the prepared teeth in relation to soft tissues. From an ethical viewpoint, when used with other teaching resources, it may reduce the number of natural teeth used for operative dentistry training.

8.10 Conclusion

The benefits of AR technology in dental education are clear. As educational tools, AR simulators can provide enhanced opportunities for students. An AR system can facilitate versatility in the learning process, as learning activities can be performed anywhere and at any time without supervision. However, there are some limitations to the use of AR. Most are expected to be overcome by technological advances. It seems that work with other technologies may enhance the function of existing AR systems (Schnelzer et al. 2012; Diana et al. 2014).

Application of AR technology can be of great benefit to students transitioning from the preclinical level to clinical practice or mastering more demanding dental procedures. This new technology provides access to educational resources, quality interaction, and lowered the cost of the overall training.

References

Balta JY, Cronin M, Cryan JF, O'Mahony SM (2015) Human preservation techniques in anatomy: a 21st century medical education perspective. Clin Anat 28:725–734

Bell H, Waag W (1998) Evaluating the effectiveness of flight simulators for training combat skills: a review. Int J Aviation Psychol 8(3):223–242

Buchanan JA (2001) Use of simulation technology in dental education. J Dent Educ 65:1225–1231

Bugarić M (2013) Wildfire surveillance systems enhanced by geographic Information System (GIS) and GIS-based Augmented Reality [dissertation]. Sveučilište u Splitu, Fakultet elektrotehnike strojarstva i brodogradnje

Chandrasekaran B, Cugati N, Kumaresan R (2014) Dental Students' Perception and Anxiety Levels during their First Local Anesthetic Injection. Malays J Med Sci 21(6):45–51

Cutler N, Balicki M, Finkelstein M et al (2013) Auditory Force Feedback Substitution Improves Surgical Precision during Simulated Ophthalmic Surgery. Investigative Opthalmology & Visual Science 54(2):1316

Diana M, Dallemagne B, Chung H et al (2014) Probe-based confocal laser endomicroscopy and fluorescence-based enhanced reality for real-time assessment of intestinal microcirculation in a porcine model of sigmoid ischemia. Surg Endosc 28:3224–3233

Dută MA, Bogdan CM, Popovici DM et al (2011) An overview of virtual and augmented reality in dental education. Oral Health Dent Manag 10:42–49

Espejo-Trung LC, Elian SN et al (2015) Development and application of a new learning object for teaching operative dentistry using augmented reality. J Dent Educ 79(11):1356–1362

Ewers R, Schicho K, Undt G et al (2005) Basic research and 12 years of clinical experience in computer-assisted navigation technology: a review. Int J Oral Maxillofac Surg 34(1):1–8

Fiset L, Milgrom P, Weinstein P et al (1985) Psychophysiological responses to dental injections. J Am Dent Assoc 111:578–583

Gandaglia G, Schatteman P, De Naeyer G et al (2016) Novel technologies in urologic surgery: a rapidly changing scenario. Curr Urol Rep 17:19

Gettman M, Rivera M (2016) Innovations in robotic surgery. Curr Opin Urol 26:271–276

Grohmann I, Raith S, Kesting M et al (2013) Experimental biomechanical study of the primary stability of different osteosynthesis systems for mandibular reconstruction with an iliac crest graft. Br J Oral Maxillofac Surg 51:942–947

Haluck R (2000) Computers and Virtual Reality for Surgical Education in the 21st Century. Arch Surg 135(7):786

Höllerer TH, Feiner SK (2004). Chapter 8: Mobile augmented reality, Telegeoinformatics: Location-Based Computing and Services, Karimi HA, Hammand A (Eds.). UK, Taylor & Francis Books Ltd

Hwang G, Yang T, Tsai C, Yang S (2009) A context-aware ubiquitous learning environment for conducting complex science experiments. Comput Educ 53(2):402–413

Jamal A, Temsah M-H, Khan SA, Al-Eyadhy A, Koppel C, Chiang MF (2016) Mobile phone use among medical residents: a cross-sectional multicenter survey in Saudi Arabia. JMIR MHealth UHealth 4(2):e61

Juan M-C, Alexandrescu L, Folguera F et al (2016) A Mobile Augmented Reality system for the learning of dental morphology. Digital Education Review 30:234–247

Kerr J, Lawson G (2019) Augmented Reality in Design Education: Landscape Architecture Studies as AR Experience. International Journal of Art & Design Education

Knipfer C, Rohde M, Oetter N et al (2018) Local anaesthesia training for undergraduate students – how big is the step from model to man? BMC Med Educ 18:308

Kühl S, Kirmeier R, Platzer S et al (2016) Transcrestal maxillary sinus augmentation: Summers's versus a piezoelectric technique, an experimental cadaver study. Clin Oral Implants Res 27:126–129

Levine AI, DeMaria S, Schwartz AD, Sim AJ, eds. (2009) The comprehensive textbook of healthcare simulation. New York, NY: Springer New York; 2013.

Liu D, Bhagat K, Gao Y et al (2017) The Potentials and Trends of Virtual Reality in Education. Smart Computing and Intelligence 105–130.

Llena C, Folguera S, Forner L et al (2018) Implementation of augmented reality in operative dentistry learning. Eur J Dent Educ 22(1):e122–e130

Ma L, Jiang W, Zhang B et al (2018) Augmented reality surgical navigation with accurate CBCT-patient registration for dental implant placement. Med Biol Eng Compu 57(1):47–57

Madan GA, Madan SG, Madan AD (2002) Failure of inferior alveolar nerve block: exploring the alternatives. J Am Dent Assoc 133:843–846

Meechan JG (2005) Differences between men and women regarding attitudes towards dental local anesthesia among junior students at a United Kingdom dental school. Anesth Prog 52(2):50–55

Mikesell P, Nusstein J, Reader A et al (2005) A comparison of articaine and lidocaine for inferior alveolar nerve blocks. J Endod 31:265–270

Mladenovic R, Cvetkovic A, Martinovic B et al (2019) Efficiency of chewable toothbrush in reduction of dental plaque in students. BMC Oral Health 19(01):58

Mladenovic R, Lap P, Djordjevic F et al (2018) The use of mobile-aided learning in education of local anesthesia for the inferior alveolar nerve block. Vojnosanit Pregl 2018:154. In press. https://doi.org/10.2298/VSP180622154M

Mladenovic R, Pereira L, Mladenovic K et al (2019) Effectiveness of Augmented Reality Mobile Simulator in Teaching Local Anesthesia of Inferior Alveolar Nerve Block. Journal of Dental Education 83(4):423–428

Moglia A, Ferrari V, Morelli L et al (2016) A systematic review of virtual reality simulators for robot-assisted surgery. Eur Urol 69:1065–1080

Nuttall NM, Bradnock G, White D et al (2001) Dental attendance in 1998 and implications for the future. Br Dent J 190(4):177–182

Oxford Advanced American Dictionary (2019) [Internet] https://www.oxfordlearnersdictionaries.com/definition/american_english/simulation. Accessed 25 Nov 2019

Pellegrino G, Mangano C, Mangano R et al (2019) Augmented reality for dental implantology: a pilot clinical report of two cases. BMC Oral Health 19(01):158

Perry S, Bridges S, Burrow M (2015) A review of the use of simulation in dental education. simulation in healthcare: J Soc Simulat Healthc 10(1):31–37

Riener A, Gabbard J, Trivedi M (2019) Special Issue of Presence: Virtual and Augmented Reality Virtual and Augmented Reality for Autonomous Driving and Intelligent Vehicles: Guest Editors' Introduction. PRESENCE: Virtual and Augmented Reality 27(1):i-iv

Robinson R (2015) Spectrum of tablet computer use by medical students and residents at an academic medical center. PeerJ 3:e1133

Rosenberg H, Grad HA, Matear DW (2003) The effectiveness of computer-aided, self-instructional programs in dental education: a systematic review of the literature. J Dent Educ 67(5):524–532

Schnelzer A, Ehlerding A, Blumel C et al (2012) Showcase of intraoperative 3D imaging of the sentinel lymph node in a breast cancer patient using the new freehand SPECT technology. Breast Care (Basel) 7:484–486

Seymour NE, Gallagher AG, Roman SA et al (2002) (2002) Virtual reality training improves operating room performance: results of a randomized, double-blinded study. Ann Surg. 236:458–463

Simon JF, Peltier B, Chambers D, Dower J (1994) Dentists troubled by the administration of anesthetic injections: long-term stresses and effects. Quintessence Int 25(9):641–646

Smith NF, Smith DW (1989) Simulators. Franklin Watts, New York

Sutherland IE (1968) Head mounted three dimensional display. In: Proceedings of the AFIPS. New York, Thompson Books

Tanzawa T, Futaki K, Tani C et al (2011) Introduction of a robot patient into dental education. Eur J Dent Educ 16(1):e195–e199

Thiel W (1992) Die Konservierung ganzer Leichen in natürlichen Farben. Ann Anat 174:185–195

Touati R, Richert R, Millet C et al (2019) Comparison of two innovative strategies using augmented reality for communication in aesthetic dentistry: a pilot study. J Healthc Eng 2019:7019046

Uzunboylu H, Cavus N, Ercag E (2009) Using mobile learning to increase environmental awareness. Comput Educ 52(2):381–389

Won Y, Kang S (2017) Application of augmented reality for inferior alveolar nerve block anesthesia: a technical note. Journal of Dental Anesthesia and Pain Medicine 17(2):129

Zhu M, Liu F, Chai G et al (2017) A novel augmented reality system for displaying inferior alveolar nerve bundles in maxillofacial surgery. Scientific Reports 7(1)

Zollhöfer M, Thies J, Garrido P et al (2018) State of the art on monocular 3D face reconstruction, tracking, and applications. Comput Graph Forum 37(2):523–550

Chapter 9
The Development of Augmented Reality Applications for Chemistry Learning

Ferli Septi Irwansyah, Efa Nur Asyiah, Dian Sa'adillah Maylawati, Ida Farida, and Muhammad Ali Ramdhani

Abstract This chapter describes the use of Augmented Reality (AR) technology in chemistry education. The chapter begins with definition analysis, development, component, working principles, steps in making AR media, and supporting applications that are related with AR in education particularly for chemistry teaching and learning process. The proposed AR system consists of three parts: computers, Head Mounted Display (HMD), and markers that use AR toolkit working principles as follows: making AR through Vuforia setting stage, making the target management, managing assets, and running processes. Additionally, Unity application also supports in AR making. There were researches in the field of education especially in chemistry teaching and learning that had used AR technology, such as the concept of crystal structure, molecular geometry, molecular chirality, and molecular hybridization.

9.1 Introduction

Since 1957, Augmented Reality (AR) has existed as one of the contributors to technological advances that can combine the real world with the virtual world (Isberto 2018). Until now, AR has played many roles in all fields, such as health, medicine, agriculture, and education (Martin et al. 2018).

F. S. Irwansyah (✉) · E. Nur Asyiah · I. Farida
Department of Chemistry Education, UIN Sunan Gunung Djati, Bandung, Indonesia
e-mail: ferli@uinsgd.ac.id

E. Nur Asyiah
e-mail: nurasyiahefa@gmail.com

I. Farida
e-mail: farchemia65@uinsgd.ac.id

D. S. Maylawati · M. A. Ramdhani
Department of Informatics, UIN Sunan Gunung Djati, Bandung, Indonesia
e-mail: diansm@uinsgd.ac.id

M. A. Ramdhani
e-mail: m_ali_ramdhani@uinsgd.ac.id

© Springer Nature Switzerland AG 2020
V. Geroimenko (ed.), *Augmented Reality in Education*,
Springer Series on Cultural Computing,
https://doi.org/10.1007/978-3-030-42156-4_9

AR is very useful in education, along with students' understanding of invisible concepts (Smith and Nakhleh 2011). In Augmented Reality (AR), education is positioned as a learning. The use of instructional media by utilizing Augmented Reality can stimulate students to think critically about problems and events that occur in their daily life since it helps students to learn autonomously (Oh and Byun 2012). Moreover, AR is used in a smartphone which most of the students are familiar with (Zan 2015). Augmented Reality media can illustrate abstract concepts to understand and arrange objects, enabling AR to become better media in accordance with the objectives of learning media (Oh and Byun 2012).

Using Augmented Reality media is very useful to improve student learning outcomes and interests (Carmigniani et al. 2011). In terms of effectiveness, many students support that the Augmented Reality media in the Android version by using smartphones in natural science lessons can help them understand and memorize scientific material so that they easily understand science lessons (Zan 2015). It also helps them to learn in their own way and increase their creativity and imagination since Augmented Reality can increase student concentration (Han 2018). Some researches in the field of education particularly chemistry education that has been carried out using AR were based on the concept of crystal structure (Irwansyah et al. 2017), molecular geometry (Irwansyah et al. 2018), molecular chirality (Jannah et al. 2019), molecular hybridization (Asyiah et al. 2019), and alkanes and cycloalkanes.

It is expected that Augmented Reality (AR) in chemistry teaching and learning will be continually developed in other submicroscopic concepts and hopefully the improvement media could be more optimal in system without markers so that it can be used easier without scanning.

9.2 Development of Augmented Reality Technology as a Learning Media on Metal Structure Concepts

Augmented Reality as a learning media on metal structure material consists of several concepts: solid structure, seven basic crystal systems, and metal structures. This study refers to the modified Computer Assisted Instruction (CAI) tutorial model design (Darmawan 2012), which consists of the analysis phase, the design development stage, and the validation stage.

Making of instructional media needs to be adapted to the material (Arsyad 2007) of metal structures, so that concept analysis and concept maps of metal structures with the connectedness of submicroscopic representations were made. This is supported by the results of the due diligence test which are declared valid and suitable for use in the aspect of material substance (Irwansyah et al. 2017).

AR on metal structure material sub microscopically represents 3D objects presented by the marker. This learning media has advantages in terms of appearance that is offered inductively to stimulate curiosity, develop students' thinking skills (Arsyad 2007), and increase motivation (Irwansyah et al. 2017) and can be adjusted to the applicable curriculum. This is evidenced by the feasibility test on the aspect of visual communication which is declared valid and quite feasible to use (Irwansyah et al. 2017).

The process of making AR learning media in metal structure material must refer to the outline to assist in creating AR media. Based on the results of concept analysis, a flowchart is produced as a reference and a storyboard as a designed outline (Darmawan 2012).

9.2.1   Start Display

The sign in view contains a camera view that will display 3D objects of metal structure when it is projected with a marker. 3D objects shown include (1) structural objects of crystalline and amorphous solids, (2) structural objects of seven basic crystal systems, (3) tightly packed packaging structures of metal, and (4) metal structures.

This learning media is assisted by smartphones and student worksheets, which direct users to develop submicroscopic representation capabilities in metal structure material. Worksheets direct students to work on questions that have been made according to indicators. The use of smartphone makes learning media effective and efficient. The process showed that it was feasible and valid. However, the function of the media must be adjusted again in the delivery of material to avoid verbalism (Sadiman 2009). Visualization of objects in the worksheet is shown in Fig. 9.1.

9.2.2   Display Learning Objectives

Display learning objectives contain learning objectives on metal structure material that must be achieved by students, namely, the ability to analyze the structure of solid substances and seven basic crystal systems based on the three-dimensional parameters of the space lattice, determine the tight packing structure of a metal. The learning objectives are arranged based on the development of students' submicroscopic representation capabilities on metal structure material and adapted to the learning media (Sadiman 2009). The purpose of this learning is to get a decent response from respondents (Irwansyah et al. 2017), which results in the media that is ready to be used as a source of learning (Sudjana 2009).

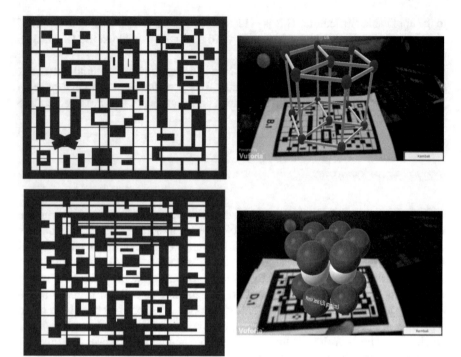

Fig. 9.1 3D object visualization

9.3 AR Technology Using Android Operating System on the Concept of Molecular Geometry

This study refers to a CAI-based tutorial (Computer Assisted Instruction) (Molenda and Januszewski 2008). AR media is made on the concept of molecular geometry through the analysis of concepts and indicators as well as the design of development stage.

The concept analysis and indicator analysis phases are based on the need for AR media production as a tool to provide real visualization. At this stage, an analysis of general molecular geometry concepts was made. The next step was arranging learning indicators for AR learning media on the concept of molecular geometry. It was intended to make students know the basis of finding an appropriate molecular shape; markers can display 3D objects in both Lewis and geometric shapes in each concept.

At the design development stage, a flowchart and storyboard were made, both can provide direction in the form of links to be addressed such as the entry menu, return menu, and the media flow start to finish, so that the objects displayed followed the directions that have been made. The next step was making of 3D molecular geometry objects and markers.

9.3.1   Display of AR Application

This display provides users with information about what will be displayed on the AR media, which contains links to be addressed, namely, learning objectives, compiler profiles, and an entry menu that includes a camera view for projecting cancer cells to appear as 3D objects. An attractive display of learning media will be able to provide a change of thought stimulation, feelings, attention, and interest in the information.

The constituent profile view aims to provide information about the data making of AR learning media making on the concept of molecular geometry. There is also a display of learning objectives that contain learning objectives on the concept of molecular geometry, namely, determining the molecular geometry of Lewis structures and formal charge, identifying the properties of compounds based on the geometric shapes of molecules, and identifying the molecular geometric shapes of various compounds. This research showed that AR learning media can modify learning objectives to be achieved and be able to adapt to the characteristics of students.

Next, there is an entry button that contains a camera view that will launch 3D objects when it is directed to the camera. This entry view provides three-dimensional submicroscopic visualization of Lewis structural and geometric shapes of molecules that have both free electrons and restricted electrons. In the use of AR media, a student worksheet has been provided, which serves as a support for AR media, in which there are some questions in line with learning indicators, each student must fill out the worksheet.

9.3.2   Worksheets and Markers

Student worksheets are supporting components of AR learning media. On the sheets, there are guidelines for the use of AR media, learning indicators, learning objectives, and several questions that guide the user (students) to understand the concept of molecular geometry. Each worksheet provides four description questions in accordance with the indicator questions that have been made, and the students were guided to determine the exact geometric shape of the molecule step by step. To get a picture or shape of 3D objects, a marker is used to support the use of AR learning media on the worksheet, and this marker can display 3D objects with suitable molecular geometry, so that the worksheet display becomes more attractive to be used. Furthermore, regarding some questions, marker shapes and 3D object shapes in the geometry concept can be seen in the following explanation.

In the first question, students were directed to count the valence electrons from the elements of Boron and Fluorine, then students were directed to choose Lewis structure images in the form of 3D objects on markers appropriately based on formal charge rules. The image of the marker and Lewis structure objects can be seen in Fig. 9.2.

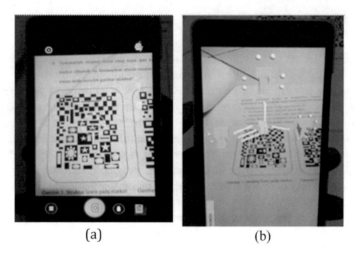

Fig. 9.2 a Display marker before using AR media. **b** Display marker after using AR media on an Android smartphone

From the Lewis structure, the students must determine which species of groups can form molecular geometries based on the species groups table that has been provided. Then students were directed to choose 3D molecular geometry marker objects from BF3 molecules appropriately, and geometric shapes can be seen in Fig. 9.3.

The next step was to differentiate it based on the elements that will determine Lewis's structure and molecular geometry. Figure 9.4 is a 3D marker and object of the Lewis structure.

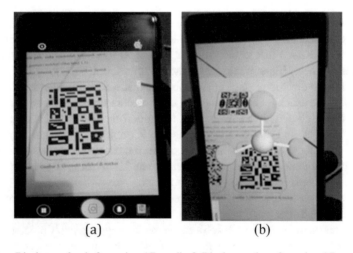

Fig. 9.3 a Display marker before using AR media. **b** Display marker after using AR media on an Android smartphone

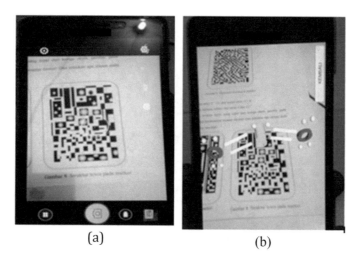

Fig. 9.4 a Display marker before using AR media. **b** Display marker after using AR media on an Android smartphone

In the third question, students were directed to analyze differences in the molecular geometric shapes of NH_3, H_2O, and CH_4, which have the same electron geometry, namely, tetrahedral. Marker images and 3D objects can be seen in Fig. 9.5.

In the fourth question, students were directed to determine the various shapes of molecular geometries on markers that have been provided from several known compounds, as well as to state the reasons for choosing these markers. The visualization of markers and 3D objects can be seen in Fig. 9.6.

Based on the results of the assessment of AR learning media on the concept of molecular geometry by expert validators on four aspects (aspect of learning, aspect

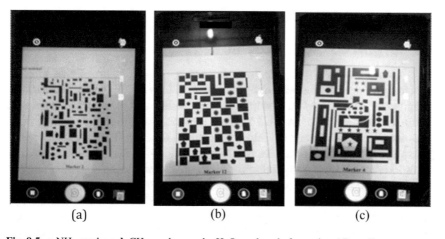

Fig. 9.5 a NH_3 markers, **b** CH_4 markers and **c** H_2O markers before using AR media

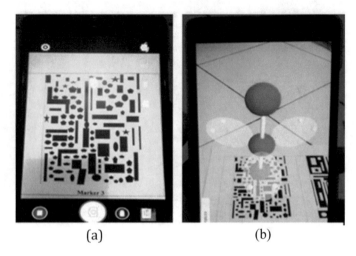

(a)   (b)

Fig. 9.6 **a** Display marker before using AR media. **b** Display marker after using AR media on an Android smartphone

of material substance, aspect of visual communication and aspect of software engineering) showed valid results with sufficient interpretation up to a high level with a count of 0.7–0.9. It indicates that AR learning media is appropriate to be used in learning or as teaching material to be taught. Moreover, the results of the experiment were limited to 10 students of chemistry education at Islamic State University (UIN) Sunan Gunung Djati Bandung. It showed an excellent response to the learning media that have been made, and it is proofed by the assessment given to the respondent and it has 70.83–92.5%. Based on the result of assessment, it is indicated that AR learning media is appropriate to be used as teaching materials or teaching aids.

9.4 Creating AR-Based Interactive Learning Media on the Concept of Molecular Chirality

This study used a DBR research design with a modified ADDIE model. The stages of creating media consist of three steps: analysis, design, and manufacture (Aldoobie 2015). The first stage, conceptual analysis and molecular chirality concept maps were made because the analytical study is the initial motion of a series of subsequent processes in making instructional media (Aldoobie 2015). However, creating analytic concepts takes a long time to get the problem formulation (Jannah et al. 2019). In line with Aldoobie (2015) which states that the analysis phase becomes the initial motion of the next set of processes because in creating a learning media, the creators must know part of the concepts that can be developed in learning media. Then construct learning indicators on the concept of molecular chirality. Moreover, the elaboration of learning indicators becomes a sub-indicator used in MFIs based on AR-based interactive learning media on the concept of molecular chirality.

The concept presented was based on the relation of submicroscopic representation in the presentation of AR-based interactive learning media on the concept of molecular chirality consisting of several sub-concepts, namely, object chirality, molecular chirality, chiral carbon atoms, (R) and (S) systems, diastereomers, meso compounds, chiral compounds. cyclic, and Fischer projections (Solomons et al. 2014).

At the development stage, a storyboard that contains a User Interface (UI) in the form of an AR application layout is generated, while a flowchart includes a User Experience (UX) between the students and an application that refers to the User Interface (UI) that has been made from the storyboard design stage to guide students' understanding in the concept of molecular chirality systematically (Yuntoto 2015). There were several obstacles in this stage; firstly in the design stage of storyboard display it was difficult to represent the scene layout in AR because the layout itself can change to the spot or point of view of the AR user camera so that it can interfere with student concentration (Irsyad 2016). Some solutions were provided by researchers to make students stay focused, i.e., the spot in detecting markers becomes one of the control variables in using an application, the AR camera spot must be in the upper corner facing the marker positioned horizontally with the best distance between the AR camera and marker around 20–60 cm (Irsyad 2016). The last thing done is creating 3D objects and markers.

Worksheets provided support tools for AR interactive learning media on the concept of molecular chirality and served as materials to present the results of molecular chirality visualizations. Worksheets contained guidelines to use the media, learning indicators, learning objectives, and questions. Worksheets cannot be separated from AR applications as worksheets direct students to use the AR application and to obtain results from the student learning process (Bertram et al. 2010).

9.4.1 Display of AR Media Interface

The display interface was made based on the flowchart and storyboard design, including opening page, main page (menu), using instructions, learning objectives, compiler profile, exit, and quiz. The first display presented the main page menu (menu), using directions, learning objectives, compiler profiles, exits, and quizzes.

The display of the AR molecular chirality application has several characteristics such as interactive coloring characteristics, and visualization of 3D objects. In contrasting coloring characteristics, the application display has different color combinations in letters, 3D objects, and backgrounds. It has a representative size and type of font to display on a smartphone (Norris 2018). This aims to emphasize the aesthetics of objects, so that they are easy to be operated by students (Da Silva in Blijlevens et al. 2017). For interactive characteristics, the display and the way to control it have the right frequency and it is sequentially based on the navigation presented, so that students can operate the application efficiently (Hinrichs et al. 2013).

9.4.2 Display Main Page (Menu)

Main menu interface contained menus related to molecular chirality content; the main menu button directs the user to the molecular chirality sub-concepts, namely, object chirality, molecular chirality, systems (R) and (S), diastereomers, meso compounds, cyclic chiral, and Fischer projections.

The sub-concepts contained in the main menu can guide users of AR-based interactive learning media on the concept of molecular chirality in running applications to observe the three-dimensional submicroscopic visualization of several concepts in molecular chirality material.

9.4.3 Display of Molecular Chirality Submenu

Chirality molecular elaboration consists of chiral molecules, chiral molecules, and chiral carbon atoms. The molecular chirality sub-concept is opened systematically and sequentially as the guide presented in the MFI, and the AR molecular chirality system was running by detecting markers through a smartphone camera. So the detected marker displayed 3D objects in accordance with the commands contained in the scene of each sub-concept.

9.4.4 Display Augmented Reality Markers

Markers are needed in AR-based learning media because the type of AR used in this media is a target image type that requires images to appear 3D objects. Additionally, the marker is used when students accomplish worksheet that has been made. The display of molecular chirality marker can be seen in Fig. 9.7.

Markers act as receptors (sensor receivers on AR cameras). In this study, only one marker was used for all questions. Meanwhile in the worksheet, there are questions according to the learning sub-indicators and students must fill out the worksheet. Beside it is a camera AR receptor, it also makes students easier to observe objects in 3D. Furthermore, the quality of the marker depends on the image on the marker itself, which affects the stability of the object that is raised (Cai et al. 2014).

The elements in the marker display consist of white space and image quality with sufficient resolution. White space is the space between one element and another element. It functions as a separator of each design element. It is in line with some theories that state that giving focus to the elements that want to be highlighted (Meggs 2011) and image quality with sufficient resolution can make it easier for AR cameras to do detection (Lin and Chen 2010). Additionally, the combination of accuracy of these two elements can improve students' understanding of observing the displayed 3D objects (Kamelia 2015).

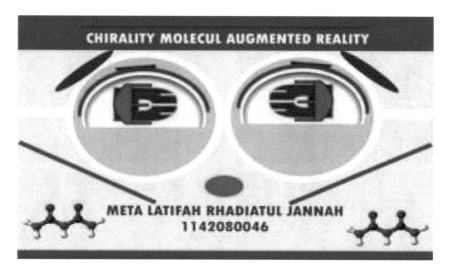

Fig. 9.7   AR Chirality molecular marker

9.4.5   Display Questions on the Student Worksheet

The student worksheets consist of nine breakdown questions according to the question indicators that have been made. These questions are close to the AR molecular chirality application. The questions provided on a worksheet guide the students to understand the concept of molecular chirality, the visualization of material, and the shape of 3D objects, presented in Fig. 9.8.

The visualization display of 3D objects in this study has the details of each 3D object adjusted to the prevalence of molecules that exist both in terms of angle and color (M. Johnson and Henley 2014). In addition, 3D objects that are developed have the impression that they can be rotated as requested (M. Johnson and Henley 2014). Judging from the characteristics of the appearance and visualization of 3D objects developed by the AR molecular chirality application can be referred to as interactive media because this application is designed to actively involve student responses (Singhal et al. 2012) and also can develop submicroscopic student representations (Irwansyah et al. 2017).

9.4.6   Quiz Display

The quiz interface contains a matter of evaluating molecular chirality, which serves to determine the extent of user understanding of molecular chirality content after using AR-based interactive learning media. The quiz button directs the user to work on the evaluation questions complete with discussion.

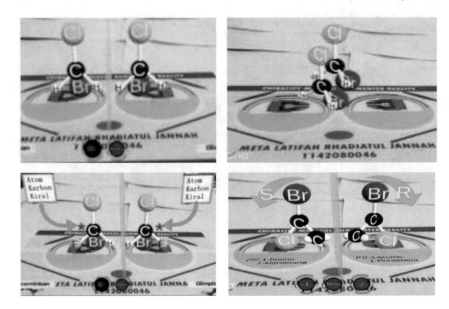

Fig. 9.8 Chiral molecules when mirrored and chiral molecules when crushed

Overall the appearance in the AR molecular chirality application has the same navigation features. After completing the development stage, the next step is the validation stage. The results of improvement are based on the results of the assessment of AR-based interactive learning media on the concept of molecular chirality by the validator and students (Septia et al. 2017). Suggestions from the validator and students were suggestions for adding instructions for the use of media in worksheet, suggestions for enlarging the size of the menu font, suggestions for color selection and size of the options button, suggestions for font sizes in applications, suggestions for improving quizzes, suggestions for adding priority order clusters to screen text, suggestions for placing object layouts in order to not obstructing screen text, and suggestions for making too effective content in the text.

The results of the feasibility test and limited experiment showed that the validator and the respondent considered that AR-based interactive learning media on the concept of molecular chirality that was made was able to meet the indicators of learning media and was suitable to use in teaching and learning process in the classroom (Irwansyah et al. 2017).

9.5 Creating AR-Based Learning Media on the Concept of Molecular Hybridization

Creating AR learning media in the formation of covalent bonds based on valence bond theory began with determining the media elements and contents that will be displayed into the application, then designing the appearance and making the application. After that, a validation test as well as a feasibility test for students was conducted by material experts and media experts.

There are two display results in each stage of creating Augmented Reality learning media in the formation of covalent bonds based on Valence Bonding Theory, in general, the result of the analysis phase and the result of design development.

The first stage of the analysis is the analysis of the needs of various journal sources on learning media, and the concept of molecular hybridization according to Salah and Dumon (2011) state that the hybridization process produces hybrid orbitals that are difficult for students to imagine. Moreover, according to Cataldo et al. (2018) hybrid orbitals are only represented by two-dimensional images. This is supported by Penny et al. (2017), which state that the molecules described in the book make the students difficult to represent it physically. It made students misunderstand in interpreting the form of hybrid orbitals (Uyulgan and Akkuzu 2016).

There were various learning media carried out on the concept of hybridization. For example manufacture of atomic model kits, this medium has a large molecular model that requires large space (Penny et al. 2017). Besides, there was also other instructional media such as the molecular model kit conducted by Smiar and Mendez (2016), the result showed that students still found difficulties in understanding the electrons contained in the molecule. Furthermore, other media, namely, three-dimensional printed molecular models was successful to help students understand atomic and hybrid orbitals, but it took more time because the three-dimensional model must be labeled (Cataldo et al. 2018). Additionally, computer technology is utilized in the concept of hybridization; for example, Macromedia flash learning media visualizes abstract concepts in the form of animations and images, which also can help students to understand about the concepts, but this media still needs improvements in appearance due to distance visibility and students lacking direct interaction with the media (Wijayanti 2018). The use of other learning media also has been carried out by displaying hybridization molecules in computers, but students have not been directly involved in them (Nassabeh et al. 2014), so it can be concluded that Molecular hybridization learning media has not been done much. Based on the previous experiment that had been done, it is imperative for us to have hybridization learning media using AR technology that hopefully can make the learning process more interactive (Carmigniani et al. 2011).

The next stage of analysis process is the analysis of concept maps and concept analysis in accordance with the curriculum. It aims to produce concepts that are appropriate with the learning media created.

Concept labels have abstract concept types and symbol concept types (Asyiah 2019). This shows that the concept of forming covalent bonds based on valence bond theory requires submicroscopic representation so that it is suitable for making AR technology-based learning media (Asyiah 2019). Furthermore, from the results of the concept analysis, a concept map was produced that aims to find out the relationship between concepts and sub-concepts.

After analyzing the concept, the next step is to compile the learning indicators used for AR learning media in the formation of covalent bonds based on the theory of valence ties in accordance with the curriculum. The material chosen was the valence bond theory. The primary competency to be achieved is that students can apply knowledge about valence bond theory and hybridization to identify the properties of compounds. Based on these necessary competencies, indicators and learning objectives are formulated to create AR learning media in the formation of covalent bonds based on valence bond theory.

The results of the analysis that have been made were used as a reference in the design phase. At the design stage, the flow of making AR learning media in covalent bond formation is based on valence bond theory in the form of flowcharts and storyboards.

The first purpose of making storyboards and flowcharts was to facilitate researchers in making AR learning media in the formation of covalent bonds based on valence bond theory. Secondly, it was intended to provide direction or guidance of the hyperlink to be addressed, such as start, return, exit menus, and others. Third, to show the flow of media from start to finish so that the menus and objects that are displayed followed the directions that had been made.

After creating storyboards and flowcharts, the next step is to develop markers and 3D objects that will be applied to the learning media of AR in the formation of covalent bonds based on valence bond theory. The results of storyboards, flowcharts, markers, and 3D objects will be used as a reference for the appearance and flow of AR media development.

9.5.1 Initial Menu Display

The initial menu display of the application contains the intended hyperlink, such as the user manual menu, KD (based competence) and aim, the writer profile, questions, exit, start menu, which includes submenus to enter the 3D object display. The initial menu display can be seen in the following Fig. 9.9.

Each display of this AR media is interconnected by using buttons, and it is intended that users can access the desired page (Kuswanto and Radiansah 2018).

This AR learning media display has several characteristics such as attractive colors and shows, and interactive. In line with Blijlevens et al. (2017), which state that attractive color designs will give users aesthetic pleasure. The characteristics of an attractive media display, in line with Nazmi (2017), which indicates an attractive media display will be able to provide stimulation of thoughts, feelings, attention, and interest in the information, so students will be encouraged to learn further. These results state that AR media is appropriate for use in learning to increase students'

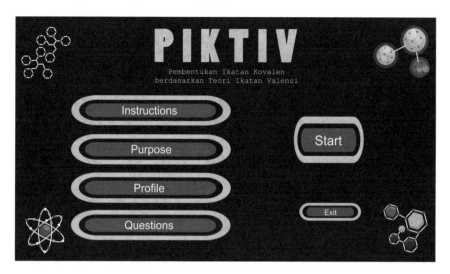

Fig. 9.9 Display the initial AR media menu on an Android smartphone

interest in learning so that they also study on the formation of covalent bonds based on valence bond theory. Besides that, an attractive appearance will increase motivation in learning (Kuswanto and Radiansah 2018). On interactive characteristics, the display is equipped with various buttons making it easier for students to use the application (Hinrichs et al. 2013). Moreover, this AR media uses Android smartphone technology that most people have, so it is effortless to use if learning media is contained in smartphones (Anshari and Almunawar 2017).

9.5.2 Display Basic Competencies and Learning Objectives

The basic competencies and learning objectives display aim to provide information about what students must achieve in learning the formation of covalent bonds based on valence bond theory (Anugrahana 2016). It obtained three indicators, namely, the sub-concept of the orbital form, the hybridization process as well as the sigma bond, and pi bond which is used as sub-concepts in the indicator (Chang 2011). In line with Hartini (2013) which states that the formulation of indicators developed at least three indicators and indicator aims to provide careful direction to the material to be taught.

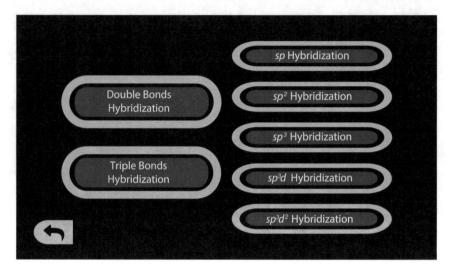

Fig. 9.10 Hybridization submenu

9.5.3 Display Main Menu (Start)

The main menu contains menus related to the content of the valence bond theory. The start button directs the user to the orbital and hybridization submenu. Orbital and hybridization submenus contained in the main menu can direct users to the next submenus to guide the user in running the application to observe the three-dimensional submicroscopic visualization of some concepts in the valence bond theory material.

9.5.4 Display of the Hybridization Submenu

Display hybridization submenu consists of sp hybridization submenu, sp^2 hybridization, sp^3 hybridization, sp^3d hybridization, sp^3d^2 hybridization, double hybridization, and triple hybridization. The hybridization submenu can be seen in the following Fig. 9.10.

9.5.5 Display Animation Hybridization Process sp

Animation of the sp hybridization process displays the sp formation of sp hybrid molecules from s and p atomic orbitals. Display animation can be seen in Fig. 9.11.

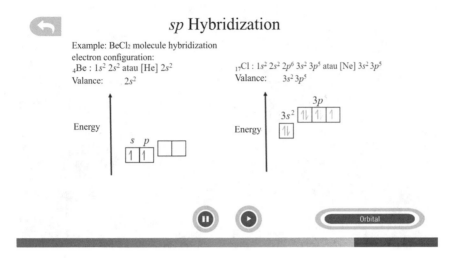

Fig. 9.11 Animation hybridization sp

In the hybridization display, there are the pause, play, back and animation progress bar buttons, and the orbital submenu. The pause button functions to stop the animation, the play button works to restart the animation, the back button functions to return to the previous menu, and the animation progress bar functions to display the extent to which the animation is running and can be clicked along the animation progress bar. The pause, play, and animation progress bar buttons aim to make it easier for users to analyze the hybridization process displayed on the animation.

This process cannot be explained on the AR camera display because AR can only display and have limitations in guidance (Mustaqim 2017). So we need guidance in the form of animation because animation can explain a concept or process that is difficult to explain with other media (Muslimin 2017), such as the concept of valence bond theory related to the hybridization process (Chang 2011).

The orbital submenu will hyperlink to the AR system. The AR system will be run by detecting markers via the Android smartphone's camera so that the detected marker will display 3D objects in accordance with the commands contained in each scene in every sub-concept. 3D objects that are displayed have an object shape that is adjusted to the normal form of the molecule in terms of angles and colors (Johnson and Henley 2015). The display of 3D objects in each sub-concept can be seen in Fig. 9.12.

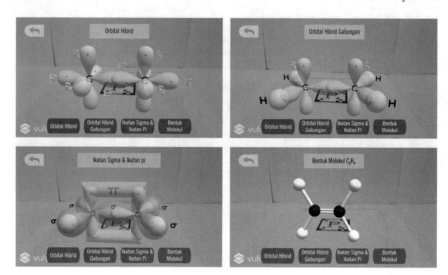

Fig. 9.12 Display of 3D objects in each sub-concept

9.5.6   Display of Question Menu

The questions menu contains a matter of evaluating valence bond theory. Evaluation questions were given to measure the ability of students to the extent of understanding learning through AR learning media that has been made (Kuswanto and Radiansah 2018). Questions consist of five problem descriptions that refer to the problem indicators. The question menu display can be seen in Fig. 9.13.

The type of AR that was used in this media is the type of target image whose operation requires images to bring up 3D objects. The picture is called a marker. In this study, only one marker was used to detect all 3D objects. The marker was made in the form of a square with a black and white image. Making markers that have varied colors is more interesting than black and white markers (Haryani et al. 2017). However, because 3D objects have color variations, if the marker has a color except black and white, it will interfere with the scanning process, because the marker will affect the stability of the object that appears (Cai et al. 2014). Besides that AR cameras are also needed with sufficient resolution for the scanning process on the marker. This was obtained from respondents' suggestions so that the scan can take place quickly. The improvement is by giving the camera autofocus on the application (Apriyani and Gustianto 2015). Because the density and speed of cameras and markers will increase students' understanding of observing the displayed 3D objects (Kamelia 2015). The marker display can be seen in Fig. 9.14.

The next step after making AR learning media was doing a validation test. The assessment aspects include aspects of learning, aspects of material substance, aspects of visual communication, and aspects of software engineering. So that by doing validation will obtain a learning media that is suitable for use in learning.

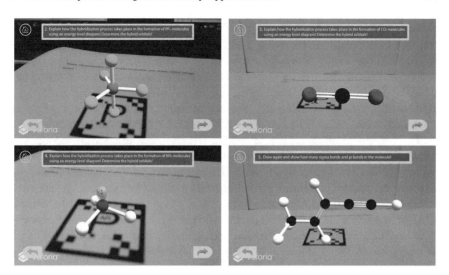

Fig. 9.13 Question menu display

Fig. 9.14 AR marker

The validation is intended to show AR learning media products and provide a validation questionnaire. The validation test was conducted on three validators. In general, AR learning media on the formation of covalent bonds based on valence bond theory is declared valid with some suggestions for improvement in certain aspects.

The feasibility test by conducting a limited experiment aims to determine the response of students to AR learning media on the formation of covalent bonds based on valence bond theory. The implementation of a limited trial began with an application given to students to be installed on a student's Android smartphone. Then students were given a guide to use media and follow the instructions of use, as stated in the instruction's menu on the AR media. Furthermore, students answer questions contained in the media. Then students were given a questionnaire to assess learning media with several aspects of the AR media. The feasibility test done by conducting a limited test resulted in several comments and suggestions from respondents. Based on the results of the feasibility of several indicators showed that this AR media can visualize the concept of abstract valence bond theory, and it is expected that the same media with different concepts can also be visualized. From all indicators obtained, it has an average value of 88.59% and it can be concluded that this media is suitable to be used as a learning media (Arikunto in Ernawati and Sukardiyono 2017).

9.6   Creating AR Learning Media on the Concept of Alkanes and Cycloalkanes

In general, based on the stages of making Augmented Reality media on the concept of alkanes and cycloalkanes, there are three display results, namely, the results of concept analysis, display of the results of design development, and validation results.

The analysis phase had been carried out in analyzing the concepts including the main concepts and sub-concepts. It was intended to produce concepts that are suitable for the learning media created. Concepts and sub-concepts have abstract concept types and symbol concept types. This shows that the concept of conformation of alkanes and cycloalkanes is a concept that emphasizes submicroscopic representations so that it is suitable for making Augmented Reality (AR) technology-based media. Furthermore, the results of the concept analysis were mapped through a concept map that aims to determine the relationship between the concepts and sub-concepts that have been analyzed.

After analyzing the concept, the next step was to compile the learning indicators used for Augmented Reality learning media. Concept labels were arranged based on the main concepts, whereas learning indicators were arranged based on sub-concepts. Learning indicators were arranged sequentially based on the level of difficulty. It aimed to facilitate students in learning the concepts of alkanes and cycloalkanes and to make learning process systematically.

At this stage, the making of learning media must pay attention to workflows based on storyboards and flowcharts. The purpose of storyboarding and flowchart is to facilitate the making of AR learning media on the concept of alkane and cycloalkanes conformation, provide direction or guidance in the form of links to the destination, such as play, exit menus, etc., and show the flow of the media start to finish so that the objects that are displayed in accordance with the directions that have been made.

After creating a storyboard and flowchart, the next step was to develop markers and 3D objects, which will later be applied to the learning media of AR on the concept of alkane and cycloalkanes conformation. The results of the storyboard, flowchart, markers, and 3D objects will be used as a reference display and flow of AR media usage. The following is the appearance and flow of the use of AR media on the concept of alkane and cycloalkanes conformation.

The menu display contains the intended links such as the hint button, profile, and play, providing the camera options for viewing 3D objects of alkane and cycloalkanes configuration on the AR media.

The purpose of making this menu display is to provide information to users about what will be displayed on the AR media. In the central display screen, there is a choice of buttons in the form of a playing display. This display aims to direct the camera display options. This display is used as an option display for users to see the 3D objects that are attached to the marker cards in the order of the numbers.

If one of these numbers is touched, an AR camera display will appear, which will then be directed to the marker so that the AR camera detects the 3D shape. In this view, there are next and previous buttons that function to see the next and previous 3D shapes of the conformational 3D shape shown. The display of each AR camera directed to the marker that matches the number of the selected marker can be seen in the following Fig. 9.15.

In each AR camera display, it presented 3D objects of different alkane and cycloalkane conformations with several different shapes as well as AR cameras from one to two display alkane conformational 3D shapes, whereas the other AR cameras display conformational 3D shapes cycloalkanes. In each 3D form show, there is a strain energy information whose function is to determine the conformational stability of ethane. However, 3D objects are not presented with a description of the name

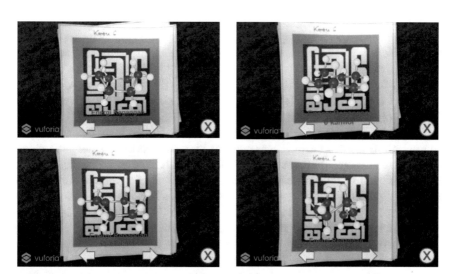

Fig. 9.15 Display each AR camera that is directed to each marker that matches the number selected

of the conformation so that users can determine their name by just looking at the shape. The function of next and previous buttons on the AR camera display is to help the user (students) in learning the amount of conformation of each compound, both alkanes and cycloalkanes.

Spreadsheets are one of supporting component for running Augmented Reality applications on various Android smartphones. On the worksheet, there are guidelines for the use of AR media, learning indicators, learning objectives as well as several questions that guide the user (students) to understand the concepts of alkane and cycloalkanes conformation. Before making a worksheet, first, we made a grid of questions that are useful as a reference in formulating a worksheet following the AR media that has been made. Inside the questions grid, there are question indicators that are in line with the learning indicators, questions in accordance with problem indicators, and the level of difficulty of the questions and answers, and scores as a reference in assessing students' work. This worksheet is very helpful in building students' understanding of the concepts of alkane and cycloalkanes conformation so that learning becomes more meaningful (Lan et al. 2013).

Question worksheets were made and it referred to indicators. The worksheets consisted of six questions, each had little description questions following the indicator questions that have been created. The user (student) is guided in stages on how to determine the conformation of each compound, describe conformation and how to determine the stability of conformation, and explain the relationship between conformational forms and the stability of the alkane and cycloalkane conformations.

The worksheet was along with a supporting marker card using AR learning media, which amounts to nine. This marker card can display 3D objects of alkane and cycloalkanes conformation accompanied by energy information of each conformation if the camera is directed at the marker, as explained in the previous discussion. The use of the marker card is to follow the instructions or questions listed on the worksheet.

Validation was carried out by showing the learning media products and providing three pieces of instruments, namely, AR learning media worksheets, MFI assessment rubric, and validation questionnaire sheets. The results of the validation were conducted on three validators. In general, the results of the validation of AR learning media on the concept of alkanes and cycloalkanes were valid with some suggestions for improvement in certain aspects.

The results of the feasibility test of the Augmented Reality learning media on the concept of alkane and cycloalkanes conformation showed that the learning media of AR on the concept of alkane and cycloalkanes conformation gets sufficient value on the indicator of the efficiency of product use in terms of time. It showed that AR learning media on the concept of alkane and cycloalkanes conformation is quite feasible and can streamline learning time (Sudjana 2009). However, to be more efficient in learning time, improvements and additions are needed so that learning runs effectively. This was explained (Mahnun 2012) that the learning media that had been made needed to be further improved so that the learning media was more efficient, reliable, and suitable to be used. Furthermore, the media makes students easy to develop their abilities and interests.

9.7   Conclusion

Research showed that Augmented Reality (AR) as a learning media is helpful in chemistry teaching and learning particularly for abstract and complex concepts that need a visualization in the learning process such as the concept of metal crystal, molecular geometry, molecular chirality, hybridization, and conformation of alkanes and cycloalkanes.

Result of feasibility test of AR showed that it has 72.5–88.33% for metal crystal material, 70.83–92.5% for molecular geometry material, and molecular chilarity has 90.12% in average. Furthermore, feasibility result of AR for hybridization is 83.33–97.50% and it is 75–87.5% for conformation of alkanes and cycloalkanes.

Based on the result above, we can conclude that AR can be used as a learning media in chemistry teaching and learning process since it helps students to comprehend the invisible concepts. Moreover, it is expected that AR in chemistry education will be continually developed in other submicroscopic concepts and hopefully the improvement media could be more optimal in system without markers so that it can be used easier without scanning.

References

Aldoobie N (2015) ADDIE model. Am Int J Contemp Res 5(6)

Anshari M, Almunawar MN (2017) Smartphones usage in the classrooms: learning aid or interference ? Educat Informat Technol 22(6):3063–3079

Anugrahana A (2016) Peningkatan Kompetensi Dasar Mahasiswa Calon Guru SD pada Mata Kuliah Pendidikan Matematika dengan Model Pembelajaran Inovatif. J Penelitian 20(2):182–187

Apriyani M E, Gustianto R (2015) Augmented reality sebagai Alat Pengenalan Hewan Purbakala dengan Animasi 3D menggunakan Metode Single Marker. J Infotel 7(1)

Arsyad (2007) Media Pembelajaran. PT Raja Grafindo Persada, Jakarta

Bertram WC et al (2010) Using media in teaching

Asyiah et al (2019) The making augmented reality technology-based learning media in molecular hybridization concept. J Phys: Conf Ser 288(1):012068. https://doi.org/10.1088/1757-899X/288/1/012068

Blijlevens J et al (2017) The Aesthetic Pleasure in Design Scale : The Development of a Scale to Measure Aesthetic Pleasure for Designed Artifacts. Psychology of Aesthetics, Creativity, and the Arts 11(1):86–98

Cai S et al (2014) Computers in Human Behavior A case study of Augmented Reality simulation system application in a chemistry course. Comput Hum Behav 37(5):31–40. https://doi.org/10.1016/j.chb.2014.04.018

Carmigniani J et al (2011) Augmented reality technologies, systems and applications. Multimedia Tools and Applications 51(1):341–377

De CR et al (2018) Hands-On Hybridization: 3D-Printed Models of Hybrid Orbitals. Journal of Chemistry Education 95(9):1601–1606

Chang R (2011) General Chemistry The Essential Concepts, 6th edn. McGraw-Hill, Rockefeller Center

Darmawan D (2012) Teknologi Pembelajaran. PT Remaja Rosda Karya, Bandung

Ernawati, I, Sukardiyono T (2017) Uji Kelayakan Media Pembelajaran Interaktif pada Mata Pelajaran Administrasi Server. Electronics, Informatics, and Vocational Education 2(2)

Han S (2018) How does The Smartphone Usage of College Students Affect Academic Performance? Journal of Computer Assisted Learning: 1–10.

Hartini S (2013) Pengembangan Indikator dalam Upaya Mencapai Kompetensi Dasar Bahasa Indonesia di Sekolah Menengah Atas Kabupaten Karanganyar Jawa Tengah. In Universitas Muhammadiyah Surakarta. Surakarta, Indonesia, p 198–214

Haryani P et al (2017) Augmented Reality (AR) Sebagai Teknologi Interaktif dalam Pengenalan Benda Cagar Budaya Kepada Masyarakat. Jurnal SIMETRIS 8(2):807–812

Hinrichs U et al (2013) Interactive Public Displays. IEEE Comput Graphics Appl 33(2):25–27

Irsyad, S (2016) Aplikasi Augmented Reality Sebagai Media Simulasi Ikatan Kimia Berbasis Android Menggunakan Metode Fast Corner Detection. In Universitas Islam Negeri Maulana Malik Ibrahim Malang

Irwansyah FS et al (2017) The Development of An Augmented Reality (AR) Technology-based Learning Media in Metal Structure Concept. Ideas for 21st Century Education. Taylor & Francis Group, London, pp 233–238

Irwansyah FS et al (2018) Augmented Reality (AR) Technology on the Android Operating System in Chemistry Learning. IOP Conference Series: Materials Science and Engineering 288(1):012068. https://doi.org/10.1088/1757-899X/288/1/012068

Isberto M (2018) The History of Augmented Reality. https://androbuntu.com/2018/12/29/pengertian-augmented-reality/. Accessed 3 May 2019

Jannah M L R et al (2019) Making Interactive Learning Media Based on Augmented Reality on the Concept of Molecular Chirality Making Interactive Learning Media Based on Augmented Reality on the Concept of Molecular Chirality. In Journal of Physics: Conference Series IOP

Johnson M, Henley J A (2014) Learning 2D Game Development with Unity: A Hands-On Guide to Game Creation. Retrieved from https://books.google.com/books?id=dgTVBQAAQBAJ&pgis=1

Johnson M, Henley J A (2015) Learning 2D Game Development with Unity: A Hands-On Guide to Game Creation

Kamelia L (2015) Perkembangan Teknologi Augmented Reality Sebagai Media Pembelajaran Interaktif Pada Mata Kuliah Kimia Dasar. Jurnal Istek 9(1)

Kuswanto J, Radiansah F (2018) Media Pembelajaran Berbasis Android pada Mata Pelajaran Sistem Operasi Jaringan Kelas XI. Jurnal Media Infotama 14(1)

Lan C, et al (2013) Mobile Augmented Reality in Supporting Peer Assessment: An Implementation in a Fundamental Design Course. In IADIS International Conference on Cognition and Exploratory Learning in Digital Age (CELDA 2013), Celda

Lin H, Chen T (2010) Advanced Concepts for Intelligent Vision Systems. Computers & Graphics 26(3)

Mahnun N (2012) Media Pembelajaran (Kajian terhadap Langkah-langkah Pemilihan Media dan Implementasinya dalam Pembelajaran). Jurnal Pemikiran Islam 37(1)

Martin J et al (2018) Augmented reality dalam pendidikan 4.0. In: 2018 IEEE-13 International Scientific dan Konferensi Teknis Ilmu Komputer dan Teknologi Informasi, CSIT

Meggs P B (2011) The Elements of Graphic Design. Type and Image: the Language of Graphic Design

Molenda M, Januszewski A (2008) Educational technology: A definition with commentary. In Association for Educational Communications and Technology (AECT)

Muslimin MI (2017) Pengaruh Penggunaan Media Pembelajaran Video Animasi terhadap Hasil Belajar Pendidikan Kewarganegaraan Kelas II SD. E-Jurnal Prodi Teknologi Pendidikan 6(1):26–34

Mustaqim I (2017) Pemanfaatan Augmented Reality Sebagai Media Pembelajaran. Jurnal Pendidikan Teknologi Dan Kejuruan. https://doi.org/10.23887/jptk-undiksha.v13i2.8525

Nassabeh N et al (2014) Dissociation of the Ethyl Radical: An Exercise in Computational Chemistry. J Chem Educ 91(8):1248–1253

Nazmi M (2017) Penerapan Media Animasi untuk Meningkatkan Minat Belajar Peserta Didik pada Mata Pelajaran Geografi di SMA PGII 2 Bandung. Jurnal Pendidikan Geografi 17(1):48–57

Norris CB (2018) Academic Writing in English. University of Helsinki, Language Services

Oh S, Byun Y (2012) The Design and Implementation of Augmented Reality Learning Systems. In: 2012 IEEE/ACIS 11th International Conference on Computer and Information Science, p 651–654

Penny MR et al (2017) Three-Dimensional Printing of a Scalable Molecular Model and Orbital Kit for Organic Chemistry Teaching and Learning. Journal of Chemistry Education 94(9):1265–1271

Sadiman AS et al (2009) Media Pendidikan: Pengertian. Pengembangan dan Pemanfaatannya, Rajawali Pers, Jakarta

Salah H, Dumon A (2011) Research and Practice Conceptual Integration of Hybridization by Algerian Students Intending to Teach Physical Sciences. Chemistry Education Research and Practice 12(4):443–453

Septia T et al (2017) Validation of Lectora based interactive module to improve the ability of junior high school students spatial in learning Geometry. Retrieved from https://umindanao.edu.ph/journal/wpcontent/uploads/2018/01/UM20172112_Validation-of-Lectora-based-interactive-modu.pdf

Singhal S et al (2012) Augmented chemistr : Interactive Education System 49(15)

Smiar K, Mendez JD (2016) Creating and Using Interactive, 3D-Printed Models to Improve Student Comprehension of the Bohr Model of the Atom, Bond Polarity, and Hybridization. Journal of Chemistry Education 93(9):1591–1594

Smith K, Nakhleh MB (2011) University Students' Conceptions of Bonding in Melting and Dissolving Phenomena. Research and Practice 12(6):398–408

Solomons TWG et al (2014) Organic chemistry. Petra, United States of Americ

Sudjana N (2009) Media Pembelajaran. Sinar Baru Algensindo, Bandung

Udin M N et al (2016) Perancangan Media Pembelajaran Menggambar Teknik Dengan Menggunakan Macromedia Flash. Indonesian Journal of Civil Engineering Education 2(1)

Uyulgan MA, Akkuzu N (2016) An insight towards conceptual understanding: looking into the molecular structures of compounds. Acta Didactica Napocensia 9(4):49–70

Wijayanti F (2018) Pembuatan Media Animasi untuk Topik Hibridisasi dengan Program Macromedia Flash. Jurnal Ilmu Kimia Dan Terapan 2(1):11–16

Yuntoto S (2015) Pengembangan Aplikasi Android Sebagai Media Pembelajaran Kompetensi Pengoperasian Sistem Pengendali Elektronik Pada Siswa Kelas XI SMKN 2 Pengasih

Zan N (2015) The effects of smartphone use on organic chemical compound learning. US-China Educat Rev A 5(2):105–113

Chapter 10
Mixed Reality Books: Applying Augmented and Virtual Reality in Mining Engineering Education

Lea Daling, Christopher Kommetter, Anas Abdelrazeq, Markus Ebner, and Martin Ebner

Abstract This chapter deals with the integration of Augmented and Virtual Reality (AR/VR) elements into academic mining education. The focus lies on the didactical approach within the EU-funded MiReBooks (Mixed Reality Books) project. The project aims to develop a series of AR- and VR-based interactive mining manuals as a new digital standard for higher education across European engineering education. By combining AR and VR technologies, it is possible to address current challenges in mining education in an innovative way. These virtual applications should make otherwise impossible and dangerous situations accessible to students. Classical paper-based teaching materials are enriched with AR content and translated into pedagogically and didactically coherent manuals for integrative use in the classroom. The authors explore how AR and VR instruments can be effectively integrated into teaching. The results of a broad evaluation of AR/VR-based lectures are presented and discussed in this chapter. The experiences and findings are summarized in a decision matrix for the use of AR/VR-based technologies in teaching.

L. Daling · A. Abdelrazeq
Institute of Information Management in Mechanical Engineering (IMA), RWTH Aachen University, Aachen, Germany
e-mail: lea.daling@ima.rwth-aachen.de

A. Abdelrazeq
e-mail: anas.abdelrazeq@ima.rwth-aachen.de

C. Kommetter · M. Ebner · M. Ebner (✉)
Educational Technology, Graz University of Technology, Graz, Austria
e-mail: martin.ebner@tugraz.at

C. Kommetter
e-mail: christopher.kommetter@gmail.com

M. Ebner
e-mail: markus.ebner@tugraz.at

© Springer Nature Switzerland AG 2020
V. Geroimenko (ed.), *Augmented Reality in Education*,
Springer Series on Cultural Computing,
https://doi.org/10.1007/978-3-030-42156-4_10

185

10.1 Introduction

The challenges in mining studies are diverse. In particular, the lack of transferability of theoretical knowledge into practical work and thus a smooth transition from university to professional life are problems that have not been sufficiently solved so far (Kazanin and Drebenstedt 2017). Many areas of mining, such as blasting, can for the most parts only be dealt with in theory. A practical and realistic demonstration of a blast is a logistical challenge. In addition, witnessing a blast with a group of students would be dangerous. Moreover, it would only be possible to watch the blasting from a safe distance, the detailed procedures would be unattainable and not easy to observe due to the fast speed of the process. Therefore, such a blasting process is limited to the presentation in the lecture hall.

Other processes, such as the loading of rubble onto trucks, can only be observed sequentially; static calculations can be simulated, but not actually tested. Visiting a mine would also only be possible to a limited extent and in small groups. An observation and guidance with a description would be unimaginable, if only because of the noise and the dangers. In summary, it can be stated that teaching that is as practice oriented as possible, which is important for a significant learning success according to Reich (2002), is difficult to implement in the area of teaching in mining education.

10.2 The Potential of AR and VR in Teaching

According to Milgram and Kishino (1994), Augmented Reality (AR), as well as Virtual Reality (VR), is understood as part of a spectrum between reality and virtuality. AR can help to overcome these challenges in mining education by merging the physical and digital worlds in real time. AR is used to expand the real world's perception with virtual objects. Thus, natural processes for interaction with virtual objects are enabled (Lee 2012). Physical activity is a basic prerequisite for conceptual understanding. The Learning outcomes are enhanced through interaction (Radu 2014). In addition to teacher-supported learning, an AR system should also offer the possibility of self-taught learning for students in order to meet their needs (Kaufmann 2003).

The use of fully immersive virtual worlds allows learners to interact naturally with objects as they are used to (Winn 1993). With fully immersive VR worlds, implemented for example with VR glasses, mines could be visited virtually by a large number of students at the same time. Processes such as drilling can be repeated at any time and viewed from close-up. Hazardous areas can be overcome during observation and the viewing angles can be freely selected. Any additional descriptions and information could be displayed on demand in the virtual mine. This ensures autodidactic learning or repetition of what has been learned at home.

Recently, there is an increasing fusion of these technologies, for example, to work with augmentations in completely immersive VR environments. For this reason, AR and VR are considered in this chapter together and also as mixed solutions, realized by different end devices. A major advantage of using AR and VR systems over conventional teaching media and materials is the ability to animate objects, respond to the user's actions, and transcend the physical boundaries of real objects (Woods et al. 2004). Many teaching media and materials can only partially satisfy the demand for a self-directed, activating, and constructing learning process (Hellriegel and Čubela 2018).

AR and VR can also improve distance learning, as interfaces that support remote actions with other learners or teachers who connect to existing objects (Mellet-d'Huart 2012). It can improve the way students learn in a creative and convenient way: for example, an ordinary building can be extended with educational content so that students are able to read things while remaining the way they are used to interact with the environment (Kaufmann 2003).

In order to increase the desired learning outcomes, collaborative interactions with adults and peers will help to achieve this by revealing the thinking process, knowledge, and skills of their peers (Thorsteinsson and Page 2007). An essential aspect of collaboration is that users can show each other facial expressions, gestures, and body language, which increases communication possibilities (Billinghurst and Kato 1999). Social interaction between students in the same physical space should be a very important goal for an educational environment (Roussos et al. 1999). AR systems can achieve this better than VR applications because they only extend the physical world, not replace it. The use of action-oriented learning can positively improve the relationship between reflection and action through collaboration (Wagner and Ip 2009). Therefore, we are interested in determining the scope of the learning environments used, whether students have used the system independently or whether they use the same virtual space for collaboration.

10.3   The MiReBooks Project: Using AR and VR Technologies in Teaching

MiReBooks is a new digital learning experience that explores the way mining is taught, applied, and changed in the future. By using traditional paper-based teaching materials and enriching them with AR- and VR-based experiences, professors, and teachers can now teach phenomena in the classroom or lecture hall and students can experience those experiences that are not normally easily accessible in the real world. The intention is to ensure that complex mining questions no longer pose a challenge to learning progress. Thus, students can complete their studies with a better understanding of their discipline. Through thoughtful didactical integration into lesson plans, students will be able to use new forms of participation appropriate to the needs of their generation. MiReBooks should change the way students are taught by enabling teachers to involve their students more effectively and to provide them with an expanded repertoire of content and increased comprehension. The range of possible examples of the industrial mining environment in which students can immerse themselves becomes endless, giving industry graduates a holistic view of the industrial context. Students will enter the labor market as digital natives and will have a significant impact on the functioning and development of the industry in the future. Implementing AR and VR seems to be a promising way to improve learning experiences through operational efficiency and innovation. The tool is therefore also attractive for industrial use in vocational training, in order to bring existing employees up to date. MiReBooks will be the lubricant for social and environmental change and innovation in mining, safe and healthy working conditions, and mining processes and equipment.

10.4   Evaluation of AR and VR Technologies in Teaching

In order to evaluate the usefulness and usability of AR and VR technologies in mining education, various technologies have been tested within the framework of test lectures at different partner universities of the MiReBooks project. Within these lectures, different sets of hardware components were included (Standalone and computer-connected VR headsets; such as HTC Vive, Oculus Go, and Oculus Quest, AR capable smartphones with and without head mounts such as Samsung Galaxy S9, and a router-based solution for interconnecting different VR headsets). During the test lectures, classical teaching materials were used (PPT, Whiteboards, Blackboard) and combined with small breakout sessions providing AR- or VR-based experiences. In total, there were 12 test lectures (four on *open pit bench blasting*, three on *hard rock underground drift development*, two on *hauling in mining*, and another three on *continuous surface mining*). Previously, all lecturers were asked to fill a storybook on their lectures containing the aim and use of the respective media for a certain learning objective.

10.4.1   *Research Design and Procedure*

While the main hypothesis of using AR- and VR-based technologies in lectures is to enable a more efficient transfer of knowledge, we aimed at getting a first insight on the usability and usefulness of the technologies for each student and teacher within the test lectures. Thus, the first question to be answered is how these technologies can be effectively integrated into teaching scenarios such as lectures, tutorials, exercises, homework, or group work in terms of time, frequency of use, as well as user acceptance, and perceived usefulness by the students.

In order to evaluate the learning and teaching experience when using AR or VR in lectures in mining, we used a combination of questionnaires (directly after the test lectures) including open questions to investigate usability of hardware as well as the possibilities for further improvements and adjustments for more efficient use of these technologies in the learning environment.

10.4.2   Questionnaires

Test lectures were evaluated using a questionnaire for both students and teachers. We collected data on general information, such as demographic data or professional background, as well as previous experiences with various technologies. System Usability Scale (SUS; Brooke 1996) was used for the evaluation of the respective technology. If several technologies were used in the lectures, SUS was filled out for each technology used. A SUS score between 60 and 80 means that the system is marginally acceptable, values above 80 show good to excellent system usability and 100 points indicate an excellent-rated system that fully meets users' expectations. Although several authors have shown that SUS is reliable and valid, the final score does not indicate why the evaluated technology has high or low usability (Sauro 2011) For this reason, the questionnaire included three additional open questions for students (What did you particularly like about the use of AR and VR in the test lecture? What benefit do AR and VR technologies offer over traditional teaching materials? What would have to be changed in order to use AR and VR successfully in teaching?), while teachers were asked to answer two more open questions (Which of the technologies listed in the table on page 1 "How often do you use the following devices?" have you already used in teaching and how? If you held this test lecture previously in other universities: "what was different this time compared to your previous test lecture(s)?").

10.4.3   Participants

In total, 120 students took part in the test lectures, either invited as participants of summer schools or via announcement within regular lectures. Out of that, 78 of the participants were undergraduate/graduate students, 36 were PhD students. 64.82% of the students were from the mining area. Five different lecturers ran the test lectures.

10.5   First Results

The analysis of the questionnaires focuses on aspects of perceived usability of the technology (student and teacher perspective) and reveals feedback on opportunities and challenges of AR and VR technologies in mining education. Since no sufficient number of answers from the teachers' perspective could be obtained, these results cannot be analyzed and presented within the scope of the paper. In order to sufficiently cover the perspective of the teachers, interviews are currently being conducted with teachers with and without technology experience. In this paper, we therefore only deal with the perspective of the students.

10.5.1   Evaluation Results

According to the SUS for tested technological equipment, Oculus Quest reaches the highest score of all VR headsets (with mean score of 79 points). Samsung Galaxy was ranked afterward (mean score of 77 points), followed by Oculus Go and HTC Vive (both with mean score of 72 points). As for AR technology, Samsung Galaxy S9 was used and rated with mean score of 79 points.

The results of the three open questions "(1) What did you particularly like about the use of AR and VR in the test lecture?", "(2) What added value do AR and VR technologies offer over traditional teaching materials?", and "(3) What would have to be changed in order to use AR and VR successfully in teaching?", are summarized in the following. The answers of the first two questions can be clustered into three categories: *Learning experience and motivation, teaching methods,* and feedback on the *use of technology.* Referring to *learning experience and motivation*, participants of the test lectures pointed out that AR/VR technologies assist greatly in transferring knowledge and enable a better understanding of the subject. Thus, students reported as a benefit to have the possibility to obtain in-field experience without leaving a classroom. Students particularly liked their active role and the interactive learning, which is perceived as more helpful to learn about more complex issues. With regard to the perception of *teaching methods*, students stated to like that several senses are addressed (sight and hearing) while using 360°VR. The better visualization with a special close look to practice, field, and machines leads in their opinion to a better imagination of theoretical issues. Furthermore, they mentioned the possibility of safe and time-saving field trips and excursions as helpful. In terms of the *use of technology* students stated to like the interaction with AR and VR content and to explore relevant objects/processes on their own. The technology is described as easy to use and turns learning into fun. Moreover, it offers more action than just sitting and looking at the blackboard.

At the same time, the evaluation of the third question revealed many approaches for improving the *technology*, as well as feedback for *structuring an AR/VR-based lecture* and *teaching conditions.* Referring to the improvements of the technology, students mainly would like to have the possibility to interact with their teacher. They would like to be better navigated by the lecturer (e.g., objects the lecturer is talking about should be highlighted or pointed somehow). Playing 360° videos should be simultaneous for every student. The quality of the videos is desired to be higher and effects such as screen flickering should be eliminated. One issue is that students cannot take notes while being in VR or using the AR App, so they have to remember what the lecturer explains. Furthermore, students would like to be informed about the impact of VR on their health. While *structuring a lecture using* AR and VR content, teachers should particularly pay attention to clearly express the learning goals. Furthermore, teachers should give time to explore the technologies and the respective environment. Special attention should be paid to create optimal teaching conditions. Thus, there should be enough space to move in the classroom and students wished for a small number of students participating in a AR/VR-based lecture. The number of headsets should be adjusted according to the number of students and a fast and stable Wi-Fi should be provided. Students also mentioned the importance of well trained and experienced lecturers here.

10.5.2   Limitations

On the one hand, a great number of students took part in the evaluation, whose answers were evaluated with regard to opportunities and limitations or AR/VR-based lectures in mining. On the other hand, not all students could be tested and interviewed under the same conditions (different lecturers, different rooms, different topics, and technologies). Under certain circumstances, the different conditions can have an influence on the evaluation of the technologies. This should be taken into account when considering the results. Furthermore, it should be taken into consideration that technical issues such as unstable WLAN connection could have affected the students' opinions. This represents more of university infrastructure issues than the tested technologies itself. The evaluation presented here shows only the results of the students due to too low response rates. In order to ask the perspective of the teachers, 1:1 interviews are currently being conducted.

10.6   Discussion

The results of the evaluation initially provide information about the user-friendliness and improvement possibilities of the technology. The evaluation results of SUS show that Oculus Quest is the most convenient among the tested VR headsets. When using AR, only one device was tested that achieved the same score as the Oculus Quest. For both media it should be considered that there is still a lot of room for improvement. When using AR technology, for example, the scaling of the model shown should be worked on so that it also provides a good overview with the smartphone. In the area of VR, it becomes clear that a high resolution and quality of the 360 videos is indispensable for the success of the application.

In addition, insights were gained into the integration of these technologies into teaching. From this it can be deduced what, from the students' point of view, has to be considered before, during and after the AR/VR-based lecture and accordingly contributes to the success of the lecture. In terms of lecture preparation, it can be concluded that the targeted use of media should be integrated into the formulation of learning objectives. The first question to be answered is which level of knowledge transfer is to be achieved before choosing which medium is to be used and when. For an initial insight and getting to know a subject, it will therefore be sufficient to simply show an environment (e.g., a video or the representation of a model in AR). If the aim is to achieve a deeper understanding, interaction possibilities with the learning object and possibilities for direct feedback should be taken into account. (e.g., the collaborative finding of a solution for a specific problem in VR). Furthermore, the conditions of the premises should not be underestimated. A stable WLAN connection is just as important as ensuring room for movement for the students. In addition, there should be enough technology available for the students or at least the possibility to follow the scenery on a screen. During the implementation it should be ensured that the teacher gives the students enough time to familiarize themselves with the technologies. In addition, the teacher should be able to resolve minor technical issues himself or herself, or get support by technical assistance. The students found it particularly helpful to have an active role in the learning process and to be able to explore the environments themselves. Many of the students reported having a lot of fun interacting with these technologies. These factors are particularly important for increasing intrinsic motivation. Furthermore, it was emphasized that the location- and time-independent possibility for field trips represents an added value. Special importance is attached to the possibility of interaction between students and teachers in VR. A simultaneous control and navigation through the learning environment as well as the giving of pointers should be made possible. In the course of the follow-up to the AR/VR-based lecture, the students consider it useful to make the content available for private use as well. In this way, specific processes can be reconstructed and refreshed at a later point in time.

In general, it can be summarized that a targeted and didactically well-designed use of AR/VR technologies can result in great added value for the students. So far, the perspective of the teachers has not been sufficiently taken into account in the current study. The changing role of acting more and more as a moderator to enable active learning processes could be a great challenge for those. The ability to feel confident in the use of the technologies should also be taken into account in a further survey.

10.7 Conclusion and Outlook

When using AR and VR technologies in an educational environment, bases such as learning object and learning outcomes as well as the level of knowledge transfer (as specified, e.g., in the learning outcome taxonomy according to Bloom in 1973), should be addressed. Furthermore, other factors such as teaching setting, technical setup, teaching method, and type of media have to be considered. The assessment of these factors makes it possible to identify new possibilities for implementing future AR and VR applications in teaching.

Derived from the evaluation's findings, the first draft for a decision matrix (see Fig. 10.1) is presented. The matrix underlines that the choice of medium should be made at the end of the decision-making chain. First, questions about the learning object and the learning outcome to be achieved should be answered. Subsequently, one has to consider questions about the setting and teaching method before deciding which technology will be used in the lecture. Each column of the decision matrix should be understood as a varying spectrum which is flexibly assignable. Thus, the matrix intended to serve as a compass to consider the most useful features in the use of AR and VR technologies. Ideally, the matrix is used starting with the learning object. Accordingly, corresponding learning objectives are formulated and assigned to the respective taxonomy levels. Then the different factors (setting, teaching method, and AR/VR technologies) have to be examined in more detail. For instance, in order to achieve a higher taxonomy level, where students are encouraged to actively learn and independently develop new topics, a smaller space with possibilities for interaction is more suitable. Here, the students can work alone or in groups with the respective technologies. On the other hand, in a large auditorium it may be more suitable to enrich the frontal teaching with demos or videos.

Nevertheless, the characteristics on the spectrum may vary, resulting in new constellations. Accordingly, a higher taxonomy level of knowledge transfer can of course also be achieved within the framework of a lecture in the auditorium—however, it

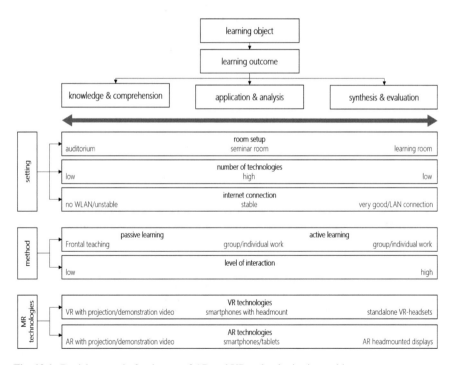

Fig. 10.1 Decision matrix for the use of AR and VR technologies in teaching

should then be taken into account how the level of interaction or the number of technologies can be adapted.

It must be emphasized that the derived matrix only reflects the findings of the previous evaluation. Only the perspective of the students was taken into account. Factors from the teachers' perspective could extend the matrix, for example, by financial aspects or factors that are related to preparatory work (e.g., technical support in the preparation of the content). In addition, settings such as flipped classroom or homework promoting active learning (Kommetter and Ebner 2019), are not listed here. This should be taken into account in the further course of the project.

Further possibility for extending the matrix is the inclusion of gamified elements in teaching. Most of the time, teaching materials are not motivating for the students to acquire. Therefore, taking a look at the computer game industry is a good choice as it manages to keep people on their chairs for hours and days (Prensky 2003). The gaming industry is also increasingly relying on AR and VR applications. Through playful elements, such as rankings, where students get points for solving a problem and duel with these points, the motivation of students can be increased, just as they are motivated to play a game. Although playful learning is also possible without any AR or VR elements, they set new standards here and offer students the opportunity to focus completely on the teaching content. If it is possible to prepare the teaching material in a game-based learning environment, the implementation can be considered with the help of AR and VR.

Furthermore, students can either complete a simple task using an AR or VR environment by supporting or improving their environment, or they can even have an immersive learning experience when an application replaces their common learning situation with AR or VR. Physical activity is associated with conceptual understanding. AR systems can build such an interactive learning environment. AR offers students a 3D view and constantly changing content through interaction, which increases their interest in learning. The complexity of a task and level of physical activity should therefore be considered in future research.

The presented evaluation of AR/VR-based lectures in the field of mining education provides new insights into the effective use of such technologies in teaching. Thus, the developed decision matrix summarizes important findings from the project and should support teachers in dealing adequately with new trends. Nevertheless, there is still a need for further research to take a holistic view of the topic. The studies on the usability and acceptance of these technologies are an essential prerequisite for the research of further (long-term) effects of AR/VR-based teaching.

Acknowledgements This activity has received funding from the European Institute of Innovation and Technology (EIT), a body of the European Union, under the Horizon 2020, the EU Framework Programme for Research and Innovation. Further information about MiReBooks: https://eitrawmaterials.eu/course/mirebooks-mixed-reality-handbooks-for-mining-education.

References

Billinghurst M, Kato H (1999) Collaborative mixed reality games. In: Ohta Y, Tamura H (eds) ISMR'99: proceedings of the first international symposium on mixed reality, Yokohama, Japan, March 1999. Springer, Berlin, pp 261–284

Brooke J (1996) SUS: A "quick and dirty" usability scale. usability evaluation in industry. Taylor and Francis, London, pp 107–114

Bloom BS, Engelhart MD, Füner E (1973) Taxonomie von Lernzielen im kognitiven Bereich. Beltz, Weinheim

Hellriegel J, Čubela D (2018) Das Potenzial von Virtual Reality für den schulischen Unterricht—Eine konstruktivistische Sicht. MedienPädagogik: Zeitschrift Für Theorie Und Praxis Der Medienbildung 18:58–80. https://doi.org/10.21240/mpaed/00/2018.12.11.X

Kaufmann H (2003) Collaborative augmented reality in education. Vienna University of Technology, Institute of Software Technology and Interactive Systems

Kommetter C, Ebner M (2019) A pedagogical framework for mixed reality in classrooms based on a literature review. EdMedia + Innovate Learning 901–911

Kazanin OI, Drebenstedt C (2017) Mining education in the 21st century: global challenges and prospects. Zap Gorn Inst 225:269–375

Lee K (2012) Augmented reality in education and training. TechTrends 56(2):13–21. https://doi.org/10.1007/s11528-012-0559-3

Mellet-d'Huart D (2012) Virtual reality for training and lifelong learning. Themes Sci Technol Educ 2(1–2):185–224

Milgram P, Kishino F (1994) A taxonomy of mixed reality visual displays. IEICE Trans Inf Syst 77(12):1321–1329

Prensky M (2003) Digital game-based learning. ACM Comput Entertain 1(1):1–4

Radu I (2014) Augmented reality in education: a meta-review and cross-media analysis. Pers Ubiquit Comput 18(6):1533–1543

Reich K (2002) Systemisch-konstruktivistische Didaktik. Eine allgemeine Zielbestimmung. In: Voß R (ed) Die Schule Neu Erfinden. Neuwied, Luchterhand, pp 70–91

Roussos M, Johnson A, Moher T, Leigh J, Vasilakis C, Barnes C (1999) Learning and building together in an immersive virtual world. Presence: Teleoperators Virtual Environ 8(3):247–263. https://doi.org/10.1162/105474699566215

Sauro J (2011) A practical guide to the system usability scale: background, benchmarks & best practices. Measuring Usability LLC, Denver, Colorado

Thorsteinsson G, Page T (2007) Computer supported collaborative learning in technology education through virtual reality learning environments. Bulletin of the Institute of Vocational and Technical Education, Graduate School of Education and Human Development, Nagoya University, Japan 4:6–19

Wagner C, Ip RKF (2009) action learning with second life - a pilot study. J Inf Syst Educ 20(2):249–258

Winn W (1993) A conceptual basis for educational applications of virtual reality. Human Interface Technology Laboratory. Technical Report TR-93–9, 1–14.

Woods E, Billinghurst M, Looser J, Aldridge G, Brown D, Garrie B, Nelles C (2004) Augmenting the science centre and museum experience. In: Spencer SN (ed) GRAPHITE '04: proceedings of the 2nd international conference on computer graphics and interactive techniques in Australasia and South East Asia, Suntec City, Singapore, pp 230–236

Part III
Educational Augmented Reality in Humanities and Art

Chapter 11
Beyond Historical Books, Names and Dates: Leveraging Augmented Reality to Promote Knowledge, Reasoning, and Emotional Engagement

Jason M. Harley, Susanne P. Lajoie, Chayse Haldane, Brea McLaughlin, and Eric G. Poitras

Abstract Research on the design and use of augmented reality (AR) systems in education is in an early stage as developers and researchers examine the affordances and constraints of this promising emerging technology. Despite the relative popularity of history among mobile AR apps, there is a lack of theory-driven empirical research and instructional design. This chapter describes our program of research that contributes to addressing these gaps by examining the ability of a location-aware mobile app and accompanying tour guide protocols to foster historical knowledge, historical reasoning, and emotional engagement. This chapter briefly introduces mobile location-aware apps before describing the theoretical frameworks that informed our instructional design, methodological decisions, and interpretations of findings. Next, we describe the mobile AR app we used in our research from two empirical studies

J. M. Harley (✉)
Department of Surgery, McGill University, Montreal, Quebec, Canada
e-mail: jason.harley@mcgill.ca

Research Institute of the McGill University Health Centre (RI-MUHC), Montreal, Quebec, Canada

J. M. Harley · C. Haldane · B. McLaughlin
Department of Educational Psychology, University of Alberta, Edmonton, Alberta, Canada
e-mail: chaldane@ualberta.ca

B. McLaughlin
e-mail: bmclaugh@ualberta.ca

J. M. Harley · S. P. Lajoie
Institute for Health Sciences Education, McGill University, Montreal, Quebec, Canada
e-mail: susanne.lajoie@mcgill.ca

Department of Educational and Counselling Psychology, McGill University, Montreal, Quebec, Canada

E. G. Poitras
Department of Educational Psychology, University of Utah, Salt Lake, Utah, USA
e-mail: eric.poitras@utah.edu

© Springer Nature Switzerland AG 2020   199
V. Geroimenko (ed.), *Augmented Reality in Education*,
Springer Series on Cultural Computing,
https://doi.org/10.1007/978-3-030-42156-4_11

described in this chapter. Our summary of findings draws on two published arti-cles and one new and unpublished paper; the latter examined instances of historical reasoning with the mobile app. We close the chapter with implications for future research, including connections with current and additional research we have carried out with different mobile AR apps: DiscoverUofU and the Edmonton Queer History App.

11.1   Introduction

Research on the design and use of augmented reality (AR) systems in education is in an early stage as developers and researchers examine the affordances and constraints of this promising emerging technology (Bacca et al. 2014; Poitras et al. 2016; Wu et al. 2013). Wu et al. (2013) offered a helpful summary of several features and affordances of AR for education: (1) learning content in 3D perspectives, (2) ubiqui-tous, collaborative, and situated learning, (3) learners' sense of presence, immediacy, and immersion, (4) visualizing the invisible, and (5) bridging formal and informal learning. These features and affordances are not necessarily unique to AR, but they do paint an enticing portrait of the potential it holds for enhancing learning and stu-dents' enjoyment of learning. In their review of AR in education, Wu et al. (2013) also proposed a helpful perspective to understand AR from: one that focuses on the applications of AR rather than specific technologies. Accordingly, we have defined AR in our research as technology that supplements reality (rather than replacing it like virtual reality [VR]) with digital information designed to be relevant to the instructional content that supports learning.

Our program of research with AR has focused on evaluating and designing mobile, location-aware AR apps. These kinds of apps utilize global positioning system (GPS) technology to track learners as they physically move throughout real-world locations to situate information in response to their location. Mobile location-aware AR apps, henceforth referred to as mobile AR apps, leverage the ubiquity of mobile phones and the opportunities they can provide from formal and informal learning. Do they work? Research has found evidence that students learn better with mobile AR apps than with low (e.g., digital book) or no technology-mediated forms of instruction (i.e., control conditions; Chang et al. 2015, 2014; Efstathiou et al. 2018; Li et al. 2013; Yoon et al. 2017). This is a promising start, but the literature is too nascent and too diverse in both the types of mobile AR technologies, uses of these technologies, and learner outcomes to provide strong instructional recommendations.

In this chapter, we outline theoretical frameworks used to evaluate cognitive and affective outcomes associated with learning history with mobile AR apps as a means to advance research in this area. We review two empirical studies that eval-uated the necessity for and effectiveness of a human tour guide to provide scripted prompts and feedback designed to foster history learning and historical reasoning. This research was conducted in order to help educators and other users of mobile AR apps make evidence-based designs for optimizing history learning with mobile

AR. These studies were timely, as little research had evaluated instructional or pedagogical approaches to using mobile AR apps (Harley et al. 2016, in press), despite findings that how mobile AR apps are used matters for learning (Chang et al. 2015; Harley et al. in press; Hwang et al. 2016; Ibáñez et al. 2016). For example, Chang et al. (2015) integrated AR with concept maps to form a scaffold and found that fifth-grade students assigned to the concept map AR condition performed significantly better than those in the standard AR condition. Hwang et al. (2016) created a competitive game approach to support AR-based learning activities in a real-world field trip and found that elementary students assigned to the game approach outperformed students in the nongame approach. Ibáñez et al. (2016) developed a version of a mobile AR app with task suggestions (based on students' individual pre-test scores) for ninth-grade students and found that those using the task suggestion version of the AR app outperformed those with the standard version.

Our program of research with mobile AR apps has also helped address another under-examined area of research with mobile AR app: emotions. Recent studies have found motivational (e.g., Chang et al. 2016; Furió et al. 2015), attitudinal (Hwang et al. 2016), and other psychological benefits (e.g., "sense of place"; Chang et al. 2015; Chen et al. 2016) from using mobile AR apps to learn, but emotions have not been a focus. Our research sought to help address this gap due to the critical associations emotions have with learning (Pekrun 2006; Pekrun and Perry 2014).

The following sections provide an overview of our findings to date with two studies examining a mobile AR app designed to educate people about the history of a large Canadian city: Montreal. We also share new findings from a mixed-methods analysis of historical reasoning during learners' interactions with the mobile AR app: The McCord Urban Museum App. The structure of the remainder of this chapter includes an overview of two theories that influenced our selection and examination of the McCord Urban Museum App, including the development of human tour guide prompt and feedback protocols to support historical knowledge and reasoning with the app. Next, we describe the McCord Urban Museum App and review key findings from two published studies evaluating learners' historical knowledge and emotional engagement from their interactions with it. An unpublished mixed-methods analysis of transcribed audio data from the tour and learner-guide interactions follows. This chapter concludes with current and future directions for educational mobile AR app research, including connections with recent research we have done with other mobile apps.

11.2 Theoretical Framework

Our mobile AR history research is guided by the control-value theory of achievement emotions (Pekrun 2006; Pekrun and Perry 2014) and a novel application of van Drie and van Boxtel's (2008) historical reasoning framework. We provide a brief overview of each theory below and how it broadly contributed to our research.

11.2.1 The Control-Value Theory of Achievement Emotions

Emotions can enhance learning by fostering motivation and focusing attention and limited cognitive resources on achievement-related activities (e.g., when experiencing the enjoyment of task), and promoting situationally appropriate information processing and self-regulation strategies (Pekrun et al. 2009; Pekrun and Perry 2014). Negative emotions such as boredom can, however, be maladaptive to achievement and undermine interest and intrinsic motivation (Pekrun et al. 2014; Pekrun and Perry 2014) as well as consume cognitive resources needed for the achievement task (Meinhardt and Pekrun 2003).

A central tenet of the control-value theory of achievement emotions (CVT; Pekrun 2006; Pekrun and Perry 2014) is the role that appraisals of control and value play as proximal antecedents of emotions. Subjective *control* is defined as one's perceived ability to effectively manage achievement activities and their outcomes. More broadly, appraisals of control target one's beliefs concerning the causal influence they exert (agency) over actions and outcomes (controllability), including the subjective likelihood of being able to obtain said outcome (probability). The app we used in our research, provided user-directed navigation (e.g., choice in what learners paid attention to, for how long, and in what order), which could enhance their perceptions of control by supporting autonomy, pacing, and self-directed inquiry. Moreover, the app leveraged learners' previous experiences by using similar and familiar technologies (e.g., Google Maps).

Subjective *value* is the second core appraisal dimension outlined in the CVT. Pekrun defines subjective value as the perceived importance of an activity or its outcome(s) to oneself (goal relevance), combined with the perception that an action or outcome is positive or negative in nature (goal congruence—event supports or hinders goal attainment; Pekrun 2006; Pekrun and Perry 2014). One of the ways the McCord Urban Museum app sought to enhance appraisals of value was by providing historical information about real-world settings that stood to be personally relevant to learners since the historical locations corresponded to physical spaces in the city they were going to university in.

Another component of the CVT that held particular relevance for our research is that achievement emotions (and their proximal antecedents) are *domain* and *subject-specific*. In other words, one might experience anxiety learning about math, but not languages (domain-specificity; Goetz et al. 2007, 2008) and trigonometry but not algebra (subdomains of math). The same applies to different tasks. Accordingly, we distinguished our measurement of emotions directed toward different aspects (object foci) of the tour: the app (technology-directed emotions), learning about the historical location (topic emotions), and the guide (social emotions). Doing so provided us with an opportunity to better understand the role of different, critical components of the tour, and learners' emotions. A richer understanding of the sources of emotions provides more opportunities and better direction to make changes to an educational environment than holistic emotional ratings.

11.2.2 Historical Reasoning

Historical reasoning is an activity where learners acquire knowledge of the past and use it to interpret phenomena from the past and present (van Drie and van Boxtel 2008). Learners can engage in historical reasoning by comparing or explaining historical phenomena, requiring them to adopt an active role in building knowledge, and an understanding of the past. The framework of historical reasoning proposed by van Drie and van Boxtel (2008) contains six components: (1) Posing historical questions, (2) using sources of information, (3) contextualization, (4) argumentation, (5) using substantive concepts, and (6) using meta-concepts. Each of our studies, including the new analysis reported on later in this chapter, incorporated all six of the core components of this historical reasoning framework (Harley et al., 2016, in press) described below.

The ability to recognize and understand *historical questions* is an essential component of historical reasoning (Schreiber et al. 2006). One type of question that can prompt historical lines of reasoning is comparison questions (van Drie and van Boxtel 2008). Depending on the study, either a companion app (MetaGuide) or a protocol used by a human tour guide can provide guidance on how and when to ask learners to compare past and present locations in order to identify differences. These open-ended comparative questions were designed to foster historical reasoning by encouraging learners to explore how locations have changed from the past to the present.

Learners can acquire information about the past from *using a variety of sources of information*, including written documents, images, videos, and other media. Reasoning with historical documents involves using information presented in documents or images (Rouet et al. 1996). The mobile AR app we used in the studies described in this chapter provided learners with a combination of text and historical images to give information about the historical location they were visiting (in person or virtually). Learners were encouraged to use this multimedia information in order to help them answer comparative questions posed by the guide.

Contextualization involves interpreting and understanding the past by applying general knowledge about the characteristics of the time period and place (van Drie and van Boxtel 2008). It also entails learners situating historical phenomena or objects in a spatial and social context in order to compare events from the past to the present. Our mobile AR app facilitated contextualization by providing information about the historical date, location, and situating learners in the present-day location. For instance, learners could view the present-day location to see the mode of transportation and compare it to the past where a horse-drawn carriage was the primary mode of transport.

Historical information is often partial and contradictory because historical representations are not perfect, complete, or absolute. Making claims about the past must therefore be supported by rational arguments and evidence (van Drie and van Boxtel 2008). Our mobile AR apps were designed to implicitly foster *argumentation* by providing partial information about the site location. For example, a participant who notes that there were more horse-drawn carriages in the 1800s might justify their claim using evidence from the image (i.e., the image depicted a horse-drawn carriage and no cars; McCord Urban Museum) or using knowledge about that time period to form a rational argument (e.g., there were more horse-drawn carriages because cars were not yet widely available). In the second study to employ human tour guides to fostering historical reasoning with a mobile AR App, we integrated causal and explanatory questions into the guide protocol to bolster this important form of historical reasoning (Harley et al. in press).

Concepts such as historical structures, persons, and periods enable learners to thematically organize historical knowledge (van Drie and van Boxtel 2008). The meaning of *substantive concepts*, however, differs according to time and place. Individuals must therefore learn how to differentiate between the *present* meaning of a concept and the *historical* meaning. The mobile AR app we used helped encourage the use of substantive concepts by asking learners to identify differences between the past and present. For example, present-day transportation is different from transportation in the 1800s. To make comparisons between transportation today and transportation in the 1800s, learners had to calibrate the meaning of the concept to be appropriate for the time period. *Meta-concepts* include evidence, time, place, and change (van Drie and van Boxtel 2008) and are important because they guide questions about historical comparisons. Our mobile AR apps allowed learners to make comparisons and assess change over time.

11.3   Highlights from Mobile AR App Research on Emotions, Historical Reasoning, and Learning

In the previous section, we summarized the primary theoretical frameworks that guided our assessment and design of mobile AR apps. Below, we review key findings pertaining to emotions, learning, and historical reasoning from two studies examining a mobile AR app: the McCord Urban Museum App. The studies are presented sequentially to illustrate how the first study helped inform the second. Interested readers are encouraged to read the associated publications (Harley et al. 2016; Harley et al. in press) for further details, as providing more detail than a summary is beyond the scope of this chapter. A brief description of the McCord Urban Museum App is provided below. Corresponding study highlights follow.

11.3.1   The McCord Urban Museum App

Studies 1 (Harley et al. 2016) and 2 (Harley et al. in press) examined the McCord Urban Museum App developed by the McCord Museum. The McCord Urban

Museum App allowed users to identify historical landmarks in the city of Montreal using GPS smartphone technology. Specifically, the app allowed users to view multimedia content (historical text and images) that illustrate how the city used to look in the past (e.g., the 1800s) in comparison to the present day. Two iconic and historical locations on McGill campus were selected: The Roddick Gates (study 1) and McGill's Arts Building (study 2). The McCord Urban Museum App used a map interface, similar to Google Maps, where historical locations were marked by pins. Learners could click on pins to read locations labels and timestamps and click on the labels to learn more: view historical pictures and corresponding historical text about the location.

The view of the locations in the historical pictures closely matched the views and geographical perspectives learners had of the contemporary locations during the guided tours. This positioning helped users to visually compare how the historical locations had changed by looking at a picture taken from the same position they were standing in long ago. Some locations, such as the Arts Building, had multiple pins that allowed users to examine the same historical location from different vantage points, focus on different sections of it, or learn about neighboring landmarks. Figure 11.1 shows a tour guide interacting with a learner while she uses the app to learn about and compare text and visual information about the historical Arts Building with the contemporary version on-site. Figure 11.2 shows the same interaction but using a different historical location, virtual setting, and a portable eye-tracker.

11.3.2   Study 1: Comparing Virtual and Location-Based Mobile AR Apps

The aim of our first, two-part study with the McCord Urban Museum App (Harley et al. 2016) was to conduct a preliminary evaluation of the effectiveness of this app, when used in conjunction with a human guide who provided scripted prompts and feedback, to foster positive emotions and history learning in a laboratory as well as an outdoor, location-based study. Our sample consisted of undergraduate students at one large North American university: $N = 13$ in our lab-based, virtually situated tour of a historic location (Part 1) and $N = 18$ in our outdoor, location-based tour (Part 2). Across Parts 1 and 2: (1) most learners were able to independently identify one of three high-level historical differences between the past and present versions of the Roddick Gates (the historical location). Most of the specific historical differences were discussed with some scaffolding support from the human guide. (2) Learners reported moderately high levels of enjoyment and low levels of boredom regarding the tour, learning, and interacting with the human guide. (3) Analyses of eye-tracking data from the lab-based (virtual tour) portion of the study revealed that learners frequently used the app-based features to help them make comparisons between the past and present-day locations.

Fig. 11.1 MTL urban museum tour on the McCord museum app being used by the learner (left) while interacting with tour guide (right) in front of contemporary version of the arts building. See Harley, Lajoie et al. (in press) for study details. Image photoshopped for illustrative purposes

Our comparison of the results from the virtual versus on-location tours revealed that learners were able to identify more differences in on-location. Moreover, they required less scaffolding to identify differences and fewer answers being provided by the human tour guide when on-location. Findings also suggested that scaffolding prompts were effective in eliciting historical differences from learners, although they were more necessary in the virtual than the on-location tour. Collectively, these preliminary findings supported our hypotheses that learners would be able to effectively and enjoyably learn about historical differences between past and present historical locations by contextualizing multimedia representations. Furthermore, preliminary findings demonstrated that the guide prompts and mobile AR apps were effective both virtually and on-location.

Fig. 11.2 Historical image from the MTL urban museum tour on the McCord museum app (top right-hand corner) being used by the learner (below) while interacting with tour guide (right) in front of a virtual, touch-enabled contemporary version of the Roddick Gates using google street view and a smartboard. The orange dot on the historical image on the mobile phone (top right) corresponds to what the learner is currently looking at. Specifically, the orange dot is from a video replay screenshot of data from portable SMI eye-tracking glasses (SMI ETG 2w; 30 Hz). See Harley, Poitras et al. (2016) for study details. Image photoshopped for illustrative purposes.

11.3.3 Study 2: Analyses 1: Comparing Historical Reasoning Prompts from Human Guides to Foster Learning and Emotions

Following the results from Study 1 (Harley et al. 2016) that revealed that posing historical comparison questions was both effective and necessary for learners to make all the key historical comparisons (in both the virtual and on-site tour contexts), we wanted to extend the prompt and feedback framework the tour guide used. The extended prompt and feedback (EPF) protocol built off of the success of what we referred to as the original comparison prompt and feedback (CPF; Harley et al. 2016) protocol. The EPF protocol was primarily enhanced with questions that supported argumentation by asking learners causal and explanatory questions related to a new historical location on McGill University's campus: The Arts Building. The primary objective of this study was to investigate whether the EPF protocol supported better (a) emotional engagement, (b) knowledge outcomes, and (c) value of history learning than the CPF condition while learners used a mobile AR app to learn about history. A second aim of the study was to compare learners' appraisals of task value (learning about the history of McGill University) before and after the guided tour.

Findings indicated that knowledge measured using a post-tour test were significantly higher in the EPF than the CPF condition, though learners in both conditions scored highly. A small effect size was observed in the same direction for learners' perceived success (subjective measure of knowledge outcome). These results provided preliminary evidence that both conditions were effective at teaching students about history with the mobile AR app. Moreover, these findings provided preliminary evidence that the guide's emphasis on a broader and deeper array of historical reasoning prompts in the EPF condition meaningfully enhanced learning over and above those prompts and feedback provided in the core CPF protocol.

Significant differences were not observed in levels of emotions or task value between EPF and CPF conditions, but both positive emotions and task value were relatively high, as hypothesized. When examining the object focus of the emotions, however, we found that learners reported significantly higher levels of enjoyment and curiosity from learning about the Arts Building (topic emotion) than from using the app itself (technology-directed emotion). Regarding task value, we found that learners reported significantly higher levels of task value after the guided tour compared to their pre-guided-tour responses.

Bolstered by the promising findings from study 1 and 2, which also generally supported our hypotheses, we embarked on further analyses of the data from the study 2 sample as well as the design of a new mobile location-aware AR app (Harley et al. 2019a, b) which we discuss in the closing section of this chapter. We now turn to examining the incidence of historical reasoning with the McCord Urban Museum mobile AR app—a first, despite the importance of historical reasoning in history education. Examining instances of historical reasoning also allowed us to expand our assessment from objective (post-tour multiple-choice or identification of correct answers during the tour) and subjective (perceived success) measures of knowledge to examine historical reasoning itself. In doing so, we sought not only to replicate findings from studies 1 and 2 but also to address some of their limitations in the process.

11.3.4   Study 3: Comparing Historical Reasoning Prompts from Human Guides to Foster Historical Reasoning and Knowledge

This study was guided by the following research questions: (1) How often did university students engage in historical reasoning during a guided tour with the McCord Urban Museum App? (2) What kinds of historical reasoning (van Drie and van Boxtel

2008) were observed? (3) Was the incidence of historical reasoning associated with the protocol (EPF or CPF) students were randomly assigned to? (4) Did students who engaged in higher levels of historical reasoning score higher on the post-tour knowledge test? Insufficient theory and empirical research were available to form detailed hypotheses for the first two research questions. We did hypothesize, however, that students in the EPF protocol would engage in more historical reasoning than those assigned to the CPF protocol because of additional prompts to engage in historical reasoning and encouragement to engage in a broader variety of historical reasoning processes. Moreover, we hypothesized that students who engaged in higher levels of historical reasoning would score higher on the post-test because they would have engaged in more cognitive activity while learning; a critical ingredient in meaningful learning (Mayer 2002).

11.3.4.1 Methods

11.3.4.1.1 Participants

Forty-five university students (32 female; 10 male) from a large North American university between 19 and 32 years old ($M = 23$; $SD = 3.1$) and enrolled in various programs volunteered to participate in this study. Student GPAs ranged from 2.20 to 4.00 ($M = 3.44$; $SD = 0.42$) out of four. Qualitative analysis was ongoing at the time of these analyses which were based on 16 of the 46 participants' data. Participants were compensated with $5 per half hour for a potential total of $10/hour. Partisscipants were recruited from either the university's online classified advertisement or a McGill University's undergraduate student Facebook group.

11.3.4.1.2 Historical Reasoning Prompt and Feedback Protocols

A trained human tour guide (undergraduate RA) provided both procedural and pedagogical support to learners as they completed the experimental protocol and used the mobile AR app to learn about the history of the McGill University Arts Building. Tours in both conditions began with the same open-ended introduction following a tutorial of how to use the app. In the CPF condition, learners were only encouraged to identify each of the four core differences between the historical and contemporary Arts Building. Once learners in the CPF condition identified this difference the guide provided them with additional context underlying the historical meaning of the difference. The EPF condition differed from the CPF condition with the provision of a historical reasoning hint designed to help learners figure out the context and meaning of the historical difference themselves. Once the difference was uncovered, the guide then provided additional historical context and facts about the difference. Please see Harley, Lajoie, et al., (in press; particularly Appendices B and C) for details on the prompt and feedback protocols.

11.3.4.1.3   Measure of Learning: Post-Tour Quiz

History learning was primarily assessed using a seven-item multiple-choice quiz (see Harley et al., in press). Each question contained five foils and was designed to assess learners' knowledge of the history of McGill University covered in the tour in relation to the Arts Building location.

11.3.4.1.4   Qualitative Analyses

In order to identify instances of historical reasoning in learners' interactions with the mobile AR app and guide van Drie and van Boxtel's (2008) historical reasoning framework was used to create a coding book and scheme that delineated six types of historical reasoning. Through the iterative, qualitative coding process the coding scheme was reduced to three categories of historical reasoning which could be reliably identified and classified in the transcripts: asking historical questions, contextualization, and argumentation. Each coder coded the segmented transcripts individually before meeting to resolve the disagreement. See Table 11.1 for definitions of the coded historical reasoning processes and example statements.

Table 11.1 Historical reasoning processes, definitions, and examples

Historical reasoning Process	Operational definition that was used (based on van Boxtel and van Drie 2008)	Example
Asking historical questions	Participant is asking questions related to history (different questions can increase the richness of the historical reasoning and can function as a catalyst for historical reasoning). Procedural questions are not historical questions	"um what would be that dome up there be used for? back then, or would it be just for looks?" (Explanatory question example)
Contextualization	Situating a historical event within a temporal, spatial, and social context in order to describe, explain, compare, or evaluate it	"And also thought it would be important that younger people got an education, or an opportunity to get a higher education in [Blinded]...?" (Contextual historical empathy])
Argumentation	Participant puts forward a claim about the past and supporting it with sound arguments and evidence through weighing different possible interpretations and taking into account counterarguments	"They had a lot of money, and they wanted to put it to public use."

Table 11.2 Frequency of condition by the level of historical reasoning

		Condition		Total
		CPF	EPF	
Historical reasoning grouping	High	1	7	8
	Low	6	2	8
Total		7	9	16

11.3.4.2 Results

Qualitative analyses revealed 173 instances of historical reasoning from 16 learners' transcripts (23,530 words in total; $M = 1,471, SD = 355$). Pre-discussion agreement was 80% and post-discussion agreement was 99% (two segments were resolved by a third coder). Of the 173 instances of historical reasoning, 17 (10%) involved the learner posing historical questions, 88 (51%) involved the learner engaging in contextualization, and 68 (39%) involved the learner using argumentation.

In order to investigate whether students' level of historical reasoning was associated with the protocol they were assigned to, we ran a Chi-Square analyses using protocol (EPF and CPF) and frequency of historical reasoning (median split used to group students into high and low groups on account of small sample). We found a significant association between historical reasoning and protocol where $x^2(1) = 4.06$, $p = 0.044$ using the Yates Continuity Correction in SPSS to accommodate our cell counts. Specifically, we found that seven out of nine learners assigned to the EPF protocol engaged in high levels of historical reasoning (see Table 11.2). Overall, learners in the EPF protocol engaged in an average of 14.5 ($SD = 6.60$; 131/173) and CPF learners in an average of 6 ($SD = 4.04$); 42/173). Figure 11.3 illustrates the mean frequency levels of each of the three different historical reasoning processes by condition.

We conducted a one-way ANOVA to examine the relationship between historical reasoning and post-test pefromance where high versus low level of historical reasoning was entered as the independent variable and post-tour quiz was entered as the dependent variable. Results failed to reveal a significant effect, but did reveal a moderate effect size, $F(1,14) = 0.79$, $p > 0.05$, $\eta^2_p = 0.05$ where learners who engaged in high levels of historical reasoning ($M = 0.86, SD = 0.13$) outperformed those who engaged in low levels of historical reasoning ($M = 0.79, SD = 0.19$).

11.3.4.3 Discussion

Our preliminary results from our ongoing qualitative analyses of collected data revealed that learners engaged in historical reasoning while interacting with the mobile AR app and a human guide. As hypothesized, protocol assignment was statistically significantly associated with the quantity of historical reasoning learners

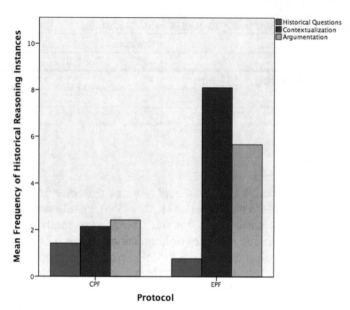

Fig. 11.3 Mean frequency level of each of the three different historical reasoning processes by protocol: EPF = extended prompt and feedback protocol; CPF = comparison-based prompt and feedback protocol

engaged in: learners randomly assigned to the EPF protocol engaged in more historical reasoning than those in the CPF protocol. While learners in the EPF protocol engaged in more historical reasoning, all learners engaged in some historical reasoning, complimenting findings from previous research that a simpler set of prompts used in conjunction with the mobile AR app fostered historical knowledge (Harley et al. 2016, in press). Our other hypothesis was partially supported by the medium effect size investigating the effect of high vs. low levels of historical reasoning on post-tour knowledge scores. The quantitative analyses run in this study were limited by the small sample size, but the patterns suggest that these effects will be strengthened as additional participants are qualitatively coded.

11.4 General Discussion, Ongoing, and Future Directions

The studies and analyses described above provide preliminary support for the use of mobile AR apps to foster historical knowledge, historical reasoning, and emotional engagement—when supported by a human tour guide. One of the questions that emerged from these studies was whether learning and emotional engagement could be achieved without the human guide or with a partially automated set of instructional prompts. Poitras, Harley, and Liu (2019) conducted a preliminary investigation of this line of inquiry using a mobile AR app, DiscoverUofU, that taught 60 under-graduate learners about the history of the University of Utah. Specifically, this study examined learners' emotions and prompts automatically generated from a different app (mObserver) to direct the guide's facilitation of the tour. In addition to identi-fying higher levels of mean enjoyment than boredom or frustration, as in previous studies, we found that learners' emotional profiles were associated with patterns of discourse moves used by the tour guide. Moreover, learners classified as belonging to the positive emotion cluster outperformed those in the negative emotion cluster in identifying distractor statements. As such, this study provided further evidence of the influence of instructional prompts delivered by a human guide during a mobile AR app-facilitated tour on knowledge and affective outcomes but using an intelligent quantitative field observation system (mObserver) rather than relying on training and an instructional roadmap. Further automatization efforts might include the use of a virtual pedagogical agent (Harley et al. 2018) and agents able to provide not only instructional but also emotional scaffolding (Harley et al. 2017).

Recently, we completed our first study with a third mobile app that taught 57 undergraduate students about queer history in the city, province, and country they attended university in: The Edmonton Queer History App (Harley et al. 2019a, b). Our findings provided further evidence that such apps support high mean levels of enjoyment and low mean levels of boredom as well as high knowledge outcomes. One of the main contributions of this study was assessing technological control with a usability questionnaire. Not only was the EQH App rated as high in technological control, but this appraisal, along with appraisals of task value, contributed to a model that significantly predicted technology-related enjoyment, as hypothesized by the CVT (Pekrun 2006; Pekrun and Perry 2014). Further, technology-related enjoyment (as well as topic boredom) significantly predicted the perceived success of learning (subjective learning outcome). These findings provided evidence that the design of the EQH App, based on the McCord Urban Museum App (Harley et al. 2016, in press), was effective for promoting learning and emotional engagement.

A follow-up study with the EQH App was recently completed that addressed several of the limitations of the previous studies. Chief among these was the lack of a pre and post-test of history knowledge and a non-app control group. Ongoing analyses of a study with a counter-balanced pre- and post-test and learners randomly assigned to either learn with the EQH App or to play a game are underway. Ongoing analyses are also extending the measurement of emotions from self-report measures to behavioral and physiological measures of emotion using techniques our team have used previously (Harley et al. 2015, 2019a, b).

One particularly important direction for future research is to conduct randomized control trials using counter-balanced pre- and post-tests that compare learning with a common (or common set) of mobile apps across formal (e.g., classroom) and informal (e.g., on-site) education settings. Such comparisons should also include learning in different instructional contexts, such as with the teacher leading a class of students through a tour, students taking the tour individually, and students working in pairs or groups. Further comparisons with automated scaffolding with human or virtual guides would also provide more evidence and insight into the role prompts and feedback designed to support historical knowledge, reasoning, and emotional engagement. Harley et al. (2019a, b) recently used M-Learning Theory (Sharples et al. 2009) to provide instructional and theoretical guidance on how these contexts might vary with mobile learning.

In conclusion, the results of our two studies with the McCord Urban Museum App, and related research, support the use of mobile AR apps as educational tools to foster historical knowledge, reasoning, and emotions that have the potential to meaningfully supplement traditional forms of history education. In particular, the EPF and CPF protocols evaluated in Study 2 of this chapter reveal the value-added from including prompts that target more sophisticated and varied forms of historical reasoning than our earlier work that focused on comparison-based prompts (Harley et al. 2016). This analysis also built on our earlier work by providing educators with examples of more types of questions: ones that can support greater levels of historical reasoning when used with similar mobile AR apps for history learning. Future research directions outlined in this chapter call for studies with more experimental control and methodological breadth in their examination of learning and emotions as the field begins to mature and move from exploratory research to robust evaluations that examine and account for an increasing amount of instructional, technological, and learner complexity.

Acknowledgments This research was supported by funding from the Social Sciences and Humanities Research Council (SSHRC) of Canada (grant number: 895–2011-1006). The authors wish to thank Daniel Beaudin for graphic illustration support for Figs. 11.1 and 11.2, and Philippe Latour for taking the picture used in Fig. 11.1. We also thank Tara Tressel, Meredith Derian-Toth, and Amanda Jarrell for posing as the tour guide or learner in Figs. 11.1 and 11.2.

References

Bacca J, Baldiris S, Fabregat R, Graf S, Kinshuk (2014) Augmented reality trends in education: a systematic review of research and applications. Educ Technol Soc 17(4):133–149

Chang HY, Hsu YS, Wu HK (2016) A comparison study of augmented reality versus interactive simulation technology to support student learning of a socio-scientific issue. Interact Learn Environ 24(6):1148–1161

Chang YL, Hou HT, Pan CY, Sung YT, Chang KE (2015) Apply an augmented reality in a mobile guidance to increase sense of place for heritage places. Educ Technol Soc 18(2):166–178

Chen CH, Chou YY, Huang CY (2016) An augmented-reality-based concept map to support mobile learning for science. Asia-Pac Educ Res 25(4):567–578

Chiang, THC, Yang, SJH, Hwang GJ (2014) An augmented reality-based mobile learning system to improve students' learning achievements and motivations in natural science inquiry activities. Educ Technol Soc 17(4):352–365

Efstathiou I, Kyza EA, Georgiou Y (2018) An inquiry-based augmented reality mobile learning approach to fostering primary school students' historical reasoning in non-formal settings. Interact Learn Environ 26(1):22–41

Furió D, Juan MC, Seguí I, Vivó R (2015) Mobile learning vs. traditional classroom lessons: a comparative study. J Comput Assist Learn 31:189–201s

Goetz T, Frenzel AC, Hall NC, Pekrun R (2008) Antecedents of academic emotions: testing the internal/external frame of reference model for academic enjoyment. Contemp Educ Psychol 39:9–33

Goetz T, Frenzel AC, Pekrun R, Hall NC, Lüdtke O (2007) Between- and within-domain relations of students' academic emotions. J Educ Psychol 99(4):715–733

Harley JM, Bouchet F, Hussain S, Azevedo R, Calvo R (2015) A multi-componential analysis of emotions during complex learning with an intelligent multi-agent system. Comput Hum Behav 48:615–625

Harley JM, Lajoie SP, Frasson C, Hall NC (2017) Developing emotion-aware, advanced learning technologies: a taxonomy of approaches and features. Int J Artif Intell Educ 27(2):268–297

Harley JM, Lajoie SP, Tressel T, Jarrell A (in press) Fostering positive emotions and history knowledge with location-based augmented reality and tour-guide prompts. Learn Instr Retri. https://doi.org/10.1016/j.learninstruc.2018.09.001

Harley JM, Jarrell A, Lajoie SP (2019a) Emotion regulation tendencies, achievement emotions, and physiological arousal in a medical diagnostic reasoning simulation. Instr Sci 47(2):151–180. https://doi.org/10.1007/s11251-018-09480-z

Harley JM, Liu Y, Ahn TB, Lajoie SP, Grace AP, Haldane C, Whittaker A, McLaughlin B (2019b) I've got this: fostering topic and technology-related emotional engagement and queer history knowledge with a mobile app. Contemp Educ Psychol 59:1–18 https://doi.org/10.1016/j.cedpsych.2019.101790

Harley JM, Poitras EG, Jarrell A, Duffy MC, Lajoie SP (2016) Comparing virtual and location-based augmented reality mobile learning: emotions and learning outcomes. Education Tech Research Dev 64:359–388

Harley JM, Taub M, Azevedo R, Bouchet F (2018) "Let's set up some subgoals": understanding human-pedagogical agent collaborations and their implications for learning and prompt and feedback compliance. IEEE Trans Learn Technol 11(1):54-66

Hwang GJ, Wu PH, Chen CC, Tu NT (2016) Effects of an augmented reality-based educational game on students' learning achievements and attitudes in real-world observations. Interact Learn Environ 24(8):1895–1906

Ibáñez MB, Di-Serio Á, Villaran-Molina D, Delgado-Kloos C (2016) Support for augmented reality simulation systems: the effects of scaffolding on learning outcomes and behavior patterns. IEEE Trans Learn Technol 9(1):46–56

Li R, Zhang B, Sundar SS, Duh HBL (2013) Interacting with augmented reality: how does location-based AR enhance learning? In: Kotzé P, Marsden G, Lindgaard G, Wesson J, Winckler M (eds) Human-Computer interaction—INTERACT 2013. Lecture notes in computer science, vol 8118. Springer, Berlin, Heidelberg

Mayer RE (2002) Multimedia learning. Psychology of learning and motivation 41:85–139

Meinhardt J, Pekrun R (2003) Attentional resource allocation to emotional events: an ERP study. Cogn Emot 17:477–500

Pekrun R (2006) The control-value theory of achievement emotions: assumptions, corollaries, and implications for educational research and practice. Educ Psychol Rev 18:315–341

Pekrun R, Elliot AJ, Maier MA (2009) Achievement goals and achievement emotions: testing a model of their joint relations with academic performance. J Educ Psychol 101(1):115–135

Pekrun R, Hall NC, Goetz T, Perry R (2014) Boredom and academic achievement: testing a model of reciprocal causation. J Educ Psychol 106:696–710

Pekrun R, Perry RP (2014) Control-value theory of achievement emotions. In: Pekrun R, Linnenbrink-Garcia L (eds) International handbook of emotions in education. Routledge, New York, pp 120–141

Poitras EG, Harley JM, Compeau T, Kee K, Lajoie SP (2016) Augmented reality in informal learning settings: leveraging technology for the love of history. In Zheng R, Gardner MK (Eds.) Handbook of research on serious games for educational applications. IGI Global, Pennsylvania

Poitras EG, Harley JM, Liu Y (2019) Achievement emotions with location based mobile augmented reality: an examination of discourse processes in simulated guided walking tours. Br J Edu Technol. https://doi.org/10.1111/bjet.12738

Rouet JF, Britt MA, Mason RA, Perfetti CA (1996) Using multiple sources of evidence to reason about history. J Educ Psychol 88(3):478–493

Schreiber W, Korber A, Von Borries B, Krammer R, Leutner-Ramme S, Mebus S, Schoner A, Ziegler B (2006) Historisches Denken. Ein Kompetenz-Strukturmodell. [Historical Thinking. A model. A model of competences] Ars una, Neuried, Germany.

Sharples M, Arnedillo-Sánchez I, Milrad M, Vavoula G (2009) Mobile learning. Technology-enhanced learning: Principles and products. Springer, Netherlands, pp 233–249

van Drie J, van Boxtel C (2008) Historical reasoning: towards a framework for analyzing students' reasoning about the past. Educ Psychol Rev 20:87–110

Wu H, Lee S, Chang H, Liang J (2013) Current status, opportunities and challenges of augmented reality in education. Comput Educ 62:41–49

Yoon S, Anderson E, Lin J, Elinich K (2017) How augmented reality enables conceptual understanding of challenging science content. Educ Technol Soc 20(1):156–168

Chapter 12
Design and Implementation of Augmented Reality for English Language Education

Danyang Zhang, Minjuan Wang, and Junjie Gavin Wu

Abstract Computer- and mobile-assisted language learning (CALL and MALL) have been gaining mainstream acceptance in second language education across the globe over the past two decades. Recently, Augmented Reality (AR)-supported learning has become a new frontier in MALL attributing to the pervasiveness of smartphones and the development of mobile technologies. However, one major research gap is that the previous studies on mobile AR, primarily relying on the case study approach to verify the effectiveness of various mobile technologies and AR products, often lack strong theoretical support such as frameworks and models. Against this backdrop, this chapter first reviews mainstream language learning theories, and then examines recent studies of AR in English Language Education (ELE). We then introduce three existing AR design frameworks in the mobile learning context, aiming to offer theoretical insights into designing and learning technology-enhanced language learning tasks. We end the chapter with design and learning principles for language teachers so as to promote the integration of this novel technology into English Language Education.

D. Zhang
Faculty of Education, University of Cambridge, Cambridge, UK
e-mail: dz298@cam.ac.uk

School of Foreign Languages, Shenzhen University, Shenzhen, China

M. Wang
Learning Design and Technology, San Diego State University, San Diego, USA
e-mail: mwang@sdsu.edu

J. G. Wu (✉)
Department of English, City University of Hong Kong, Hong Kong, China
e-mail: junjiewu4-c@my.cityu.edu.hk

© Springer Nature Switzerland AG 2020
V. Geroimenko (ed.), *Augmented Reality in Education*,
Springer Series on Cultural Computing,
https://doi.org/10.1007/978-3-030-42156-4_12

12.1 Introduction

Augmented reality (AR) increasingly penetrates into our personal lives in various forms, including mobile games (e.g., *Pokémon GO*), TV dramas (e.g., *Memories of the Alhambra)*, professional skill training (e.g., providing automobile technicians on-the-job knowledge transfer), Global Positioning System (GPS) (e.g., *AR GPS Compass 3D*), and so on. In this chapter, we adopt the definition proposed by Wang and her colleagues (2018), in which AR is "a combination of technologies that superimposes computer-generated content over a real word environment" (Wang et al. 2018, p. 1391), which interactively connects the real and the virtual worlds and appears at three dimensions (Azuma 1997).

Due to the development of new technologies and the pervasiveness of smartphones, mobile-assisted language learning (MALL) has developed rapidly within the past decades. Educators and researchers conducted empirical research on MALL (e.g., Rosell-Aguilar 2017; Zhang and Pérez-Paredes 2019) and promoted the use of mobile tools in English Language Education (ELE), such as instant messaging apps (e.g., *WeChat*, Wu 2017, 2018b) and self-developed learning software (Wang et al. 2009). As various existing AR software relies on the use of mobile technology, it is considered one type of mobile learning (Greenwood and Wang 2018). More specifically, AR in ELE falls into the scope of MALL, which enables the continuity or spontaneity of access and interaction across various language teaching and learning contexts (Kukulska-Hulme and Shield 2008). Other than conventional classroom learning, AR can combine the real scene perceived by the learner with the virtual scene generated by mobile devices, so as to build a semi-realistic world and to enhance the motivation to learn a foreign language learning motivation (Liu and Tsai 2013).

Yet, there have not been a wide range of reports exploring the topic of AR in language education, especially in teaching English. In particular, MALL studies have been criticized for the lack of theoretical support because many MALL researchers are teaching-oriented (Miller and Wu 2018). There is a need to examine relevant language learning theories and practices that are suitable for supporting AR-based learning, before integrating AR technology into language teaching and learning on a large scale. According to Saforrudin et al. (2011), many language teachers do not possess sufficient knowledge of AR and are not familiar with this new technology. Considering both theoretical and practical needs, this chapter offers suggestions on how to improve instructors' preparedness of using new technologies in their language teaching and to provide theoretical guidance for future AR research. Firstly, we review some of the well-acknowledged and widely adopted language learning theories, including constructivism, sociocultural theory (SCT), and connectivism. We then showcase several illustrating case studies from various ELE contexts, including (1) an AR-based mobile English composition learning material, (2) a place-based AR mobile game, and (3) an AR-enhanced context-aware ubiquitous learning environment. Drawing on three existing AR design frameworks, we propose instructional design and learning principles for language teachers, to enable their better use of this novel technology in teaching.

12.2 Learning Theories and Illustrating Case Studies

In this section, we introduce three classic language acquisition theories, namely constructivism, sociocultural theory (SCT), and connectivism. They are believed to be able to theoretically guide the use of AR in ELE, with some characteristics aligning with the features of the AR technology. We also describe case studies to showcase how each of their theories influences the use of AR in ELE.

12.2.1 Constructivism: An AR-based Mobile English Composition Learning Material

Constructivists perceive learning as a dynamic process, arguing that learners not only acquire knowledge from instructional approaches but also actively construct their perspectives based on their previous knowledge and experiences (Bruner 1996; Dewey 1916; Jonassen 1991; Piaget 1973). The constructivist theory centers the diversity of learners in the learning process (Dewey 1916), elucidating learners' active engagement in the authentic and meaningful learning practices (Aljohani 2017; Kaufman 2004). As an overarching learning theory, many contemporary well-recognized learning theories such as discovery-based learning, situated learning, and problem-based learning are rooted in constructivism (Wang et al. 2018). The afford-able AR-supported learning (Wang et al. 2018), which aligns with the essence of constructivism, is also rooted in constructive learning. With the support of AR tech-nology, learners can acquire contextualized linguistic and content knowledge from the AR-based language learning materials, internalize and construct the knowledge, and then use the obtained knowledge in productive tasks (Liu and Tsai 2013).

Guided by the notion of constructivism and AR-based MALL technologies, Liu and Tsai (2013) designed contextualized and learner-oriented AR-based mobile English learning materials, serving as an aid for college EFL (English as a Foreign Language) learners to write English compositions.

In this study, the researchers invited a group of five undergraduate English majors to take a path-fixed campus trip with the assistance of the AR-based mobile learning material on their smartphones. Combining and applying GPS and AR techniques, learners were situated in the real environment and obtained knowledge generated by the AR technique. During the trip, when participants directed the camera to one of the predefined locations, a description of this location would be shown on their smartphone screens. They could further click the scenic spot to access more detailed information. Upon the completion of the trip, they were required to write a composition to introduce their campus by describing the scenery and to complete an open-ended questionnaire to reflect on their experiences with AR-supported learning.

The results of Liu and Tsai (2013) study are optimistic, demonstrating students' progress in grasping both linguistic and content knowledge. For example, a number of linguistic expressions from the AR learning material were found in students' essays, providing evidence for their receptive and productive vocabulary knowledge development. In addition, they demonstrated enhanced knowledge of the campus. According to the questionnaire results, students were generally satisfied with this type of material, highlighting its advantages in helping them acquaint the campus scenic spots and expanding their vocabulary repertoire. Besides, they also reported the challenges in using this new-born technology due to their lack of digital literacy skills, which is in line with Conole and Pérez-Paredes's (2017) study. Since learners in constructivist learning should be equipped with awareness and strategies of taking charge of his or her learning (Aljohani 2017), it will be crucial to provide instructions and training to help them effectively use the AR-infused learning materials.

Driven by the AR-based mobile technology, place-based language learning practice (Godwin-Jones 2016) can facilitate learners' participatory learning process and motivate them to actively engage in language learning activities (Lee 2012). With a similar design, scholars have attempted to conduct AR-enhanced place-based language learning research in relation to different language skills (e.g., speaking abilities: Boonbrahm et al. 2015; vocabulary knowledge: Santos et al. 2016; intercultural and communication skills: Liu et al. 2016). Clearly, constructivism has become one of the most supported approaches in language learning (Aljohani 2017). However, social constructivism, which highlights the importance of social interaction and collaboration, is not reflected in these studies. In the next section, we will provide an example under the guidance of social constructivism and sociocultural theory (SCT), in order to highlight the importance of social and cultural factors in mediating student's language learning experience.

12.2.2 Sociocultural Theory (SCT): A Place-Based AR Mobile Game—ChronoOps

As mentioned in the previous section, the significance of social and cultural factors in language acquisition has been widely recognized by language educators and researchers. Against this backdrop, sociocultural theory (SCT) in language education has become increasingly popular in the past decades. Among others, Lantolf and Thorne's (2006) seminal work offers educators and researchers valuable insights into the development of human language from a psychological perspective. The recent definition of SCT by Lantolf et al. (2015) describes SCT as a theory of mind that acknowledges "human mental functioning is fundamentally a *mediated* process that is organized by *cultural artifacts*, activities, and concepts" (p. 207, original emphasis). This definition denotes several key constructs in SCT, including mediation, internalization, Zone of Proximal Development (ZPD), and so on. Rather than conducting a thorough review of the influential learning theory (see detailed discussions in Lantolf and Poehner 2014; Lantolf and Thorne 2006), this chapter briefly discusses two key constructs of SCT in relation to AR, respectively named (1) mediation and (2) ZPD.

Vygotsky believed that human mental development is not only a result of interweaving factors of the biological elements but also impacted by the "culturally constructed auxiliary means" (Lantolf and Thorne 2006, p. 59) that includes cultural artifacts (e.g., AR tools), activities (e.g., moving about a place for searching information), and concepts (e.g., the knowledge about directions). To accomplish learning tasks, social interactions and mediation are of prime importance. As Lantolf and Thorne (2006) believe, cognitive development benefits from "a dialogically produced interpsychological process through which learners internalize knowledge" (p. 282). This idea reflects the second construct in this section, namely ZPD.

In the past decades, scaffolding is no longer restricted to teachers, but has been extended to learners (e.g., student peers, Wu and Miller 2019) and tools (e.g., mobile dictionary, Zhang and Wu 2019). Through a collaborative mode of inquiry, learners are able to poll their strengths and weaknesses in order to construct and internalize new knowledge. However, Lantolf and Thorne (2006) caution that over-scaffolding would decrease student's learning agency and learners should be supported to regulate their learning from other-directed to self-directed. Under this view, teachers should *gradually* develop learners' autonomy to effectively plan, carry out, and evaluate their own learning (Hafner and Miller 2019). Nonetheless, this transformal view of education may be challenging to implement particularly in examination-oriented societies where a significant emphasis is placed on final test scores over learning processes (Miller and Wu 2018; Wu 2017, 2018b).

AR place-based technology (e.g., mobile games) has the benefits in extending learning beyond bricks-and-mortar environments, creating opportunities for collaborative learning, and providing contextual information for learners (Thorne and Hellermann 2017). These affordances are in line with the mediation and ZPD concepts in SCT in that (1) learning is mediated by AR technology and placed in a contextualized setting, and (2) place-based AR games usually require a group of team players to participate. In Portland State University, Thorne et al. (2015) conducted a research project to investigate how a project-based AR game (*ChronoOps*) facilitated learners' English language proficiencies.

In this study, participants were given a scenario that the earth was undergoing severe environmental issues. Students were sent back to the year of 2015 as agents to learn about green technology. Turning the university campus into a virtual world, students would receive multimodal AR information in English to help them accomplish various tasks (e.g., verbally recording of their observations, taking videos, producing written reports, and oral presentations) when they reached a certain spot. As an exploratory study, Thorne et al. (2015) found that the use of AR technology and the coordination among social, physical, and informational surroundings mediated/facilitated the entire learning process. Thorne and Hellermann (2017) further examined two excerpts from the pre-planning stage for making reports in this project.

They reported that learners made use of the physical environment (e.g., the fountain) and initiated the physical movement to accomplish their collaborative learning tasks. Both language and non-verbal language (gaze and gesture), as well as the physical contexts are intertwined and support each other in meaning co-construction and learning activities coordination.

In language learning, speaking serves as a constructive activity for learners to outwardly and inwardly regulate thinking and behavior (Lantolf and Thorne 2006). Outwardly speaking, a speaker can regulate other people's behavior via linguistic or non-linguistic signs such as directing students' attention to a certain piece of information. Inwardly speaking, linguistic artifacts provide affordances in regulating individuals' behavior and thinking (e.g., forcing himself/herself to use English for communication). Taken together, it is clear that in this study the learners' learning was co-constructed among peers as well as mediated by their cultural artifacts (e.g., (verbal/non-verbal) language and AR games), physical environments, and cultural concepts (e.g., the subject knowledge), which in turn augmented learners' learning processes.

Traditional schooled literacy, which focuses on the development of reading and writing as an individual learner's task (instead of collaborative work) via the paper–pen mode, has been criticized for quite a long time due to its decontextualization and the insufficient authenticity of learning (Lantolf and Thorne 2006). By contrast, the aforementioned AR projects made good use of learners' environmental contexts. Contuxualized learning has been embraced as an effective way of teaching and learning (Ferguson et al. 2019). It is time for language educators to recognize and highlight the important role of context in developing curriculum and in facilitating out-of-class language learning.

12.2.3   Connectivism: An AR-enhanced Context-Aware Ubiquitous Learning Environment

Most of the conventional learning theories (e.g., behaviorism, cognitivism, constructivism, and SCT) were developed before the digital age. According to Siemens (2005), learning could also reside in non-human appliances, which connects various information sources. In tandem with the broader constructivist theory (Sect. 12.2.1), connectivism, as a successor of theories mentioned above and an evolution of pedagogical paradigms in the digital era, guides the development and implementation of new technologies including AR (Greenwood and Wang 2018; Wang et al. 2018). As Greenwood and Wang (2018) describe, connectivism in technology-enhanced learning underscores how technologies create new learning opportunities for learners to access, acquire, and share knowledge, which stimulates interactive and collaborative learning within seamless networked learning contexts. The networked world requires people to improve their ability in accessing information and synthesizing connections with other individuals, groups, systems resources, and communities

(Bell 2009), which is assumed to be more critical than their possession of information. As such, connectivism supporters believe learning happens in many ways from the networks, in which students are decision-makers in gathering, classifying, prioritizing, or filtering information (Al-Shehri 2011).

Beyond the limitation of time and place, mobile technologies enable learners to instantly access various learning resources (Pachler et al. 2010). AR technology extends the potentials, giving learners more exposure to the combined actual and virtual language learning environment. To illustrate connectivism in AR-enhanced ELE, we exemplify an AR-based context-aware ubiquitous learning environment called *Handheld English Language Learning Organization (HELLO)* designed by Liu (2009). Aiming at enhancing EFL learners' speaking and listening skills, *HELLO* constructs a contextualized English learning environment by combing the conventional technologies (e.g., sensors and ubiquitous computing, information technologies) and the emerging technologies (e.g., AR). In *HELLO,* teachers control the management system, in which they can input learning materials and assessments and view students' portfolio. Equipped with a PDA (Personal Digital Assistant) phone, students can access all the learning materials via the *u-Browser,* talk to the virtual tutor via the *u-Speaker,* and take tests via the *u-Test.* Besides, they can picture the 2-D bar code attached in the real preset location via the *u-Camera* and *u-QR code* to obtain new information. Even though this project was from a decade ago, the method it used is still exemplary and reflects a good integration of emerging technology into teaching.

Liu (2009)'s case study aims to leverage the potentials of *HELLO* to enhance students' communicative abilities, i.e., listening and speaking skills. The eight-week course targeted school campus, involving three main study phrases: (1) "*Campus Environment*"—a self-study phrase in which students listened to the audio materials; (2) "*Campus Life*"—a context-aware immersive learning activity phrase in which students followed the mobile guide map to perform learning activities; (3) "*Campus Story*"—a task-based collaborative learning activity phrase in which students attended a "story relay race" to make a story together. According to the post-listening and speaking test scores, the experimental group performed significantly better than the control group in all the learning tasks, demonstrating the effectiveness of using *HELLO* in improving their communicative skills. In the interviews, most participants showed positive attitudes toward *HELLO*, agreeing that such an AR-based context-aware ubiquitous learning environment could not only benefit their new linguistic knowledge acquisition but also motivate them to continue developing their communicative competence in the future.

Different from the place-based language learning material created by Liu and Tsai (2013), Liu (2009) designed and implemented a more complicated and comprehensive English language learning environment by holistically integrating various types of English learning resources, tasks, and interactions. In line with the connectivism theory, *HELLO* is an epitome in AR-enhanced language learning. It offers students richer learning experiences by providing multiple types of learning materials, helping them establish connections between the physical and the virtual world (e.g., talking

with virtual teachers and obtaining information from the bar code in specific locations), and practice language skills (e.g., listening and speaking skills). However, we
agree with Al-Shehri (2011) that despite the potential of connectivism in advancing various mobile learning activities, both of the connectivism theory and language
learning theories and principles should be taken into account. In practice, we expect
to see learners' longitudinal progress afterwards in evaluating the long-term effects
of the AR-enhanced language learning environment. As the author indicates, more
pedagogical efforts should be made to (1) overcome the constraints of devices and
technology, (2) help students become more familiar with the emerging technologies (e.g., AR technology), and (3) work with school teachers to further assess the
practicality of this environment in satisfying students' various learning needs.

12.3   Three Existing AR Design Frameworks

In this section, we will review three existing AR design frameworks from the perspectives of (1) learner (the potential model for the design of mobile-AR curation
exercises, Novak et al. 2012), (2) designer (the mobilegogy model, Machun et al.
2012), and (3) technology (the SAMR model, Puentedura 2006) to consolidate the
theoretical foundation of implementing AR in ELE. We will again use the three case
studies in Sect. 12.2, to analyze the advantages and limitations of AR products and
to generate pedagogical principles for educators and language teachers.

   In 2012, Novak, Wang, and Callaghan proposed a four-circle model for designing
mobile-AR curation activities in art and science museums, which are frequently at
the forefront of technological integration and education, and are prime spaces for
informal learning experiences. They argue that AR-supported "amateur curation"
activities can greatly increase visitors' learning interests and help them learn more
from the visits.

   As shown in Fig. 12.1, the inner circle *Theme Development* refers to instructions
for guiding students to develop a learning theme at the first step. This process is
beneficial in helping students select artifacts and resources. Afterwards, instructors
will lead learners through the activities, so that they can (1) understand the artifacts,
(2) identify and strengthen the relationship between the artifacts, and (3) synthesize
and implement their understanding of the artifacts in meaningful and organized ways.
Finally, the outer circle of this model considers the sociocultural context surrounding
the learners, by encouraging peer interactions and discussions.

   This model (Fig. 12.1) pioneers a new learner-centered teaching approach,which
can be used to promote language learning activities and to increase learner autonomy
during the learning process. By comparison, the AR-based context-aware ubiquitous
learning environment *(HELLO)* reviewed previously could be more learner-oriented.
More effort should be invested to encourage learners to actively participate both
in the learning and designing stages, and to contribute instructional materials. In
addition, learners should be allowed to interact with the AR technologies in a more
active way, for example, encoding language learning (e.g., words and phrases for

Fig. 12.1 A model for designing mobile-AR curation exercises (Novak et al. 2012)

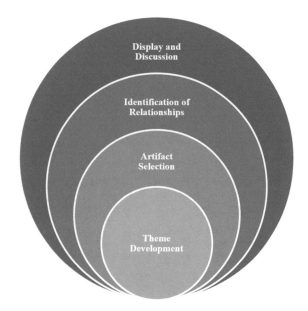

communication) and evaluative items (e.g., quiz) into the QR code, then printing and putting the code at certain places as suggested by Novak et al. (2012).

When we attempt to situate AR in the mobile learning context, it is of great necessity to understand the strategies that are unique to the mLearning environment. Xiao et al. (2011) were the first to create an mLearning design model, named LTCS (*Location, Technology, Culture, and Satisfaction*). All effective mobile learning should consider the LTCS factors. Based on this model, Machun et al. (2012) proposed the mobilegogy model, featuring five factors—*Location, Technology, Culture, Satisfaction,* and *Design* (LTCSD) in mobile learning. At the center of this model are learning outcomes, which are directly impacted by design decisions related to these five factors. The two outer circles in Fig. 12.2 respectively illustrate instructional adaptations and learning experience expansions suitable for mobile learners.

We believe that the mobilegogy model still applies to English Language Education (ELE). For instance, mobile AR can accommodate the changing language learning environment, achieving a high level of ratings in *Location*. The three case studies reviewed earlier in this chapter are convincing examples, which all demonstrate that portable mobile AR platforms can enable mobile language learning. However, despite the rapid advance in AR technology and AR-based learning design with the provision of user-friendly operations and multimodal stimuli, it is an indisputable fact that this type of technology is still germinating. *Technology* and *Design* are the two aspects that still need more investment, for example, improvements in cross-device compatibility, content delivery options, and limited scrolling. *Culture is* an even more critical factor in ELE. More effort should be in place to assist learners to overcome the potential cultural barriers in their language learning.

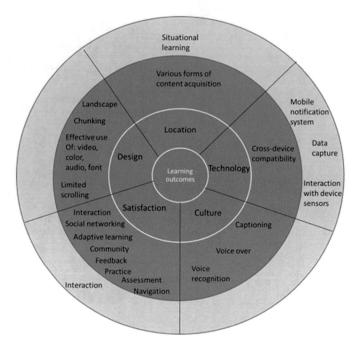

Fig. 12.2 The mobilegogy model (Machun et al. 2012)

Although the three case studies we reviewed have considered the importance of contexts, future design should strive to position learners in real language learning settings, making efforts to localize their language learning problems and offer them in-time support. In terms of *Satisfaction*, even though many existing mobile AR platforms, including the three case studies, have already taken many elements (e.g., adaptive learning, practice, assessment, real world applications, and learner attention) into consideration, some elements like social interactions, learner controlled pace, and formative feedback that could contribute to the creation of the interactive, collaborative, and learner-centred AR-enhanced language learning environment should be featured and integrated into future product design.

Reflecting a human-centered design approach, the mobilegogy model (in Fig. 12.2) serves as a guide for designers to tailor technology-enhanced learning for the mobile realm and to maximize the capabilities of mobile devices for effective mobile learning. Equipped with AR technologies, mobile platforms can further take learners out of the traditional classroom, helping them take active part in different learning contexts, and interact with well-designed learning content at the convenience of their fingertips.

Differing from the previous two models that focus more on the designing and planning stage, the SAMR model (Fig. 12.3), originally proposed by Puentedura (2006), consists four classifications (*Substitution, Augmentation, Modification,* and *Redefinition*) of technology use. This model was designed to guide educators and

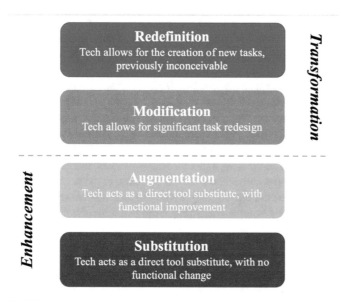

Fig. 12.3 The SAMR Model (Adapted from Puentedura 2006)

teachers to evaluate how well mobile learning activities meet the goal of transforming learning, so as to further enhance the quality of technology-enhanced education. Scholars such as Hockly (2013) has encouraged the use of SAMR model in MALL, especially in the context of ELE.

According to Puentedura (2006) and Hockly (2013), *Substitution* is the simplest way to implement technologies (e.g., mobile technologies) into learning. At this level, learning activities could also be accomplished without the implementation of technologies. Going beyond the *Substitution* level, technologies can not only substitute other learning activities, but also can offer more functional improvements over what traditional approaches could have been achieved at the *Augmentation* level. As Puentedura (2013) argues, learning activities at the *Substitution* and *Augmentation* level can only enhance learning, but learning activities fall within the *Modification* and *Redefinition* level can transform learning. Apart from allowing the learning activities to be redesigned in which the *Modification* level fits into, at the *Redefinition* level, the technology-enhanced language learning tasks are unique and could not be completed without the support of the technology.

In the current mobile learning implementation, some learning activities still stay at the *Substitution* and/or the *Augmentation* level. Besides, there are many successful practices going beyond these two levels, providing learners with more benefits at the two higher levels. The three AR-enhanced cases reviewed in Sect. 12.2 are examples that fall into the *Redefinition* level, offering language learners connected, situated, and personalized learning experience (Romrell et al. 2014). For instance, Liu and Tsai's (2013) study verified the success of using mobile AR technologies to redefine language learning. With the support of GPS and AR technologies, learners in their study were connected to new knowledge, situated in the real language learning contexts, and acquired new knowledge in a personalized way. In these cases, traditional teaching and learning approaches would not be able to create such a novel experience for learners.

The above three existing frameworks offer theoretical insights in designing, implementing, and evaluating AR-based language learning activities. The current AR practices, falling into the *Redefinition* level of the SAMR model, have surpassed many approaches driven by other technologies (e.g., mobile-based SMS delivery). However, there remains a long way to go, not merely in the advance of design and technologies, but also in creating a more learner-centered, interactive, and collaborative language learning environments for our learners. In the next section, we present pedagogical principles to help language instructors and students better position themselves in AR-enhanced language learning settings and to effectively learn a foreign langauge.

12.4   An Ecology of AR-enhanced Language Learning and Pedagogic Principles

As Ellis (2010) suggests, a good learning theory should be insightful and informative for teaching practice. In a similar vein, Lantolf and Poehner (2014) elucidate that "[t]he relationship between theory and practice can be reciprocal rather than a one-way street…the relationship is cyclic: theory–practice-theory, etc. or indeed, practice-theory–practice, etc." (p. 5). Synthesizing the theoretical and pedagogical review in Sects. 12.2 and 12.3, we propose a new and comprehensive model, an ecology of AR-enhanced language learning as depicted in Fig. 12.4. Following we

The ecology of AR-enhanced language learning

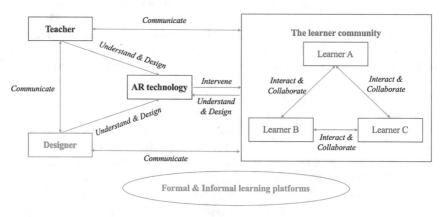

Fig. 12.4 The ecology of AR-enhanced language learning

describe this ecology in detail and suggest how it can be used to guide language teaching and learning using new technologies such as AR.

This ecology model (Fig. 12.4) is based on the abovementioned learning theories, design frameworks, and case studies. This model describes the major relationship among Teacher, Designer, AR technology, and the Learner Community, in both formal and informal learning settings.

The left side of the model shows how teacher and designer can work together to understand user needs, understand the capacities of AR technology, and then design immersive learning experiences for their students. The right side of the model illustrates how individual learners can communicate and collaborate by using AR technology. They will provide feedback to teacher and designer, who will further revise the learning activities. Thus, this ecology aligns with the current design thinking model, which has been widely used in designing user-centered and innovative learning solutions.

In line with the five key steps (empathize, define, ideate, prototype, and test) of the widely used design thinking model, we describe step-by-step pedagogic and learning design principles that can be derived from the ecology model.

12.4.1 Understanding and Identifying Learners' Language Learning Needs and Current Knowledge Gaps

As the current AR-enhanced materials cannot take account of learners' differences, ELE would be much better served if an instructor can position himself/herself as a facilitator, supporter, and guide, who not merely help students in linguistic knowledge acquisition, but also consider learners' language learning needs and identify their current knowledge gaps. At this stage, instructors should ask themselves why learners have such problems and needs and the underlying issues. In addition, designers also have responsibility before developing the AR learning environment. Besides, instructors and designers should work together to further narrow the focus of the learning design, identify key problems, and shortlist existing resources. Several questions should be considered:

(1) What do we know about our learners?
(2) What data and assessment information do we have that might inform our design?
(3) What are our constraints in technology and curriculum design?
(4) What are the key capabilities we need to focus on?

In particular, in the interactive and collaborative AR-enhanced language learning environment, learners are encouraged to share their opinions with instructors and designers. As presented in the ecology model (Fig. 12.4), learners in the AR-enhanced language learning environment can communicate with teachers and designers by using the synchronous and asynchronous discussion forums and social networking sites. Instructors and designers should work actively with each other to synthesize learners' responses, in order to identify the core problems and the main goals they currently have.

12.4.2 Sketching Out and Designing an AR-enhanced Language Learning Environment

To generate as many creative ideas as possible before formulating a solution, instructors could encourage learners to brainstorm ideas on synchronous and asynchronous discussion forums and social networking sites. They could design collaborative activities, asking every group of learners to present their prototype of the design to the whole class. When the design is sketched out, learners from other groups could offer critical feedback and suggestion for future improvement.

As the model (Fig. 12.4) indicates, designing the AR-enhanced language learning environment is not only the designer's responsibility. Instructors, especially those who are tech-savvy, should consider taking upon the dual role as a language teacher and AR technology designer so that they can better evaluate their students' needs and customize the technology in their teaching. However, as the development and proliferation of technology do not mean that instructors can use it effectively in their language teaching (Zhang 2019), they should at least familiarize themselves with the use of AR technology (e.g., knowing the affordances and limitations of AR, answering basic questions regarding AR) in English language teaching before getting involved in the designing process.

As learning in the digital age has become more autonomous and student-oriented (Hafner and Miller 2019), teachers should acknowledge that the Internet connects and allows learning to occur in the "unstructured learning environment" (Miller and Wu 2018, p. 2). Under this circumstance, the learning environment should empower learners in the holistic language learning process, such as allowing them to access various online resources in the networked language learning environment. Teachers should make full use of AR technology in designing and implementing more interactive and collaborative language learning activities, in order to improve the networked language learning environment and to encourage students to better connect with others, including expressing opinions, sharing ideas, and constructing meanings. More importantly, learners should be empowered in decision-making (Novak et al. 2012), being able to "efficiently search for, critically evaluate, and creatively use" (Wu 2018a, p. 393) information both from the physical and virtual layers of the AR-based materials to develop their knowledge system.

12.4.3 Testing and Refining the Optimal Language Learning Experience

After implementing, the AR-enhanced language learning environment should be tested and evaluated. Instructors and designers should see how the AR-enhanced language learning environment works, tracking learning and considering how it might be refined, scaled, or evolved. As with prototyping, this process can be repeated several times to enhance the user experience. During this process, instructors and designers should not only observe how AR technologies facilitate learners' language development, but also debrief by exchanging opinions and comments. It is also important to offer opportunities for learners to express their perceptions of learning in such environments and to provide feedback and critiques. Rather than an end, instructors and designers can make further iterations, returning to previous stages to discover more problems and make modifications.

12.5 Concluding Remarks

English fever is, to a large extent, a *fait accompli* in many EFL countries and regions (e.g., East Asia, Wu 2019). With the proliferation of technologies, many educators are taking actions in exploiting them to further augment their students' language learning experience. Among other technologies, AR has captured educators' attention and interests in (1) promoting learner-oriented language learning, (2) creating interactive and collaborative learning environments, (3) stimulating learners' motivation in learning a language, and (4) facilitating their language learning outcomes.

The chapter opens with an introduction to the concept and features of AR technology, followed by a discussion of three key learning theories—constructivism, sociocultural theory, and connectivism. We further illustrate these three learning theories with recent case studies in ELE. Afterwards, we introduce three existing frameworks, obtaining theoretical insights for future AR-enhanced language learning design and development. The chapter ends with an ecology of AR-enhanced language learning for language educators to better make use of the AR technology in practice. As the AR technology increasingly advances, we expect to see more AR-based language learning products that can "argument" the "reality" of current English language learning. Moreover, we also suggest that researchers, instructors, and practitioners pay more attention to understanding the essence and emphases of different learning theories, in order to optimize their future academic research and pedagogical practice in English Language Education.

References

Aljohani M (2017) Principles of "constructivism" in foreign language teaching. J Lit Art Stud 7(1):97–107

Al-Shehri S (2011) Connectivism: a new pathway for theorising and promoting mobile language learning. Int J Innov LeadShip Teach Humlties 1(2):10–31

Azuma RT (1997) A survey of augmented reality. Presence: Teleoperators & Virtual Environ 6(4): 355–385

Bell F (2009) Connectivism: a network theory for teaching and learning in a connected world. Educ Developments Mag Staff Educ Dev Assoc. https://usir.salford.ac.uk/id/eprint/2569/1/ConnectivismEdDev.pdf. Access 16 Sept 2019

Boonbrahm S, Kaewrat C, Boonbrahm P (2015) Using augmented reality technology in assisting english learning for primary school students. International conference on learning and collaboration technologies. Springer, Cham, pp 24–32

Bruner JS (1996) The culture of education. Harvard University Press, Cambridge

Conole G, Pérez-Paredes P (2017) Adult language learning in informal settings and the role of mobile learning. In: Yu S, Alley M, Tsinakos A (eds) Mobile and ubiquitous learning: An international handbook. Springer, New York, pp 45–58

Dewey J (1916) Democracy and education. The Free Press, New York

Ellis R (2010) Second language acquisition, teacher education and language pedagogy. Lang Teach 43(2):182–201

Ferguson R, Coughlan T, Egelandsdal K et al (2019) Innovating pedagogy 2019: Open University Innovation Report 7. The Open University, Milton Keynes

Godwin-Jones R (2016) Augmented reality and language learning: From annotated vocabulary to place-based mobile games. Lang Learn Technol 20(3):9–19

Greenwood AT, Wang M (2018) Augmented reality and mobile learning: theoretical foundations and implementation. In: Crompton H, Traxler J (eds) Mobile learning and higher education: challenges in context. Routledge, New York, pp 41–55

Hafner CA, Miller L (2019) English in the disciplines: a multidimensional model for ESP course design. Routledge, London

Hockly N (2013) Technology for the language teacher. Mob Learn ELT J 67(1):80–84

Jonassen D (1991) Objectivism versus constructivism: do we need a new philosophical paradigm? ETR&D 39(3):5–14

Kaufman D (2004) Constructivist issues in language learning and teaching. Annu Rev Appl Linguist 24:303–319

Kukulska-Hulme A, Shield L (2008) An overview of mobile assisted language learning: from content delivery to supported collaboration and interaction. ReCALL 20(3):271–289

Lantolf JP, Poehner ME (2014) Sociocultural theory and the pedagogical imperative in L2 education: Vygotskian praxis and the research/practice divide. Routledge, New York

Lantolf JP, Thorne SL (2006) Sociocultural theory and the genesis of second language development. Oxford University Press, Oxford

Lantolf JP, Thorne SL, Poehner M (2015) Sociocultural theory and second language development. In: VanPatten B, Williams J (eds) Theories in second language acquisition. Routledge, New York, pp 207–226

Lee K (2012) The future of learning and training in augmented reality. InSight: J Sch Teach 7: 31–42

Liu PHE, Tsai MK (2013) Using augmented-reality-based mobile learning material in EFL english composition: an exploratory case study. Br J Edu Technol 44(1):E1–E4

Liu TY (2009) A context-aware ubiquitous learning environment for language listening and speaking. J Comput Assist Learn 25(6):515–527

Liu Y, Holden D, Zheng D (2016) Analyzing students' language learning experience in an augmented reality mobile game: an exploration of an emergent learning environment. Procedia—Soc Behav Sci 228:369–374

Machun P, Trau C, Zaid N, Wang MJ, Ng J (2012) MOOCs: Is there an App for that? IEEE/WIC/ACM international conferences on web intelligence and intelligent agent technology, 3, 321–325. Macau, China

Miller L, Wu J (2018) From structured to unstructured learning via a technology-mediated learning framework. EAI Endorsed Trans E-Learn 5(17):1–9

Novak D, Wang M, Callaghan V (2012) Looking in, looking out: A discussion of the educational affordances of current mobile augmented reality technologies. In: Jia JY (ed) Educational stages and interactive learning: From kindergarten to workplace training. IGI Publishing, Hershey, pp 92–106

Pachler N, Bachmair B, Cook J, Kress G (2010) Mobile learning. Springer, New York

Piaget J (1973) To understand is to invent: the future of education. Grossman, New York

Puentedura RR (2006) Transformation, technology, and education in the state of Maine. https://www.hippasus.com/rrpweblog/archives/2006_11.html. Accessed 1 Oct 2019

Puentedura RR (2013) SAMR: Moving from enhancement to transformation. https://www.hippasus.com/rrpweblog/archives/000095.html. Accessed 1 Oct 2019

Romrell D, Kidder L, Wood E (2014) The SAMR model as a framework for evaluating mLearning. J Asynchronous Learn Netw 18(2):1–15

Rosell-Aguilar F (2017) State of the app: a taxonomy and framework for evaluating language learning mobile applications. CALICO Journal 34(2):243–258

Saforrudin N, Zaman HB, Ahmad A (2011) Technical skills in developing augmented reality application: teachers' readiness. In: Zaman HB et al (eds) Visual informatics: sustaining research and innovations. Springer, Heidelberg, pp 360–370

Santos MEC, Taketomi T, Yamamoto G, Rodrigo MMT, Sandor C, Kato H (2016) Augmented reality as multimedia: the case for situated vocabulary learning. Res Pract Technol Enhanc Learn 11(4):1–23

Siemens G (2005) Connectivism: Learning as network-creation. ASTD Learn News 10(1):1–28

Thorne SL, Hellermann J (2017) Mobile augmented reality: hyper contextualization and situated language usage events. In: Colpaert J, Aerts A, Kern R et al (ed) Proceedings of the XVIII international CALL conference: CALL in context. University of California at Berkeley, Berkeley, pp 721–730

Thorne SL, Hellermann J, Jones A, Lester D (2015) Interactional practices and artifact orientation in mobile augmented reality game play. PsychNology J 13(2–3):259–286

Wang M, Callaghan V, Bernhardt J, White K, Peña-Rios A (2018) Augmented reality in education and training: pedagogical approaches and illustrative case studies. J Ambient Intell HumIzed Comput 9(5):1391–1402

Wang M, Shen R, Novak D, Pan X (2009) The impact of mobile learning on students' learning behaviours and performance: report from a large blended classroom. Br J Edu Technol 40(4):673–695

Wu J (2017) Teacher's presence in synchronous mobile chats in a Chinese university. J Asia TEFL 14(4):778–783

Wu J (2018a) Antiplagiarism and L2 students' online writing. TESOL J 9(2): 393-396

Wu J (2018b) Mobile collaborative learning in a Chinese tertiary EFL context. TESL-EJ 22(2): 1-15

Wu J (2019) JINHYUN CHO, english language ideologies in Korea: interpreting the past and present. Cham: Springer, 2017. pp 181. Hb. € 93.59. Lang Soc 48(1): 166–167

Wu J, Miller L (2019) Raising native cultural awareness through WeChat: a case study with Chinese EFL students. Comput Assist Lang Learn. 10.1080/09588221.2019.1629962. Access 16 Sept 2019

Xiao J, Wang M, Li X (2011) A comprehensive model for designing mobile learning activities and resources. Mod Educ Technol 21(123):15–21

Zhang D (2019) Christoph A. Hafner and Lindsay Miller: English in the disciplines: a multidimensional model for esp course desIGN Appl Linguist. 10.1093/applin/amy067. Access 16 Sept 2019

Zhang D, Pérez-Paredes P (2019) Chinese postgraduate EFL learners' self-directed use of mobile English learning resources. Comput Assist Lang Learn . 10.1080/09588221. Access 16 Sept 2019

Zhang D, Wu J (2019) Learning across contexts: a multiple case study of mobile dictionary in Chinese EFL learners' incidental and intentional vocabulary learning. In: Proceedings of the 18th world conference on mobile and contextual learning, TU Delft, Delft, pp 4–11

Chapter 13
Iberian Cultures and Augmented Reality: Studies in Elementary School Education and Initial Teacher Training

Jose-Manuel Saez-Lopez and Ramon Cozar-Gutierrez

Abstract Augmented reality (AR) allows an educational application that promotes and makes possible a series of interactions in the classroom. In this chapter, we explored the opportunities of integrating augmented reality applications into elementary school education in Spain. The process was centered on the exploration of figures through augmented reality devices—the group work was focused on pre-Roman artworks, trying to identify their characteristics. We also applied this approach to higher education, namely to initial teacher training in Castilla-La Mancha University, Spain. We concluded that our approach brings curiosity and satisfaction to the students, and also enhances their motivation because of its active and collaborative nature.

13.1 Introduction

From an analysis of publications in journal citation reports and SCOPUS, it is concluded that the number of published works on augmented reality in education has increased considerably in recent years (Fombona and Pascual 2017; Radu 2014; Tekedere and Göker 2016).

Azuma (1997) defines augmented reality as the fusion of a direct or indirect vision of a physical environment (real world), whose elements are combined with digital objects to create a mixed reality in real time.

Its main features are:

- combination of the real with the virtual.
- real-time interaction.
- 3D registration.

J.-M. Saez-Lopez (✉)
Faculty of Education, UNED, Spanish National University of Distance Education, Madrid, Spain
e-mail: jmsaezlopez@edu.uned.es

R. Cozar-Gutierrez
Faculty of Education, Universidad de Castilla-La Mancha, Albacete, Spain
e-mail: ramon.cozar@uclm.es

© Springer Nature Switzerland AG 2020
V. Geroimenko (ed.), *Augmented Reality in Education*,
Springer Series on Cultural Computing,
https://doi.org/10.1007/978-3-030-42156-4_13

Mullen (2012, p. 13) emphasizes that "Augmented reality is to combine what is not there with what does exist imperceptibly and offer users an enhanced or enhanced representation of the world around them." On the other hand, Barroso and Cabero (2016), based on proposals from different authors (Cabero and Barroso 2016; Cabero and García, 2016; Fombona et al. 2012; Fundación Telefónica 2011; Muñoz 2013), synthesized it as "the combination of digital information and physical information in real time through different technological devices."

In addition, Fombona and Pascual (2016) highlight, in their documentary review, greater performance in student learning, linked to their creative, motivational potential by the immersive sense of the experience.

In the different studies and cases analyzed, in primary education and higher education, some researchers found improvements when using these resources (Cózar et al. 2015; Cózar-Gutiérrez and Sáez-López 2016; Sáez-López et al. 2018).

In primary education, it is important to understand the students' level of motivation and to identify the instructional materials that can motivate or demotivate them and thus take the necessary measures to improve participation. In recent years numerous resources and applications have been incorporated in educational realities, highlighting advantages mainly in student motivation (Cózar-Gutiérrez and Sáez-López 2016; Han et al. 2015; Huang et al. 2016; Kamarainen et al. 2013; Kerawalla et al. 2006; Klopfer and Squire 2008; Klopfer et al. 2009; Knaus 2017; Squire et al. 2005; Squire and Klopfer 2007; Sáez-López et al. 2015, 2016, 2019; Sáez-López and Ruiz-Gallardo 2013).

13.2   Initial Teacher Training and Augmented Reality

Ramón Cózar Gutierrez is the director of the "LabinTIC AB" research group. Participants in this group have been carrying out experiences and interventions of interest in relation to educational technology. In particular, contributions and experiences have been made in the initial teacher training in various groups in elementary education teacher training, in the subject of social sciences teaching, in the Faculty of Education of Albacete, at the University of Castilla-La Mancha. From these approaches, students are expected to know the educational possibilities offered by the use of augmented reality applied to 3D objects from sculptures of Iberian peoples (see Figs. 13.1, 13.2 and 13.3).

Coherently with the competences of the degree, a series of practical activities is proposed in which the students handle applications to obtain the objects and later integrate them into the Aumentaty program, and in this way use the resource and favor the educational integration of Iberian sculptures (pre-Romans) as essential historical content. The intention is to virtualize the scenes of AR through photographs and software; this handling in order to take photographs allows capturing images that later will become a 3D object in.obj format. Once this object is acquired, the Aumentaty Author program can be joined, or the object can be imported into .dae with SketchUp.

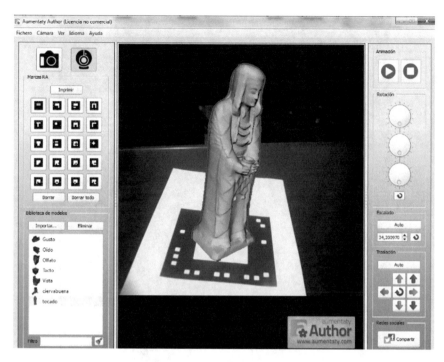

Fig. 13.1 Iberian sculpture. Screenshot from "Aumentaty Author"

Once the process is described from a technical point of view, with management and use of technologies, it focuses on the pedagogical application with respect to the active role of students who then create educational resources that they can adapt and highlight in their future pedagogical activities. Therein lies the importance of the approach for future teachers in this context of initial teacher training.

The contents of the activity are obtained from archaeological collections of Iberian art (Spanish and pre-Roman) housed in the Provincial Museum of Albacete. This pedagogical activity lasts 3 weeks in the context of higher education and has a collaborative approach, with groups of 4 students working from a script that detail the competencies, objectives, tasks, and specific support material for each of the tools to use with the teacher's supervision. Finally, each group presents the materials, results, and achievements of their project in an evaluation session.

The educational use of augmented reality favors ubiquitous learning because it makes the physical space a stimulating scenario, in addition to fostering experiential learning, increasing motivation, satisfaction, and even academic results according to several studies. Another advantage of the use of these materials and approaches is their flexibility since they can be used at different educational levels and in different disciplines by applying different models and didactic methodologies such as project-based learning, game-based learning, or gamification, which helps to optimize times in training contexts and create interactive content (Sáez-López et al. 2015, 2016).

Fig. 13.2 Middle ages Spanish sculpture. Photo in Albacete museum by the authors

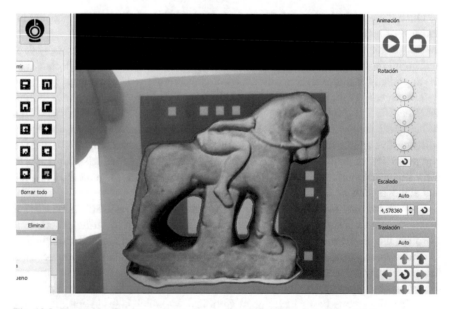

Fig. 13.3 Horse rider. Iberian sculpture. *Source* Screenshot from aumentaty author

Some studies (Radu 2014) highlight the usability difficulties of augmented reality—inefficient integration in the classroom and differences in learning—as we observe improvements in students who tend to have a high performance. One difficulty in the integration of augmented reality is the systematic abuse of traditional and rote approaches in the curricula. There is also a difficulty in using the interfaces and the management of programs that require prior digital literacy on the part of students and a comprehensive technological, technical, and pedagogical training on the part of the teachers. We must also bear in mind the possibility of loss of interest, inherent to passing fashions, which may cause it to stop being so motivating in subsequent courses. In short, we will see in the coming years the interest and potential of this resource, which is so motivating and beneficial, with an increasingly favorable environment due to the growing training and digital literacy of teachers and students.

13.3 Augmented Reality in Elementary School

From several investigations (Cózar-Gutiérrez et al. 2018) the integration of augmented reality as an emerging technology in educational contexts in elementary education is valued. In this way, these technological tools are integrated into the 5th year of primary education in the Spanish educational system. The students are 10–11 years old in this course. A didactic unit in 3 phases using Iberian art models through augmented reality as an educational resource is proposed (coherently with the initial teacher training taught and described in the previous section). In the aforementioned investigations, a descriptive analysis is provided, as well as a quasi-experimental design with mixed methods. The data of 73 students are analyzed, applying the Wilcoxon test, the Mann Whitey U test, the signs test, and participant observation.

The pedagogical approach has enabled group work to motivate and satisfy students, with the possibility of developing digital competence, research skills, and particularly in the selection of key information (Cózar-Gutiérrez and Sáez-López 2016; Sáez-López et al. 2018).

In the Spanish context, the curricular framework is based mainly on content, evaluation criteria, and learning standards in primary school (Ministry of Education and Culture [MECD] 2014) and key competences throughout life (European Parliament and Council 2006). In this context, a didactic methodology centered on the student is carried out (Ausubel et al. 1983), based on collaborative learning (Johnson 2003, 2006) which fosters active work centered on the student.

In addition to sharing content through augmented reality, content and presentations are organized as a result of students' group work, in which they approach the different terms and theoretical contents through a participatory and group methodological approach.

Furthermore, there are clear benefits to working with these resources with respect to the development of digital competence, resource management, and multimedia language. On the other hand, there are tasks to search and analyze information; so, it is essential to use critical thinking skills, comprehensive thinking, and different cognitive skills of a higher order.

The way of working in this context is structured in phases (Cózar-Gutiérrez et al. 2018). In the didactic unit, contents related to the Iberian peoples and their sculptures are explored with this approach and organization:

Phase I: Explore images through augmented reality with mobile devices and computers. Try to identify the different sculptures from first contact and motivation.

Phase II: Collect information related to art, culture, and society of the pre-Roman peoples and the motives behind those figures through group work. Students obtain detailed information about each of them.

Phase III: Identify the general characteristics of Iberian art through the comparison of different works. Religious elements, forms (almond eyes, animal body, sphinxes, etc.)

To begin, the first phase allows the use and exploration of the augmented reality scenes (Figs. 13.1, 13.2, 13.3, and 13.4) from the models employed and designed by the research group "LabinTic: Laboratory of integration of ICT in the classroom," from the University of Castilla-La Mancha. As described in the previous section, these models have been used in the initial teacher training at the teacher training school and correspond to the most representative works of Iberian art from the southern half of Spain in pre-Roman times.

Fig. 13.4 Hind. Iberian sculpture. *Source* Screenshot from Aumentaty Author

To facilitate interaction and visualize the contents in the classroom, each model is linked to a QR code and pointing to a paper marker that has been printed; you can see and manipulate the images on the mobile device.

In the following phases (II and III), the students look for information about each of the augmented reality scenes manipulated and try to understand their artistic and cultural value as well as their funerary and religious purpose. We then proceed to the search and selection of information through the Internet and as well as the group work that allows us to discuss, analyze, and contrast the information.

For greater efficiency, work with these resources requires clear and simple instructions that allow all students to perform a task without complications and without the need to have extensive technological training as a prerequisite. The instructions are clear: install the Aumentaty application on Google play; download the bookmarks in a link provided by the teacher; open the mobile phone with Aumentaty; and point to the paper marker with the camera to see the figures (Fig. 13.5).

From the analysis of the results, it is concluded that the students positively value the use and integration of augmented reality due to its advantages of active participation. Although there are no statistically significant improvements with respect to academic performance, there are improvements regarding the level of interest, enthusiasm, commitment, and motivation of the students.

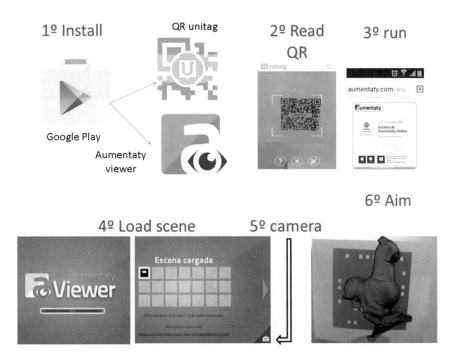

Fig. 13.5 Steps to use the Aumentaty viewer. *Source* Cózar-Gutiérrez and Sáez-López 2016 and Cózar and Sáez-López

This proposal highlights the importance of the development of cultural and artistic competence, with the possibility of addressing contents related to the history of art and significant periods of local history. Through these methods and appropriate pedagogical approaches, students have the opportunity to manipulate artistic objects, which allows them to better analyze content in art history. These experiences highlight improvements in participation, interest, enthusiasm, commitment, fun, motivation, recognition of artistic content and collaborative work in the learning process.

The possibility of active participation centered on the students by working on the contents in groups and manipulating the historical models that will allow them to understand the concepts and fundamental terms in history and art is evident and remarkable since, when manipulating the objects, the students understand that the figures worked are usually funerary, with cavities in the back to deposit the ashes of the deceased. It is important to highlight the social class of the subjects and the religious character of the sculptures.

It is interesting to perceive the style such as, for example, the almond-shaped eyes. From these examples, it is understood that students have the opportunity to analyze the figures in greater detail. The ability to manipulate the sculptures with 3D models on the mobile device allows for analysis.

In short, other important advantages stand out in relation to the satisfaction of students who have worked with these approaches. They include greater curiosity and the possibility of manipulating historical models and sculptures important to the history of local art. The possibility of being able to manipulate artistic works in detail allows the artistic expressions and fundamental sculptural details to be understood.

13.4   Conclusions

Factors and elements beneficial to pedagogical practice stand out. Mainly, the factor with greater presence and which is more decisive is motivation, which stimulates and promotes improvements in learning. The manipulation of various figures arouses the interest and curiosity of the student so that activities that students enjoy, have fun with, and which advance the contents of the social sciences are highlighted, thereby improving satisfaction in learning (Cózar-Gutiérrez and Sáez-López 2016).

The approach of using technological resources allows for certain dynamics and interactions in the classroom that are consistent with active pedagogical assumptions centered on the student. The student should look for information on the different figures and maintain an awake and active attitude. These processes allow the development of digital competence; the act of seeking and including information related to art history content requires a search for knowledge that promotes improvement in skills with technologies. In the analysis of cognitive competencies, their importance is valued in processes aimed at understanding, generating and analyzing information, as well as processes focused on decision-making and problem-solving (Cózar-Gutiérrez and Sáez-López 2016).

On the other hand, the approaches oriented toward collaborative learning are essential since they enable activities in which the student learns to work in a team. In this context, social skills, communication skills, an active attitude, and the ability to participate are stimulated. In the application of these techniques, it should be taken into account that the correct planning and design of the activities are necessary since the functioning of the groups needs supervision to facilitate group communication and avoid possible errors stemming from students who do not participate or from excessive leadership. In short, the benefits and advantages highlighted in the integration of augmented reality are mainly:

- Motivation
- Interest
- Curiosity
- Satisfaction
- Active approaches
- Comprehensive thinking
- Critical thinking

With respect to initial teacher training, it is concluded that it favors the teaching–learning process, motivates students, and facilitates the understanding of content. There are many possibilities offered by the use of AR for the preparation of teaching materials and learning activities, and, specifically, as we have shown, when studying and exposing the contents related to the history and history of art of our closest environment (Cózar et al. 2015).

We can bring museums to our classrooms, rebuild historical sites, recreate different moments of history, show emblematic monuments, among many other resources, at zero cost. The procedures used do not involve an excessive effort for teachers since, with certain basic notions of computer science that are relatively easy to access today, together with the use of free and easily accessible applications on the network, we can manipulate the scenes of RA that we find in the repositories and even create those that interest us. However, we are aware that a greater incidence in the training and improvement in ICT is essential in the initial training of teachers (Cózar et al. 2015; Sáez-López et al. 2019).

In this sense, it is not surprising that more than half of the respondents manifest a need for initial training in this tool. The answers obtained from a qualitative approach are in line with the disposition of respondents toward ICT in education.

The results are satisfactory due to the degree of novelty, implication, motivation, and challenge that the educational instrumentalization of AR supposes for the students. All have agreed that it is a good resource to present and explain the curricular contents of the social sciences in an attractive, innovative, and motivating way at any educational level by highlighting the numerous alternatives that it contributes which favor interactive learning in teaching–learning processes and which they have experienced for themselves (Cózar et al. 2015).

It is positive to be innovative, to incorporate novelty into our classrooms but without losing sight of the fact that the mere incorporation of the novelty does not lead to the success of the educational process. It is necessary to take into account what kind of students we address and what are the specific objectives that we intend to achieve by introducing these virtual elements into our teaching so that they do not cease to be a means to an end and become the end. For this, it is convenient that technological innovations be introduced in the classroom together with an appropriate didactic and disciplinary approach. It is our responsibility as teachers to train our students in the pedagogical and disciplinary use of these emerging technologies so that they teach their students in equal conditions in their future teaching practice (Cózar et al. 2015; Sáez-López et al. 2019).

References

Ausubel DP, Novak JD, Hanesian H (1983) Psicología Educativa Un punto de vista cognitivo. Trillas, México

Azuma R (1997) A survey of augmented reality. Teleoperators Virtual Environ 6(4):355–385

Barroso J, Cabero J (2016) Evaluación de objetos de aprendizaje en realidad aumentada: estudio piloto en el grado de medicina. Enseñanza & Teaching 34(2):149–167

Cabero J, García F (coords) 2016 Realidad aumentada Tecnología para la formación. Síntesis, Madrid

Cabero J, Barroso J (2016) The educational possibilities of augmented reality. NAER New Approaches Educ Res 5(1):44–50

Cózar-Gutiérrez R, Moya M, Hernández J, Hernández J (2015) Tecnologías emergentes para la enseñanza de las Ciencias Sociales. Una experiencia con el uso de Realidad Aumentada en la formación inicial de maestros. Digital Education Review, 27, 138–153. https://www.revistes.ub.edu/index.php/der/article/view/11622/pdf

Cózar-Gutiérrez R, Sáez-López JM (2016) Realidad aumentada, proyectos en el aula de primaria: experiencias y casos en Ciencias Sociales. EDMETIC 6(1):165–180

Fombona J, Pascual MÁ (2016) La producción científica sobre Realidad Aumentada, un análisis de la situación educativa desde la perspectiva SCOPUS. EDMETIC 6(1):39–61

Fombona J, Pascual MA, Madeira MF (2012) Realidad aumentada, una evolución de las aplicaciones de los dispositivos móviles. Pixel-Bit Revista de Medios y Educación 41:197–210

Fundación Telefónica (2011) Realidad Aumentada: una nueva lente para ver el mundo. Fundación Telefónica-Ariel, Madrid

European parliament and council (2006) Key competences for lifelong learning–A

European framework. Off J Eur Union on 30 Dec 2006/L394. https://www.eur-lex.europa.eu/LexUriServ/site/en/oj/2006/l_394/l_39420061230en00100018.pdfd

Huang CSJ, Yang SJH, Chiang THC et al (2016) Effects of situated mobile learning approach on learning motivation and performance of EFL students. J Educ Technol Soc 19(1):263–276. bitly/2Q0oNDT

Johnson DW (2003) Social interdependence: interrelationships among theory, research, and practice. Am Psychol 58(11):934–945

Johnson G (2006) Synchronous and asynchronous text-based CMC in educational contexts: a review of recent research. TechTrends: Link Res Pract Improv Learn 50(4):46–53

Johnson L, Adams Becker S, Cummins M et al (2016) NMC Horizon Report: 2016 higher, education. Austin Texas, The New Media Consortium

Kamarainen AM, Metcalf S, Grotzer T et al (2013) EcoMOBILE: integrating augmented reality and probeware with environmental education field trips. Comput Educ 68:545–556. https://doi.org/10.1016/jcompedu201302018

Kerawalla L, Luckin R, Seljeflot S et al (2006) 'Making it real': Exploring the potential of augmented reality for teaching primary school science. Virtual Rity 10(3):16–174. https://doi.org/10.1007/s10055-006-0036-4

Klopfer E, Squire K (2008) Environmental detectives: the development of an augmented reality platform for environmental simulations. Educ Technol Res Dev, 56(2):203–228 https://doi.org/10.1007/s11423-007-9037-6

Klopfer E, Osterweil S, Salen K (2009) Moving learning games forward. Cambridge, MA, Educ Arcade. https://www.bit.ly/2Gxjr0L

Knaus T (2017) Pädagogik des digitale: phänomene, potentiale, perspektiven In Eder S, Mikat C, Tillmann A (eds), Software takes command. Kopaed, München, pp 40–68. https://www.bit.ly/2Gxjr0L

Ministerio de Educación y Cultura y Deporte, MECD (2014) Real Decreto 126/2014, de 28 de febrero, por el que se establece el currículo básico de la Educación Primaria. https://www.boe.es/boe/dias/2014/03/01/pdfs/BOE-A-2014-2222.pdf Mullen T 2012

Muñoz JM (2013) Realidad aumentada, realidad disruptiva en las aulas. Boletín SCOPEO, 82

Radu I (2014) Augmented reality in education: a meta-review and cross-media analysis. Pers Ubiquit Comput 18(6):1533–1543

Squire K, Klopfer E (2007) Augmented reality simulations on handheld computers. J Learn Sci 16(3):371–413. https://doi.org/10.1080/10508400701413435

Squire K, Giovanetto L, Devane B et al 2005 From users to designers: Building a self-organizing game-basedlearning environment. TechTrends 49(5):34–42. https://doi.org/10.1007/BF02763688

Sáez-López JM, Cózar R, Domínguez-Garrido MC 2018 Realidad aumentada en Educación Primaria: comprensión de elementos artísticos y aplicación didáctica en ciencias sociales. Digital Education Review 34:59–75. greavubedu/der/

Sáez-López JM, Ruiz-Gallardo JR 2013 Enseñanza de las ciencias, tecnología educativa y escuela rural: un estudio de casos. Revista electrónica de enseñanza de las ciencias, 12 (1): 45–61. https://www.reec.uvigo.es/volumenes/volumen12/reec_12_1_3_ex666.pdf

Sáez-López JM, Miller J, Vázquez-Cano E et al 2015 Exploring application, attitudes and integration of video games: minecraftedu in middle school. Educ Technol Soc 18(3):114–128.https://www.ifetsinfo/journals/18_3/9pdf

Sáez-López JM, Román-González M, Vázquez-Cano E 2016 Visual programming languages integrated across the curriculum in elementary school. A two-year case study using scratch in five schools. Comput Educ 97:129–141. https://doi.org/10.1016/jcompedu201603003

Sáez-López JM, Sevillano-García ML, Pascual-Sevillano MA 2019 Application of the ubiquitous game with augmented reality in primary education. Comunicar, preprint. https://doi.org/10.3916/C61-2019-06

Tekedere H, Göker H (2016) Examining the effectiveness of augmented reality applications in education: a meta-analysis. Int J Environ Sci Educ 11(16):9469–9481

Chapter 14
The Educational Use of the 'Harry Potter: Wizards Unite' Augmented Reality Application

Alberto Ruiz-Ariza, Sebastián López-Serrano, Sara Suárez-Manzano, and Emilio J. Martínez-López

Abstract After the great success of the augmented reality game Pokémon GO, the same company (Niantic, Inc) has recently launched a new game based on another media saga. This game is called 'Harry Potter: Wizards Unite', and it is a location-based augmented reality game inspired by J. K. Rowling's wizarding world and the Harry Potter franchise. Players are able to actively explore real-world surroundings to unravel a global mystery, cast spells and encounter fantastic beasts and iconic characters along the way. But how could 'Harry Potter: Wizards Unite' be applied in the educational system? In this chapter, we address the possible impact of the creation of augmented reality on those players within the educational framework, as well as some practical proposals for its adaptation and possibilities as a didactical tool.

14.1 Introduction

The impact of New Technologies on our society has led to the emergence of new forms of economic, social, political, and cultural organisation, resulting in new ways of working, communicating and learning. As a direct consequence of this development, we are faced with a new socio-educational paradigm organised around New Technologies. Educational systems have been affected by this transformation, since New Technologies have significant potential to create new educational experiences

A. Ruiz-Ariza (✉) · S. López-Serrano · S. Suárez-Manzano · E. J. Martínez-López
Faculty of Humanities and Educational Sciences, Group HUM-943: Physical Activity Applied to Education and Health, University of Jaen, Jaen, Spain
e-mail: arariza@ujaen.es

S. López-Serrano
e-mail: slserran@ujaen.es

S. Suárez-Manzano
e-mail: ssuarez@ujaen.es

E. J. Martínez-López
e-mail: emilioml@ujaen.es

© Springer Nature Switzerland AG 2020
V. Geroimenko (ed.), *Augmented Reality in Education*,
Springer Series on Cultural Computing,
https://doi.org/10.1007/978-3-030-42156-4_14

and opportunities that allow the development of more motivated and meaningful learning. The scientific literature indicates the importance of including novel teaching methodologies related to the current features of our social context in the educational system, which includes the use of New Technologies (Ruiz-Ariza et al. 2018). It has been shown that their advantages are more beneficial than those used in a more traditional methodology (Sánchez et al. 2014).

New Technologies are not in themselves a guarantee for effective, meaningful and contextualised learning. Incorrect implementation and use can actually be detrimental to learning or can attract more attention to the tool than to the desired didactic content. It is therefore essential to design these experiences to develop their full potential. Here, the role of the teacher becomes vital, since in their process of continual training, non-face-to-face training approaches and the use of New Technologies become increasingly important. In this process, the acquisition of social strategies is a key for the prevention and solving of conflicts related to bullying or cyberbullying. Besides, it could be used as a source of learning and personal enrichment. We must keep in mind the term of 'digital natives', that is, generations of students who have been born immersed in the digital language and who naturally inhabit the domain of smartphones, computers and video games (Prensky 2011). Some research, such as that conducted by Spikol and Eliasson (2010), indicates that younger people adapt quickly to these skills. Therefore, current students can take advantage of the options offered by New Technologies for the acquisition and development of critical knowledge, using these tools as a permanent source of entertainment and learning.

Within the emergence of these New Technologies, we must highlight mobile learning (m-learning), defined as 'learning across multiple contexts, through social and content interactions, using personal electronic devices, for example smartphone or tablet' (Crompton 2013). M-learning allows us to provide learning opportunities beyond the traditional methods used in classrooms, such as the ability to extend the learning space from a formal context (i.e. a classroom) to an informal context (i.e. social networks). That is, the educational place moves to a virtual environment focused on the student. These characteristics relate this work to more informal learning since at any time and place it may be necessary to resolve an issue that requires access to different sources of information, which generates new formative interactions between students in different scenarios beyond educational centres (Jeno et al. 2019).

If we focus more on educational aspects, the m-learning methodology affects the way of explaining concepts and exploring certain curricular content. In addition, we must highlight the motivational component, which can be one of the greatest attractions for students due to the inherent interest and enjoyment of the learning activity (Jeno et al. 2017) or the positive climate that it can generate in the classroom (Valverde et al. 2013). On the other hand, m-learning can have other additional benefits, such as increasing student mastery of learning tasks, facilitating faster learning and feedback by offering efficient ways to access information and providing greater opportunities to interact with the content of the class (Hashemi et al. 2011).

14.2   Augmented Reality: What Is It?

Within the multiple contexts generated by m-learning, special account must be taken augmented reality (AR). This technology enables the enhancement of human senses (vision, aural and tactile) with virtual information (invisible to the naked eye), superimposed on top of the real world by digital means (Azuma 1997). Martín-Gutiérrez et al. (2015) show that AR promotes collaborative and autonomous learning in education. According to Azuma et al. (2001) AR systems are characterised by three properties

(1)   Combining real and virtual objects in a real environment. The use of different display and tracking technologies might cause different degrees of physical immersion. For instance, head-mounted or spatial displays foster a higher degree of immersion than handheld displays, such as PDAs or smartphones (Carmigniani et al. 2010; Krevelen and Poelman 2010).

(2)   Aligning real and virtual objects to interact with each other. Digital information is superimposed on the real environment from the user's perspective. The user's point of view changes and they need to know where they are, where everything is located and how to get to particular objects or places, i.e. the navigation process. Although navigation is not the main objective of a user in a virtual or augmented environment, it has direct implications on the way users interact with a pervasive computing landscape (Burigat and Chittaro 2007; Kye and Kim 2008; Narzt et al. 2005), and also contributes to the feeling of immersion (Huang et al. 2010).

(3)   Running interactively, and in real time. Azuma's third AR property is directly related to real-time interactivity. Several authors emphasise the importance of this kind of interaction to foster cognitive tasks such as understanding, memory and imagination, among others (Dalgarno 2010; Neumann and Majoros 1998).

Within the AR categories, we highlight Azuma's second property, the only one that uses GPS or geolocation. Under this idea, some AR active games (ARG) are appearing. For example, Pokémon GO was released for smartphones in the summer of 2016, and became one of the greatest AR successes by implementing this type of geolocation in the search for game creatures in different parts of a city (Anderson et al. 2016; Clark and Clark 2016). The app makes use of a map of the physical space in which the user finds themselves, generated by GPS, and requiring physical exercise to explore and advance in the game (Clark and Clark 2016; Tateno et al. 2016). It could be said that the objective of ARG is to provide real-world objects with attributes that allow the user to interact with the objects, through displacement and physical exercise.

14.3   The Integral Benefits of Augmented Reality Active Games

Pioneering research has shown that AR could be an interesting way of increasing important educational variables, such as quality of writing (Wang 2017), mathematical abilities (Sommerauer and Müller 2014), or learning a foreign language (Hsu 2017). Regarding ARG, an educator's challenge is to use the physical immersion characteristic of this technology to foster student engagement in learning activities. In education, ARG is one of the technological advances with a higher level of impact, allowing the creation of content that can be shown to students, offering greater interactivity and the possibility of including new concepts, such as three-dimensionality. Through its use, we can perceive improvements in the teaching-learning process and in the acquisition and development of digital competence for both students and teachers (Badia et al. 2016).

One of the most famous ARG examples is Pokémon GO, which has been shown to have important benefits for health. For example, it can help to avoid sedentarism and make people more physically active (LeBlanc and Chaput 2017; Nigg et al. 2017), with a positive effect on fitness and cardiometabolic health (Krittanawong et al. 2017; Sharma and Vassiliou 2016) and decreasing levels of obesity (Smith 2016). Beyond physical benefits, Pokémon GO can also affect psycho-cognitive, social and family variables (De Oliveira-Roque 2016; Ruiz-Ariza et al. 2018; Serino et al. 2016). Some recent research has shown that Pokémon GO is useful in minimising the effects of social withdrawal in younger people (Kato et al. 2017; Tateno et al. 2016) or to prevent anxiety and depression (McCartney 2016). One study carried out in Spain showed that Pokémon GO can increase attention span, concentration and sociability in adolescents playing this game over a period of 8 weeks (Ruiz-Ariza et al. 2018). The authors analysed this result independently of important confounders such as age, sex or educational level of mothers. Ruiz-Ariza et al. (2018) also found that participants play for around 40 min per day, usually with other colleagues. They concluded that Pokémon GO is a novel and motivational way of encouraging daily physical activity and affecting socio-cognitive variables.

14.4   The Appearance of the Augmented Reality Game 'Harry Potter: Wizards Unite'

With the same dynamic of Pokémon GO, the ARG 'Harry Potter: Wizards Unite' was released in June 2019. This game is immersed in the magical world created by the writer J. K. Rowling, and combines the history and characters of Harry Potter and the 'Fantastic Beasts' movies. The premise of this game, developed by the Niantic company, is similar to Pokémon GO. That is, users must move through the physical space in search of different elements or events related to the magical world (magical objects, characters from books, fantastic animals), which allow them to complete different missions and go up a level as a wizard or witch. Each time the player finds one object, they must perform a spell to capture that object. For example, if they find a captured animal, they must cast a spell in order to release it.

During the Harry Potter ARG, players must prepare potions, work with other wizards and witches and cast spells to return an 'incontratus' (magical creatures or artefacts) to the magical world, when they appear in the game in locations real world, such as parks, banks, buildings, university, libraries, monuments, zoos and museums. Players can choose between one of the following professions: auror, magizoologist or teacher, who all have different skills. In addition, they must cooperate with other players in magical challenges, real-time multiplayer fighting and finding the rarest incontratus. When returning an incontratus, a player receives unique rewards that will be seen in the game registry. When spells are cast, magical energy is consumed and players must visit taverns regularly, which are located in Muggle locations distributed throughout the planet, to collect food and drink that restore this energy. Magical challenges also take place in the fortresses including real-time multiplayer battles against Death Eaters or werewolves (Fig. 14.1).

Fig. 14.1 'Harry Potter: Wizard Unite' development. *Source* https://www.imore.com/harry-potter-wizards-unite-beginners-guide

14.5 Practical Applications of Augmented Reality in Education

With the aim of facilitating the practical application of ARG in an educational context, we show several examples with didactical options. As on example, this section is targeted to the third cycle of Primary Education (students are aged 10–12 years). We have chosen this age range because it is the time when young people have easy access to their own mobile devices, but it is not assumed that they use them appropriately and correctly. This proposal is primarily located in the subject area of Physical Education, because another of the current concerns of society is the continuous increase of physical inactivity in young people; from an early age they invest the time in sedentary activities, such as playing sedentary video games.

The proposal is a gamified project on the Harry Potter theme (Fig. 14.2). All teachers who teach in the group will collaborate and work in coordination. The project will take place at the beginning of the academic year, coinciding with the first teaching unit of each subject. For this project, teachers in each area will adapt

Fig. 14.2 The presentation and initiation poster of the project

and include their activities in the fantasy context created in the classroom. Among all the elements and mechanics of gamification, we will focus on the main ones.

We will start with thematisation, making the classroom a 'fantastic' place, where magic appears. From the subject area of plastic arts, the decoration of the classroom and door will be designed, as well as the notebooks that will be used, identification cards, and other tasks associated with the subject. From the language and literature subject area, 'enigmas of magic' or 'hidden messages' will be created; all the participants will have a 'magician's notebook', keep it up to date and write down all the activities proposed by the teacher. From the subject area of mathematics or 'alchemy', students must write down all the 'formulae to create magic potions', and the teachers will theme their classes to this subject.

In summary, all subject areas will be adapted to the ARG theme and each teacher will collaborate in adapting their activities and motivating the students. Likewise, everybody will collaborate in the scoring and evaluation of the activities carried out by the 'magician apprentices'. Each student will have a personal card and there will be a public ranking in a secure area, called the 'magic meter' (Fig. 14.3).

There will be various ways to acquire points and we propose several activities:

- Levels reached in the 'Harry Potter: Wizards Unite' application, creating weekly challenges according to number of steps, kilometres walked and other active challenges.
- Excellent grades obtained in the tasks of magician apprentices.
- Reflection of positive values: friendship, companionship, empathy, punctuality, fair play, material collection.

Likewise, it is possible to assign scores that cancel out the positive ones, due to disruptive behaviour.

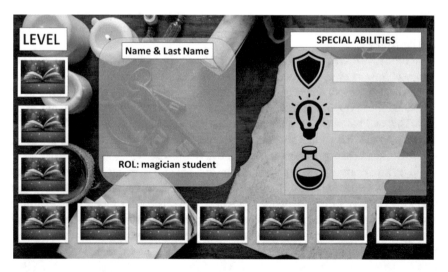

Fig. 14.3 The magic meter

We propose that these points be used as instruments to make potions, ingredients, magic texts, or other tools that can be used during training as magicians. To facilitate their identification, the corresponding score-cards, potions and other elements that can be obtained will be created.

Like any gamification dynamic, we present a general objective that will guide our entire story to the students. In this case, due to the versatility of the sports hall, we will start the gamification in this place. A video will be shown to the group, which will explain that all the students present have been selected to study in the 'school of magicians', but this school is in danger, because the Dementors want to take over their power, with the aim that evil magic rules the Earth. The Dementors tell the students that they have captured the 'Director of the school of magic', to steal his magic and knowledge to become more powerful and to dominate the world. Therefore, the goal of our students will be to find the Director and release him. But, at the same time, they must prevent the Dementors from entering the school, because they also want to steal the magic books from the library.

The teaching unit will last 4 weeks. Students will have the option of getting up to level three of magician apprentice. Each level will be represented with a broom. When students have three brooms, they will be considered magicians. To get each level they must get at least 20 magic points at the end of the week. All teachers can give up to two magic points every day. Each Monday will begin with the counter to level up to zero. From Monday to Friday they will have a challenge in which the application will be used (number of steps, steps climbed, stairs lowered, time at a certain intensity of running, running time at moderate intensity and many more). These challenges will reach students every morning through a QR code that will be hidden in the recreation area. In this way the students are forced not to remain seated during that time of rest, but to be continuously moving around the centre talking to each other and cooperating to find it. From the second week, the challenges must be carried out with two or more partners. This will create links, and all work towards the same goal. The mobile application that will be used to unveil daily challenges will be HPreveal.

In the second week there will be a gymkhana. In this activity, there will be as many stations as areas of knowledge. Each of these work stations will be planned by the teachers responsible for teaching the area of knowledge. All activities will be motivated by an important fact: an owl has arrived with a map attached to one of its legs. This owl belongs to the Director of the school of magicians and The Director has to send the owl so that the magician apprentices know how to get to the place where he is held as a prisoner and they can help him escape.

To facilitate circulation, students will be divided into as many groups as workstations and will go from one to the text, with a maximum time allowed at each. The teachers in charge of each workstation will be responsible for monitoring that time and should allow students to finish their task. To do this, the teachers can give out clues. In these activities the students will review the content they have seen in class during the previous sessions. In addition, in some of these activities, New Technologies may be used. At the end of this activity participants will receive a letter stating that the Director has been transferred to another place, but he will soon send them

Fig. 14.4 Educational escape room

the necessary information so they can rescue him; as motivation, each student will receive a badge 'for value contributed and teamwork'.

The last day of the project will be the day of graduation to magicians; it will be a special day, because an 'escape room' will be prepared (Fig. 14.4). Following the thread of the narrative, at this moment in the story, the students have already managed to reach the fortress in which the Dementors have imprisoned the Director but now the problem he faces is that they have all been trapped and must escape. This test will consist of different phases. In a first phase, a new video will be displayed in which the dynamics, the rules and some tricks to the activity will be explained, so that the students can find clues and know how to use them.

The place where this activity takes place will be set in a fortress, there will be clues that allude to the history that they have been living throughout the gamification process and in each of the stages of the escape room they must use the content, competences and skills acquired during the previous classes.

It is very important that there are enough tracks and padlocks so that all students can work at the same time. In the case of having few resources or being a very large class, an alternative option could be chosen. Instead of making one escape room, two 'break outs' could be planned. The main characteristics of the escape room versus the break outs are

- Activity in a single group, compared to activity divided into at least two groups working at the same time.
- Only one group of students works and in the case of having to divide the students into different groups it would have to be done in shifts, once all the tracks and elements have been relocated in their corresponding place, meaning there is the

possibility of two or more groups working at the same time and even in the same place.

- In the escape room there would only be one test set, however, in the other activity there would be different tests set for each group. A different colour ink or folio or a brand can differentiate between the tests and tracks. As this gamification is inspired by the world of Harry Potter, the names of the different school houses could be used.

In both alternatives all digital locks will be used through AR. Only the last lock will be physical to be able to place more reality in the situation. Some of the clues will be QR codes that the students will have to scan with their smartphones and will help them visualise 3D images with AR glasses or using a prism that they themselves must manufacture. This activity can include as many instruments as teachers consider appropriate. It is very important to control the time, so that it does not cause discomfort among the students, but it is not too fast. At the end of this activity, a graduation ceremony will be held in which each student will be awarded a new badge and will be given a 'magician diploma'.

Attached to the whole project will be the 'books of the travelling magician'; two books that students will take home every day, in which they will write or draw something about their experience as a magician's apprentice. Two will be provided so that it is possible for each student to take home free at least once.

We should not forget that the limits of gamification and the ability to motivate students is only the limits of imagination and work capacity that teachers have in creating a learning environment adapted to students' curiosity and abilities. The main objective, in our case, is to increase the level of physical activity, manage responsible and moderate use of New Technologies, while teaching the students how useful they can be if used with the correct objective.

14.6 Limitations and Strengths of This Proposal

Regarding the limitations of this proposal, we would recognise that the support and specific training of a teacher involved is highly important. Moreover, it might be that some educational centres cannot have New Technologies for economic reasons. An alternative could be that children without smartphones share with other classmates or that teachers design group activities with one or two school phones, which would at least increase knowledge of this technology.

On the other hand, the use of an ARG, such as Harry Potter, across different subjects as Physical Education, could be a powerful instrument to increase physical activity, active homework and motivation towards education. Some strategies such as gymkhanas with AR or the creation of escape rooms or break outs, are current active methodologies very attractive for students.

14.7   Conclusion

After the great success of the ARG Pokémon GO, 'Harry Potter: Wizards Unite' has recently appeared as a new active game for smartphones. Players can cast spells, encounter fantastic beasts and iconic characters in this AR world. This chapter has addressed the impact of the Harry Potter ARG in an educational context, as well as a practical proposal for its adaptation and options as a teaching tool. The use of AR and the modalities of ARG are a great attraction for students and teachers. Its incorporation into the educational system is a significant challenge, because it gives the opportunity to motivate the didactic process during class and to participate in some subjects as Physical Education, for example with physically active homework.

References

Anderson N, Steele J, O'Neill LA, Harden LA (2016) Pokémon go: Mobile app user guides. Br J Sports Med *2016e096762*. http://doi.org/10.1136/bjsports-2016–096762

Azuma RT (1997) A survey of augmented reality. Presence: Teleop Virt Envir 6(4):355–385. https://doi.org/10.1162/pres.1997.6.4.355

Azuma RT (2001) A survey of augmented reality. Presence: Teleop Vir 6(4):355–385

Badia A, Chumpitaz-Campos L, Vargas-D'Uniam J, Suárez-Díaz G (2016) The perception of the usefulness of technology conforms its use to teach and learn. Electr of educ res 18(3):95–105

Burigat S, Chittaro L (2007) Navigation in 3D virtual environments: effects of user experience and location-pointing navigation aids. Int J Hum Comput Stud 65(11):945–958. https://doi.org/10.1016/j.ijhcs.2007.07.003

Carmigniani J, Furht B, Anisetti M et al (2010) Augmented reality technologies, systems and applications. Multimed Tools Appl 51(1):341–377. https://doi.org/10.1007/s11042-010-0660-6

Clark AM, Clark MT (2016) Pokémon GO and research: qualitative, mixed methods research, and the supercomplexity of interventions. Int J Qual Methods 15(1):1609406916667765. https://doi.org/10.1177/1609406916667765

Crompton H (2013) A historical overview of m-learning: toward learner-centered education. In: Berge ZL, Muilenburg LY (eds) Handbook of mobile learning. Routledge, New York, pp 3–14

Dalgarno B, Lee MJ (2010) What are the learning affordances of 3-D virtual environments? Br J Educ Technol 41(1):10–32. https://doi.org/10.1111/j.1467-8535.2009.01038.x

De Oliveira-Roque F (2016) Field studies: could Pokémon GO boost birding? Nature 537(7618):34. https://doi.org/10.1038/537034e

Hashemi M, Azizinezhad M, Najafi V, Nesari AJ (2011) What is mobile learning? Challenges and capabilities. Procedia Soc Behavior Sci 30:2477–2481. https://doi.org/10.1016/j.sbspro.2011.10.483

Hsu T-C (2017) Learning English with augmented reality: Do learning styles matter? Comp Educ 106:137e149. https://doi.org/10.1016/j.compedu.2016.12.007

Huang H-M, Rauch U, Liaw S-S (2010) Investigating learners' attitudes toward virtual reality learning environments: based on a constructivist approach. Comp Educ 55(3):1171–1182. https://doi.org/10.1016/j.compedu.2010.05.014

Jeno LM, Grytnes J-A, Vandvik V (2017) The effect of a mobile-application tool on biology students' motivation and achievement in species identification: a self-determination theory perspective. Comp Educ 107:1–12. https://doi.org/10.1016/j.compedu.2016.12.011

Jeno LM, Adachi PJ, Grytnes JA, Vandvik V, Deci EL (2019) The effects of m-learning on motivation, achievement and well-being: A self-determination theory approach. Br J Educ Technol 50(2):669–683. https://doi.org/10.1111/bjet.12657

Kato TA, Teo AR, Tateno M, Watabe M, Kubo H, Kanba S (2017) Can Pokémon GO rescue shut-ins (hikikomori) from their isolated world?. Psychiat clin neuros 71(1):75–76. https://doi.org/10.1111/pcn.12481

Krevelen DWFV, Poelman R (2010) A survey of augmented reality technologies, applications and limitations. Int J Virtual Real 9(2):1–20

Krittanawong C, Aydar M, Kitai T (2017) Pokémon GO: Digital health interventions to reduce cardiovascular risk. Cardiol Young 1e2. https://doi.org/10.1017/S1047951117000749

Kye B, Kim Y (2008) Investigation of the relationships between media characteristics, presence, flow, and learning effects in augmented reality based learning augmented reality. Inter J 2(1):4–14

LeBlanc AG, Chaput JP (2017) Pokémon GO: A game changer for the physical inactivity crisis? Prev Med 101:235–237. https://doi.org/10.1016/j.ypmed.2016.11.012

Martín-Gutiérrez J, Fabiani P, Benesova W, Meneses MD, Mora CE (2015) Augmented reality to promote collaborative and autonomous learning in higher education. Comput Human Behav 51:752–761. https://doi.org/10.1016/j.chb.2014.11.093

Narzt W, Pomberger G, Ferscha A, Kolb D, Müller R, Wieghardt J et al (2005) Augmented reality navigation systems. Univ Access Infor Soc 4(3):177–187. https://doi.org/10.1007/s10209-005-0017-5

Neumann U, Majoros A (1998) Cognitive, performance, and systems issues for augmented reality applications in manufacturing and maintenance. In: Proceedings IEEE 1998 virtual reality annual international symposium. Cat No98CB36180. IEEE Comput. Soc. Atlanta, GA, USA, 1998, pp. 4–11

Nigg CR, Mateo DJ, An J (2017) Pokémon GO may increase physical activity and decrease sedentary behaviors. Am J Public Health 107(1):37–38. https://doi.org/10.2105/AJPH.2016.303532

McCartney M (2016) Margaret McCartney: Game on for Pokémon GO. BMJ 354. https://doi.org/10.1136/bmj.i4306

Prensky M (2011) Enseñar a nativos digitales. SM, Madrid

Ruiz-Ariza A, Casuso RA, Suarez-Manzano S, Martínez-López EJ (2018) Effect of augmented reality game Pokémon GO on cognitive performance and emotional intelligence in adolescent young. Comp Educ. 116:49–63. https://doi.org/10.1016/j.compedu.2017.09.002

Sánchez J, Ruiz J, Sánchez E (2014) Las clases invertidas: beneficios y estrategias para su puesta en práctica en la educación superior

Serino M, Cordrey K, McLaughlin L, Milanaik RL (2016) Pokémon GO and augmented virtual reality games: A cautionary commentary for parents and pediatricians. Curr Opin Pediatr 28(5):673e677. https://doi.org/10.1097/MOP.0000000000000409

Sharma P, Vassiliou V (2016) Pokémon GO: Cardiovascular benefit or injury risk? Oxf Med Case Reports (10):omw085. https://doi.org/10.1093/omcr/omw085

Smith DR (2016) A walk in the park: Is Pokemon Go foreshadowing the future of biodiversity research and scientific outreach? EMBO Rep 17(11):1506e1509

Sommerauer P, Müller O (2014) Augmented reality in informal learning environments: A field experiment in a mathematics exhibition. Comp Educ 79:59e68

Spikol D, Eliasson J (2010) Lessons from designing geometry learning activities that combine mobile and 3D tools. In: 2010 6th IEEE International Conference on Wireless, Mobile, and Ubiquitous Technologies in Education, IEEE, Kaohsiung, 2010, pp. 137–141

Tateno M, Skokauskas N, Kato TA, Teo AR, Guerrero APS (2016) New game software (Pokémon GO) may help youth with severe social withdrawal, hikikomori. Psychiatry Res 246:848e849. https://doi.org/10.1016/j.psychres.2016.10.038

Valverde J, Fernández MR, Revuelta FI (2013) El bienestar subjetivo ante las buenas prácticas educativas con TIC: su influencia en profesorado innovador. https://doi.org/10.5944/educxx1.16.1.726

Wang Y-H (2017) Exploring the effectiveness of integrating augmented reality-based materials to support writing activities. Comp Educ 113:162e176. https://doi.org/10.1016/j.compedu.2017.04.013

Chapter 15
Making Inside the Augment: Augmented Reality and Art/Design Education

Patrick Lichty

Abstract This chapter deals with the developing genre of Augmented Reality (AR) design from architecture to fine arts. Although a great deal of literature exists in this area within the architectural field, this chapter will seek to delve into more holistic approaches to the use of AR in art and design. This will engage the HCI-based issues of handheld device compared to headset (HoloLens, Magic Leap) technologies in terms of Lichty's theory of immersive gesture. Differences between these platforms, as well as AR's distinctions from other immersive media offer insights into the development of pedagogical models in the creative disciplines. Of particular interest is the use of AR in Design Education, allowing future possibilities for hybrid models of creative expression, like augmented overlays on physical models/artworks, to the use of AR as a tool in material work. This chapter aims to look at the current literature, draw inferences through analyzing case studies how educational models are being constructed through the theory of gesture and consider models for the use of these technologies in improving the creative disciplines.

15.1 Introduction

Pedagogy in art, design, and architecture which implements AR has become a topic of interest as it is also implemented in areas of engineering, medicine and psychology. While the use of AR in disciplines such as architecture is well documented, the use of this medium in areas such as engineering still develops, its use in areas of design and visual arts education are still in earlier stages. Secondly, the heterogenous nature of AR's forms, such as delivery via headset, handset or across Mixed Reality, leads to a multitude of approaches to AR's applications in Design Education. In considering approaches to these genres using forms of augmentation, this discussion will look at the representative practices and aesthetics of augmentation, examine works and case studies as illustrations of pedagogical and didactic models. Lastly, speculative

P. Lichty (✉)
College of Arts and Creative Enterprises, Zayed University, Dubai, United Arab Emirates
e-mail: patrick.lichty@zu.ac.ae

© Springer Nature Switzerland AG 2020
V. Geroimenko (ed.), *Augmented Reality in Education*,
Springer Series on Cultural Computing,
https://doi.org/10.1007/978-3-030-42156-4_15

261

approaches to art and design learning strategies will be considered. This is for two reasons; that the writer's disciplines are more aligned to art and design, and that fields like architectural education is far more well explored in AR. While this discussion will touch on disciplines like landscape architecture, the emphasis will be far more on arts and design. And lastly, in that the use of AR in arts education in the area of the humanities (i.e. history), is also well travelled, a focus on the plastic/design practices will be the primary focus. Our entry point into this exploration will be an expansion on this author's ideas on the representational practices of AR, gestural aesthetics, and how these inform pedagogical strategies in AR and Immersive Media.

15.2 The Translation of Art and Design into Augmented Environments

In the chapter *The Translation of Art in Virtual Worlds* (Lichty 2014a, b), four gestures of the creation of art and now arguably design in virtual worlds were described. In order to expand this thought on creativity in AR, we will revisit the idea of engagement with the subject in immersive environments (of which AR is one). It is important to distinguish here between virtual worlds and virtual reality, in that virtual reality immerses the field of view, and in the case of environments like the CAVE, the entire body within the virtual environment. Conversely, virtual worlds, while in the cases of environments like Second Life, High Fidelity or Sansar, can be experienced as VR, also have levels of immersion that vary in that they can also be experienced through the conventional computer screen. Conversely, AR, especially in the case of device-oriented media, enforces a definite frame for experience, and virtual environments in the case of headset-based work integrates media fully into the human environment, and this will be a necessary distinction in considering the creative gesture in augmented space.

In *Translation,* four modes of communication in virtual worlds were defined, and this frames discourse on the representational quality of AR. One was the evergent, relating to virtually native content. The second is, for example, installations that look into virtual worlds at full scale, like *The Gate, or Hole in Space, Reloaded* (Antoine et al. 2007) which opened a full-sized projective gateway into the virtual world. And lastly there are the gestures that are consistent only with their root worlds, and not seeking to bridge, such as virtual art in virtual galleries, or artists who are not engaged tightly with virtual environments making images for contemporary galleries, such as Eva and Franco Mattes and their *Thirteen Most Beautiful Avatars* (Eva and Franco Mattes 2007) or *Kristine Shoemaker's Gracie Kendal Project* (Shoemaker 2008) Each of these have a specific intention, or experiential vector, from environment to environment (or not) and this imposes very specific formal properties on that experience (Fig. 15.1). In the case of AR, this experience is complicated by the imposition of the physical world onto the virtual, or the other way around. This, much like art and design in virtual worlds, imposes certain formal qualities on the

Fig. 15.1 Diagram of experiential vectors between physical and virtual worlds

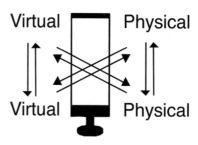

media experience. One example that elaborates on the cross-modal gesture between virtuality and the physical is Perry Hoberman's (1998) work, *Systems Maintenance.*

Perry Hoberman's (1998) installation, *Systems Maintenance* (Hoberman 1998) is an early AR-like work that illustrates the formal qualities of augmentation. To quote the description of the work, "An ensemble of life-sized furniture occupies a large circular platform on the floor, a virtual room is displayed on a computer monitor, and a 1/8 size physical scale model of the room is presented on a small pedestal (Fig. 15.2). Each version is imaged by a camera (either video or virtual), and the three resulting images are combined into a single large-scale video projection. By moving the furniture and camera viewpoints for each of the three rooms, visitors can match or mismatch the components of each of the rooms as they appear in the projected image. There is an implicit goal: to line up the three versions of each piece of furniture, to

Fig. 15.2 *Systems Maintenance* (Hoberman 1998)

bring them into harmony." (Brouwer et al. 1998) While Hoberman's novel model of augmentation in *Systems Maintenance* plays with the larger environment, an imposed subject, and the attempt to resolve the two.

15.3   Headset Versus Handheld Methods in AR (Architecture, Industrial Design, Art)

One of the key aspects of AR as educational tool or learning environment is its phys-icality, and this is expressed in different modalities. As stated by Bacca et al. (2014) Technology Enhanced learning (TEL) embraced a number of ways of interaction, such as mobile device-based learning (m-learning), ubiquitous learning (u-learning), of which Augmented Reality is a subset. Currently, (ca. 2020) the primary ways of experiencing AR are through headsets like the Meta, HoloLens (1, 2), Magic Leap, and mobile devices, although many other applications exist that use webcams, cam-eras and so on (like Hoberman, Berry, et al.). The location of the display (head/hand) and the method of gestural capture for interaction are key elements to the experience and haptics of the given application.

As with the writings in *The Translation of Art in Virtual Worlds* (Lichty 2014a, b), and *The Aesthetics of Liminality* (Lichty 2014a, b), crucial elements in the experience of immersive media constitute the vector of experience between the interactor and the media (*Translation*), and how the overlay (augment) is placed and experienced (*Liminality*). In the case of the experiential vector, for the case of VR this is relatively simple; whether the intended semiotics between the media and the interactor or audience is in the same space (physical/virtual) or crossing from one to the other. In the case of AR, XR, MR, and so on, the notion is that the interactor has a form of virtual media overlaid onto the physical environment in a synchronized fashion. The difference between development and deployment of mobile (handset) and ubiquitous media (headset) is linked to the situation of the camera (hand or head-mount) and the gestural nature of the interaction. The notion of experiencing the augment through a window or through the line of sight is essential for the experience of augments at scale. This is the difference between throwing a ball at a Pokémon and walking through a full-scale Sketchup moquette. In addition, the genres of design education relating to software design, use of AR as creative space, and its use as educational tool require investigation. These are described as the modalities of augmented/ubiquitous education (didactic, developmental, and demonstrative).

The second component of the augmented experience is not only the delivery of the image, but the method of interaction, with different models for headsets and handsets. For headsets like the HoloLens and Meta, gaze and finger tracking offer surprisingly nimble and intuitive interfaces that are learned rapidly through pinches, drags, and points. In terms of the Magic Leap, the device in part uses an Oculus Go-style puck that limits the forms of interaction to "air-mouse" and slider disc operations, which at best, encumbers the pointing hand. In the case of the handset not only is the hand encumbered with the phone/pad, the other hand now becomes the interacting one, more often than not. The point to this discussion is that as media moves toward ubiquity in its delivery, the handset versus headset have their ergonomic limitations that shape the media experience they provide. This has to do with the aesthetics of the gesture in the augmented environment.

15.4 Aesthetics of the Gesture

While conventional definitions of the aesthetic relate to the notion of beauty, in the context of interaction design, perhaps redefining this in a context of efficiency or elegance in creating with gesture or creating one of interaction. The creative gesture in AR, or any computational environment or that matter, will depend on two factors— ubiquity of the environment, and the invisibility of the interface (Stephenson 2018). The first relates to the invisibility of the environment, as computation moves toward ubiquity with devices like the HoloLens 2, and the invisibility of the interface, with Apple's iOS having changed the interface from a device to a set of processes and gestures. This is also evident with the HoloLens, but unless the device serves a clear metaphorical or haptic purpose (other than the airmouse/puck, the ipencil is a good example) the device can be either a contrivance or an encumbrance. Of course, this stance privileges the headset over the handset, and the universality and form factor of these platforms is still in developmental stages. With this in mind, there is a full understanding that as of 2020, the pad/handset is still the main platform for AR. In the following studies, a series of projects are explored for all their aspects; teaching AR design (developmental), AR-based design (didactic), and AR-based educational software (demonstrative), the modes of which will be termed as such.

15.5 Developmental, Didactic, and Demonstrative AR in Design Education

As with any medium, Augmented Reality reveals itself as having different modalities as an educational channel. Among these modalities, these are defined by the author as the developmental (teaching AR design), didactic (AR as creative/educational tool), and demonstrative (illustrative, which one will distinguish from the didactic). The use of each of these has a different communicative quality that assist in the education of design principles. These modes are similar to saying "Show me", "Give me a sandbox where one can test these ideas". And "Tell me". While AR is powerful in its ability to show, explain, and act as tool, a distinction shows useful differences in usage that can allow for the creation of novel applications. In the following studies, these distinctions will be made and contextualized as to how they can be used in the (extended) classroom. For added clarification, when the "extended" classroom is implied, this includes a broad range of educational applications, from the institutional to public to informal/implicit audiences.

15.6   Developmental Methodologies: Maya3D and HoloLens

One key application for the use of AR in the design industry is the integration of AR headset and gesture-based spatial computing into design tools. In the mid-2010s Autodesk integrated support for the HoloLens into modeling and design software like Maya 3D and Fusion 360 (O'Connor 2015). A video from the Augmented World Expo 2016 illustrated real-world integration using the Maya model of a motorcycle prototype not only as a desktop model, but also as a full-scale overlay on the motorcycle being redesigned (Fig. 15.3). As the speaker demonstrated the placement of handlebars in differing configurations, the prototype also showed notes from designers sharing the model from other studios also working on the design.

From an educational perspective, not only could the student prototype be marked for critique, but the Mixed Reality overlay methodology is extremely useful for team-based design projects. Furthermore, the annotation functions are essential for communication, everywhere from student notes, team communications during asynchronous or multiple location sessions, and for educator feedback. The full-scale Mixed Reality overlay functions are also essential for final prototyping. The full-scale aspect of AR in the educational realm is also essential in the areas of Architecture and Interior Design.

Architecture and Interior Design are early applications for AR-based education as one of the first architectural visualization plugins for the HoloLens 1 is a streaming app for Google for the 3D architectural visualization program, Sketchup. The demonstrations by Sketchup for HoloLens app programmer Trimble Systems (Tyrsina 2016), illustrate one of the most important abilities of Immersive technology—the ability to manipulate scale. The straightforward notion of being able to examine an architectural model is not so innovative, but when the model is pinched and scaled up to human scale, the potential becomes clear (Fig. 15.4). For example, in our Interior Design program at Zayed University, the use value of being able to

Fig. 15.3 Microsoft HoloLens and AutoDesk/Maya demo (Autodesk 2015)

Fig. 15.4 SketchUp visualization for HoloLens (Trimble Systems 2015)

explore Sketchup mockups of designs places the student in a 1:1 situation, which is so far from the "model on table" scenario. In a video demonstrating the HoloLens to the Royal Institute of British Architects (Trimble 2015) the gestural move from table scale to human scale is implied by the portrayed wonder of the users. Although the actual scenarios being seen by the architects in the short film, there is a scene implying seeing a model on a table and then another with one standing, making pinching gestures (one of the standard HoloLens gestures) and smiling as if they are standing within the architectural model itself. Whether this is the case or not, the plausibility of that representation, in context with the Trimble video, reflects the wonder of AR's depiction of human-scale geometry as a compelling tool for exploring student projects.

15.7   Demonstrative Explorations: Kerr and Lawson's *Master of Time*

As with many AR-based educational projects, projects develop their own developmental pedagogy as well as the delivered on if the product is one of didactic or demonstrative pedagogy. In Kerr and Lawson's reflection of their project *Master of Time* (Kerr and Lawson 2019) which "was created to educate first year students and non-designers on the foundational principles of landscape architecture." It uses a form of AR using the *Story City* locative storytelling platform in six sites throughout the Brisbane City Botanic Gardens, because of the location near Kerr and Lawson's Queensland University of Technology (QUT). One of the discoveries that the team found is that the bibliography for AR in Landscape Architectural Education in relation to AR as of 2019 is not as deep as for other disciplines and the field of AR development in general is a relatively new field in tertiary education, according to Kerr and Lawson. For this reason, *Master of Time* created innovations in methodology and form with this app.

A challenge in the creation of *Master of Time* related to debates regarding the didactic nature of educational narratives in software design. Kerr and Lawson outline this in a discussion of two apps for Landscape Architectural education, the *Garden Guide* at the Chicago Botanical Gardens (GardenGuide 2019), and the "fairy hunting" app for the Melbourne Botanic Gardens (GardenDrum 2014). The Chicago app used GPS tracking to deliver a pragmatic informational experience, including a plant finder that has a database of over two million species, as well as a robust set of self-guided educational materials. Conversely, the Melbourne app features the co-authored "Disney Fairies Trail" that leads the audience through the gardens as they hunt for the fairies. This story-centric approach has been criticized for stressing experience over content (Partland 2014), despite psychological studies linking narrative memory to emotional states (Kensinger 2009). In attempt to balance the merits of both approaches, Kerr and Lawson attempt with *Master of Time* "to seamlessly combine a story-driven, fiction-based narrative experience with a more traditional fact-based and walking guide-based approach".

To complement the interdisciplinary, inter-genre approach, the QUT team developed *Master of Time* using new approaches for the University. In response to the multiple disciplines needed to produce the app, representatives from interactive, communication, and interior design teamed with the Landscape Architecture faculty in creating the app. This coalition also developed a unique co-design approach that split teams into parallel production streams, streamlining workflow and increasing efficiency with limited resources. In addition, alumnus-founded design firm assisted with project management, expanding the engagement from faculty and first-year students to graduates. Such an approach leads to community pipelines for potential workforce expansion and institutional growth.

Master of Time also used novel production approaches which also made effective use of the creative and technical resources at hand. Instead of using a code-heavy app environment like Unity, *Master of Time* utilized *Storycity*, an open platform that allows for the creation of GPS-driven "choose your own adventure" stories (Story City 2019). While not an AR experience in the modality of *Pokémon Go*, it does allow for a landscape-driven narrative using GPS to drive content delivery. When the interactor is at the site on QUT where *Master of Time* begins, they are presented with a text and video narrative by a mysterious guide that takes them through the story, consisting of six sites. Each of these like the lily ponds or banyan trees offers a story revealing a different aspect of the Gardens, like the cultural or ecological components of the area (Fig. 15.5). In so doing, the QUT team felt that they achieved their goals of engaging with narrative, creating an impact on learning, connecting with the landscape through visualizations in an easy and intuitive fashion. Although

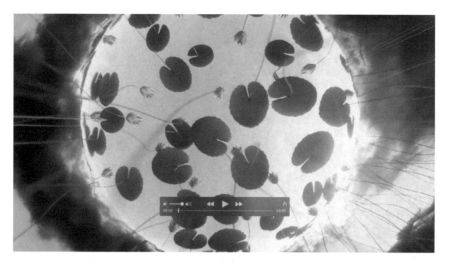

Fig. 15.5 *Master of Time* (Kerr and Lawson 2019)

a highly disparate scenario from the next example, *Master of Time* is an influence on our current mars Habitat project at Zayed University.

15.8 Demonstrative/Developmental Counterpoint: Mars Habitat Project (Zayed/AUS)

As part of the celebrations leading up to the Dubai Expo 2020 and the Golden Jubilee of the UAE, Interior Designer Camilo Cerro of the American University of Sharjah along with the author are creating a student-partnered Mars habitat simulation in a 4 m Sublime Immersive portal. Patterned from the educational initiatives from the UAE Space Agency's Sirius Mars Habitat project, (Nasir 2019) the Mars Geosphere Initiative introduces students to space science, gaming engines, speculative design that mixes popular genres of science fiction design (Minority Report, Star Trek, 2001 A Space Odyssey) with hard science (Cerro and Lichty 2019). As of this writing, a simulation of areas near the Hellas Basin from NASA data has been built, lit and is ready for the initial designs by Cerro and Lichty to be implemented by the team. This is the developmental part of the pedagogy.

The demonstrative education through the project is implemented after full implementation of the environment. The notion is that due to the building limitations put upon a Mars mission by cosmic radiation from Mars' weak magnetic field, habitat builds will be in underground spaces such as lava tubes (David 2019). From a simulations perspective, the space will be created level by level, optimizing simulation engine performance and simplifying interaction, developing in VR, then expanding into AR (Fig. 15.6). The environment will be constructed using tightly

Fig. 15.6 Mars geosphere initiative, prototype landscape (Cerro and Lichty 2019–)

proscribed scripting and player guidance using lines of sight and chokepoint guidance. From this, each of the visitors would be sure to engage all of the instructional stations and demand interaction to obtain information about the project, much like the Kerr/Lawson project. The design program of building the sites along with creating media for public education (educational design) is an exciting prospect for institutional/public partnerships. Another application for AR in education at the tertiary level is the implementation of installation-based art/design, such as sculpture.

15.9 Arabian Case Studies: Pieces in the UAE

The extension of Zayed University alumnus AlAnood Obaidly's Sharjah Art Foundation March Project sculptures for Dubai's 2017 ECHO Media Festival (*Reconstructing Sculpture*) is not necessarily a student project, but one that could have been one under different contexts. Abu Dhabi artist Obaidly was first recognized for small found object assemblages that were colorful, geometric, and diminutive (often under 30 cm in height). When the Sharjah Art Foundation commissioned her in late 2017 to create monumental versions of the sculptures, two nearly 30 cm sculptures were refabricated at nearly 350 cm. These sculptures remained on display for the duration of the exhibition, and Zayed University wanted to create a new commission at the same scale for the university's display at the Abu Dhabi Art fair. However, logistics with fabricators and engineers could not accommodate the narrow production windows, so the author, along with colleagues Lina Ahmad and Walter Willems acquired the moquette, remodeled it in 3D, and created an AR sculpture garden scenario that was both seen at the fair and in a partnership with the Maraya Foundation's 1971 Design Center in Sharjah, was produced for the ECHO festival

Fig. 15.7 *Reconstructing Sculpture* (Anood Obaidly 2017)

(Fig. 15.7) (1971 Design Space 2017) and Sharjah's Innovation Week festival in 2018. The work retained its material qualities, the back of it being an enameled teal, and the central elements being wood and plastic colored shapes. However, when one put the HoloLens on, the sculpture appeared in four locations around the user at the full 3.5-meter scale.

While not strictly an educational scenario, consider if the Obaidly sculpture garden were being done as a senior level architectural site design, at the scale of Mel Chin's *Wake* and *Unmoored,* which are discussed later. The project is researched and sketched by the student and developed like any other site survey. Design cycles of critique and revision until the prototype is ready for its first commit. The creation of the 3D prototype is of some question, depending on the representation desired. Although the representational quality of Trimble's Sketchup plugin is acceptable in many cases, many audiences typically wish to see a prototype that is as close to the final iteration as possible, as early as possible. Therefore, we created the full-scale moquette in AutoCAD and 3D Studio Max. Maya would have possible worked better for its existing integration with the HoloLens, but due to the platform dominance of the software platforms with the Interior Design and Architectural industries in the UAE, we produced using 3DS Max and Unity/Vuforia. In addition, the network requirements to implement the Maya prototype workflow was hard to guarantee in the field, so the stand-alone approach was necessary. The simplicity of the workflow from modeling/texturing, FBX import and placement within the Unity environment and compile of code to the HoloLens showed the potential of use of the technology in our classroom. In addition, with the addition of direct compiling to the HoloLens 2 from the Unreal Engine environment, this process continues to improve.

15.10   Case Study: Teaching Information Physicalization in AR

In the previous examples, we explored direct applications of AR within the design process, sculptural, architectural, and for product design. Physical data visualizations are fairly common in the age of laser cutting and 3D printing, and artists like Scott Kildall have been mapping out datasets from exoplanets to city infrastructural distributions for years (Kildall 2015). In addition, album art like Joy Division's iconic *Unknown Pleasures,* in which designer Peter Saville used a diagram of radio waves from Pulsar CP 1919, from *The Cambridge Encyclopedia of Astronomy* (Grow 2018). In this case, the students had a challenge of a two-week window to collect, learn a new workflow to depict a dataset of their choosing, and execute that workflow. This presented a number of unusual challenges that led to an agile workflow utilizing AR.

Because of the project being at the end of the semester, and time of being of the essence, two critical points came into play. First, as Interior Design and Visual Arts students were hard at work at the laser cutters and 3D Printers, a non-material approach was necessary. For that matter, Adobe Aero had come out publicly about three weeks before the deployment of the project, and the workflow was streamlined enough that the initial studies could be explored in under an hour, and the final project executed easily in the two weeks required. The workflow is described in the diagram below.

The students were instructed to select a basic dataset and choose a visualization (Bar, scatter plot, pie) to use the z-axis scattering function of aero. For the majority of the class, generic pie and bar charts showed basic proficiency with the technology, but two outstanding projects used the tool with elegance, and another turned the process into a highly artistic one. Sara Al Balooshi created an infographic using Statistical data detailing the adult reading preferences of the US literary audience. The infographic held a portrait of a reader in which a 3D model of a book was placed in front, and a scatter plot of the genres involved (Fig. 15.8). What was unique about this particular work was that it integrated 2- and 3D contextual art in a cohesive scheme that communicated the idea with a unified metaphor.

Another project in this class took a radically different approach. Rather than taking a statistical approach, this project created a dimensional graphic artwork inspired by a local Augmented Reality art exhibition displayed by the ImagineNation Gallery at the Nations Towers in Abu Dhabi (Staff 2019) which offered several animated and dimensional designs. In her case the piece was a floating island similar to that of a Roger/Martyn Dean album design, combined with a rainbow and classical architecture (Fig. 15.9). Although the piece broke with the design brief proper, it showed understanding of spatial visualization as well as a spatial form of graphic illustration. The demonstration of the aesthetic process in the AR medium after such a short learning curve was extremely heartening to see.

Fig. 15.8 *Data Physicalization 1* (Sara Al Balooshi 2019)

15.11   AR-Based Art as Allegorical Space

Mel Chin: *Wake and Unmoored:* A Lesson for the Times. One of the most spectacular AR-based projects that integrates artistic and informative elements is MacArthur Award recipient Mel Chin's *Unmoored* and *Wake.* A partnership with Microsoft and UNC Asheville's STEAM Studio, these works are a poignant commentary on climate change that speculates on a world where the polar caps have melted, and New York City's Times Square is twenty meters underwater (Microsoft Stories 2018). Visitors begin with *Wake,* a 7-meter-tall physical sculpture that intertwines the shipwreck

Fig. 15.9 Data Physicalization 2 (Khadeeja Ali Sawad 2019)

of the clipper ship U.S.S. Nightingale with a whale skeleton and its figurehead of legendary singer Jenny Lind that was fabricated in Asheville. Above the physical installation, *Unmoored* looms over the visitors as ships cruise overhead on the post-Melt sea (Fig. 15.10). As Chin states, "The use of cellular devices, phones, and laptops has resulted in a decrease in empathy", (Castro 2019) and that evident phenomena placed within technology could help humanity rekindle that empathy. Installed as part of Queens Museum's *All Over the Place* exhibition, (nolongerempty.org 2018) these works engage institutionally with UNC Asheville and Microsoft and shares the outcome as an allegory for the visitors in NYC. The multiple levels of engagement are an example of the Developmental aspects (UNC Asheville), and a demonstrative metaphor in its installation site in New York City.

15.12   Humann and Thiel: Further Allegories

Two projects, while perhaps not strictly educational in themselves are worthy of mention for the didactic component/potential of the work. Tamiko Thiel's *Unexpected Growth*, (Huffman 2018) commissioned for the Whitney Museum's *Programmed* exhibition, (Meier 2019) and Richard Humann's *Ascension,* as part of the *Art Has No Limits* exhibition on the High Line in Manhattan (Gannon 2019). *Unexpected Growth* playfully engages two very serious threats to ocean ecosystems: ocean borne

Fig.15.10 Unmoored (Mel Chin 2019)

plastic waste and coral bleaching caused by global warming. The installation shows a future (?) in which plastic has outstripped organic matter in the oceans and has resulted in strange symbioses of corals and plastic forks that spread throughout the gallery (Fig. 15.11).

Conversely, Humann's re-envisioning of constellations along modern mythologies, such as Marilyn Monroe as "The Tragic Queen" as a modern analogy to Cassiopeia (Fig. 15.12). This installation reflects on Western pop and consumerist culture, but the GPS-based image placement app Membit (now redesigned as Aery for art-specific purposes) (Van Buren 2019) could overlay historical, cultural, and other didactic information in public spaces. Both of these works point toward a broader vision for a public form of education or communication of provocative/evocative content, and point toward models of art as education through the use of AR and educational design.

15.13 Conclusion

In this chapter, we have engaged the subject of AR, design, and education from a revisiting of the author's theories of interaction in relation to content delivery, experience, and gestural engagement. This led to a suggestion that the potential of AR lies in the coming of ubiquitous computing and the invisibility of the environment/interface. The educational elements of AR involve aspects of its design (developmental), potential as teaching environment (didactic), and explanatory medium. The case studies engaged in this discussion were chosen for their engagement with these aspects of AR-based education, where projects like Kerr and Lawson's *Master of Time* involved

Fig. 15.11 *Unexpected Growth*, (Tamiko Thiel et al. 2018). Commissioned by the Whitney Museum of American Art

Fig. 15.12 *Ascension* (Richard Humann 2017–19)

multiple perspectives (developmental/didactic). Other projects where the author has used AR to facilitate creativity in the classroom or creation of student/alumni projects, much like Autodesk's integration of HoloLens support to the Maya3D software environment. This combination of aspects reveals AR's multimodal power as educational tool/environment. Conversely, it is also hoped that through the variety of case studies, an implicit landscape of AR's usability as educational tool, creative tool, and developmental environment is illustrated. Also, of note are the adolescent aspects of educational AR/AR education, although it is rapidly maturing as of ca. 2020, although AR is also well established in many educational genres. Through this discussion, it is hoped that our focus on art and design in AR-based education resonates with the author's ongoing theories of AR-based experience/design, and points towards future directions in the integration of education in AR design/AR-based design/AR-based educational design.

References

1971 Design Space (2017) Echo: reconstructing sculptures. https://1971design.ae/en/learn/events/1691/echo-reconstructing-sculptures/

Antoine Y, Bernard Y et al (2007) "Exhibition > work." The gate, or hole in space reloaded, iMAL.org. https://legacy.imal.org/iMAL_opening/en/The-Gate.html

Bacca J, Baldiris S, Fabregat R, Graf S, Kinshuk K (2014) Augmented reality trends in education: a systematic review of research and applications. Educ Technol Soc 17(4):133–149

Brouwer et al (1998) The art of the accident. NAI Publishers, V2 Organisatie

Castro J (2019) Time to make a stand: a conversation with mel chin. Sculpture. https://sculpturemagazine.art/time-to-make-a-stand-a-conversation-with-mel-chin/

Cerro C, P Lichty (2019) How design will help humanity become an multiplanetary species. Proposal to UAE Space Agency/Roscosmos

David L (2019) Living underground on the moon: how lava tubes could aid lunar colonization. Space.com. Space https://www.space.com/moon-colonists-lunar-lava-tubes.html

Gannon D (2019) New virtual art exhibition at high line nine highlights multiple artists at once. www.6sqft.com/new-virtual-art-exhibition-at-high-line-nine-highlights-multiple-artists-at-once/

GardenGuide (2019) GardenGuide|Chicago Botanic Garden. https://www.chicagobotanic.org/app

GardenDrum (2014) Disney fairies trail app launch-RBG Melbourne. https://gardendrum.com/2014/11/29/disney-fairies-trail-app-launch-rbg-melbourne/

Grow K (2018) The science behind Joy Division's 'unknown pleasures' cover. Rolling stone. https://www.rollingstone.com/music/music-news/joy-divisions-unknown-pleasures-cover-the-science-behind-an-image-191126/

Hoberman P (1998) Systems maintenance, Perry Hoberman. V2_Lab for the Unstable Media, Netherlands. https://v2.nl/archive0/articles/systems-maintenance

Huffman KR (2018) Unexpected growth by Tamiko Thiel at Whitney Museum of American art *Digicult*. https://digicult.it/internet/unexpected-growth-by-tamiko-thiel-at-the-whitney-museum-of-american-art/

Kerr J, Lawson G (2019) Augmented reality in design education: landscape architecture studies as AR experience. Int J Art Des Educ. https://doi.org/10.1111/jade.12227

Kensinger EA (2009) Remembering the details: effects of emotion. Emot Rev: J Int Soc Res Emot. U.S. National Library of Medicine. https://www.ncbi.nlm.nih.gov/pmc/articles/PMC2676782/

Kildall S (2015) Bad data. Scott Kildall. https://kildall.com/archives/project/bad-data

Lichty P (2014a) The translation of art in virtual worlds. In: Grimshaw M (ed) The Oxford handbook of virtuality. Oxford University Press, New York

Lichty P (2014b) Geroimenko V (ed) The aesthetics of liminality: augmentation as an art form. Augmented reality art. Springer International Publishing, Switzerland, pp 99–125

Mattes E, Franco L (2007) 13 most beautiful avatars. https://0100101110101101.org/show-13-most-beautiful-avatars/

Microsoft Stories (2018) 'Unmoored': times square installation shows how artists can anchor storytelling with mixed reality.https://news.microsoft.com/features/unmoored-times-square-installation-shows-how-artists-can-anchor-storytelling-with-mixed-reality/

Nasir S (2019) UAE-Russia experiment to explore survival in martian conditions. Khaleej Times. https://www.khaleejtimes.com/uae/dubai/uae-russia-experiment-to-exploresurvival-in-martian-conditions

Nolongerempty.org (2018) Mel chin: wake & unmoored. https://www.nolongerempty.org/exhibition/mel-chin-wake-unmoored/

O'Connor F (2015) Microsoft pitches HoloLens to businesses creating 3D models. PCWorld. IDG News Service. https://www.pcworld.com/article/2947632/microsoft-pitches-hololens-to-businesses-creating-3d-models.html

Partland L (2014) Parents divided over new botanic gardens fairy-hunting app for children. ABC News. https://www.abc.net.au/news/2014-12-22/parents-divided-melbourne-botanic-gardens-fairy-finding-app/5984216.

Shoemaker K (2008) The Gracie kendal project. https://www.kristineschomaker.net/the-gracie-kendal-project

Staff, Time Out Abu Dhabi (2019) An augmented reality art exhibition has launched in Abu Dhabi. Time Out Abu Dhabi. https://www.timeoutabudhabi.com/news/421182-an-augmented-reality-art-exhibition-has-launched-in-abu-dhabi

Stephenson H (2018) How to design invisible interfaces. Creative Bloq. https://www.creativebloq.com/features/how-to-design-invisible-interfaces

Story City (2019). www.storycity.com.au/

Trimble Systems (2015) Microsoft HoloLens RIBA architects and mixed reality. YouTube. https://www.youtube.com/watch?v=cxN4U0hbrz8

Tyrsina R (2016) SketchUp viewer is the first commercial app for the HoloLens. Windows report|Error-free Tech Life. WindowsReport. https://windowsreport.com/sketchup-viewer-app-holo-lens/

Van Buren J (2019) AERY – Membit's app for fine art. Membit Inc. www.membit.co/2019/11/26/aery-membits-app-for-fine-art/

Chapter 16
The Romantic App: Augmented Reality in Fine Art Education

Claudia Hart

Abstract This chapter explores *The Romantic App* an ongoing project in the School of the Art Institute of Chicago. It is a custom application for smartphone or tablet made especially for the nineteenth and twentieth century paintings of the European Painting and Sculpture wing in the Art Institute of Chicago. Art Institute students designed and executed *The Romantic App* in the Fall semester of 2015, with a second iteration produced in Spring, 2019. It is intended both as a teaching vehicle but also as an art work, allowing young people to engage collaboratively with mentors from another time and period. Augmented Reality was chosen as a medium for this project because it functions in parallel to the grand painting tradition of the nineteenth century, that moment when photography had its first dizzying impact on Parisian culture. Like so many of the optical viewing devices of that époque, *The Romantic App* also reveals illusions and phantasmagoria hidden beneath the surface of the visible world. When the app is open, one can glimpse visions and optical illusions through the interface of a device, integrated into a curated selection of paintings scattered throughout the Museum. Using one's phone as a kind of magical mirror or optical lens, users are encouraged to examine individual paintings, to see hidden animations, enactments and other kinds of moving pictures subtly mixed into their surfaces.

16.1 Introduction

Since 2007, when I started working at the School of the Art Institute of Chicago, I've taught a class entitled *Virtual Installation* to a mixed bag of advanced graduate and undergraduate students. At the time of this writing, 13 years later, what this

C. Hart (✉)
Department of Film, Video, New Media and Animation, School of the Art Institute of Chicago, Chicago, IL, USA
e-mail: chart2@saic.edu

© Springer Nature Switzerland AG 2020
V. Geroimenko (ed.), *Augmented Reality in Education*,
Springer Series on Cultural Computing,
https://doi.org/10.1007/978-3-030-42156-4_16

evocative catch phrase—"virtual installation"—might actually signify has metamorphosed yearly, shifting platforms as our innovation culture has driven computer-graphics software forward at a dizzying pace, to become obsolete every year and then replaced by a newer version with even more hyper-realist capacities.

16.1.1 About this Chapter

When I started teaching *Virtual Installation*, I used *Photoshop* software to manipulate "captured" images by integrating virtual-reality 3D simulations to create still frames that mixed the fantastical and the imaginary into realistic, documentary photos. Several years later, I used even more sophisticated video-tracking software, again integrating more or less realistic simulations into footage shot on digital-video cameras. In the fall of 2015, I proposed that we try a different tactic. I asked my students to re-imagine *Virtual Installation* as an augmented-reality app that would superimpose an exhibition of moving-image art works created by them, to float over the canonical nineteenth and early twentieth-century painting collection of the Art Institute of Chicago.

The nineteenth and early twentieth-century painting collection, presided over by Gloria Groom, then nineteenth-century Painting Curator and now European Painting and Sculpture Chair, seemed both to provide a significant learning opportunity and also to create a profound content and context for a collective art work by both my students and I, acting in the capacity of curator and creative director. I described our historical condition as one of standing on the threshold of a digital age, just as the Impressionists and the related movements of that earlier time—from Manet, Corot and the PreRaphaelite resistance, until Seurat and Matisse—stood on the threshold of the age of mechanization and photography (Benjamin 1937). I imagined us all as "paradigm-shift" artists and therefore asked each student to curate a collection of works within the larger Art Institute painting collection, and then to produce image-based animated augments using their collections as trackables. I thought then, and still do, of standing on these master's shoulders, in conversation and collaboration with them. What we produced in 2015, was *The Romantic App*. Four years later, my 2019 *Virtual Installation* class and I produced *The Romantic App 2.0*, here merged with the original group. This chapter is a selected documentation of the ensuing work.

16.1.2 About the Romantic App

The Romantic App is a custom augmented-reality application for smart-phone or tablet made especially for the eighteenth and nineteenth century paintings of the European Painting and Sculpture Wing in the Art Institute of Chicago. It was a class project, created in conversation with European Painting and Sculpture Chair

Gloria Groom and her curating staff. With support from Research Associate Allison Perelman and Collections Manager Devon Lee Pyle-Vowles, Art Institute students designed and executed *The Romantic App* in the Fall Semester of 2015 and again in the Spring Semester of 2019.

This high-tech augmented-reality application functions in the grand tradition of the nineteenth century, that moment when photography had its first dizzying impact on Parisian culture. Like so many of the optical viewing devices of that époque (Huhtamo 2013), *The Romantic App* also reveals illusions and phantasmagoria hidden beneath the surface of the visible world. When the app is open, one can glimpse visions and optical illusions through the interface of one's smart device, integrated into a curated selection of paintings scattered throughout the museum. Using their phones as a kind of magical mirror or optical lens, visitors may examine individual paintings to discover hidden animations, enactments and other kinds of moving pictures integrated into their surfaces.

Augmented reality is an emerging technology that permits users to see media embedded in physical objects or linked to specific locations in the real world. It is currently available only through custom applications, but will soon be a common feature in every smart device. Just like turning on "wireless' reception, users will turn on "augmented reception." How this works is quite logical: an object or image can be designated as a "trackable." An augmented app can scan this image as if it were a common QR code, which then links the specific app to a particular stream of information coming from the Internet Cloud.

Augmented reality is a subset of a larger group of simulations technologies, all grouped together under the aegis of the virtual. *The Romantic App* is intended to create a dialog between the virtual world of the present and the paintings of the nineteenth century that so strongly reflect the cultural impact of photography and film (Clarke et al. 2019). Impressionist painters along with the Realistic painters of that same epoque, were marked by the impact that the dramatic new scientific discoveries of that time had on the public imagination.

Like that earlier time, our own twenty-first century is experiencing a paradigm shift (Rubinstein 2019), one in which computer-generated realities augment and metamorphosize our vision of what actually might be considered real. As in the nineteenth century, in the twenty-first, the boundary between the fantastical imaginary and the physical or concrete are experiencing a process of evolution and erosion. *The Romantic App* is meant to address that fact by inviting our students, the first denizens of post-Internet culture, to express this transformation in their own ways.

16.2 The Proof of Concept

The Romantic App was predicated on several projects in which I personally intervened in the Art Institute of Chicago European Painting and Sculpture collection wearing my "artist's hat" rather than the hat of a pedagog. To do so, I chose two works, one by Antonio Canova (1757–1822) and the other by Dante Gabriel Rossetti (1828–1882). I produced my own animated augments as in-class demos for the 2015 *Virtual Installation* class, in order to walk my students through the technical, aesthetic and conceptual decision-making process involved in the production of a work made in a museological context.

I chose these particular historical paintings both because they influenced my personal practice as a feminist digital-artist living in the twenty-first century, and also because of where they stand on the art-history timeline. Even before 2015 and *The Romantic App* project, I had produced art inspired by Canova and Rossetti, because I think of them as poetic paradigms of the Romantic canon.

Antonio Canova's *Head of the Medusa* (1801) (Fig. 16.2) is important because it is a brilliant work but also because of its mythological source material, the Medusa, a s/hero with particular contemporary relevance in terms of feminist liberation politics. In Hesiod's *Theogony* (Hesiod and Most 2018), Perseus cut off the head of Medusa and springing from her blood came Chrysaor and Pegasus, Chrysaor being a golden giant and Pegasus the famous white winged-horse. Medusa rests as a symbol of female empowerment, a true warrior princess.

Canova's Medusa was my first augment—a self-portrait animation entitled *Channeling Medusa* (2015) (Fig. 16.1). Canova's sculpture *Medusa* left me breathless in

Fig. 16.1 Claudia Hart, *Channeling Medusa*, 2015

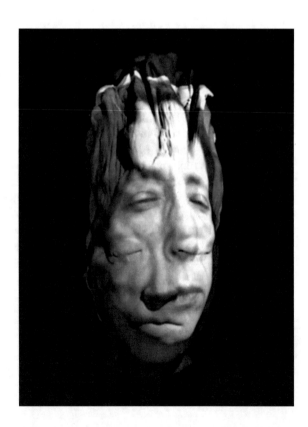

Fig. 16.2 Antonio Canova,
The Head of Medusa, 1801

2007, on my first visit to the Art Institute. Medusa is the symbol of all things feminine, of the queen, and is a form of the Greek word metis—"feminine wile"—that which the male gods strove to obtain. Nine years later, I piled my own images on top of the Canova: a selfie video, shot in my editing room at school, and then digitally projected (Fig. 16.3) onto my own interpretive 3D digital model, built using *Maya* 3D animation software, in 2010 (Fig. 16.2).

I was interested in the *Beata Beatrix* (1871–72) by Dante Gabriel Rossetti because of Rossetti's significant role in the *Luddite* movement. The *Luddites* were a conservative resistance movement to industrialization that took command of Europe in the late nineteenth century. In Great Britain, Pre-Raphaelite painters expressed the *Luddite* philosophy, supporting a return to Medievalism and handicraft and eschewing any form of industrial production. They were anti-Modernist. In response to this history, I created a work, *Desire*, (Fig. 16.4) consisting of a slide-show of related works, meant to be projected on top of Rossetti's painting. The model for the *Beata Beatrix* was Elizabeth Siddal, Rossetti's muse and wife. Siddel also modeled for a host of the other *Luddite* Pre-Raphaelite painters (Hawksley 2013), and was herself an unacknowledged but accomplished poet, long abused by the philandering Rossetti. She died young at 31, of tuberculosis. My augment is a slideshow of other works for which she modeled by a half a dozen of her male peers for whom she represented a romantic heroine and a paradigm of female enchantment.

Fig. 16.3 *Channeling Medusa* by Claudia Hart, 2015, over *The Head of Medusa* by Antonio Canova, 1801, as seen through *The Romantic App*, 2015–2019

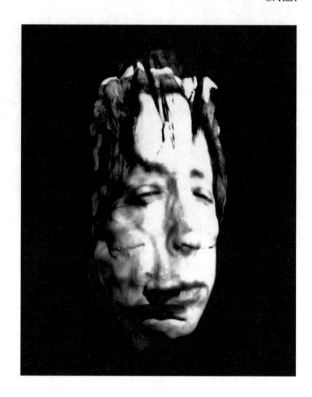

16.3   Art Institute of Chicago, Romantic-App Walk-About

In 2015, my students and I conceived of our augmented-reality application as a more or less permanent exhibition within the context of the permanent collection of the Art Institute. As an extension of that project, we also developed a "museum tour" performed by the students as if they were doscents. We thought of our augmented-reality app, installed on the smart phone of a normal museum visitor as a contemporary parallel to the nineteenth-century optical toys popular at the time that photography first had its impact on Western culture. They were "magic mirrors," a new-fangled version of the the Zoetrope or Magic Lantern (Huhtamo 2013), peeked through by the public as they strolled through the museum (Fig. 16.5).

My intentions in *The Romantic App* were historical, and as a pedagog, I personally appreciate the irony of layering by means of the *Layar* app, a new-media equivalent of a nineteenth-century optical toy, a high-tech animation on top of a nineteenth-century painting in a nineteenth-century museum. The Art Institute of Chicago was founded as both a museum and school for the fine arts in 1879, a critical era in the history of Chicago as civic energies were devoted to rebuilding the metropolis that had been destroyed by the Great Fire of 1871 (Larson 2004). Historically, the Art Institute is a significant example of an architecture standing on the threshold of Modernism. László Moholy-Nagy (American, born Hungary, 1895–1946) who

Fig. 16.4 Claudia Hart, *Desire*, 2015 on Dante Gabriel Rossetti, *Beata Beatrix*, 1871–72, as seen through *The Romantic App*, 2015–19

emerged as a professor at the *Bauhaus* art school in Germany (1923–28), fled to Chicago in 1937, where he founded the *New Bauhaus*, a school that continues today as the Institute of Design at the Illinois Institute of Technology. My pedagogic idea for *The Romantic App* was informed by this illustrious history.

We thought of *The Romantic App* as a liminal interface, a site on the threshold of the twenty-first-century, the epoque of digital technology, and the Art Institute—and the urban site of Chicago—as symbols of the American, industrial twentieth-century and Modernism. With this in mind, my students, lead by Jarad Solomon, a gifted student, both graphic designer and artist now known for his hybrid augmented-graphic projects, designed a booklet (Fig. 16.6), guiding visitors through Gloria Groom's glorious Impressionism collection at the Art Institute. In the spring of 2015, we lead School of the Art Institute board members through our augmented collections, fully cognizant of them as dramatic photo opportunities. In addition to

Fig. 16.5 *The Romantic App as Historical Enactment,* The Art Institute of Chicago, photo: Cass Davis, 2015

designing a booklet guiding visitors through the augmented collection defined by *The Romantic App*, and referring to the graphical tropes established by the German Bauhaus, Solomon also produced a profound series of augments connecting and blending works adjacent to one another in the museum (Fig. 16.7). He visualized conceptual curatorial space by connecting works that the Art Institute curators had also connected spatially, using animated graphics driven by an algorithm tracing a path between a color in one object to the identical color in an adjacent one (Fig. 16.8). Solomon's goal was to illustrate and re-define curatorial relationships, but at the same time, he also produced resonant and hypnotic works of augmented-reality art.

16.4 Student Projects

The Romantic App was created in two versions, four years apart, in the School of the Art Institute of Chicago, spring semester of 2015, and again in the spring semester of 2019. A selected group of outstanding student projects are compiled in this chapter, along with students' descriptions of their augments, my class assignment. Subtle shifts in both the students' and my own conceptual orientation differentiated 2015 and 2019 versions, due to the broader impact of augmented-reality on culture after the

Fig. 16.6 *The Romantic App* Catalog designed by Jarad Solomon, 2015

Niantic *Pokémon GO* augmented-reality mobile game was released in 2016, going viral.

What changed in the 5 years, as evidenced by the way the students framed their own work and wrote about it, constitutes a reframing of the way we imagined an augmented work to exist "in perpetuity," of particular significance in the context of the Art Institute of Chicago where the collections trace medieval through contemporary art-history. When we produced *The Romantic App* 2015, we used the mobile browser-app *Layar*, a company six years old at that time that I naively imagined as relatively stable. I asked the students to think of their work as a smaller exhibition sitting in virtuality on top of the permanent collection of that august institution. Although I knew museums rehang, loan, and remove works for conservation, I imagined the augmented app as functioning within that context, a thing that could be upgraded and conserved. I thought of *Layar* as a fixed-frame software, like Photoshop or the 3D animation product Maya, classic standards that I also imagined as being conserved in a contemporary art museum. The student writings for *The Romantic App* 2015, therefore expressed my own assumptions, that the students were producing a "permanent" collection within the Art Institute of Chicago's own stable collection.

A few weeks before my *Virtual Installation* class scheduled to produce the Romantic App 2019 was to begin, *Layar*, and its parent company *Blipp*, were suddenly liquidated. So much for permanence! Improvising, I decided to use *SnapChat*, a popular

Fig. 16.7 Chair and *Portrait of Anna Maria Dashwood* by Thomas Hope and Sir Thomas Lawrence, as seen through *The Romantic App* in an augment by Jarad Solomon, 2015

social media site with a sophisticated augmented function and a public software. The problem with *SnapChat* in the context of a permanent collection in an august art history museum is that *SnapChat* augments only remain on their app for 2 weeks. After that they are deleted by the company. The students and I discussed the implications of this hyper-impermanence in terms of how to imagine this version of *The Romantic App* in perpetuity. We decided that which was lasting could only be our documentation of the work, that would include the app assets and a short description of each individual augment. The "work" as it would exist in the future, could only be an image of the trackable, based on the trackable—high resolution scans provided

Fig. 16.8 X-frame armchair and *Wounded Stag and Dog* by Lewis Nockalls Cottingham and Sir Edwin Henry Landseer, as seen through *The Romantic App* in an augment by Jarad Solomon, 2015

by the Art Institute on their public website—and their augment—Gifs made by the students, in the form of a multilayer Photoshop Document. We felt that these were the most stable forms that we could currently identify in the digital domain. This is apparent in the way that the students described their works in *The Romantic App* 2019 group.

16.4.1   Anthony L. Blackwood

Anthony L. Blackwood, BFA, 2016
The Romantic App, 2015
Tracking: Paul Gauguin, *The Ancestors of Tehamana or Tehaman Has Many Parents (Merahi Metua No Tehamana)*, 1893

Using visual and experimental media from our own time, I want to generate and allude to the energy that evolves culture and the social space, created by technological change and development. It moved Gauguin to explore new visual territories, beyond the limitations of human perception (Fig. 16.9). It also moves me. For this piece (Fig. 16.10), I used a photograph found in the archives of the Art Institute, of the real child bride of Gauguin and placed her in an animated environment to critique and question Gauguin's racist and patriarchal values.

Fig. 16.9 Paul Gauguin, *The Ancestors of Tehamana or Tehaman Has Many Parents (Merahi Metua No Tehamana)*, 1893

Fig. 16.10 Anthony L.
Blackwood on Paul Gauguin,
2015

16.4.2   Daniel Brookman

Daniel Brookman, BFA, 2017
The Romantic App, 2015
Tracking: Claude Monet, *The Petite Creuse River*, 1889

   Current and popular new media tropes can easily be connected to previous conventions found in the European Painting and Sculpture wing, particularly in works from the nineteenth century. Notably, these trends include: a fixation with antiquated and exotic imagery, a continual infatuation with the construction of impeccable fantasies, along with sentiments and aesthetics born out of a widespread anxiety towards a variety of sociological rationalizations for the vast technological changes sweeping through Europe at that time. The body of work that I have developed here augments these 19th-century works, and seeks to show direct parallels with our own time, also wrought by technological upheavals, by visually melding with the earlier works and at the same time showing a contemporary equivalent. For my Monet piece (Fig. 16.11), I used the MetaCreations Corporation *Bryce*, a mass-market software made to model 3D fantasy landscapes, reconstructing the Monet as a high-tech artifact (Fig. 16.12).

Fig. 16.11 Claude Monet, *The Petite Creuse River*, 1889

Fig. 16.12 Daniel Brookman on Claude Monet, 2015

16.4.3   Savario Caponi

Savario Caponi, BFA, 2016
The Romantic App, 2015
Tracking: Jean Victor Bertin, *Entrance to the Park at Saint-Cloud*, 1802

Architecture and other urban spaces such as parks and landscapes were symbols of the ideal (Fig. 16.13) in the 19th-century. But they also are the inspiration for environments commonly found in all kinds of 3d games, from the apocalyptic to mystery and shooter games. In this augment, I made the connection by making an animation using the Bertin painting as a backdrop and inserting animated galloping horses on top (Fig. 16.14). I found the animation free on the Internet by "Googling": *free 3d-horses*. I think of it as a contemporary painting.

Fig. 16.13   Jean Victor Bertin, *Entrance to the Park at Saint-Cloud*, 1802

Fig. 16.14 Savario Caponi on Jean Victor Bertin, 2015

16.4.4 Jessica Ceuvallos

Jessica Ceuvallos, BFA 2019
The Romantic App, 2019
Tracking: Edvard Munch, *The Girl by the Window*, 1893

Munch painted *The Girl by the Window* (Fig. 16.15) after a trip from Paris in 1893. In keeping with that time period, I incorporated vintage footage from one of the Lumière brothers' short films in Paris in 1895, found on the Internet, shot in front of Notre Dame. I wanted to keep the voyeuristic aspect of the painting intact. We are also voyeurs, watching a girl watching a scene made in the same epoque (Fig. 16.16).

In my body of augmented works, I explore the idea of fleeting moments that can be found in photographs, in art works and also in dreams. The paintings in the European galleries of the Art Institute of Chicago are like windows onto the past, capsules of what the artists then viewed around them. By taking these paintings and installing videos in them with connections to that past, it expands the world of the painting itself, making it more real, but also more surreal at the same time.

Fig. 16.15   Edvard Munch,
The Girl by the Window,
1893

16.4.5   Cindy Chang

Cindy Chang, BFA, 2021
The Romantic App, 2019
Tracking: Ferdinand Hodler, *The Grand Muveran*, 1912

   The Grand Muveran by Ferdinand Hodler (Fig. 16.17) was known for its distinctive art style and symbolic expression. Instead of using the *en plein air* style which focuses on the retinal reproduction of the subject, Hodler painted more fantastical and symbolic pictures. His work has an artificial feel because it also reflects that his artwork is artificially created, an internal world rather than a recreation of reality. To emphasize the artificiality, I created the virtual "behind the scenes" of this painting. I built 3D models of the "mountains," outlining the shapes appearing in the painting, and layered them together. It creates a *trompe-l'oeil* effect. Through the app, but from the side rather than a frontal view, observers can see panels traced from the mountain shapes, stacked in virtual space on top of one another (Fig. 16.18). But

Fig. 16.16 Jessica
Ceuvallos on Edvard Munch,
2019

from the front, the 3D objects seem to be the actual 2D painting. I am questioning
what is real and what is unreal in art.

16.4.6 Muyeol Choe

Muyeol Choe, BFA, 2020
The Romantic App, 2019
Tracking: Franz Ludwig Catel, *Inside the Colosseum, 1818–1828*
Life in Nowhere, 2019
　　When Georges-Eugène Haussmann rebuilt Paris, all the old alleyways and narrow
streets were destroyed (Fig. 16.19). For this work, I'm imagining animistic spirits
from the old Medieval world, that might have haunted these alleys as being evicted
out of their homes. Dispossessed, they occupied romantic paintings, squatting in the
works of art, forever yearning for where their lives breathed, struggled, and dreamed.

Fig. 16.17   Ferdinand Hodler, *The Grand Muveran*, 1912

This project comes from an idea I am dubbing the *animism of space*: the spaces we all inhabit have spirits of their own. Baudelaire expressed the idea in his poem, *The Swan*. A swan is freed from a cage. It walks on the dry pavements of twentieth century alienated Paris. It yearns for water just as Baudelaire longed for old Paris. If where life once breathed and struggled and dreamed is gone, then life leaves with it. In the poet's mind, The alleyways live, and his swan was the spirit of the old alleys.

To me, trying to capture the "spirit of life," lost with the fabric of medieval Paris due to Haussmann's reconstruction drove romantic painting and all of the optical toys and seances that characterized the culture at that time. Augmented space does not replace the physical. It starts where the physical meets the imagination. It is a symbol of the human desire to restore the forgotten; a refuge where the human mind may dream. That dream, in this case, is life itself (Fig. 16.20).

16.4.7   Cassandra Davis

Cass Davis, MFA, 2017, Fibers and Material Studies
The Romantic App, 2015
Tracking: Ferdinand Hodler, *Day (Truth)*, 1896–98

Fig. 16.18 Cindy Chang on
Ferdinand Hodler, 2019

    In my recent work, created in dialog with the nineteenth and twentieth century painting collection of the Art Institute of Chicago, I have been exploring cloth as shroud, to help visualize the frightening inevitability of death, but also the possibility of rebirth and a transcendent experience.

    In Hodler's *Truth* (Fig. 16.21), a mystical figure holds a burial shroud, possibly foreshadowing her own death or acting as a harbinger of death. I have layered on top of it a video of a nude model holding a fluttering veil. The wind from the cloth seems to swirl from the mountaintop painted by Hodler on the canvas beneath, creating a figure that feels both two and three dimensional, as this shroud both obscures and reveals the body beneath (Fig. 16.22).

Fig. 16.19   Franz Ludwig Catel, *Inside the Colosseum, 1818–1828*

16.4.8   Nick Flaherty

Nick Flaherty, BFA, 2017
The Romantic App, 2015
Tracking: George Seurat, *A Sunday Afternoon on the Island of La Grande Jatte*, 1894

The thousands of carefully placed paint strokes that Seurat carefully painted 120 years ago, as a part of his serious scientific investigations into perception, over a score of years of museum blockbusters and museum gift shop commercialization, amounts to an image that gets photoshopped and parodied hundreds of times. All of these ads and parodies are actually collected by the Art Institute museum, to become fodder for my animation, as one Seurat marketing add or Youtube video parody melts into the next (Fig. 16.23), a cheap entertainment for the scores of teenagers inhabiting selfie-land. What do you think? Thumbs up or down?

Fig. 16.20 Muyeol Choe on Franz Ludwig Catel, *2019*

16.4.9 Xavier Hughes

Xavier Hughes, BFA, 2021
The Romantic App, 2019
Tracking: John Phillip Simpson, *The Captive Slave*, 1827
    Retrospective-1, 2019
    The Captive Slave by the English painter, John Simpson (Fig. 16.24), is a hybrid
between portrait and genre painting. It depicts a shackled, dark-skinned man, thought
to be modeled by the American-born actor Ira Aldridge. The painting is an abolitionist
statement. To complicate and propel this painting into an expanded conversation,
I've reinterpreted the work by digitally collaging it with a portrait of an aristocratic
woman by John Singer Sargent (Fig. 16.25). The motif of "the enslaved" present in
the original piece becomes less literal in a way and more contemplative of possibly
an institutional enslavement; but also, the implied interaction between the male and
female figures (Fig. 16.26) and the clear dichotomy of class presents a complexity
that parallels the original sentiment of the painting.

Fig. 16.21 Ferdinand
Hodler, *Day (Truth)*,
1896–98

16.4.10   Insun Kang

Insun Kang, BFA, 2020
The Romantic App, 2019
Tracking: Edgar Degas, *Portrait after a Costume Ball (Portrait of Madame Dietz-Monnin)*, 1879
    Adèle: Two letters from the Art Institute Research Files, 2019
    Adèle: Two letters from the Research Files uses augmented reality to layer the lesser known stories about the making of the painting and the art historical interpretations that followed the completion of the work to let them all exist in the same time and space.

Fig. 16.22 Cass Davis on
Ferdinand Hodler, 2015

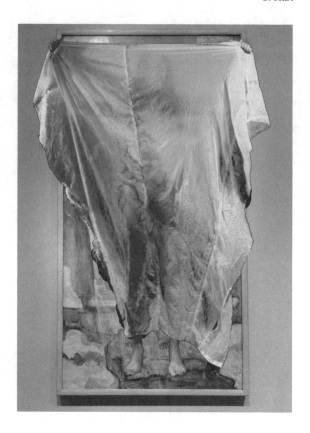

In creating the series of three augmented reality lenses for the European Paintings at the Art Institute of Chicago, I used the research files at the museum extensively as sources of both material and inspiration. These files contain myriads of visuals and texts that allow a revealing glimpse into how museum works are maintained, contextualized, researched, of how ownership transferred and transmitted around the globe.

I found some lovely personal stories hidden amongst those dense research materials, such as the one letter from the great-granddaughter of "the" Madame Dietz-Monnin subject of this painting (Fig. 16.27). Contrasting that letter to another by Degas, written to but never sent to Mme. Dietz-Monnin, her granddaughter Victoire reveals her take on the Degas, in a second letter, revealing why her great-grandmother so disliked the portrait, a fact disturbing to Degas, as seen expressed by his letter.

Fig. 16.23 Nick Flaherty on George Seurat, 2015

Fig. 16.24 John Phillip
Simpson, *The Captive Slave*,
1827

Fig. 16.25 John Singer
Sargent, *Mrs. George
Swinton (Elizabeth
Ebsworth)*, 1897

Below is the unsent letter from Degas that I found in the Art Institute research files, that I copied in full, followed by a short excerpt from Victoire's handwritten letter. The augmented reality work that I created merges them with a copy of a pastel sketch that I also found the the research files, and a photo of the framed sketch sitting on a piece of furniture, part of a small packet containing Victoire's letters, and the portrait by Degas. With all of these images transparently layered over one another, I created an ambient animation, semitransparent through which a viewer can also see Degas actual painting beneath it (Fig. 16.28). It is an ode to the archives and a representation of all museums as living beautiful archives and gateways to the past.

Fig. 16.26 Xavier Hughes and John Singer Sargent on John Phillip Simpson, 2019

Unsent letter from Degas to Mme. Dietz-Monin:

To Mme Dietz-Monin,

Let us leave the portrait alone, I beg of you. I was so surprised by your letter suggesting that I reduce it to a boa and a hat that I shall not answer you. I thought that August or M. Groult to whom I had already spoken about your last idea and my own disinclination to follow it, would have informed you about the matter.

Must I tell you that I regret having started something in my own manner only to find myself transforming it completely into yours? That would not be too polite and yet…

But, dear Madame, I cannot go into this more fully without showing you only too clearly that I am very much hurt.

Outside of my unfortunate art, please accept all my regards (undated).

Fig. 16.27 Edgar Degas, *Portrait after a Costume Ball (Portrait of Madame Dietz-Monnin)*, 1879

Letter excerpted from Victoire Gilbaud, Great-granddaughter of Mme. Dietz-Monin, found in the research files of the Art Institute of Chicago, dated 1980:

She was a gay widow. It is said that in the portrait, she was in a nightdress, …and drunk. Others say she was painted as a prostitute, waiting for a client. (That is why she did not like it!) (excerpt—dated 1980).

16.4.11 Amanda Konkol

Amanda Konkol, BFA, 2018
The Romantic App, 2015
Tracking: Alberto Pasini, *Memory of the Orient*, 1880

Fig. 16.28   Insun Kang on Edgar Degas, 2019

I chose my collection of paintings based on a keen interest in conflict. For me, these still images are representative of the liminal space between thoughts and actions (Fig. 16.29). Animating, in this context, is to continue the actions implied within the paintings but never performed. Repetition and rhythm are the reigning qualities of my GIFs, as they extend the natural motion of the paintings while creating new images which underscore the historical content within each piece (Fig. 16.30).

16.4.12   Ferrell Lamonth

Ferrell Lamonth, BFA, 2016
The Romantic App, 2015
Tracking: Vincent Van Gogh, *The Drinkers*, 1890

I chose The Drinkers by Vincent van Gogh (Fig. 16.31), and the Acrobats at the Cirque Fernando (Francisca and Angelina Wartenberg) because, quite simply, I was simply struck by them artistically. They captured my attention as soon as I saw them.

Fig. 16.29 Alberto Pasini, *Memory of the Orient*, 1880

I was strongly attracted by their compositions and by their subject matters that felt immediate and almost "captured." In working on and with them, I tried to find my own way and my own meaning behind these works. I tried to manipulate what was happening within each painting to try to find the deeper meaning of the painting itself. The most striking of these is the Van Gogh, that is a profound work but at the same time has become a kitsch cultural symbol. Both in the Art Institute Museum and additionally online, I found dozens of tote bags, pillows and other cheap consumer products decorated with images of this painting (Fig. 16.32). I made an animation popping one on top of another, until they finally "eat" the original work alive.

Fig. 16.30 Amanda Konkol on Alberto Pasini, 2015

16.4.13 Yoo-Jin Lee

Yoo-Jin Lee, BFA, 2016
The Romantic App, 2015
Tracking: Antoine Etex, *Bust of the Duke of Orleans*, 1833

In the Romantic period, many artists became politicized and painted pictures symbolizing the radical positions that ultimately lead to the French Revolution. In my augments, I picked more conventional works, sculptures of aristocrats (Fig. 16.33) in the traditional academic style. I layered on top of these animations I made of disenfranchised others. In this case, a crowd of veiled Moslem women. I am portraying these so-called realistic sculptures itself as representing a more real truth: the gap between the ideal and reality (Fig. 16.34).

Fig. 16.31 Vincent Van Gogh, *The Drinkers*, 1890

16.4.14　Sharon Pak

Sharon Pak, BFA/BA, 2016
The Romantic App, 2015
Tracking: Édouard Manet, *Fish (Still Life)*, 1864
　flesh + bodies [embodiment/disembodiment] + as vessels + apparatus + automata], 2015

This collection of work focuses on kinesthesia, a state of perception altering a representation by means of the limits of the flesh. I began this work thinking about my religious history and the relationship I have with the spiritual—much of which is dependent on experiences that heavily rely on intangibility (a lot like the digital realm). As a byproduct of this relationship (Figs. 16.35 and 16.36), I realized how much I fetishize the tactile and visceral and created these works keeping in mind the still very real provocations and affective repercussions that come out of the digital image.

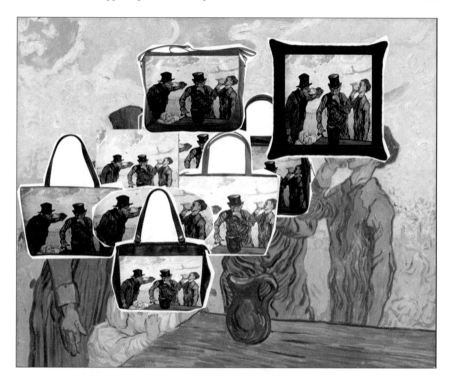

Fig. 16.32   Ferrell Lamonth on Vincent van Gogh, 2015

16.4.15   Christen Shea

Christen Shea, Post Baccalaureate, 2016, Film, Video, New Media, and Animation + Ceramics
The Romantic App, 2015
Tracking: Henri Fantin-Latour, *Corner of a Table*, 1873
   Pour Latour, 2015
   Looking across to the culture that so influenced this period with its gardens and woodblock prints, here we recall Japanese Shinto themes of inanimate spirituality. The portrayed scenes (Fig. 16.37) are haunted by the spirits of dormant objects and impressions of activities in past and future moments. Enchanted objects transcend their state of suspense and dynamic action breathes life into stillness (Fig. 16.38).

Fig. 16.33   Antoine Etex, *Bust of the Duke of Orleans*, 1833

16.4.16   Emily Shoebey

Emily Shoebey, BFA, 2020
The Romantic App, 2019
Tracking: Dante Gabriel Rossetti, *Beata Beatrix*, 1871–72
    Siddal and the Cult of the Lady, 2019
    Beata Beatrix (Fig. 16.39) is a painting honoring the memory of Elizabeth Siddal, the model for this and many other Pre-Raphaelite paintings and sketches, made by her husband. She is depicted as Beatrix from *The Divine Comedy*, the monomaniacal subject and avatar of light that inspired Dante Aligheiri to write as a character within *The Comedy*.

Fig. 16.34 Yoo-Jin Lee on
Antoine Etex, 2015

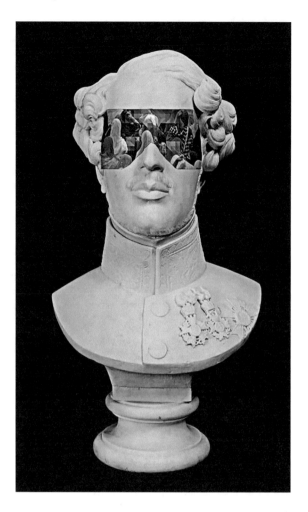

This sort of glorification of Siddal as *Beatrix* (and many other figures she has been painted by the other Pre-Raphaelites, as she was embraced as the muse of the whole movement) has ties to the Cult of the Madonna of the Middle Ages, that the Pre-Raphaelites very likely drew inspiration from. However, deifying someone also makes them less human. Siddel was, sadly, taken more as an object to love and be infatuated with rather than as a person. I am memorializing the real Siddal here, as a young woman from one century to another from an earlier one (Fig. 16.40).

Fig. 16.35 Édouard Manet, *Fish (Still Life)*, 1864

16.4.17 Jarad Solomon

Jarad Solomon, MFA, 2016, Art and Technology Studies
The Romantic App, 2015
Tracking: Claude Monet, *Veteuil*, 1901

The work I've done for *The Romantic App* is divided between four of Monet's haystacks, two of Monet's paintings of the village of Vétheuil, and two pairs of chair/portrait couples. My process connects and blends adjacent works (Fig. 16.41), filling the space between with a color analysis of the connected pieces. The goal of the project is to illustrate and re-define curatorial relationships.

Fig. 16.36   Sharon Pak on Édouard Manet, 2015

16.4.18   Kalan Strauss

Kalan Strauss, BFA, 2020
The Romantic App, 2019
Tracking: Henri Fantin-Latour, *Still Life: Corner of a Table*, 1873
    Compressionism, 2019
    We live in a digital age where the majority of art exists and is viewed on digital platforms, such as Instagram and Twitter. Art is also the marketing around it and those platforms are important in the artworld as marketing tools, both by galleries and by the artists themselves. But many artists use social media in unique ways both as a tool to promote themselves and make unique projects specific to the social media platform which functions as their stage and also their museums. Beginning with the Dutch painters of the seventeenth century, still life paintings were a sought-after genre

Fig. 16.37   Henri Fantin-Latour, *Corner of a Table*, 1873

by aristocratic collectors and were easier for artists to sell. They provided painters
a way to monetize their work and sustain their artistic careers. Still lives have been
around for hundreds of years by now, so also provide a consistent, timeless structure
for artists to display their own unique style and view on painting and on life itself.
Using imagery that is familiar to mostly everyone (Fig. 16.42), allows artists to show
off their skills and depict the world according to their own subjective desires. I am
doing the same as the artists of the nineteenth century, now as an artist of the twenty-
first century, but using the glitches and compression artifacts native to my medium
(Fig. 16.43), to create a visual style interpreting 19th-century still lives culled from
the Art Institute, a museum of also from the nineteenth century, now repositioned on
the Internet—my museum of the twenty-first—and with the hope of also marketing
and eventually selling them!

Fig. 16.38   Christen Shea on Henri Fantin-Latour, *2015*

16.4.19   Jessica Walters

Jessica Walters, MA, 2021, Art Therapy and Counseling
The Romantic App, 2019
Tracking: Claude Monet, *Branch of the Seine near Giverny (Mist)*, 1897
   Tribute to Berthe Morisot II: The Artist's Body, 2019

Berthe Morisot was a female painter who participated in the first French impressionist group with Claude Monet, Camille Pissarro, Alfred Sisley, Pierre-Auguste Renoir, Edgar Degas, Paul Cezanne, and Armand Guillaumin. Despite multiple exhibitions and a long career as a professional artist, Morisot's death certificate states that she was "without profession." It is my belief that Morisot's obscurity, during her lifetime and currently, is tied to her social status as a woman in the 1800s.

My three-part virtual installation series, *Tributes to Berthe Morisot*, uses the paintings of Morisot's contemporaries to bring attention to Morisot and her artwork.

In *Tribute to Berthe Morisot I*, shadows of two hands sprinkle crushed flowers over Renoir's *Lunch at the Restaurant Fournaise (The Rowers' Lunch)* (1875). The shadows and flowers represent femininity and are a tribute to Morisot's signature use of crushed petals in her paint. I encourage viewers to ponder why Morisot was overshadowed by her contemporaries.

Fig. 16.39 Dante Gabriel
Rossetti, *Beata Beatrix*,
1871–72

In *Tribute to Berthe Morisot II: The Artist's Body*, a ghostly, translucent hand covered in blue paint, gently sprinkles flower petals (Fig. 16.45) over Claude Monet's *Branch of the Seine near Giverny (Mist)* (Fig. 16.44), from the series *Mornings on the Seine* (1897).

Some believe that Morisot is scarcely known because of her status as an upper class elite bourgeois artist. Monet, however, one of the world's most renowned Impressionists, was also a member of the upper-class. In my augment, I imitate Morisot by mixing crushed flowers into my paint as a way to honor her. But also using Monet in the background rather than in the historical foreground that he actually occupies.

Fig. 16.40 Emily Shoebey on Dante Gabriel Rossetti, 2019

Fig. 16.41 Jarad Solomon on Claude Monet, 2015

Fig. 16.42 Henri Fantin-Latour, *Still Life: Corner of a Table*, 1873

Fig. 16.43   Kalan Strauss on Henri Fantin-Latour, 2019

16.5   Conclusion: Augmented Reality as Allegory and Pedagogy

Mid semester, spring 2019, Kalan Strauss, a talented student, asked me, with a certain degree of anxiety, whether it was "enough" to "just" make a contemporary digital landscape out of a historical one (Fig. 16.46), layering it by means of *The Romantic App* on top of the original. He meant "enough" to mean "good art." His anxiety was a critical response to the the techno-formalist critique often leveled against digitally processed abstraction. His anxiety reflects generally the pedagogic position embraced at the School of the Art Institute, which is Conceptual. It is not uncommon for undergraduates to make many intertextual and theoretical references in their work.

I took Kalan's anxiety seriously, hesitating before responding, as I shared a bit of it. I projected forward in time, to imagine how *The Romantic App* might be regarded in the future, answering him with a resounding "yes." Yes, it is enough.

Fig. 16.44   Claude Monet, *Branch of the Seine near Giverny (Mist)*, 1897

The depth of meaning of the works done by young artists within the historic context of the Art Institute of Chicago has much to do with the structural nature of augmented reality technology and its deep impact and effectiveness as a pedagogical tool. Augmented apps actually integrate an editorial evaluation—a subjective response—with the object of that gaze. Instead of creating a hierarchical relationship between subject and object, augmented apps necessitate a dialogical one, where subject and object engage in conversation. This is why users of all ages tend to greet a view of the world through an augmented lens with such delight! Augmented information does not present as pedantic, but by layering one point of view over another and integrating them into a new whole, is collaborative: a very different approach to the pedagogical "problem" than earlier authoritarian or clearly hierarchical versions. Students and other users don't feel like they are being taught, but rather that they are participants in a conversation. Dialogic conversation—the Socratic method—is also, in my experience, the most effective way to teach. Augmented apps create community through conversation. And community is the ground of all good teaching and learning environments.

Fig. 16.45 Jessica Walters on Claude Monet, 2019

In the specific case of *The Romantic App*, the conversation between past and present, youth and age, the historical and institutionalized, and the emergent and contemporary, make it convincing as an art work. It functions as both pedagogy and also as a metaphor for the process of art history particularly, but also of the grand narrative of History itself, as established positions become irrelevant, decay and are replaced by emergent ones, ad infinitum.

The Romantic App and all artistic augmented apps are *gesamtkunstwerk*, a total work of art. Its individual augments are its elements, like brush strokes on the surface of a painting, its form a collection of gestures made by young artists positioned on the threshold of the digital age (Fig. 16.47). An app is a museological filter, optical

Fig. 16.46 Claude Monet, *Apples and Grapes*, 1880

glasses for viewing a distant past, from the time and place of a less distant one, whenever that might be: the "future." *The Romantic App* embodies, or actually dis-embodies, the profound possibilities implied by the structure of the apparatus, an open digital application acting as a filter on the camera of a twenty-first- century "smart" device. It is liminal. *The Romantic App* proposes augmentation as a structure, as art, but also pedagogy as art. And in that, community discourse as art, process as art, and ultimately, the process of art history as art. It also implies obsolescence as the generative force behind History, and in so doing is the vehicle of its own unmaking.

Claudia Hart
December, 2019

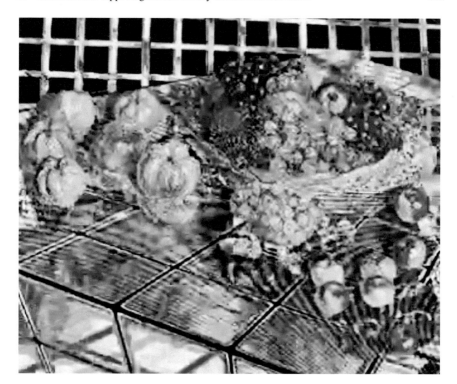

Fig. 16.47   Kalan Strauss on Claude Monet, 2019

References

Art institute of Chicago (2019) The Collection. https://www.artic.edu/collection

Benjamin W (1937) The work of art in the age of its technological reproducibility. In: Eiland H, Jennings M (eds) Walter Benjamin Selected Writings, vol 3, 1935–38. Harvard University Press, Cambridge, pp 99–133

Clarke J, Hunter M, Rubin J, Johnson M (2019) In: Shields, C (ed) Impressionism in the age of industry. Art Gallery of Ontario, Toronto and DelMonico Books, Oxford, New Zealand

Hawksley L (2013) Lizzie Siddal: the tragedy of a pre-raphaelite supermodel. Andre Deutsch, London

Hesiod (700 BC) (2018) The theogony: works and days, testimonia (Trans: Most G). Loeb Classical Library. Harvard University Press, Cambridge

Huhtamo E (2013) Illusions in motion: media archaeology of the moving panorama and related spectacles. MIT Press, Cambridge

Larson E (2004) The devil in the white city. Crown, London

Rubinstein D (ed) (2019) The new paradigm. Routledge, London, pp 1–7

Part IV
Augmented Reality in Environmental and Special Education

Chapter 17
Augmented Reality for Outdoor Environmental Education

Julie Ducasse

Abstract Over the last decade, mobile learning has become one of the most important trends in education. Leveraging on the technological capabilities of mobile devices, researchers and teachers have investigated the use of mobile devices in a variety of disciplines, including environmental education, in order to design innovative educational material such as augmented reality (AR) apps. Designing technologically enhanced learning activities for environmental education is particularly challenging because they often take place in informal settings and outdoors, for example through field trips or visits to parks. In this chapter, we discuss the potential of augmented reality for outdoor environmental education. More specially, we: (i) give a brief overview of learning theories that promote learning in context; (ii) describe a number of illustrative examples of augmented reality mobile apps for environmental education; (iii) and discuss the purpose and forms of digital augmentations in the context of environmental education.

17.1 Introduction

Over the last decade, a number of innovative ways of teaching have been employed in order to take advantage of the pervasiveness of technologies, but also to leverage on students' expectations and willingness to learn with technology. Mobile learning is one of them (Wu et al. 2012). It takes advantage of the ever-growing availability of mobile devices to open new perspectives in terms of pedagogical activities, which may result in various learning outcomes and better attitudes towards learning (e.g. Kljun et al. 2018).

Interestingly, mobile devices also provide support for the implementation of Augmented Reality (AR) systems. The mobile device is used as a see-through display, through which students can see the real word enhanced with digital information, such

J. Ducasse (✉)
Faculty of Mathematics, Natural Sciences and Information Technologies,
University of Primorska, Koper, Slovenia
e-mail: julie.ducasse@famnit.upr.si

© Springer Nature Switzerland AG 2020
V. Geroimenko (ed.), *Augmented Reality in Education*,
Springer Series on Cultural Computing,
https://doi.org/10.1007/978-3-030-42156-4_17

329

as virtual objects or textual annotations. Although mobile devices are not the only devices that support AR, their availability and cost make them good candidates for the implementation of AR-based learning activities (Specht et al. 2011; Nincarean et al. 2013).

In addition, due to their technological capabilities and portability, mobile applications, whether AR-based or not, are particularly interesting for informal learning such as outdoor learning. As such, they fall within the scope of situated learning or place-based learning, two theories that promote learning in context in order to increase students' engagement and facilitate the acquisition and transfer of knowledge from school to real-life situations. Mobile devices can also support the implementation of different pedagogical approaches, such as inquiry-based learning (Suárez et al. 2018).

Environmental Education is one domain that can benefit from the use of technologically enhanced situated or place-based learning activities. Environmental Education aims to raise students' awareness regarding their environment and the evolution of their environment, but also to teach them a number of skills that will enable them to better understand the environmental challenges that society is facing. Because Environmental Education is a complex topic, which usually requires students to explore and understand complex biotopes that can evolve across space and over time, it is often taught through organised field trips and can be ever more facilitated by the use of technology, such as mobile devices and/or AR apps.

In this chapter, we will first highlight three educational theories that encourage learning in context, and highlight how these theories are related with environmental education and the use of technology to enrich outdoor activities. We will then review different augmented reality applications for environmental education in order to see how AR was used so far, and whether and how it could be used differently.

17.2   Theoretical Framework

17.2.1   Environmental Education and the Value of Outdoor Learning Activities

The Environmental Protection Agency defines Environmental Education as "a process that allows individuals to explore environmental issues, engage in problem solving, and take action to improve the environment".[1] Environmental Education encourages critical thinking and gives individuals "the skills to make informed and responsible decisions".[2] It is a multidisciplinary field that aims to encourage humans to live in a more sustainable way by giving them the tools and skills to understand

---

[1] EPA - United States Environmental Protection Agency. What is Environmental Education? https://www.epa.gov/education/what-environmental-education.

[2] Ibid.

how their actions may impact, positively or negatively, the ecosystems that surround them, and to take decisions accordingly. Although not always a subject per se, Environmental Education has been promoted by the UNESCO and also by the United Nations Environment Program (UNEP) (Leicht et al. 2018).

With climate change becoming a growing concern, it is important to promote environmental education as a way to develop students' interest in their environment but also as a way to encourage students to play an active role in the protection of their environment. As stated by Jennings (2009), "education may be an important factor in the instillation of the youth and in the empowerment of their morality in order to understand and solve energy-related environmental problems". Environmental education is therefore of crucial importance.

Environmental education can take several forms, such as trips to national parks, green clubs and sustainability projects. Examples of environmental education activities also include the creation and management of botanic gardens, bird-watching, but also ecotourism or participation in NGOs activities.

Field trips, defined as trips "arranged by the school and undertaken for educational purposes, in which the students go to places where the materials of instruction may be observed and studied directly in their functional setting" (Krepel and DuVall 1981) are particularly common and their positive impact on learning is well documented (e.g. Farmer et al. 2007, Jose et al. 2017). They enable teachers to involve students into less traditional and formal learning activities that the ones usually organised within the classroom. Therefore, students can feel more engaged and motivated but they can also apply theoretical concepts learnt in the classroom to real-world problems (Behrendt and Franklin 2014). Outdoor experience can also positively affect students' relations and connection to nature and make them more emotionally engaged (Drissner et al. 2010). For example, Kossack and Bogner (2012) observed that after spending one afternoon in a botanical garden, students become more aware of the impact of human activities on the nature and developed a stronger "inclusion of nature in self" than other students. In addition, various studies reported positive results in terms of learning when the activities were conducted outside (see Dillon et al. 2006, Behrendt and Franklin 2014 for reviews of research on field trips and outdoor learning).

17.2.2 Theories of Learning

In this section, we present the core principles of three learning theories that have paved the way of informal learning and more precisely of outdoor learning: situated learning, place-based learning and experiential learning. In addition, given the prevalence of inquiry-based learning activities in the applications that we describe in the following section, we also give a brief overview of this pedagogical approach.

17.2.2.1 Situated Learning

Situated learning was first discussed by Lave et al. (1991), who advocated that learning activities should take place in the same context as which it is applied, i.e. in an authentic context. Situated learning theory considers that learning is a "social process" during which knowledge is shared in a community of practice that includes people with different levels of expertise. Communication, collaboration and interaction between these members are key aspects of knowledge sharing. In other words, knowledge is not individualised and un-contextualised but distributed across the members of the community. As the physical or social context changes, learners are encouraged to develop new methods or approaches, which result in learners acquiring knowledge. In situated learning activities, and unlike in traditional or classroom settings, theoretical and abstract knowledge is not the ultimate goal. Rather, learners are encouraged to work on concrete and practical problems and to learn by doing and experiencing the real world.

Although apprenticeships are often quoted as an illustrative example of situated learning, other types of learning situations echo the core principles of situated learning, such as workshops, visiting professionals, field trips, activities within greenhouses, garden or national parks or role plays. In addition, the learning activities themselves are often very practical and can rely on a variety of pedagogical approaches such as problem-based learning, project-based learning or case-based scenarios.

17.2.2.2 Experiential Learning

Experiential learning theory was introduced by Kolb (2014): it posits that hands-on or learning-by-doing activities are part of the learning process and emphasises that it is important to let students reflect upon their own learning experience. Learning occurs when students integrate new experiences within their pre-existing knowledge. As a result, experiential learning "emphasizes independent judgment, free thinking, and personal experience". Kolb's experiential learning cycle is composed of four phases through which students must go in order to complete the learning experience: (i) concrete experience—through which learners are facing new experiences; (ii) reflective observation; (iii) abstract conceptualization—during which students propose form new ideas based on reflection; and (iv) active experimentation, through which students can test their idea(s) in a new situation and reflect upon the results. Each of these stages require different activities: concrete experience is about "feeling"; reflective observation is about "observing" or "watching", abstract conceptualization is about "thinking" and active experimentation is about "doing".[3]

---

[3]https://www.learning-theories.com/experiential-learning-kolb.html.

17.2.2.3 Place-Based Learning

Place-based learning is strongly associated with situated learning. Place-based learning also emphasizes the importance of community in the learning process, but in
that case communities refer to the students' local communities and their historical,
social or cultural background (Smith 2002). Placed-based learning, also referred to
as community-placed learning, can be seen as an immersive learning experience that
"places students in local heritage, cultures, landscapes, opportunities and experiences, and uses these as a foundation for the study of language, arts, mathematics,
social studies, science and other subjects across the curriculum.".[4] The learning context is provided by the community itself or by some problems or events encountered at
a local level. It encourages students' involvement and commitment within their local
community. Placed-based learning activities are often conducted outdoors and are
usually interdisciplinary. Examples of activities include the visit of local and historic
landmarks that reflect how people used to live or their traditions (Staff 2017).

17.2.2.4 Inquiry-Based Learning

Place-based learning activities are often inquiry-based. Inquiry-based learning differs from traditional learning during which teachers provide students with a certain
number of predefined concepts. Inquiry-based learning relies on the active role of the
students, who are asked to reflect upon what they need to learn in order to solve one
problem that can be of an economic, ecological or socio-political nature. Although
there exist various levels of inquiry, the general idea is that students formulate their
own research questions on a specific topic and then try to develop methods in order
to collect data that will enable them to answer that question. The teacher's role is
to be a mediator and to provide on-time cues or pieces of advice that will guide
students in their inquiry process, which is often composed of four steps (Pedaste
et al. 2015): (i) orientation (understanding and discussing the key ideas at stake); (ii)
conceptualization (generating questions and hypothesis); (iii) investigation (e.g. by
collecting data and analysing the results); conclusion (putting data together to come
up with a valid explanation/answer to the main question). Inquiry-based learning is
often used in science education as it reflects scientific approach to problem-solving.

17.2.2.5 Situated and Placed-Based Outdoor Environmental Education

Both situated and place-based learning theories are particularly relevant for environmental education (Woodhouse and Knapp 2000). Indeed, it seems intuitive for
environmental concepts or facts to be taught at the place where they occur so that
students can grasp these concepts more easily and see it in their real context instead

---

[4]https://k12teacherstaffdevelopment.com/tlb/what-is-place-based-learning-and-how-can-it-be-
used-in-your-curriculum/.

of in decontextualised class books. It is also important for students to have some knowledge about their local environment (e.g. the fauna and flora) if we want them to develop a sense of attachment to it and to later play an active role in its protection. Environmental issues can also affect one community at different levels (economical or even it terms of health): enabling students to discover and understand these causal effects at the place where they actually occur and within their local community can therefore be a key feature of the learning process. Experiential learning theory has also been successfully applied to design outdoor learning activities for environmental education (Jose et al. 2017).

However, and despite their potential, field trips or outdoor learning activities can be difficult to organise and/or be limited to somehow traditional approaches, e.g. activities during which the teacher or an instructor guides the students through different places and delivers explanations. This can lead students to be relatively passive in their learning experience. One way to enrich field trips is to leverage on the opportunities offered by technological tools, such as mobile phones or other devices (e.g. Bursztyn et al. 2017b). Over the last decade, mobile learning in particular has indeed proved to be a major breakthrough for the future of education as it offers a large palette of opportunities to enrich learning experiences. Mobile technologies promote students' collaboration and support innovative instructional materials— teachers can design multimedia content that can be delivered at different times, encouraging students to learn collaboratively and/or at their own pace. The use of mobile integrated technologies, such as camera, microphone, GPS sensors, etc. can also enrich the learning process by encouraging the active participation of the students in the learning activity.

Therefore, it is not surprising that the use of mobile devices for outdoor education has been increasingly investigated (Schneider and Schaal 2018). For example, Zimmerman and Land (2014) proposed a set of design guidelines for the implementation of place-based learning activities outdoors. Other studies focused more precisely on the learning outcomes or students' learning attitudes towards such applications. As summarised by Schneider et al. (2017), it has been shown that "the use of [mobile devices] proved to be beneficial for fostering environmental attitude, environmental knowledge, pupils' interaction with their classmates and the topic and inquiry-based learning". The capabilities of mobile phones have also led researchers to investigate the potential of Augmented Reality based mobile applications for outdoor environmental education.

17.3 Enriching Field Trips with AR: Examples of Existing AR Projects for Outdoor Environment Education

Augmented Reality is becoming more and more popular in the field of education and a number of studies have already shown its potential to enrich environmental education learning activities. In this section, we describe examples of AR projects that have been developed to enhance outdoor activities in the context of environmental education (cf. Table 17.1). By doing so, we aim to provide an overview of the most common usages of AR for outdoor environment education. This will enable us to discuss what has been investigated so far and what could be further investigated.

The examples listed below are not a comprehensive review of existing systems, nor are they all AR apps stricto sensu. Indeed, AR apps should in theory fulfil the three following criteria (Azuma 1997): (i) they must combine real and virtual objects; (ii) they must be interactive in real time and (iii) they must be registered in a 3D space. As we will discuss, very few of the systems we describe match all three criteria. However, they were all presented and discussed as augmented-reality apps in the sense that they provide students with an augmented/enriched view of the environment. We therefore chose to describe these systems in order to later discuss the untapped potential of "real" Augmented Reality for outdoor learning experiences.

17.3.1 Inquiry-Based Learning with AR

Mad City Mystery (Squire and Jan 2007) is an AR game that was designed to better understand the effects of such games on learning and how they affect students' scientific thinking. Through the app, students were asked to investigate the causes of a mysterious death that happened at a lake. The AR game invited students to combine different sources of information (interviews, water quality samples, etc.) in order to come up with a feasible explanation. There are multiple causes of the death that involve a combination of lifestyle factors (depression, alcoholism) and environmental issues (excessive exposure to chemicals such as TCE, PCBs, and mercury). Students had to take on different roles (medical doctor, environmental scientist or government official) in order to access a variety of digital content (i.e. pieces of evidence). Based on their location at the lake, students were asked to solve some challenges, to listen to interview, to take measurements, etc. The application was evaluated with three groups of students through a series of interviews and questionnaires regarding students' attitudes, understanding of environmental issues and ability to solve similar problems. The evaluation revealed that particular game mechanics (e.g. challenges and roles) lead students to engage in scientific argumentation and to play unusual roles (e.g. active investigators instead of passive students). The authors also emphasized the importance of place-based activities, which enabled students "to draw on pre-existing knowledge, such as the physical lay-out of space and known potential toxins in the environment". This is one core idea of place-based learning. The place-based activities also played a crucial role in making students aware that scientific facts can also affect their lives and the life of their community, and in engaging students into the game. In fact, the mapping between the physical locations and the virtual interviews were considered as important by both the students and the teachers.

"Mystery at the lake" (Georgiou and Kyza 2018) was designed to help students understand "scientific concepts related to the lake ecosystem, such as food chains, eutrophication, and bioaccumulation". Students had to use various features of the

Table 17.1 List of systems described in the following section

System name	References	Learning outcomes/concepts	Learning strategies and approaches
Mad City Mystery	Squire and Jan (2007)	Scientific thinking, geochemical water cycles	Place-based learning; game-based learning[a]; inquiry-based learning
Mystery at the Lake	Georgiou and Kyza (2018)	Lake ecosystems: food chains, eutrophication and bioaccumulation	Immersion as a key for learning; inquiry-based learning
Environmental Detectives	Klopfer (2005)	Ground water contaminants	Game-based learning; probeware; inquiry learning
Opera2222	Smørdal et al. (2016)	Socio-scientific issues related to climate change	Situated knowledge building
EcoMOBILE Water Quality	Kamarainen et al. (2018)	Water quality and graph interpretation	Situated learning theory; probeware
EcoMOBILE Atom Tracker	Kamarainen et al. (2016)	Cycling of matter in ecosystems (oxygen and carbon); processes of photosynthesis and respiration;	Game-based learning
Save Elli	Koutromanos et al. (2018)	Environmental issues of an island	Situated-learning theory; game-based learning
Butterfly Garden Game	Hwang et al. (2016)	Ecology of butterflies (growing cycle, appearance features, enemies, host plants)	Game-based learning
Butterfly Ecology Learning System	Tarng et al. (2015)	Butterflies' life cycle and role in the food chain	Game-based learning
Botanical Garden/EcoDiscovery Learning System	Huang et al. (2016)	Plants	Experiential learning theory
Tree investigators	Zimmerman and Land (2014)	Biodiversity of trees—local/non-native trees; evergreen/deciduous trees	Place-based learning
Grand Canyon	Bursztyn et al. (2017a)	geologic time; geologic structures; hydrologic processes	Game-based learning
Ambient Wood	Rogers et al. (2004)	Scientific inquiry; woodland habitat	Probeware

[a] According to Qian and Clark (2016), "game-based learning describes an environment where game content and game play enhance knowledge and skills acquisition, and where games activities involve problem solving spaces and challenges that provide players/learners with a sense of achievement". See De Freitas (2006) for a review of game-based learning.

app to provide an evidence-based explanation of the decline of mallard duck at the lake. The application prompted students to collect data samples at different hotspots and delivered content based on their locations, such as videos, tables or images. The video-based characters were also used to trigger students' critical thinking. This application was developed to better understand how student motivation and immersion could predict learning outcomes. It was evaluated through a range of standard questionnaires, with 135 10th graders. Pre- and post-exams showed moderate learning gains, and engagement-defined as a level of immersion-, proved to be a good predictor of learning gains.

In a similar fashion, *Environmental Detectives* (Klopfer 2005) required students to gather factual evidence in order to investigate how to tackle "a simulated chemical spill on a watershed". Once again, the AR application was used to deliver information to students, e.g. about toxicology or hydrology, but also to enable them to gather data about the environmental issue. Through an iterative design process, the authors explored various game mechanics (e.g. cascading events, or roles) and design alternatives and observed how they created diverse game experience. For example, groups of students perceived the game differently: some focused mainly on the quantitative aspects of the contamination and ignored social aspects; others tried to "collect" as many interviews as possible. Students failed to come up with satisfactory solutions and teachers had to intervene to trigger deeper discussions on the topic. However, framing up the story within students' community triggered students' motivation.

17.3.2 Other Pedagogical Approaches

Other applications mentioned in Table 17.1 do not strictly follow an inquiry-based approach. In the following examples, students' exploration of the outdoor environment is less structured and rather aim at triggering questions and observations.

Opera2222 (Smørdal et al. 2016) used situated simulation (Liestøl 2011) to augment the environment, i.e. a full-screen simulation of the environment on a handheld device with "a distinct (although minor) difference between the artificial (audio–visual) perspective via the device and the real perspective of the user".[5] Students must move to different hotspots located near the Opera House of Oslo in order to access situated simulations that show how the Opera House looks like in 2222—at that time, the city is abandoned, and the sea level has dramatically raised (cf. Fig. 17.1). Students must gather information from these different hotspots in order to explain the reasons behind such a change—climate change being one of the reasons. Observations showed that the different cues given through the simulations triggered questioning and hypothesis-making, but also collaboration. The analysis of the presentation that students had to give after experiencing the situated simulation showed that "the students were very engaged with the environment, in terms of wanting to

---

[5]https://sitsim.no/.

Fig. 17.1 Example of
situated simulations used in
Opera2222 (Smørdal et al.
2016)

find all the questions and cues, and wanting to build knowledge that could support their explanations." (Smørdal et al. 2016).

Various applications for outdoor environmental education were developed as part of the EcoMOBILE research project.[6] One of them, called EcoMOBILE Water Quality Measurement (Kamarainen et al. 2013), was composed of pre-field, field and post-field trip activities for classes of sixth graders. Students could use a mobile application as well as various probe ware to learn and understand the role of organisms near a pond ecosystem. The probeware enabled them to compile various measures, such as the temperature or pH of the water. The mobile app had multiple purposes: it helped students to navigate from one hotspot to the other; it provided instructions and information; it enabled students to enter values; it provided immediate feedback based on the values entered by the students. At some locations, the AR app delivered various media to the students, such as texts, videos but also 3D visualizations. After collecting all the measurements, each student discussed with their teacher various aspects of the pond ecosystem—e.g. is the water healthy for fish? How could acid rain affect the pond?

This project was evaluated with five classes, mainly in terms of content learning and students' attitudes. Findings revealed that students' scores strongly increased between the pre- and post-questionnaire and that students' perception of the field trip were positive, especially when the activities included technological features (e.g. 3D visualization and interactive questions). As for teachers, they "reported high levels of student engagement with the technology, and also with science". They also valued the use of technology as a way to encourage students' independence in learning, which in turn enabled teachers to act more as facilitators.

The EcoMOBILE Atom Tracker (Kamarainen et al. 2016) used a similar approach and was "designed to help students better understand the cycling of matter in ecosystems, with a focus on the concept of conservation of matter and the processes of photosynthesis and respiration". Students could follow the cycle of a carbon or oxygen atom through their environment. Prompts were delivered by the application to invite students to physically explore their environment and follow the atom, while

---

[6]https://ecolearn.gse.harvard.edu/ecoMOBILE/design.php.

QR codes were also used to deliver explanations to students (e.g. videos, images or animations) and "visualize otherwise hidden processes including transpiration, photosynthesis, and respiration". Students also had to ask a number of questions in order to continue their experience: if students' answers were incorrect, additional information was provided.

The AR app "Save Elli! Save the Environment" (Koutromanos et al. 2018) is a location-based game that takes place on the island of Santorini, Greece, at five different locations. On each hotspot, students were provided with information related to one environmental issue as well as with a multiple-choice questionnaire that they had to correctly answer in order to retrieve a secret code that enabled them to save the turtle Elli. Information was delivered through images, videos or a website. The evaluation of the application with 40 students enabled authors to better understand how attitudes, social influence, usefulness and enjoyment could explain students' motivation to play the game.

Hwang et al. (2016) developed an AR competitive game to help students engage with an educational activity that took place in a butterfly garden. The aim was to teach students basic concepts regarding the ecology of butterflies (e.g. their growing cycle, the hosting plants, etc.). It provided instructions to move from one hotspot to another, and at each hotspot students were asked to play a mini-game that was part of the learning process. Games were triggered when the students scanned a QR code. For example, a shooting-game enables students to understand what are the natural enemies or predators of butterflies (cf. Fig. 17.2). Students had to make real-world observations in order to progress within the game. Additional game mechanics included a system of scoring (the list of the top 10 players can be accessed) and a board game. An evaluation was conducted to compare the use of the AR game to a regular AR application without gaming. Results showed that the gaming approach led to better learning achievements and also had a positive impact on students' learning attitudes towards the natural science course.

Another application (Tarng et al. 2015) was developed to help students understand butterfly's life cycle, their roles in the environment and how they can be threatened

Fig. 17.2 Illustration of a mini-game used in Hwang et al. (2016) to teach students about the ecology of butterflies

by humans' activities. It combined real-word host plants with virtual butterflies. The main motivations behind this project was to offer students access to a butterfly garden that would otherwise be costly and difficult to maintain. In addition, the observation of virtual butterflies made it possible to control when students could breed them or see them pupate or break the pupas, which would be much more unlikely in a real butterfly garden. The system was composed of two main features: (i) the use of smartphones to breed and observe virtual butterflies that appear close to their host plant, as well as their natural enemies; (ii) a virtual butterfly garden that students could freely explore and in which they could catch a butterfly in order to get more details about its life cycle. The application also included some questions: when correctly answered, students received virtual money that they could use to buy new eggs. The evaluation of the system showed increased learning effectiveness for the student group using the AR system, suggesting that navigating through the virtual butterfly garden helped students to understand and remember different concepts that they were taught. In fact, students appreciated the possibility to replay the animations for breeding, to capture butterfly and also felt immersed.

In Huang et al. (2016), a botanical garden was used as the core of mobile AR app that relied on the four stages of experiential theory: concrete experience, reflective observation, abstract conceptualization and active experimentation. Thanks to the mobile app, students were guided towards the different areas of the botanical garden and could access information regarding the different plants (cf. Fig. 17.3). An evaluation was conducted to compare the learning gains in three different conditions: the AR app only; the AR app and a commentator; a commentator only (i.e. guided tour of the garden). Results showed that the AR commentator group presented higher learning gains and emotional affect than the group of students who had to follow the commentator only. Overall, the two groups who could access the AR app had more positive emotions, and especially the group who could access the AR app and follow the commentator.

Zimmerman and Land (2014) designed Tree Investigators based on a series of guidelines for place-based education. The Tree Investigators project enabled students "to observe trees like a botanist" and to compare local versus non-native species of

Fig. 17.3 Screenshot of a virtual plant (Huang et al. 2016)

trees, but also deciduous and evergreen tree species. Using a set of QR codes placed on different trees, students could access various information, such as pictures of leaves, needles and fruits or video clips of animals or insects that would not be visible in the actual season. The application also enabled students to take pictures of the trees or plants and annotate them. The overarching goal was to promote the collection and sharing of data, while encouraging discussions among learners.

Although designed for geoscience and not environmental education, the mobile AR apps described in Bursztyn et al. (2017c) are also worth mentioning. The collection is formed by three game-based apps aimed to teach students concepts about geologic time, geologic structures and hydrologic processes through an augmenting Grand Canyon field trip. The Grand Canyon was actually scaled down to a 100-m-long playing ground; as students navigated within this space, they could interact with their smartphone at ten different stops in order to answer questions or perform some tasks (e.g. identify a geologic feature). Each module was designed according to one storyline—for example, when learning about hydrologic structures, the app invited students to take part in a "raft trip [...] with a [...] water monitoring crew, along the way taking measurements and conducting surveys of changes in water flow rates, pathways and usage".

The last application described, Ambient Wood (Rogers et al. 2004), was designed to enable students to explore and experiment the woodland surrounding them through various forms of digital augmentations.[7] Students were encouraged to explore the woodland freely in order to make various observations and discoveries. Several pieces of information or explanations were provided through videos, sounds, images or visualizations of dynamic processes, and could be either triggered by students (on-demand) or by the system, for example when students reached a hotspot area. The experience also used a variety of devices: a PDA, a probe tool to gather measurements of light and moisture, a standalone viewing tool to access video clips, loudspeakers and a horn that students could use to listen to various sounds. Observations were made during two studies. They showed that information delivered on-demand by the students were particularly "effective at promoting collaboration, reflection and hypothesising", while information provided automatically by the system was not as effective, mainly because students did not pay attention to the ambient sounds or because they were already engaged in another activity. In addition, the probe tools encouraged students to explore the area extensively.

---

[7]This learning experience was not described as an AR experience; we nonetheless chose to mention it as it shares various similarities with other examples of applications.

17.4   Discussion

17.4.1   Role of Digital Augmentations

Different examples that we described so far cover a large palette of digital augmentations. In EcoMobile Water Quality Measurement (Kamarainen et al. 2013), digital content was delivered to help students understand the cycle of water and the role of organisms—two concepts that are not directly perceivable, either because they take place at different time and space, or because they deal with entities that are not visible to the human eye. In Kamarainen et al. (2016), augmentations were used to show students the path followed by an atom, which would otherwise remain invisible. In Mad City Mystery (Squire and Jan 2007) and Mystery at the Lake (Georgiou and Kyza 2018), additional digital content was mainly used to provide students with audio or video stories at the right time, as if they were actually participating in an investigation case. Opera2222 (Smørdal et al. 2016) differs from other applications as the digital content was used to deliver students a view of the future of an actual place. The two apps that were developed on the topic of butterflies (Tarng et al. 2015; Hwang et al. 2016) used augmentation for a variety of purposes, the main one being the display of virtual butterflies instead of or in addition to real butterflies that can be difficult to observe. In these two projects, the digital augmentation provided students with a view of different species of butterflies, but also of butterflies at different stages of their life cycles. In Huang et al. (2016), digital augmentations were also used to provide students with additional details about plants—details that are not naturally visible from the sole observation of the plants. The same approach was used in Ambient Wood (Rogers et al. 2004) and Tree investigators (Zimmerman and Land 2014)—videos clips and images were used to provide explanations and details. In addition, these two projects also used digital media to encourage students to perceive what they could usually not perceive (e.g. sounds, vegetation hidden below a tree, insects that are only visible during another season, etc.).

   In all of these examples, digital content is provided to reveal the complexity of the environment by showing it from various perspectives, by giving detailed and scientific information about the environment, or by "revealing the invisible". This possibility to provide students with different prisms through which they can perceive and understand their environment might be the most interesting affordance of Augmented Reality for environmental education. Based on the review of the examples presented above, we discuss the main roles of digital augmentation of environment in the context of environmental education: change of time; change of scale; change of perceivability and change of levels of analysis (cf. Fig. 17.4).

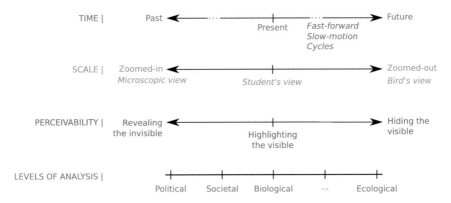

Fig. 17.4 Digital augmentations can be used to provide students with various perspectives/alternative views of their environment. The scale dimension is also discussed in Kamarainen et al. (2016)

17.4.1.1 Change of Time

One key opportunity afforded by AR is to augment the actual environment with content showing how it was in the past or how it could be in the future. This is particularly important as ecosystems are subject to dynamic processes that take place over different periods of time: past actions affect today's environment, and today's actions affect our future environment. By revealing these temporal aspects, AR can enhance student's understanding of dynamic and temporal processes.

The timespan covered by digital augmentations can range from millions of years (e.g. to show the evolution of a landscape at different geological eras, cf. Bursztyn et al. 2017c) to months (e.g. to show how the local fauna changes according to the seasons, cf. Zimmerman and Land 2014), or even hours (e.g. to show the different state of a flower depending on the day, cf. Huang et al. 2016). Changes in time perspective can also allow students to see events that usually occur during the night and are therefore difficult to observe. When augmenting the environment with futuristic content, teachers can help students to get a better idea of the actual impact of one factor on the ecosystem in several years and make it more real/plausible. In that sense, Opera2222 (Smørdal et al. 2016) is a good example: by showing students a dystopic vision of their surroundings, the authors were able to trigger "better explanations and more coherent understandings" related to climate change. In addition, the ability to "tweak" the time perspective can be used to provide students with slow motions animations (e.g. in Tarng et al. 2015 students were eager to replay some animations showing the butterflies at different growing stages) or to skip time (for example to see how a tree would look like in a couple of years). In ECOMobile Atom tracker, "students were 'transported back in time' to see what might have happened to their carbon atom if it had been a part of a starch molecule buried in the mud of a pond 62 Mio. years ago". In the case of inquiry-based activities such as Mystery at the Lake (Georgiou and Kyza 2018), augmentations can be used to replay what happened at a particular moment in time. There are other examples of "time travel" AR games that were not necessarily intended for formal education but encouraged informal learning. For example, Time-wARp Xplorer allowed users to collaboratively build a time warp experience (add their own historical photos and stories) that encouraged other users' exploration of the city of Lancaster by travelling back in time and space based on the players physical location (Lochrie et al. 2013).

This temporal dimension of digital augmentations has been discussed in two existing typologies of AR applications. Normand et al. (2017) distinguish between applications: (i) that represent past situations; (ii) that augment the world with present information and iii) that "are dedicated to foreseeing the future state of a given location". Hugues et al. (2011) identify the possibility to create an artificial environment as one of two main functionalities of AR. In that case, they posit that AR can be used to: (i) "imagine reality as it could be in the future"; (ii) "imagine reality as it was by associating the real and the virtual" and (iii) "imagine an impossible reality". They identify two ways to achieve this goal: either by encrusting virtual objects in/on real images or by encrusting real objects in/on a virtual environment.

17.4.1.2   Change of Scale

Digital augmentations can also be used to reveal what is out of student's field of view. Ecosystems are complex and are often depending on process that take place in distant places that students do not know and/or cannot see. By revealing what cannot be directly seen, AR applications enable students to connect together different places and to have a bird's view of the whole ecosystem and its connections to other natural or human elements. In other words, AR enables students to switch from a local/egocentric point of view to a global/allocentric point of view.

Additionally, AR can be used to give students access to microscopic observations, as in EcoMOBILE Atom Tracker (Kamaraisen et al. 2018) through which students can follow the course of an atom—the goal was to enable students to "'zoom-in' to see molecular processes manifest at different scales—providing students with interactive 'x-ray' molecular vision to see the atoms and molecules within physical objects". In that case, digital augmentations therefore offer a zoomed-in view of the environment.

Another opportunity related to a change of scale is illustrated in Bursztyn et al. (2017c): students are able to gain a better understanding of the Grand Canyon by studying in their school's playground. In fact, one can use the real environment as a physical frame onto which a distant and virtual environment can be displayed. This is particularly useful when distant places cannot be easily accessed and/or would be too dangerous to explore by a group of students. Similar to the idea of using augmentation to shrink/expand time, Augmented Reality can therefore also be used in to shrink/expand distances.

17.4.1.3   Change of Perceivability

In the aforementioned prototype, AR was used to alter the students' perception of their environment, be it by displaying things that did not exist in the environment (e.g. butterflies in Tarng et al. 2015) or by highlighting things that students would otherwise pay little attention to (e.g. hidden vegetation in Ambient Wood). In Tree investigators (Zimmerman and Land 2014), students were encouraged to look at parts of the tree that deserved particular attention. Therefore, AR can be used to augment the real environment with new elements or to highlight existing elements. Interestingly, in Ambient Wood (Rogers et al. 2004), natural sounds were played when students entered a hotspot area—this shows that changes of perceivability can relate to different modalities, e.g. seeing and hearing. In Opera2222 (Smørdal et al. 2016), the simulation showed the environment in the future and therefore with new elements (e.g. signs, buildings, sea) but also with elements that would change over time (e.g. damaged roof). Another feature that relates to a change of perceivability and that has not been used in the described examples is the possibility to use AR to hide objects. One good example would be to "hide" a forest to show students the potential effects of deforestation. Another instance of this change of perceivability is to reveal what is inside some objects, i.e. to provide students with an X-ray/see-through vision (Lochrie et al. 2013) that can help them to better understand the various phenomena at stake in their environment. This aspect is also discussed in the work of Tonnis and Piecher (2011) who distinguish "between objects that are directly shown, information about the existence of concealed objects […], and guiding references to objects outside the field of view that might be visible if the user would look towards that direction".

17.4.1.4   Change of Levels of Analysis

Students can gain understanding of a phenomenon by looking at it from different systemic levels. For example, the colour of an element can be described using qualitative words, but can also be explained by a quantitative analysis of its chemical composition. For example, in Mad City Mystery (Squire and Jan 2007), the water quality could be assessed by visual analysis only, but students were asked to use probeware to make quantitative measures. In the context of environmental education, micro levels of analysis can refer to the analysis of microorganisms, bacteria, molecules, etc. whereas macro levels of analysis can refer to large phenomena such as wind or water flows but also to political or social aspects. While students may tend to focus on what is visible and the scale at which it is visible, enabling them to look at the same object but through different prisms can trigger critical analysis and scientific inquiry. For example, the mysterious death that students investigated in Mad City Mystery is not a result of one cause only, but rather a combination of political, social and biological factors—all of them being difficult to identify and explore without the help of the AR mobile app.

17.4.2 Forms of Digital Augmentations

As discussed earlier, a number of the prototypes that we described are not Augmented-Reality systems per se, as they rely on digital augmentations that are neither mapped on real objects nor registered in 3D (e.g. video clippings in Squire and Jan 2007; textual explanations or instructions in Georgiou and Kyza 2018). Other systems did use 3D anchored virtual objects, such as the plants in Huang et al. (2016), the butterflies in Tarng et al. (2015) or the simulations in Smørdal et al. (2016). In all cases, the strongest link between the digital content and the physical environment was the mapping of the location, i.e. information about one plant would appear when students would be close to that plant only. However, different forms of digital augmentations could trigger different levels of immersion or engagement. Based on existing taxonomies, we discuss various dimensions of digital augmentations that could be taken into account when designing learning activities for environmental education, including spatial mapping, amount, realism, type and media of digital augmentations (cf. Fig. 17.5).

In order to describe handheld AR systems, Vincent (2012) proposed a framework describing two spatial mappings. The first spatial mapping, which refers to "the coupling of the viewpoint of the representation with the handheld device pose in the physical world", can be conformal (viewpoint controlled by the device), relaxed (viewpoint partially controlled) or non-existent. The second spatial mapping, which refers to the coupling between the representation and the augmentation itself, can also be conformal (augmentation is mapped onto the physical object), relaxed or non-existent. Most of the applications that we described displayed textual instructions or visual explanations once the user came close to a hotspot. For these applications,

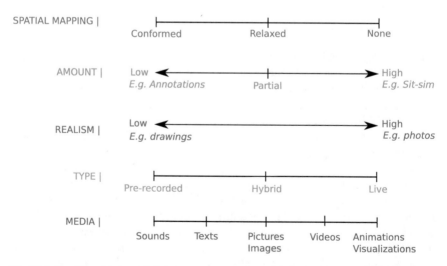

Fig. 17.5 Possible variations of digital augmentations. The first dimension (spatial mapping) refers to Vincent (2012); the last two dimensions (type and media) refer to Rogers et al. (2004)

there was no spatial mapping between the representation of the physical world and the augmentation. In fact, the physical world itself was not represented. On the other hand, some systems used a relaxed mapping between the representation and the physical world, e.g. to display virtual butterflies or plants. Opera2222 used a particular and different approach—situated simulations, which can be considered as one type of "indirect augmented reality", in which the spatial mapping between the physical world and its representation is almost conformal (as there is a slight offset between the camera's pose and the user's point of view), while the spatial mapping between the representation of the physical world and its augmentation is fully conformal. By varying the degree of spatial mappings from none to conformed, especially using the generative power of the framework proposed by Vincent (2012), one could design different digital augmentations that could lead to a higher sense of immersion and/or to a higher understanding of one concept.

Similarly, the number of virtual objects displayed on top of the representation of the physical world and their degree of realism could also significantly affect the learning experience of students. However, rendering real-time and realistic environments can be challenging, as several parameters must be taken into account: light, shadow, differences of colours between the physical world and its representation—cf. Kolivand and Sunar (2014) for an extended review of the computer graphics literature on rendering for outdoor AR. One approach is to voluntarily downscale both the representation of the physical world and the augmentations, e.g. by applying a set of stylisation techniques. By doing so, the annotations and the representation are merged into a unified view (see Fischer et al. 2005, 2006 for examples of brush stroke techniques or cartoon-like rendering for AR). For example, in Huang et al. (2016), simple silhouettes are used to display the plants. On the other hand, it is possible to design highly realistic augmentations. For example, Tarng et al. (2015) carefully design the animations of the butterfly, taking into account different textures but also various parameters to mimic the movements of a butterfly flying or foraging. A higher degree of realism can also lead to an increased sense of place. For example, Ghadirian and Bishop (2008) used realistic landscape visualization to show the spread of blackberries and their landscape over several years.

Finally, digital augmentations can also vary in terms of type and media, as discussed by Rogers et al. in Ambient Wood (Rogers et al. 2004). Augmentations can be either pre-recorded data that is played, or live data that is probed, such as readings. This type of augmentation is particularly interesting in the context of environmental education as probes can support scientific enquiry. Different media can also be used to deliver content, but, as emphasised by Rogers et al. (2004), "the digital augmentation provided should not distract the students from what they are doing but provoke and trigger them to think of how it relates to what is around them and what it means". Possible media include videos, images, sounds, audio or textual explanations, visualizations, animations, etc.

We believe that by taking into account and varying these different parameters, it is possible to design a large range of digital augmentation that could serve various purposes, create different levels of immersion and support several types of learning activities. The different dimensions that we identified are not specific to AR for environmental education; however, they can serve as a tool to design, improve or investigate various forms of digital augmentations while taking into account the specific context in which they are used. For example, designing augmentations that are mapped in a "relaxed manner" to the physical world might be more suitable in order to take into account variations in light that may occur outdoors.

17.4.3 Challenges

17.4.3.1 Technological Challenges

In order to implement genuine AR applications for outdoor learning, i.e. applications that render virtual objects combined with the real world, interactive in the real time and 3D rendered, a number of challenges must be addressed (Zendjebil et al. 2008). Outdoor conditions can change greatly from one day to another, resulting in a variety of lightning conditions that should be taken into account to ensure that the content being rendered remains visible. Noisy environments can also affect students' experience. Although headsets can be provided, they hinder the natural exploration of the environment and are not suitable for collaborative activities. On a practical level, the use of mobile devices can also hinder students' physical experience with their surroundings. For example, in Ambient Wood, the authors reported that "[students'] hands get full, making it difficult for them to touch and pick things up in the woodland" (Rogers et al. 2004). Although one could consider additional devices such as Head-Mounted Display, these devices are still less widespread and more expensive, which make their use for outdoor education unlikely.

Localization accuracy is also crucial to track users' position and display content accurately and on-time. Zendjebil et al. (2008) also identified "the limited processing power and low storage space" of handheld devices a challenge for outdoor AR, alongside the availability of a 3D model of the environment (if required) and the interaction techniques with the device. Finally, losing access to mobile data can also be a problem, as reported in Efstathiou et al. (2018).

Another key challenge of outdoor AR relates to the techniques used to trigger the events. Two main types of mobile AR applications exist (Amin and Govilkar 2015): (i) marker-based AR systems rely on the use of visual markers (e.g. QR codes) that users can scan; (ii) location-based AR systems rely on the combination of devices' accelerometer, compass and GPS to detect the users' position and orientation and trigger the digital augmentations accordingly. While the first method is easier to implement, it requires teachers to equip the environment with the markers, the detection of which can be altered by light conditions. As for the second method, it depends on the quality of the GPS and makes it necessary to map the environment. Interestingly, this second approach can be used in combination with the recognition and identification of real-world objects, either based on some of their characteristics (e.g. colour, shape, texture) or thanks to previously acquired 3D models of the object. When the object is identified, it can be augmented with digital content.

17.4.3.2   Pedagogical Challenges

One major challenge of using technologies outdoors is to find a good balance between real-world observations and on-screen observations. In Ambient Wood (Rogers et al. 2004), the authors acknowledged that "there is also the danger [PDAs] can end up focusing the student's attention on the technology". This concern was also mentioned in Schneider and Schaal (2018), when the attention required by the screen could distract students from fully experiencing their natural surroundings. As one of the key benefits of Environmental education is to expose students with nature, AR apps should be carefully designed so as not to overcome this benefit.

In fact, the design of educational activities for AR is one of the main barriers to the widespread adoption of AR for education. Designing reliable application is time-consuming and require some skills. However, a number of authoring tools exist that can assist teachers and educational content creators in the design of their AR apps (see Cubillo et al. 2015, Mota et al. 2016 for reviews of existing tools and propositions of new authoring tools).

Outdoor learning activities also come up with a large range of information sources—from the environment but also from students' interaction with each other and from the mobile/AR devices themselves. This could lead to some type of "information overload" that needs to be carefully considered and addressed when designing the pedagogical content. This aspect is particularly crucial when the activities also require students to make observations using additional devices or to draw sketches of what they see. The multiplication of material and sources of information should not become detrimental to students' attention and learning.

17.5   Conclusion

Environmental education not only helps students understand how nature works but it also helps them to better understand how human activities can affect it, be it in a negative manner (e.g. through deforestation) or in a positive manner (e.g. by taking actions). Understanding environmental issues is a challenging task that require students to critically think about various factors, such as social ecological, economic, cultural or political issues. In this chapter, we discussed how Augmented Reality can be used to support students during environmental education activities.

We first described a number of learning theories that promote learning in context and highlighted the importance of outdoor learning (and in particular of field trips) for environmental education. Through the description of 12 research prototypes, we then emphasised how mobile devices can be used in learning situations to provide students with digital content that can affect the learning experience, e.g. by providing explanations of complex natural phenomena, helping students navigate their environment or asking them to perform various activities. These prototypes covered a large range of topics, including the ecology of butterflies, the cycling of matter in ecosystems, biodiversity or climate change. Reflecting upon these examples, we discussed the various roles and forms that digital augmentations can take in the context of outdoor AR for environmental education. In particular, we discussed how AR can help students look at their environment from various and varying perspectives, in order to reveal what is not immediately perceptible. For example, we discussed how digital augmentations can show the environment at different times (e.g. past), scales (e.g. microscopic) or through different levels of analysis (e.g. biological or social). We hope that this discussion will encourage the development of AR apps for environmental education and the assessment of the role and forms of digital augmentations in terms of learning outcomes, immersion or motivation.

References

Amin D, Govilkar S (2015) Comparative study of augmented reality SDKs. Int J Comput Sci Appl 5:11–26

Azuma RT (1997) A survey of augmented reality. Presence Teleoperators Virtual Environ 6:355–385

Behrendt M, Franklin T (2014) A review of research on school field trips and their value in education. Int J Environ Sci Educ 9:235–245

Bursztyn N, Shelton B, Walker A, Pederson J (2017a) Increasing undergraduate interest to learn geoscience with GPS-based augmented reality field trips on students' own smartphones. GSA Today 27:4–10. https://doi.org/10.1130/GSATG304A.1

Bursztyn N, Walker A, Shelton B, Pederson J (2017b) Increasing undergraduate interest to learn geoscience with GPS-based augmented reality field trips on students' own smartphones. GSA Today 27:4–11

Bursztyn N, Walker A, Shelton B, Pederson J (2017c) Assessment of student learning using augmented reality Grand Canyon field trips for mobile smart devices. Geosphere 13:260–268. https://doi.org/10.1130/GES01404.1

Cubillo J, Martin S, Castro M, Boticki I (2015) Preparing augmented reality learning content should be easy: UNED ARLE—an authoring tool for augmented reality learning environments. Comput Appl Eng Educ 23:778–789

De Freitas S (2006) Learning in immersive worlds: a review of game-based learning

Dillon J, Rickinson M, Teamey K et al (2006) The value of outdoor learning: evidence from research in the UK and elsewhere. Sch Sci Rev 87:107

Drissner J, Haase H-M, Hille K (2010) Short-term environmental education-does it work?—An evaluation of the 'Green Classroom.' J Biol Educ 44:149–155

Efstathiou I, Kyza EA, Georgiou Y (2018) An inquiry-based augmented reality mobile learning approach to fostering primary school students' historical reasoning in non-formal settings. Interact Learn Environ 26:22–41. https://doi.org/10.1080/10494820.2016.1276076

Farmer J, Knapp D, Benton GM (2007) An elementary school environmental education field trip: long-term effects on ecological and environmental knowledge and attitude development. J Environ Educ 38:33–42

Fischer J, Bartz D, Straßer W (2005) Stylized augmented reality for improved immersion. In: Proceedings - IEEE virtual real. https://doi.org/10.1109/vr.2005.71

Fischer J, Bartz D, Straßer W (2006) Artistic reality: fast brush stroke stylization for augmented reality. In: Proceedings of the ACM symposium on virtual reality software and technology VRST 2006, pp 155–158

Georgiou Y, Kyza EA (2018) Relations between student motivation, immersion and learning outcomes in location-based augmented reality settings. Comput Hum Behav 89:173–181. https://doi.org/10.1016/j.chb.2018.08.011

Ghadirian P, Bishop ID (2008) Integration of augmented reality and GIS: a new approach to realistic landscape visualisation. Landsc Urban Plan 86:226–232. https://doi.org/10.1016/j.landurbplan.2008.03.004

Huang TC, Chen CC, Chou YW (2016) Animating eco-education: to see, feel, and discover in an augmented reality-based experiential learning environment. Comput Educ 96:72–82. https://doi.org/10.1016/j.compedu.2016.02.008

Hugues O, Fuchs P, Nannipieri O et al (2011) New augmented reality taxonomy : technologies and features of augmented environment. To cite this version: HAL Id : hal-00595204 New augmented reality taxonomy: technologies and features of augmented environment

Hwang GJ, Wu PH, Chen CC, Tu NT (2016) Effects of an augmented reality-based educational game on students' learning achievements and attitudes in real-world observations. Interact Learn Environ 24:1895–1906. https://doi.org/10.1080/10494820.2015.1057747

Jennings P (2009) New directions in renewable energy education. Renew Energy 34:435–439

Jose S, Patrick PG, Moseley C (2017) Experiential learning theory: the importance of outdoor classrooms in environmental education. Int J Sci Educ Part B 7:269–284

Kamarainen AM, Metcalf S, Grotzer T et al (2013) EcoMOBILE: integrating augmented reality and probeware with environmental education field trips. Comput Educ 68:545–556. https://doi.org/10.1016/j.compedu.2013.02.018

Kamarainen A, Metcalf S, Grotzer T, et al (2016) Atom tracker: designing a mobile augmented reality experience to support instruction about cycles and conservation of matter in outdoor learning environments. Int J Des Learn 7

Kamarainen A, Reilly J, Metcalf S et al (2018) Using mobile location-based augmented reality to support outdoor learning in undergraduate ecology and environmental science courses. Bull Ecol Soc Am 99:259–276

Kljun M, Pucihar KC, Solina F, others (2018) Persuasive technologies in m-learning for training professionals: how to keep learners engaged with adaptive triggering. IEEE Trans Learn Technol

Klopfer E (2005) Environmental detectives—The development of an augmented reality platform for environmental simulations. Educ Res Technol Dev 50

Kolb DA (2014) Experiential learning: Experience as the source of learning and development. FT press

Kolivand H, Sunar MS (2014) Realistic real-time outdoor rendering in augmented reality. PLoS One 9. https://doi.org/10.1371/journal.pone.0108334

Kossack A, Bogner FX (2012) How does a one-day environmental education programme support individual connectedness with nature? J Biol Educ 46:180–187

Koutromanos G, Tzortzoglou F, Sofos A (2018) Evaluation of an augmented reality game for environmental education: "Save Elli, Save the Environment." In: Research on e-Learning ICT in education 231–241. https://doi.org/10.1007/978-3-319-95059-4_14

Krepel WJ, DuVall CR (1981) Field trips: a guide for planning and conducting educational experiences. Analysis and action series. ERIC

Lave J, Wenger E et al (1991) Situated learning: legitimate peripheral participation. Cambridge university press, Cambridge

Leicht A, Heiss J, Byun WJ (2018) Issues and trends in education for sustainable development. UNESCO Publishing

Liestøl G (2011) Situated simulations between virtual reality and mobile augmented reality: designing a narrative space. In: Furht B (ed) Handbook of augmented reality. Springer, New York, pp 309–319

Lochrie M, Čopič Pucihar K, Gradinar A, Coulton P (2013) Time-wARpXplorer: creating a playful experience in an urban time warp. Phys Digit Games Play

Mota JM, Ruiz-Rube I, Dodero JM, Figueiredo M (2016) Visual environment for designing interactive learning scenarios with augmented reality. Int Assoc Dev Inf Soc

Nincarean D, Alia MB, Halim NDA, Rahman MHA (2013) Mobile augmented reality: the potential for education. Proc-Soc Behav Sci 103:657–664

Normand J, Servières M, Moreau G et al (2017) A new typology of augmented reality applications To cite this version : HAL Id : hal-01521375 A new typology of augmented reality applications

Pedaste M, Mäeots M, Siiman LA et al (2015) Phases of inquiry-based learning: definitions and the inquiry cycle. Educ Res Rev 14:47–61

Qian M, Clark KR (2016) Game-based Learning and 21st century skills: a review of recent research. Comput Human Behav 63:50–58

Rogers Y, Price S, Fitzpatrick G, et al (2004) Ambient wood: designing new forms of digital augmentation for learning outdoors. In: Proceedings of the 2004 conference on Interaction design and children: building a community, pp 3–10

Schneider J, Schaal S (2018) Location-based smartphone games in the context of environmental education and education for sustainable development: fostering connectedness to nature with Geogames. Environ Educ Res 24:1597–1610. https://doi.org/10.1080/13504622.2017.1383360

Schneider J, Schaal S, Schlieder C (2017) Geogames in education for sustainable development: transferring a simulation game in outdoor settings. In: Proceedings of 2017 9th international conference on virtual worlds and games for serious applications VS-Games 2017, pp 79–86. https://doi.org/10.1109/VS-GAMES.2017.8056574

Smith GA (2002) Place-based education: learning to be where we are. Phi Delta Kappan 83:584–594

Smørdal O, Liestøl G, Erstad O (2016) Exploring situated knowledge building using mobile augmented reality. Qwerty - Open Interdiscip J Technol Cult Educ 1:26–43

Specht M, Ternier S, Greller W (2011) Dimensions of mobile augmented reality for learning: a first inventory

Squire KD, Jan M (2007) Mad city mystery: Developing scientific argumentation skills with a place-based augmented reality game on handheld computers. J Sci Educ Technol 16:5–29. https://doi.org/10.1007/s10956-006-9037-z

Staff GS (2017) What is place-based education and why does it matter. Accessed 4 March 2017

Suárez Á, Specht M, Prinsen F et al (2018) A review of the types of mobile activities in mobile inquiry-based learning. Comput Educ 118:38–55

Tarng W, Ou KL, Yu CS et al (2015) Development of a virtual butterfly ecological system based on augmented reality and mobile learning technologies. Virtual Real 19:253–266. https://doi.org/10.1007/s10055-015-0265-5

Toennis M, Plecher DA (2011) Presentation principles in augmented reality classification and categorization guidelines

Vincent T (2012) Classifying handheld augmented reality: three categories linked by spatial mappings. Work classifying AR present Sp ISMAR 2012

Woodhouse JL, Knapp CE (2000) Place-based curriculum and instruction: outdoor and environmental education approaches. ERIC Digest

Wu W-H, Wu Y-CJ, Chen C-Y et al (2012) Review of trends from mobile learning studies: A meta-analysis. Comput Educ 59:817–827

Zendjebil I, Ababsa F-E, Didier J-Y et al (2008) Outdoor augmented reality: state of the art and issues. In: 10th ACM/IEEE virtual reality international conference (VRIC 2008), pp 177–187

Zimmerman HT, Land SM (2014) Facilitating place-based learning in outdoor informal environments with mobile computers. TechTrends 58:77–83. https://doi.org/10.1007/s11528-013-0724-3

Chapter 18
Augmented Reality in Environmental Humanities Education

Dragoş Gheorghiu, Livia Ştefan, and Mihaela Moţăianu

Abstract Environmental humanities is an emerging multidisciplinary field of research focused on identifying the impact of modern human (including cultural) activities on the environment, as well as of environmentally friendly solutions. Environmental damage can have serious consequences for the present, as well as for the past, as in the case of archaeological sites, whose investigation becomes difficult and whose process of decay is accelerated. As these issues have not yet been addressed through effective and systematic educational solutions, this chapter proposes, as part of the environmental humanities strategy a digital humanities educational solution centred on the technology of Augmented Reality (AR). The IT application proposed aims to identify the areas of ecological risk and provide detailed information on the destruction processes, as well as the ability to connect with networks of specialists. The authors' aims are to stimulate critical thinking focused on environmental issues, provide a solution for continuous learning for both specialists and the public, thus contributing to the protection of the environment and of archaeological subjects, and to further the development of sustainable activities through education and awareness.

D. Gheorghiu (✉)
Doctoral School, National University of Arts, Bucharest, Romania
e-mail: gheorghiu_dragos@yahoo.com

Earth and Memory Institute (ITM), Quaternary and Prehistory Group of the Geosciences Centre, Coimbra, Portugal

L. Ştefan
Bucharest, Romania
e-mail: livia.stefan@yahoo.com

M. Moţăianu
National University of Arts, Bucharest, Romania
e-mail: mihaela.motaianu@gmail.com

© Springer Nature Switzerland AG 2020
V. Geroimenko (ed.), *Augmented Reality in Education*,
Springer Series on Cultural Computing,
https://doi.org/10.1007/978-3-030-42156-4_18

18.1   Introduction

The recently emerged, new perspective on the changing world, the Anthropocene (Edgeworth et al. 2014), as well as the ecological perspective, point to the fact that we are living in an era of continuous site formation and taphonomy (Edgeworth 2013).

This process is unfolding under our very eyes and sometimes with adverse effects on the historical past. We are referring here to those heritage sites, whose destruction is brought about both by humans and Nature (Micle 2014), thus becoming a mere source of material which contributes to the stratigraphy process of the Anthropocene.

Sites at risk, whether natural or man-made, are subject to destruction through conscious action or neglect (Spiridon et al. 2017) and require for their salvation a holistic approach that Environmental Humanities (EH) can provide (Hutchings 2014).

18.2   Environmental Humanities

EH represents a synthesis of science and the humanities, involving both critical heritage studies (Witcomb and Buckley 2013), the merging of natural and cultural heritage pedagogies (Hutchings 2014), as well as community building (Bird-Rose et al. 2012). It is a perspective that combines both technological, ecological and pedagogical approaches in a unifying vision.

In the case of monuments at risk, this relational perspective between Nature and culture puts archaeology in relation to various ecological, environmental and pedagogical approaches.

It is well-known that archaeology itself connects humanistic disciplines with science (Parikh and Hall 2012) and that in the last decade there has been a propensity of this science to art (Gheorghiu and Barth 2019) due to similar cognitive structures (Gheorghiu 2020), the contribution of art to science nowadays being obvious (Malina 2016).

The educational value of art can help make EH's message more accessible to local communities, while environmental art (or eco-art[1]) will become a current tool for shaping a new mindset.

---

[1] https://www.plushbeds.com/blog/green/what-is-eco-art/ [accessed 20.11.2019].

18.3 Archaeology: Bridging Social and Natural Sciences

From an EH perspective archaeology must become even more a holistic science, imposing a "cross-epistemological dialogue" between high culture and local communities (see Domańska 2015). And this dialogue must have a pedagogical component, especially in regards to the contemporary attitude towards Nature.

We will try to illustrate this new attitude of archaeology in the case of monuments at risk, bringing into discussion two diametrically opposed cases of the relation of culture with Nature.

The examples relate to two archaeological sites located on the banks of the Danube River, in the south of Romania. The first case, the Palaeolithic site of Malu Roşu, is the one of an anthropic destruction of Nature, and the second, the Byzantine site Păcuiul lui Soare, illustrates the damage caused by Nature itself, when the sites are left neglected in the wild.

The Palaeolithic settlement of Malu Roşu is located on a lower terrace of the Danube River and was excavated in the 1980s and 1990s. Although the site revealed a rich Aurignacian lithic industry, in the 1990s Malu Roşu was transformed into the garbage dump of the nearby city (Păunescu and Alexandrescu 1997), which not only put an end to all subsequent archaeological campaigns, but also produced a very dense stratigraphy of very un-perishable materials, such as concrete, plastic or glass. This archaeological site in which prehistoric layers have been overlapped by contemporary recycled materials and domestic garbage is an obvious example of continuous site formation in the Anthropocene, due to an aggressive attitude towards Nature.

An opposite case, that of the aggressive attitude of Nature towards culture is that of the site Păcuiul lui Soare. Situated on a small island on the Danube River, the tenth century Byzantine fortress with walls of ashlar blocks positioned on deep oak beams foundations (Caraivan et al. 2016) is attacked by both aquatic erosion and the dense vegetation of the island. The river annually destroys the masonry on the shores, but a more effective destruction is caused by the vegetation that dislocates the blocks in the areas untouched by water.

How could EH get involved in these cases? First of all, by triggering an alarm signal, to create awareness both within the scientific community and the local communities.

Using contemporary IT technologies, educational applications can be created that visualize the respective sites, and with the help of AR and visual art one can promote awareness raising messages focused on the destruction processes.

For example, in the case of the Malu Roşu site, we propose to present in the AR application, in the form of an animation, a visual scenario in which the contemporary site will be completely covered by garbage. The visual result, which resembles Edward Burtynsky's photographs, such as "Oxford Tire Pile # 8" (see Giesecke and Jacobs 2012, p. 106), has a strong impact on the viewer.

For Păcuiul lui Soare, we present with the help of the AR application the process of destruction produced by the vegetation that has grown uncontrolled over the ruins of the fortress.

Consequently, this chapter proposes the development of an application with educational value, designed to alert the user to the existence of monuments or sites at risk and then to present through different visual narratives the issues confronting them. In addition, the application allows the creation of a network of different organizations or bodies dealing with EH problems around the world, to inform the user about this phenomenon. In the case of the "monuments at risk" described we have chosen the journal *Ecocene: Cappadocia Journal of Environmental Humanities*, with which we collaborate.

For the AR application, called EnviHum.AR, we have used a symbolic logo, that of a junction between "environment" and "humanities".

18.4 Augmented Reality State of the Art

18.4.1 New Technologies in Education: Augmented Reality

Augmented Reality (AR) is a computer-mediated reality, i.e. standing in between reality and virtuality within a "continuum" (Milgram et al. 1994). Due to the technological advancements toward smarter and more powerful mobile devices, AR glasses or headsets, AR is currently more interactive and immersive and closer to the term of "mixed reality". Author Ashford-Rowe (2019, p. 36) considers that mixing reality is not a new concept as "[it] plays into a deep and longstanding capability of the human mind to aggregate the physical and the imagined".

Despite the fact that AR is currently an affordable and popular technology among creators and users, the traditional paradigm according to which AR as an informal education technology providing contextual and experiential learning is not sufficiently explored and it is not yet extended to a mainstream level.

On the other hand, the way in which AR technology can be used in relation with other technologies or with new societal challenges has changed. Azuma (2015) considers that "ultimate uses of mixed reality (MR) and augmented reality (AR) will be to enable new forms of storytelling that enable virtual content to be connected in meaningful ways to particular locations, whether those are places, people or objects" (p. 259).

18.4.2 Augmented Reality Technology and Tools

Augmented Reality is both a concept and a technology. The concept refers to enhancing the perceived reality by adding artificial or simulated content. The concept was first demonstrated by Morton Heillig who, as a cinematographer, patented in 1962 a simulator called Sensorama, mixing visual, acoustic, vibration and smell information and creating a simulated reality.

As a technology, AR refers to different technical means to overlap the simulated content on top of a real worldview, in an interactive manner, with the purpose to provide missing and explanatory information. By unifying the real and the added information, a new and information-richer reality is created having a higher cognitive impact, i.e. the understanding of the reality being thus much improved.

An ideal AR process is the one that clears the differences between the real world and the created world. The placement of the digital information is not a trivial process but one mediated by computer devices and sensors, respectively by means of the AR-tracking process. The technical advances, such as miniaturisation and the development of the mobile devices, which could integrate video camera and sensors, defined a new range of AR category, i.e. the mobile AR (MAR), which is today the most popular and affordable AR-enabled device. The main component is the video camera which fusions information from other sensors, such as the accelerometer, gyroscope, GPS, and employs advanced techniques, such as computer graphics or computer vision, to augment the content on the camera view in real-time and correlated with the user's moving status (Azuma 1997; Azuma et al. 2001).

The earliest usage of the AR, still a typical one, is concerned with augmenting the vision of a surrounding reality or of a static image, which is called either *marker* or *marker-less image-recognition AR*, including *location-based AR*, in which case the targets are geographically defined.

Available tools for marker or marker-less AR relying only on a digital camera are the software library kits (SDK) such as OpenCV (https://opencv.org) for computer vision, ARKit (https://developer.apple.com/documentation/arkit), Vuforia (https://developer.vuforia.com/), AUGMENT (https://www.augment.com/), Google ARCore for Unity3D and Android (https://developers.google.com/ar), Wikitude (https://www.wikitude.com) for Android, iOs, Unity 3D and web, ARGON4 a web browser (https://app.argonjs.io/).

Location-based AR, as another category of AR, allows augmented visualizations in pre-defined points-of-interest (POIs), which define geographic contexts. This type of AR is supported by fewer commercial tools, among which Wikitude and Layar (www.layar.com).

One of the most revolutionary AR scenarios is based on techniques to perform recognition and mapping of spatial data, i.e. of an entire environment, not only of specific POIs or images. Recently, this technique was advanced by means of a 3D depth sensing camera and graphic algorithms, able to analyse and map spatial environments. The technique is called *simultaneous localization and mapping* (SLAM) and has as a result a set of data points called "point clouds". This technique was first performed by robots but currently was made available by AR software tools, for regular AR-enabled devices and platforms. Even if currently discontinued, Metaio AR platform was one of the first to offer to public users such advanced AR features (Gheorghiu et al. 2014, p. 21). Currently, Google ARCore is able to perform SLAM, nonetheless it requires at least Android 7.0 and more powerful and expensive mobile devices.

The AR technology has greatly advanced while facilitating for users the creation of AR applications. Users can concentrate on designing the AR application and content, since the SDKs take-over the challenges of dealing with advanced hardware of the current mobile devices and also on features included in the main mobile operating systems, i.e. Android and iOS.

18.4.3 Augmented Reality Current Status in Education

There is almost no domain in which AR not to be taken into consideration, from digital cockpits as navigation tools, anatomy, medical field and emergency, travel and tourism, art and museums, history, engineering, astronomy, geography, military, entertainment, advertising, television, games and recreation. Almost all categories of AR projects have an educational purpose, even if not declared.

Due to the fact that educational technologies have to be addressed from a multi-disciplinary perspective and theories and styles, it can be considered that education is the most relevant and complex domain in which AR to be applied.

The AR technology currently supports more complex scenarios, mainly as a "mixed-reality", including headsets and special AR/VR equipment. These diverse scenarios rely on mobile and experiential learning, learning by doing (with tasks and activities), learning by playing, collaborative learning, self or peer assessments.

To be effective for formal learning, AR and MR have to "be integrated into teaching and learning [process] and become familiar to the instructional designers and instructional technologists [...] so that they can help instructors integrate MR into their pedagogy (Horizon Report 2019).

On the other side, authors such as Radu and MacIntyre (2012) researched "how can children's developmental psychology be used to the design and usability of the AR applications".

Radu (2014) made a meta-analysis "comparing AR versus non-AR applications [and] identifies a list of positive and negative impacts of AR experiences on student learning, and factors that may cause them", considering that "although previous research has shown that AR systems have the potential to improve student learning, the educational community remains unclear regarding the educational usefulness of AR and regarding contexts in which this technology is more effective than other educational mediums".

Location-based AR scenarios resulted in many and very popular implementations, in domains such as heritage and archaeology (Gheorghiu and Ştefan 2012, 2014, 2015, 2016, 2017, 2019). Pokémon GO (Zsila et al. 2017) is a special and successful case of location-based AR application, even if its educational level is not relevant.

18.4.4   Augmented Reality in Archaeological Education

In contemporary archaeology AR is mainly used as a research tool for reconstruction and interpretation. The importance of digital technologies lead to the creation of a new discipline called Virtual Archaeology (Barceló et al. 2000; Niccolucci 2002).

Archaeologists can take advantage of the AR applications to visualize and analyse different information in their real context and on a just-in-time basis (Trapp et al. 2012; Papagiannakis and Magnenat-Thalmann 2007).

AR/MR technologies are taken into consideration due to their capability to create "presence" and "immersion" (Heeter 1992; Wagner et al. 2009; Witmer and Singer 1998; Zahorik and Jenison 1998).

Eve (2012) considers that AR in archaeology "provide[s] a timely way to combine the strengths of a computer-based approach (reproducibility, experimentation, computer reconstruction) with archaeological phenomenology (embodied experience in the field)".

18.5   EnviHum.AR—An Application for Education and Environmental Awareness

For our research, three main AR capabilities were taken into consideration, along with a creative design of the educational content: (a) location-based information and alerts; (b) recognition and augmentation of a defined natural environment; (c) immersion of the users in a 3D animated simulation.

Using a mixture of AR technology capabilities, an AR application was designed as an educational tool able to alert and inform people on endangered archaeological sites and make them more aware on the impact of different factors of human or natural negligence that may put in danger the overlooked archaeological sites.

EnviHum.AR is an educational application that can identify the areas of ecological risk, provides immediate information under the form of augmentation, as well as the possibility to connect with networks of specialists.

To implement the proposed application the authors took into consideration Wikitude AR toolkit (SDK) for Xamarin framework.

Xamarin framework (Xamarin website) is a Microsoft open-source framework that facilitates the development of cross-platform mobile applications, i.e. which can function both on Android and iOS.

18.5.1   EnviHum.AR Functionalities

In EnviHum.AR marker-based AR processes are used. An image-recognition of the two considered sites can trigger specific augmentation, i.e. information on the

Fig. 18.1 EnviHum.AR
logo and mobile application

evolution in the state of the sites. Alternatively, the geographic coordinates were used as special location-based AR "markers" that can be shown in the AR view and trigger the same augmentations.

Motion tracking, as the fundamental AR process, is supported by Wikitude SDK, in order to correctly position the augmentation within the user's surrounding space while the user is moving the camera (Fig. 18.1).

18.5.2 Malu Roşu—Augmented Content

The augmentation is triggered when the user either scans an image or is coming into the site's premises, i.e. two types of targets are used—images and POIs.

This augmentation was designed as an animated GIF and represents the deposition of garbage on the surface of the site.

Fig. 18.2 Augmentations for Malu Roşu

The animation takes place in a frame with dimensions: 2208 pixels × 2208 pixels; the aspect of the frame is in the ratio 1:1 and has been chosen to respond more easily to different formats (landscape or portrait).

All the visual elements (images of worn objects) are placed randomly on a transparent background and are positioned in the frame so as to create the feeling of depth.

The difference between the near and the far plane is given by their size, so the visual elements in the near plane have larger dimensions and those in the far distance have smaller dimensions; the elements appear successively in the frame and multiply until they occupy all the visible space.

From a technical point of view, the entire visual construction is made of layers that become visible at 1-s intervals; the animated GIF was created with Adobe Photoshop CC 2019.

As the AR does not support animated GIF, this was split in several frames that were put into the AR view with delays, thus suggesting a progressive deterioration of the site, covered by garbage.

Alternatively, when the user is coming into the site's premises, a POI is displayed with a label "Malu Roşu -endangered site. Turn the camera towards the clay terrace" (Fig. 18.2).

18.5.3 Păcuiul lui Soare—The Augmented Content

The augmentation is triggered when the user either scans an image or is coming into the site's premises, i.e. two types of targets are used—images and POIs.

This augmentation was designed as an animated GIF and represents the site deterioration by the vegetation.

The animated GIF is made of four images presented in the form of a slideshow with 2-s interval between frames; the animation was realised with Adobe Photoshop CC 2019.

As the AR does not support animated GIF, the animation was converted into a video.

Fig. 18.3 The Byzantine fortress Păcuiul lui Soare

Fig. 18.4 Augmentations for Păcuiul lui Soare

A special motion-tracking feature supported by Wikitude was implemented, called video snapping, i.e. the video is attached to a visual element of the camera and it continues to run even after the image target is no more in front of the camera.

Alternatively, when the user is coming into the site's premises, a POI is displayed with a label "Păcui -endangered site. Turn the camera towards the fortress walls" (Figs. 18.3 and 18.4).

18.5.4 Networking

Near the augmentations a button is displayed with the message "LEARN MORE". When clicked, a web page is opened, with the link of the *Ecocene: Cappadocia Journal of Environmental Humanities* (Fig. 18.5).

Fig. 18.5 The link of the
Ecocene Journal

18.6   Conclusions

The experiments performed with the users of the EnviHum.AR application have demonstrated the pedagogical value of this tool, which has created an awareness among the urban population for the communities with sites at risk and an awareness on the relationship between culture and Nature in the communities near the sites in question.

The application aims to achieve a state of entanglement (in Hodder 2012 sense) between people and the local heritage and to create an inter-community and international solidarity regarding the risks to the environment. Our intention is also to launch an e-network that supports EH ideas.

Last, but not least, the application aims to be an efficient contribution to the eco-art, which will produce a reaction in this regard towards the perception of the relation with Nature.

In conclusion, the authors intend to stimulate the holistic EH spirit, to offer a continuous learning solution for both specialists and the public, to contribute to the protection of archaeological or natural objectives, and to the development of sustainable activities through education and awareness.

Acknowledgements The authors thank Professor Vlad Geroimenko for the kind invitation to contribute to this book. Thanks also to the students and villagers who participated in the experiments with the AR application and to Mr. Răzvan Clondir for allowing the access to the Păcuiul lui Soare Island. Last, but not least, many thanks to M. Bogdan Căpruciu for the useful comments and to Mrs. Cornelia Cătuna for the editing of the text.

Photos by Mihaela Moţăianu.

References

Ashford-Rowe K (2019) Augmented and mixed reality: the why, when, and how of situating learning in authentic contexts. Educause Horizon report, 2019 Higher Education report, p 36

Azuma RT (1997) A survey of augmented reality. Presence: Teleoperators Virtual Environ 6(4):355–385

Azuma RT (2015) Location-based mixed and augmented reality storytelling. In: Barfield W (ed) Fundamentals of wearable computers and augmented reality, 2nd edn. CRC Press, Boca Raton, pp 259–276

Azuma R, Baillot Y, Behringer R, Feiner S, Julier S, MacIntyre B (2001) Recent advances in augmented reality. IEEE Comput Graph Appl 21(6):34–47

Barceló JA, Forte M, Sanders DH (eds) (2000) Virtual reality in arc. BAR international series, vol 843. Archaeopress, Oxford

Bird-Rose D, van Dooren T, Chrulew M, Cooke S, Kearnes M, O'Gorman E (2012) Thinking through the environment, unsettling the humanities. Environ Humanit 1:1–5

Cappadocia J Environ Humanit. https://ecocene.kapadokya.edu.tr/Anasayfa.Aspx. Accessed Nov 2019

Caraivan G, Dumitriu R, Chera C, Chercea C (2016) New geoarchaeological researches around the Danubian island Păcuiul lui Soare. Pontica XLVIII–XLIX:489–495

Domańska E (2015) Ecological humanities. Tekxty Drugie 1:186–210

Edgeworth M (2013) The relationship between archaeological stratigraphy and artificial ground and its significance in the Anthropocene. In: Waters CN, Zalasiewicz J, Williams M, Ellis M, Snelling AM (eds) A stratigraphical basis for the Anthropocene. Lyell collection special publications, vol 395. The Geological Society Publishing House, Bath, pp 91–108

Edgeworth M, Benjamin J, Clarke B, Crossland Z, Doman'ska E, Gorman AC, Graves-Brown P, Harris EC, Hudson MJ, Kelley JM, Paz VJ, Salerno MA, Witmore C, Zarankin A (2014) Archaeology of the Anthropocene. J Contemp Archaeol 1(1):73–132

Educause Horizon Report (2019) Higher education report. https://www.k12blueprint.com/news/2019-horizon-report-here

Eve S (2012) Augmenting phenomenology: using augmented reality to aid archaeological phenomenology in the landscape. J Archaeol Method Theory 19(4):582–600

Gheorghiu D (2020) Art in the archaeological imagination. Oxbow Books, Oxford

Gheorghiu D, Barth T (eds) (2019) Artistic practices and archaeological research. Archaeopress, Oxford

Gheorghiu D, Ştefan L (2012) Mobile technologies and the use of Augmented Reality for saving the immaterial heritage. In: The 13th international symposium on virtual reality, archaeology and cultural heritage VAST2012, 19–21 Nov 2012, Brighton, UK

Gheorghiu D, Ştefan L (2014) Augmenting the archaeological record with art. In: Geroimenko V (ed) Augmented reality art. From an emerging technology to a novel creative medium . Springer series on cultural computing. Springer, Cham, pp 255–276

Gheorghiu D, Ştefan L (2015) Preserving monuments in the memory of local communities using immersive MAR applications as educational tools. In: Vlada M, Albeanu G, Adascalitei A, Popovici M (eds) Proceedings of ICVL 2015 (ISSN 1844–8933, ISI Proceedings) – the 10th international conference on virtual learning. University of Bucharest Publishing House, Bucharest, pp 440–446

Gheorghiu D, Ştefan L (2016) Virtual palimpsests: augmented reality and the use of mobile devices to visualise the archaeological record. In: Quagliuolo M, Delfino D (eds) Quality management of cultural heritage: problems and good practices, proceedings of the U.I.S.P.P. congress 2014. Archaeopress, Oxford, pp 35–48

Gheorghiu D, Ştefan L (2017) A fractal augmentation of the archaeological record: the time maps project. In: Geroimenko V (ed) Augmented reality art, from an emerging technology to a novel creative medium, 2nd edn. Springer International Publishing, pp 297–316

Gheorghiu D. Ştefan L (2019) Invisible settlements: discovering and reconstructing the ancient built spaces through gaming. In: Geroimenko V (ed) Augmented reality games II. Springer Nature Switzerland AG.

Gheorghiu D, Ştefan L, Rusu A (2014) E-learning and the process of studying in virtual contexts. In: Ivanovic M, Jain L (eds) E-learning paradigms. E-learning paradigms and applications. agent – based approach. Studies in computational intelligence, vol 528. Springer, Berlin, pp 65–95

Giesecke A, Jacobs N (2012) Earth perfect? nature utopia and the garden. Black Dog, London

Heeter C (1992) Being there: the subjective experience of presence. Presence: Teleoperators Virtual Environ 1(2):262–271

Hodder I (2012) Entangled. An archaeology of the relationships between humans and things. Willey-Blackwell, Malden

Hutchings R (2014) Understanding of and vision for the environmental humanities. Environ Human 4:213–220

Malina RF (2016) An annotated bibliography. Art J 75(3):64–69

Micle D (2014) Archaeological heritage between natural hazard and anthropic destruction: the negative impact of social non-involvement in the protection of archaeological sites. Procedia – Soc Behav Sci 163:269–278

Milgram P, Takemura H, Utsumi A, Kishino F (1994) Augmented reality: a class of displays on the reality-virtuality continuum. In: SPIE, Telemanipulator and telepresence technologies, vol 2351, pp 282–292

Niccolucci F (2002) Virtual archaeology, proceedings of the VAST conference in Arezzo, Italy. BAR international series 1075. Archaeopress, Oxford

Papagiannakis G, Magnenat-Thalmann N (2007) Mobile augmented heritage: enabling human life in ancient Pompeii. Int J Archit Comput Multi-Sci Publ 5(2):395–415

Parikh D, Hall K (2012) Science and the material record. Archaeol Rev Camb 27(1):3

Păunescu A, Alexandrescu E (1997) Rezultatele preliminare ale cercetărilor privind aşezarea Aurignaciană de la Giurgiu-Malu Roşu, (campaniile 1992 - 1996). Cultură şi civilizaţie la Dunărea de Jos XV:16–59

Radu I (2014) Augmented Reality in education: a meta-review and cross-media analysis. Pers Ubiquit Comput 18:1533–1543. https://doi.org/10.1007/s00779-013-0747-y

Radu I, MacIntyre B (2012) Using children's developmental psychology to guide augmented-reality design and usability. In: 2012 IEEE international symposium on mixed and augmented reality (ISMAR), pp 227–236

Spiridon P, Sandu I, Stratulat L (2017) The conscious deterioration and degradation of the cultural heritage. Int J Conserv Sci 8(1):81–88

Trapp M, Semmo A, Pokorski R, Herrmann CD, Döllner J, Eichhorn M, Heinzelmann M (2012) Colonia 3D communication of virtual 3D reconstructions in public spaces. Int J Herit Digit Era 1(1):44–74

Wagner I, Broll W, Jacucci G, Kuutli K, Mccall R, Morrison A, Schmalsteig D, Terrin JJ (2009) On the role of presence in mixed reality. Presence: Teleoperators Virtual Environ 18(4):249–276

Witcomb A, Buckley K (2013) Engaging with the future of 'critical heritage studies': looking back in order to look forward. Int J Herit Stud 19(6):562–578

Witmer BG, Singer MJ (1998) Measuring presence in virtual environments: a presence questionnaire. Presence: Teleoperators Virtual Environ 7(3):225–240

Zahorik P, Jenison RL (1998) Presence as being-in-the-world. Presence: Teleoperators Virtual Environ 7(1):78–89

Zsila Á, Orosz G, Bőthe B, Tóth-Király I, Király O, Griffiths M, Demetrovics Z (2017) An empirical study on the motivations underlying augmented reality games: the case of Pokémon GO during and after Pokémon fever. Personal Individ Differ. https://doi.org/10.1016/j.paid.2017.06.024. Elsevier

Application Websites

ARGON4 a web browser. https://app.argonjs.io/. Accessed Nov 2019
ARKIT. https://developer.apple.com/documentation/arkit. Accessed Nov 2019
AUGMENT (https://www.augment.com/). Accessed Nov 2019
Google ARCore. https://developers.google.com/ar. Accessed Nov 2019
Layar. https://www.layar.com/. Accessed Nov 2019
OPENCV. https://opencv.org. Accessed Nov 2019
VUFORIA (https://developer.vuforia.com/). Accessed Nov 2019
Wikitude. https://www.wikitude.com. Accessed Nov 2019
Xamarin. https://dotnet.microsoft.com/apps/xamarin. Accessed Nov 2019

Chapter 19
Interacting Across Contexts: Augmented Reality Applications for Developing the Understanding of the Anthropocene

Lili Yan, McKay Colleni, and Breanne K. Litts

Abstract Augmented reality (AR) provides new ways that humans can engage with the world. The affordance of AR to mediate human–environment relationships addresses some major challenges people face in understanding the idea of the Anthropocene, which refers to the current geological stage of our planet, where human impact is the dominant force. This is important because being aware of how human activities change the planet is constructive to building the human–environment relationship that is sustainable for the future. As a result, with the growing popularity of mobile AR applications, pioneering designs in the last decade attempt to integrate AR with the Anthropocene. In this chapter, we present a systematic review of these AR applications guided by qualitative content analysis methods. Results indicate that AR creates multiple learning opportunities across contexts for understanding the Anthropocene based on particular forms of interaction. Implied in these interactions are two major approaches (exploration and creation) that the designers adopted to engage users with the theme context of the Anthropocene. The findings of the review can inform the future design of AR applications that mediate more meaningful interactions with the Anthropocene.

19.1 Introduction

New technologies are transforming how humans engage with the world around them. Some scholars argue that "a fundamental shift is afoot in the relationship between human and natural systems" (Allenby and Chester 2018, p. 58). For over a decade,

L. Yan (✉) · B. K. Litts
Department of Instructional Technology and Learning Sciences, Utah State University, Logan, UT, USA
e-mail: liliyan@aggiemail.usu.edu

B. K. Litts
e-mail: breanne.litts@usu.edu

M. Colleni
Department of Mechanical and Aerospace Engineering, Utah State University, Logan, UT, USA
e-mail: mckaycolleni@gmail.com

© Springer Nature Switzerland AG 2020
V. Geroimenko (ed.), *Augmented Reality in Education*,
Springer Series on Cultural Computing,
https://doi.org/10.1007/978-3-030-42156-4_19

multiple concepts have been proposed to describe this shift in human–environment interactions, such as the Anthropozoic era, Psychozoic, and Noosphere (Hamilton and Grinevald 2015), but these concepts do not effectively capture the human drive in the Earth processes (Autin 2016). There is a growing awareness that the human–environment relationship is significant in our understanding of how people engage with the world around us. One idea that scholars use to better capture this shift is the Anthropocene, which describes this recent geological epoch with human impact as the dominant force (Lewis and Maslin 2015). This contrasts the anthropocentric views, which separate humans from nonhuman and justify human exploitation of the environment.

Just as it is critical to the understanding of the human-relationship, it is important to investigate the methods and perspectives that emerging technologies have made possible for the conceptualization of the Anthropocene. Augmented reality (AR) is an emerging technology that enhances human interactivity with the physical environment through overlaying digital worlds on top of physical worlds to "augment" the real environment (Milgram et al. 1994). As a result, AR opens up the possibility of exploring what it means about human observation. Taking AR as a new medium, MacIntyre et al. (2001) suggest that the personal nature of the human–computer interface distinguishes AR from earlier media. By blending the virtual and real environment, AR displays can enhance a user's personal perception of the world (MacIntyre et al. 2001). For example, a user is able to control the point of view of the augmented experience while wearing or holding an AR device. Therefore, the human–environment relationship is inherent in AR.

Given these affordances of AR, there is an emerging trend to design AR applications in response to the emerging concept of the Anthropocene, which creates learning opportunities to understand the newly proposed concept. The necessity of promoting the general knowledge of the Anthropocene is called on by pioneering educators. For example, Laird (2017) argued that contemporary education should be geared towards learning to live in the Anthropocene. Collectively, we are responsible for the world's future in the Anthropocene. The recognition of the conscientious human agency demand that we rethink education (Laird 2017) and design learning opportunities to explore the role of humankind from diverse perspectives.

Although AR applications designed for AR are at a nascent stage, it is necessary to draw experience from current practice and thus inform future design. The purpose of this systematic review is to provide a landscape of the existing AR applications that are designed for understanding the Anthropocene. It also examines what design features are critical to engaging users across contexts. In particular, this chapter addresses the following two research questions: "What AR applications explicitly integrate the theme of the Anthropocene?" And "in what ways do these AR applications engage the Anthropocene?".

19.2 Background

19.2.1 Augmented Reality and Environmental Education

The potential of AR in promoting the understanding of the Anthropocene can be supported by its diverse applications in environmental education. Previous research has explored the roles and ways of AR that can be integrated into environmental education. Similar to video games and simulations that have been used in environmental education with unanticipated benefits, AR opens up the opportunities to establish meaningful relationships between the user and the place.

With the increasing popularity of handheld devices, it is predictable that there will be more AR platforms for both education and entertainment purposes (Klopfer and Squire 2008). Empirical studies as follows further confirm the potential of leveraging in environmental education, which shares substantial similarity with the understanding of the Anthropocene.

Researchers have pointed out that AR can effectively engage children (Hawley 2018), the inseparable audience of the Anthropocene. Hawley pointed out that similar to traditional media such as films and television, AR has been used to authenticate environmental messages. The investigation of the *dirtgirlworld*, an AR mobile app, indicated that the child audience could be considered as "agents of change" (Hawley 2018, p. 162) within both natural and digital spaces.

Besides the population of youth, AR has also been used to promote environmental education among educators. In their study, Alahmari et al. (2019) focused on investigating the environment awareness of faculty in Saudi Arabian universities, when the faculty were engaged with AR to learn about economic and environmental sustainability issues. A survey questionnaire was used to collect responses of the participants to the statements on a five-point Likert scale. The findings from the study indicated that the educational values of AR in learning the sustainability issues were well recognized among participants.

AR has been integrated with learning in environment-related disciplines. In order to address the challenges of environmental awareness in marine education, Lu and Liu (2015) integrated AR technology to the marine learning program. Using a quasi-experimental design, the researchers gained insights from students' engagement. Results confirmed the knowledge gain and students' growing confidence. Bursztyn et al. (2017) designed AR field trips to provide experiential learning to a broader audience of geoscience. They examined the learning gains of students from five colleges with the AR field trip to Grand Canyon. Results showed that the completion of the AR field trips was the predictor of learning success centered around topics of geologic time, geologic structures, and hydrologic processes.

AR has also been employed to build students' learning skills. Dede et al. (2017) explored AR along with other immersive media that have the affordances to promote deeper learning strategies such as case-based learning, diagnostic, multiple varied forms of representation, apprenticeship, interdisciplinary knowledge, and collaboration. Students will be able to work beyond academic knowledge and be prepared with the skills needed for life and work in the twenty-first century.

19.2.2 Challenges in the Understanding of the Anthropocene

The concept of the Anthropocene is comparatively foreign to both educators and the general public. An apt understanding of the idea of the Anthropocene is greatly in need to respond to timely issues. Researchers have identified several challenges of understanding the Anthropocene. For example, Leinfelder (2013) outlines three major challenges: (1) understanding the state of the planet, (2) understanding systemic interactions and feedback in a one-world system, (3) understanding time-related issues. Although the fact that human beings exert influence on natural systems is widely recognized, few are aware of the "magnitude of these effects" (Leinfelder 2013, p. 10). Environmental problems are often presented as isolated, connections and interactions are hard to identify. Human-induced temporal changes in nature are less presented than societal changes.

Implied in Leinfelder's (2013) arguments is the critique of anthropocentric observation. Awareness of the environment is often ego-centric and restricted in the immediate surroundings. For example, research data generalizing global environmental changes do not always arouse the sentiment of self-reflection, as it seems usually detached from one's community. Perceptions of the influence of human activities from the alternative perspective (e.g. the nonhuman animals) or longer time span are not readily available experience. Such perceptions are fundamental to building human–environment relations for sustainability future in the Anthropocene, based on which the human reflexivity can lead to the utility, withdrawal, and modification of human force (Leinfelder 2013).

Accordingly, Stratford (2019) argues that "the Anthropocene is a crisis in the way we think" (Stratford 2019, p. 149). It challenges the individualistic and anthropocentric assumptions fundamental to our socioeconomic structures (Brown and Timmerman 2015). There is an emerging realization that much more responsibilities of humanity have been expected than ever before. Facing the uncertainty of the future, we need to reflect on our stewardship to the nonhumans (Laird 2017). Responding to the need to consider our interconnected natural, social and intellectual systems more carefully, education should make the changes and adopt new forms and means to prepare the current and future generations for the new epoch.

Imperatives of recognizing the Anthropocene is in contrast to the lack of related learning opportunities provided by formal education. Li (2017) argues that modern formal education should embrace the concept of human vulnerability. Ranging from terrorist attacks to climate change, human vulnerability increases in the global–local ecological systems. Modern schooling should pay attention to the interconnectedness of humans and the environment in the Anthropocene.

Olvitt (2017) investigated the humans' ethico-moral engagement with the Anthropocene and explored the types of learning processes that help people to understand, live in, and co-create the Anthropocene. Olvitt (2017) further suggested that a reorientation of education systems, which responds to the rethinking of human–environment relations, should be made regarding ethico-moral challenges. Therefore, learning processes that are "relational, humble, interdisciplinary, multi-perspectival, systemic, reality-congruent and contextually responsive" (Olvitt 2017, p. 396) will better prepare individuals in the Anthropocene.

More importance of learning has been attached to the Anthropocene by scholars such as Laird (2017). Laird (2017) believes that the survival of the Anthropocene lies in learning, and argued that "learning is such a basic form of human agency consequential for Earth's habitability" (Laird 2017, p. 268). The most difficult educational challenge in the Anthropocene is to cultivate the changed ways of living for the purpose of maintaining the habitability of our planet, where children can survive and learn.

Given the potential of AR to address human–environment relations, we were interested in investigating the ways that AR enables understanding of the Anthropocene by dealing with the challenges identified in conceptualizing the Anthropocene, and what related learning opportunities can be created by the emerging technology.

19.3 Methods

Although some scholars have explored the potential of AR to engage learners of diverse levels in the Anthropocene discourse, less is known about the experience of current practices of designing AR projects pertaining to the Anthropocene. To address this need, we conducted a systematic review guided by the aforementioned research questions. Taking up Cooper's (1998) research synthesizing framework, we employed a qualitative content analysis method (Hsieh and Shannon 2005) to explore what AR applications have been designed to engage users in Anthropocene and how they engage users. We conducted this analysis by adapting Cooper's (1998) framework for reviewing AR applications: (1) collecting information of AR applications and deciding on the inclusion of AR applications, (2) further deciding on whether or not to include the AR applications based their information sources, (3) coding and summarizing results, and (4) interpreting themes.

19.3.1 Data Collection

We obtained information about the possible AR applications from both academic and non-academic venues. First, we began by searching the related articles in Google Scholar. Using a combination of keywords "Augmented Reality" and "the Anthropocene", we identified 9 projects about or include an AR application among 415

Table 19.1 Inclusion and exclusion criteria of the information sources

	Inclusion	Exclusion
Timeliness	Published in the last decade (2009–2019)	Published before 2009
Quality	Published in scholarly journal, book chapter, news report, website of the project (or designer (s)'s website, etc.)	Personal/user's blog posts or website
Language	Written in English	Not written in English
Providing related details of the AR applications	Including at least one of the following information: • Link to download the AR app • The description of the project • The discussion of the design features • The implementation of the project	Without specific information about the project (e.g. advertisements)

results entries. Projects were excluded if they were not related to AR or did not explicitly express an intent to approach the theme of the Anthropocene. Next, following the same criterion, we continued with search by applying the keywords to Google and collected five more projects. As a result, we included 14 projects of AR in this study.

19.3.2   Evaluating the Credibility of Information Sources

Altogether a variety of information sources of the selected projects were collected, such as news reports, blog posts, and academic articles. In order to create a collection of more credible information for further analysis, we excluded information sources that did not meet the inclusion/exclusion criteria described in Table 19.1. Projects without any supporting information would be dropped from this review.

19.3.3   Framework and Analysis

In our analysis, we were interested in the diverse contexts that each AR application was engaged with. Specifically, we focused on (1) the design context, (2) the user's context sources, and (3) the Anthropocene theme context. We first coded each AR application in these projects for release status and design purposes. In order to obtain an overview of when these applications become publicly accessible, we coded the year of release and whether these applications are publicly available by the time we conducted this review. To understand the design purposes of each application, we coded for what settings these applications were designed for. From this process, we were able to understand the design context of each application.

Apart from the design context, AR makes use of the user's current context sources (e.g. location) to generate targeted meaning (Grubert et al. 2016). The interactions enabled by the AR system is one of the major factors to understand how AR utilizes context sources. For the purpose of gaining insights into the kinds of interactions afforded by the AR applications, and how these interactions can engage users with the grand narrative of the Anthropocene, we proposed a model for our analysis. Our model is based on Nam's (2015) model of the various levels of interactivity in AR narratives. Specifically, Nam built on digital narrative theory (Ryan 2011) and proposed two layers of interaction, (1) the outer exploratory layer, where user can navigate the predetermined storyline with limited impact on the story, and (2) and inner ontological layer, where the story is created through the interaction between the user and the application. On the basis of the two layers of interaction, we proposed the following model to guide our coding.

Figure 19.1 shows our model to understand the ways that users can be engaged with the theme context of the Anthropocene through interactions. We used the term theme context in this chapter to refer to the environment and experience that are designed for potential understanding of the Anthropocene through interactions. We take the AR interaction as a circular process, which starts from the input and completes when the augmented effects (e.g. AR scene) get back to the user. Features of the interaction are based on the unique characteristics of input and output.

To investigate the features of the interactions, we coded input and output factors under two sub-categories respectively. For the input, we coded whether the app is utilizing direct input or indirect input. We defined direct input as the user's choice of action captured by the device that supports the application, such as the user's clicks

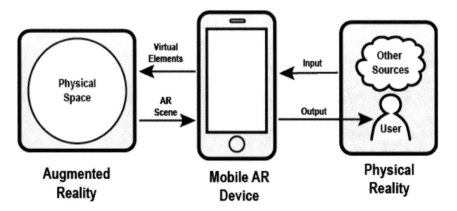

Fig. 19.1 Model for the coding of this review

on buttons, body motion or camera movement. By indirect input, we were looking for whether the input consists of external data sources. We took the input as indirect if it used data collected by a third-party research institution about the place that users are located. Another type of external data source can be the user's personal data, either detected by an additional sensor or data owned by the users and provided to an AR application.

Because of limited access to some of the projects, we only reviewed the textual and visual output. We also coded whether the output was direct or indirect in our review. For direct output, we defined it as objective information showing up about the Anthropocene, such as facts and figures. For the indirect output, we focused on virtual objects that are interpretable for users, which indirectly represents the Anthropocene, such as fictional or exaggerated images that can overlay the physical environment.

The analysis of the theme context was built on the analysis of the possible narrative layers, which was complemented by coding whether the theme of the Anthropocene can be identified in the physical environment. The purpose of this analysis is to understand how the theme context of the Anthropocene is generated based on the interactions afforded by AR.

We further developed categorized these features according to the research questions, which were used to grouping AR applications with shared or similar characteristics together. The first two authors manually coded each AR application according to the categories. Discrepancy was resolved through constant discussions between the two coders.

19.4 Results and Findings

In this section, the results of the study are presented by focusing on the themes emerged in the analysis. The design context is presented in terms of timeline, general designed AR experience, and related learning settings. The user's context source is demonstrated in terms of the types of interactions that the AR applications enable. Lastly, findings of the theme context are discussed.

19.4.1 Overview of the Collected AR Applications

19.4.1.1 Timeline

Altogether we identified 14 applications that meet our inclusion criteria from the projects we collected. An overview of the general information of these applications (Table 19.2) shows that these applications are very up-to-date, ranging from the year 2012 to 2019.

Table 19.2 Summary of collected applications

Number	Project	Developers	Year of Release	Availability
1	"Biomer Skelters"	Thiel and Pappenheimer	2013	Publicly available
2	"Gardens of Anthropocene"	Tamiki Thiel	2016	No longer available
3	"States and Territories"	David Rousell	2013	No longer available
4	"E-Waste"	Samaa Ahmed	2018	No longer available
5	"O-Tu-Kapua"	"TEMP_Air" team	2018	No longer available
6	"STE[A]M Park"	Brenda Laurel	2015	Only concept available
7	AR for the Anthropocene Museum Show (Canada)	The Anthropocene Project	2018	Publicly available
8	AR for the Anthropocene Museum Show (Italy)	The Anthropocene Project	2019	Publicly available
9	AR for Anthropocene Education Program	The Anthropocene Project	2019	In development
10	AR for Anthropocene Book	The Anthropocene Project	2018	Publicly available
11	"Anthropocene Extinction"	Linda Cheung, Reinier Gamboa, Juan Carlos Gallo, and Dane Myers	2018	Publicly available
12	"After Ice"	Justin Brice Guariglia	2017	Publicly available
13	"Making Tellus"	Nina C. Young	2015	Publicly available
14	"Mar Menor Research"	Clara Boj Tovar, Diego Garcia, and Jose Diaz	2012	No longer available

These 14 applications differ in availability. Two applications have not been released yet. The AR experience in the AR education program is under development and will be released in November 2019. And we only found information about the concept and design of "STE[A]M Park" from the designer's published book chapter (Laurel 2015). Seven of the applications are publicly available, while five of the applications are no longer in use at the point of this review.

19.4.1.2 General AR Experience

The reviewed applications are either attached to a particular project or as independent creations. Some applications are designed as the technology components to enhance the experience of a larger project. Taking *Anthropocene: The Human Epoch* (2018) at the Art Gallery of Ontario as an example, users can use mobile devices installed with AVARA app to engage with the AR experience of large-scale photographs by photographer Edward Burtynsky and filmmakers Jennifer Baichwal and Nicholas de Pencier. In these projects, the AR applications are dependent on larger projects, which makes the original project more interactive.

Some applications can offer stand-alone AR experience as a way to express the designer's perspective to approach the Anthropocene. "Gardens of the Anthropocene" (2016) (Fig. 19.2) is the independent work by Tamiko Thiel as an artistic representation of the Anthropocene. The location-based application was originally designed to be used in Seattle Art Museum's Olympic Sculpture Park and later modified to include other locations. As users are located in the designated place, they can find some virtual mutated plants imposed on the surrounding physical environment. The "surreal and dystopian scenario" (Bendor 2018, p. 140) of mutated plants feeding off man-made traffic signs and mobile devices' electromagnetic radiation is generated by the individual AR artwork without serving the purpose of a larger project.

Fig. 19.2 Gardens of the Anthropocene (Image from Thiel 2016)

These projects are responsive to the growing awareness of the Anthropocene in the past decade. As the precursor efforts to create interactive experiences of the Anthropocene, these applications offer new learning opportunities for the concept. The AR experience in *Anthropocene: The Human Epoch* (2018) is considered "an excellent educational tool for understanding how we get to this new planetary era" (Valenti 2019, p. 3). However, five of the applications, due to the limited scale of implementation or the termination of the dependent projects, are not being used any more by the time we conducted this review. In the next section, we are going to talk about the formal and informal learning opportunities created around the applications.

19.4.1.3 Learning Opportunities Across Settings

A variety of learning opportunities are supported by the applications we collected. Marsick and Watkins (2001) defined informal learning as opposed to formal learning, which is usually "institutionally sponsored, classroom-based, and highly structured" (Marsick and Watkins 2001, p. 25). Informal learning, however, is not classroom-based, and the learner has more flexibility to control their learning process. One typical kind of informal learning is incidental learning, which is the byproduct of an activity, during which learning occurs unconsciously (Marsick and Watkins 2001).

Most of the applications we collected are used outside the classroom and reveal diverse informal learning opportunities. Users can unconsciously acquire knowledge or sensation of the Anthropocene in informal learning spaces, such as parks (e.g. "Gardens of the Anthropocene" 2016), theatre ("Making Tellus" 2015), or even their familiar neighborhood (e.g. "After Ice" 2017).

Only two applications have been used in the school setting, however, they are designed for innovative learning experiences within the formal learning setting with the use of AR. "O-Tū-Kapua" (2017) is one example. As the design intention is to create a world of place-based educative narrative (Penetito 2009), students were actively engaged in making creative artwork of fictive forest with flora and fauna sharing their local environment. AR makers were made by students as they were drawing parts of the virtual world. The by-product of the artistic activity is the learning of concepts of atmospheric science that were integrated with ecological thinking and literacy (e.g. Sterling 2005). Anchored in the virtual world, the novel learning opportunities could help the students to explore the concept of the Anthropocene by being exposed to the narrative of their environment told from a different perspective. Students were able to use mobile devices such as tablets and smartphones with a hand-drawn magnifying glass to locate AR makers. Once AR was triggered, students would be shown facts of human influence on the earth from a nonhuman perspective. One of the markers is a tree stump. When seeing from the AR device, the virtual image of a tree overlays the maker and shows the environment conditions in Auckland from the perspective of a tree (Fig. 19.3).

The process of quest-based exploration is considered self-regulated, as students have more flexibility to determine their trajectory of learning while using the AR

Fig. 19.3 Tree stump AR maker of O-Tū-Kapua (left), and the triggered AR output (right) (Jowsey and Aguayo 2017)

application. Informal learning also occurs in the social interactions between the kids, as AR enables the novel and collective experience in the augmented-reality space.

"States and Territories" (2013–2017) is another project located on campus. The purpose of the project is to challenge the traditional learning environment. As was expressed by its designer David Rousell, "the States and Territories is an artistic and philosophical inquiry which aims to collectively re-imagine university learning environments for the Anthropocene epoch" (Rousell 2018b). The project is a prototype of the posthuman learning environment. Rousell (2018a) was critical about the hierarchy existed between the human and data and believed that the current relationship was anthropocentric and problematic in the epoch of the Anthropocene, where humans and nonhumans were entangled more than ever before. In response to the posthumanist conceptualization of data, Rousell (2018a) designed twelve photographic cube installations across a regional university. Each cube had images reflecting its exact location. When viewed with AR devices, an archive of information would be presented to the users. The archive consists of data generated through participatory research (Fig. 19.4). Users were able to respond to the displayed "data events" through inputting their poetry, drawing, mapping or photography.

Both projects are complementary to formal learning setting by creating novel learning opportunities for users to understand the concept of the Anthropocene. The structured curriculum featured with subject division is has the limitation for the exploration of the Anthropocene that is essentially interdisciplinary. The intersectionality of the Anthropocene is further demonstrated by the way that these two projects include diverse expertise in the design.

The participation of users in the creation of the two projects implies the special role of AR in engaging people in the Anthropocene. By creating AR makers or contributing data to AR output, users take the dual role of *making* and *consuming*,

Fig. 19.4 The cube installation and triggered display using AR devise (Rousell 2018a)

which corresponds to the essential part of the concept of the Anthropocene in terms of human activities. In this way, participation also means to include more people to participate in the discourse of the Anthropocene. Rather than having the concept only for scientists and critics, less privileged populations such as youth have greater opportunities to actively explore the concept of the Anthropocene, when engaged with AR activities, forming a citizen-oriented critique of the emerging concept (Wright 2018). In the next section, we are going to discuss the emergent patterns of interactions afforded by the AR applications in particular.

19.4.2   Interactions Afforded by AR

An examination of the interactions enabled by AR demonstrates how users can engage with the Anthropocene through the AR experience. In order to investigate the designed interactions, we coded the input and output of each application. Input and output factors are essential components of the interactive AR system. Input factors refer to the different ways users can give information to the AR system (Grubert et al. 2016). Typical input modalities include gesture (e.g. touch screen) and voice (speech directions). Output factors describe the information presented to the user (Grubert et al. 2016). Visual output can be the variance in resolution, sizes and spatial layout to realize intended effects. Other modalities such as audio and tactile output can also be integrated with visual output.

Table 19.3 Five types of interactions afforded by AR

	Input	Output	AR application
Type 1	Both	Indirect	"Biomer Skelter"; "Mar Menor Research", "Making Tellus"
Type 2	Direct	Indirect	"Gardens of the Anthropocene"
Type 3	Direct	Both	"States and Territories"; "O-Tū-Kapua", "Anthropocene Extinction"-Augmented Realities Murals; AR for the Anthropocene Museum Show (Canada); AR for the Anthropocene Museum Show (Italy); AR for the Anthropocene Book
Type 4	Direct	Direct	"E-waste", "STE[A]M Park"
Type 5	Both	Both	"After Ice"

As described in the methods section, we coded the input for whether it is direct (the user's choice of action captured by the device, such as clicks on buttons) or indirect (external data sources, such as third-party research data). We also coded whether the output was direct (for example, showing facts or figures) or indirect (for example, displaying fictional or exaggerated virtual objects).

Results showed that both types of input/output could be found among these applications, and their combinations showed the variety of interaction enabled by AR applications. Based on our coding, we identified five types of interactions (Table 19.3).

Indirect input is an important design feature that represents the human influence in the Anthropocene. Three applications were identified as using indirect ways as part of their input factors. External research data were used as the input in "Mar Menor Research" (2012) and "After Ice" (2017). The Mar Menor monster is a fictional animal to be captured in the AR environment when using the Mar Menor Research application. The monster could evolve in relation to the research data collected from its surroundings. By observing monster changing size, shape, and location, the users had a novel way to visualize research data on human influence on a specific location. Similar to "Mar Menor Research" (2012), "After Ice" (2017) incorporated ice melting data and visualized the possible sea level projected in the 2080s overlaying their environment via AR.

Indirect input from user's personal data contributes to the metaphorical representation of human impact. "Biome Skelter" (2013) captured the user's heartbeat with the Zephyr heart rate monitor. The personal physiological data would trigger a virtual biome that can grow in real-time situation along with the frequency of the input heart rate. A relatively relaxed pace is designed as the trigger of the planting process. The indirect input of "Biome Skelter" (2013) serves as the metaphor of human impact on nature. Being enclosed in the urban environment makes people less attentive to such influence. As users walk along the urban street augmented by virtual plants, an experience of traversing the design of urban environments that are detached from nature (Wright 2018) is enabled.

An examination of the output factors showed major rhetorical strategies that these AR applications used to interpret the Anthropocene. Similarities of rhetorical strategies between traditional media and AR have been identified by researchers. For example, traditional rhetorical concepts such as logos and pathos shape AR texts (Blevins 2018). Logos and pathos are also applied to persuade environmental issues (Higgins and Walker 2012). We defined the logos in AR as presenting information components suggestive to the reasoning (Higgins and Walker 2012) of the theme, and pathos in AR as the strategies that could trigger the user's feelings and emotions (Aho 1985).

Direct output factors are used in applications that tend to employ logos when presenting the idea of the Anthropocene. That is more likely in the cases with a more salient educational purpose. As indicated earlier, "States and Territories" (2013) and "O-Tū-Kapua" (2018) use direct output such as environmental information of specific locations as part of their output and thus promote a data-informed understanding of the Anthropocene.

Indirect output factors are features of AR applications that identify themselves as artworks. Rather than presenting facts about the Anthropocene, applications using indirect output intend to create the pathos in responses of the users. The sensation of survival or crisis is inevitable, when users are engaged with these interactions. The effects of pathos are shared by applications such as "Gardens of the Anthropocene" (2016), where human vulnerability is depicted by augmenting plants that are beyond the control of human beings.

"Anthropocene Extinctions" (2018) incorporates both logos and pathos in their output. Located on a street wall in Miami, the AR murals bring images of several extinct animals to life, thus using a direct (logos) output. While using this AR application, users can be engaged with the experience of walking among these animals in the AR environment, which generates emotional responses caused by the indirect (pathos) output. The combination of pathos and logos illustrate the way the designers interpret the Anthropocene.

Based on these types of interactions, the further understanding of the way users can engage with the theme can be drawn, when considering the theme context, which will be discussed in the following section.

19.4.3 The Theme Context of the Anthropocene

As mentioned in the methods section, there are two layers of interactions supported by AR when investigating AR narratives (Nam 2015), the outer layer (users explore the storyline) and the inner layer (users create parts of the story). Considering the grand narrative of the Anthropocene, we were interested in examining the relationship between the users and the theme context of the Anthropocene.

We use the term "theme context" to indicate the environment and experience in the user's place that embodies the theme of the Anthropocene. The place is defined as the experience of the user's engagement with the physical location (Chauhan et al.

2019). As perceptions are enhanced in AR, the virtual effects change how users can be engaged with the theme of the Anthropocene when seeing virtual objects overlay the physical environment (Milgram and Kishino 1994).

In order to understand the role of AR in terms of the theme context, we coded each AR application in terms of whether there is an existent theme of the Anthropocene in the physical environment. Results of the coding suggested that nine applications had a pre-existing theme of the Anthropocene, while the physical place of the rest of the four applications was not designed with the indication to the Anthropocene.

Based on the coding and the findings of interaction types in the previous section, we identified two ways that the user can engage with the theme context. (1) *The user can explore the theme context.* In the nine applications with the pre-existing theme in the physical environment, the user takes the role as an explorer of the theme context. In addition, these applications also fall into the categories of either Type 3 or Type 4 interactions, which is also suggestive that direct input is related to this role. A combination of pre-existent theme and direct input is one design feature of AR that posits users in the role to explore the theme.

By using AR applications in the place with the pre-existing theme of the Anthropocene, users are flexible to explore the theme context at their own choice of the sequence action of direct input (e.g. clicking buttons or moving cameras). The theme context is an augmented version of the physical environment. For example, the users of the AR applications for the Anthropocene museum exhibitions (2018) (2019) are explorers of the theme context, where they can have augmented experience while learning about the theme of the Anthropocene that is pre-existed in the physical exhibition.

(2) *The user can co-create the theme context they are exploring.* For those applications without the pre-existing theme in the physical place, users' interactions with AR devices are an indispensable part of the creation of the theme context. Indirect input is contributive to creating the theme context, which serves as the representation of human activities, while the output that constructs the theme context shows the impact of human activities. When using applications designed with such input, the actions of the user can trigger the theme context upon the physical environment, which is previously without such a theme. The reflexivity of the Anthropocene is strongly demonstrated when the indirect input takes the form of the user's personal data (e.g. "Biomer Skelter" with indirect input of the user's heart rate).

19.5   Discussion

Our review of the recent AR applications designed for developing the understanding of the Anthropocene reveals that AR affords multiple layers of engagement with Anthropocene across contexts. At the outer layer, users are engaged by participating in the making of parts of the AR activities (e.g. "O-Tū-Kapua" 2018). At the inner layers, we identified diverse interactions afforded by AR, and the users' roles of exploring and co-creating in the theme context. These design features respond to the challenged human–environment relationship that is critical to the understanding of the Anthropocene. By either showing the effects of human activities to the users, or having users co-creating the theme, AR affords the roles of human users beyond passive observers of the environment. Much as the Anthropocene critics challenge the passive observation of the global change in the new epoch, designers of these applications have creatively built the interactions to engage users in the conceptualization of the Anthropocene.

19.6 Limitations

Our review has several limitations. Because of the emerging status of both the technology and the concept of the Anthropocene, our review was based on a relatively small sample size. AR applications that did not identify themselves with the design purpose for the Anthropocene but with the potential for learning about the Anthropocene were not included in our review.

Most of the applications we collected are not widely accessible. When compared to *Pokémon GO*, the iconic AR game that can reach a great population, the applications we reviewed have limited access. For some applications, the location requirements prohibit broader participation in the afforded experiences. Some applications are part of larger projects, such as a museum exhibition, and their users are mostly restricted to the visitors of the exhibition. Needing access to either the event or the location resulted in the fact that most applications are less famous. Most of the information we collected for each application was based on reading. By only focusing on the ideation features of the design (Norman 2002) that show the intended way to engage with the Anthropocene, we were not able to fully capture the AR experience from the user's perspective. More in-depth analysis should include the users' experience when using the applications. Nevertheless, these identified design features would inform future designs that target broader users.

19.7 Conclusion

Our chapter presents a systematic review of 14 AR applications that are designed for developing the understanding of the Anthropocene. By conducting a qualitative content analysis, we identified multiple layers of engagement that are enabled by these AR applications. Novel learning opportunities are supported by the use of AR. By using different combinations of direct and indirect input/output factors, these AR support diverse user interactions. Based on these interactions, users can explore or co-create the theme context of the Anthropocene when using the applications. These design features illustrate the ways that AR makes use of multiple contexts to generate meaning and promotes the conceptualizing of the Anthropocene, which can inform the design of relevant AR applications in the future.

References

Aho J (1985) Rhetoric and the invention of double entry bookkeeping. Rhetor J Hist Rhetor 3:1–43. https://doi.org/10.1525/rh.1985.3.1.21

Alahmari M, Issa T, Issa T, Nau SZ (2019) Faculty awareness of the economic and environmental benefits of augmented reality for sustainability in Saudi Arabian universities. J Clean Prod 226:259–269. https://doi.org/10.1016/j.jclepro.2019.04.090

Allenby B, Chester M (2018) Reconceptualizing infrastructure in the Anthropocene. Issues Sci Technol 34(3):58–63

Autin WJ (2016) Multiple dichotomies of the Anthropocene. Anthropocene Rev 3(3):218–230. https://doi.org/10.1177/2053019616646133

Bendor R (2018) Imagination. In: Interactive media for sustainability. Palgrave Macmillan, Cham, pp 129–164. https://doi.org/10.1007/978-3-319-70383-1_5

Blevins B (2018) Teaching digital literacy composing concepts: focusing on the layers of augmented reality in an era of changing technology. Comput Compos 50:21–38. https://doi.org/10.1016/j.compcom.2018.07.003

Bursztyn N, Walker A, Shelton B, Pederson J (2017) Assessment of student learning using augmented reality Grand Canyon field trips for mobile smart devices. Geosphere 13(2):260–268. https://doi.org/10.1130/GES01404.1

Brown PG, Timmerman P (eds) (2015) Ecological economics for the Anthropocene: an emerging paradigm. Columbia University Press, New York. https://doi.org/10.7312/brow17342

Chauhan A, Lewis W, Litts BK (2019) Location and place: two design dimensions of augmented reality in mobile technologies. In: Zhang Y, Cristol D (eds) Handbook of mobile teaching and learning. Springer, Berlin, Heidelberg. https://doi.org/10.1007/978-981-13-2766-7_104

Cooper HM (1998) Synthesizing research: a guide for literature reviews, 3rd edn. Sage Publications, Thousand Oaks, CA

Dede C, Grotzer TA, Kamarainen A, Metcalf S (2017) EcoXPT: designing for deeper learning through experimentation in an immersive virtual ecosystem. J Educ Technol Soc 20(4):166–178

Grubert J, Langlotz T, Zollmann S, Regenbrecht H (2016) Towards pervasive augmented reality: Context-awareness in augmented reality. IEEE T Vis Comput Gr 23(6):1706–1724. https://doi.org/10.1109/TVCG.2016.2543720

Hamilton C, Grinevald J (2015) Was the Anthropocene anticipated? Anthropocene Rev 2(1):59–72. https://doi.org/10.1177/2053019614567155

Hawley E (2018) Children's television, environmental pedagogy and the (un) natural world of dirtgirlworld. Continuum 32(2):162–172. https://doi.org/10.1080/10304312.2017.1347913

Higgins C, Walker R (2012) Ethos, logos, pathos: strategies of persuasion in social/environmental reports. Account Forum 36(3):194–208. https://doi.org/10.1016/j.accfor.2012.02.003

Hsieh HF, Shannon SE (2005) Three approaches to qualitative content analysis. Qual Health Res 15(9):1277–1288. https://doi.org/10.1177/1049732305276687

Jowsey S, Aguayo C (2017) O-Tū-Kapua ("what clouds see"): a mixed reality experience bridging art, science, technology in meaningful ways. Teach Curric 17(2):95–102. https://doi.org/10.15663/tandc.v17i2.166

Klopfer E, Squire K (2008) Environmental detectives—the development of an augmented reality platform for environmental simulations. Education Tech Research Dev 56(2):203–228. https://doi.org/10.1007/s11423-007-9037-6

Laird S (2017) Learning to live in the Anthropocene: our children and ourselves. Stud in Philos and Educ 36(3):265–282. https://doi.org/10.1007/s11217-017-9571-6

Laurel B (2015) Looking into nature: learning and delight in a STE [A] M park. In: Geiger J (ed) Entr'acte. Palgrave Macmillan, New York, pp 157–171

Leinfelder R (2013) Assuming responsibility for the Anthropocene: challenges and opportunities in education. Trischler H, Anthropocene: envisioning the future of the age of humans. RCC Perspect Munich 3:9–28

Lewis SL, Maslin MA (2015) Defining the anthropocene. Nature 519(7542):171–180. https://doi.org/10.1038/nature14258

Li HL (2017) Rethinking vulnerability on the age of Anthropocene: toward ecologizing education. Educ Theory 67(4):435–451. https://doi.org/10.1111/edth.12264

Lu SJ, Liu YC (2015) Integrating augmented reality technology to enhance children's learning in marine education. Environ Educ Res 21(4):525–541. https://doi.org/10.1080/13504622.2014.911247

MacIntyre B, Bolter JD, Moreno E, Hannigan B (2001) Augmented reality as a new media experience. In: Proceedings IEEE and ACM international symposium on augmented reality. IEEE, pp 197–206

Marsick VJ, Watkins KE (2001) Informal and incidental learning. New Dir Adult Contin Educ 89:25–34. https://doi.org/10.1002/ace.5

Milgram P, Kishino F (1994) A taxonomy of mixed reality visual displays. IEICE T Inf and Syst 77(12):1321–1329

Milgram P, Takemura H, Utsumi A, Kishino F (1994) Mixed reality (MR) reality-virtuality (RV) continuum. Syst Res 2351:282–292

Nam Y (2015) Designing interactive narratives for mobile augmented reality. Cluster Comput 18(1):309–320. https://doi.org/10.1007/s10586-014-0354-3

Norman D (2002) The design of everyday things. Basic Books, New York

Olvitt LL (2017) Education in the Anthropocene: Ethico-moral dimensions and critical realist openings. J Moral Educ 46(4):396–409. https://doi.org/10.1080/03057240.2017.1342613

Penetito W (2009) Place-based education: catering for curriculum, culture and community. N Z Annu Rev Educ 18:5–29. https://doi.org/10.1007/978-1-4419-0585-7

Rousell D (2018a) Mapping the data event: a posthumanist approach to art| education| research in a regional university. In: Rousell D (ed) Arts-research-education. Springer, Cham, pp 203–220. https://doi.org/10.1007/978-3-319-61560-8_12

Rousell D (2018b) The project. https://www.statesandterritories.org/orientations

Ryan ML (2011) The interactive onion: layers of user participation in digital narrative texts. In: New narratives: stories and storytelling in the digital age, pp 35–62. https://doi.org/10.2307/j.ctt1df4h49.7

Sterling S (2005) Linking thinking, education and learning: an introduction. In: Scotland W (ed) Linking thinking: new perspectives on thinking and learning for sustainability, vol 1. WWF-UK, Panda House, Surrey, England

Stratford R (2019) Educational philosophy, ecology and the Anthropocene. Educ Philos Theory 51(2):149–152. https://doi.org/10.1080/00131857.2017.1403803

Thiel T (2016) Tamiko Thiel. http://tamikothiel.com/gota

Valenti JM (2019) Tools from Sundance for environmental education and science communication. Appl Environ Educ Commun 18(2):191–194. https://doi.org/10.1080/1533015X.2019.1590254

Wright R (2018) Post-human narrativity and expressive sites: mobile ARt as software assemblage. In: Geroimenko V (ed) Augmented reality art. Springer, Cham, pp 357–369. https://doi.org/10.1007/978-3-319-69932-5_20

Chapter 20
Alaskan Timeosaurs and Interplanetary Human Spaghetti: A Regional Look at Augmented Reality in Special Classrooms

Nathan Shafer

Abstract This chapter looks at how augmented reality (AR) has been used as an enrichment activity in special education and other classrooms in Alaska, with a regional focus, including the integrating of Indigenous knowledge. Examples of integrated augmented-reality enrichments and Indigenized replacement curriculum for special education with a critical examination of the way that third party educational programs are permeating the educational system, creating less regional diversity, in lieu of standardization. Examples of differentiated education in augmented reality artist Nathan Shafer's Peer Art program, part of the Structured Learning Classroom (a classroom for students on the autism spectrum) at Wendler Middle School in Anchorage, Alaska, are anecdotally examined, with an emphasis on ways to use Indigenous thinking over top of special education programs such as Social-Emotional Learning, Social Stories and Social Thinking. Specific analysis of the Dena'ina Athabascan notion of 'evil' in their storytelling traditions is overlaid on the way Structured Learning classrooms develop routines to help students on the autism spectrum negotiate their school days.

20.1 Peer Art: Augmented Reality as Enrichment

The author of this chapter is a Special Education teacher in Anchorage, Alaska. He teaches in a Structured Learning Classroom, which is a program for students on the Autism Spectrum. His Structured Learning Classroom uses a partially Indigenized curriculum, with integrated new media art units. This program offers a 'Peer Art' class, where general education students come into the Structured Learning Classroom (SLC) and do year-long art projects with the Structured Learning students. This chapter was written during the second year the program has been running. In the first year, the Peer Art students collaboratively worked on an augmented reality videogame

N. Shafer (✉)
Structured Learning Classrooms, Anchorage School District, Anchorage, Alaska, USA
e-mail: shafer_nathan@asdk12.org

Wintermoot Shared Universe, Anchorage, Alaska, USA

© Springer Nature Switzerland AG 2020
V. Geroimenko (ed.), *Augmented Reality in Education*,
Springer Series on Cultural Computing,
https://doi.org/10.1007/978-3-030-42156-4_20

called *Timeosaurs*. In the second year, the students are producing augmented reality comic books.

The Peer Art program was developed to provide enrichment activities for special education students, as most of them do not get to participate in elective classes during their middle school years (grades 7, 8). Their elective classes are mostly special education classes (social skills, affective skills, study skills, etc.), and tend to ignore a humanities based education, instead providing extra classes that augment their disabilities with special education curriculum. In the Peer Art program the assignments are yearlong collaborative projects requiring learning many different new media techniques and software programs, as well as engage them in the social skills curriculum that is designed specifically for them. We will get into specifics with the Peer Art class later on in this chapter, as we begin talking about the designing of new media curricula for special education classrooms, specifically augmented reality.

Augmented reality (AR), or any other new media formats for that matter, provide an opportunity for enrichment in the education of K-12 students that are not be measured in terms of standardized test scores or improved grades. New media/augmented reality as a pedagogical tool is not an answer to solving any disabilities or substandard academic performances or scores, rather as an assist to connecting with school. The role that augmented reality plays is one that can situate itself in other academic areas that are not part of standardized evaluations. In Alaska, this translates more into the realm of culture and the humanities. AR is significant in that it is a format better suited to knowledge from the Oral Traditions, and other ways of telling stories outside of the standard western cannon, which for the most part are novels and textbooks. For example, Alaska Native languages, of which there are over 20 in the Alaska region, were not written languages. The notion of teaching them with books is a bit of a disservice to the thousands of years these languages have existed and were successful in educating children and helping people learn about their worlds, thriving in the Circumpolar North.

Alaskan stories were originally intended for in-person auditory processing, and new media offers a way of connecting them to students in a format more suited to their actual usage, what the European model of novels and textbooks cannot do. In the context of a special education classroom for students on the autism spectrum, deficits in communication and functional language can be augmented through storytelling and digital theater. Digital storytelling and virtual theaters offer alternative ways for students with autism to participate in social interactions.

Analysis of augmented reality inside of a classroom here will be anecdotal, as placing enrichment activities for special education students, or Alaska Native students, into a format that needs to prove its worth by improving academics. Enrichment activities by their nature are auxiliary addenda added to a core curriculum to enliven and compound non-academic interests to students' academic careers. New media enrichments for students, whether they are in a special education program, in advanced placement classes, or for neurotypical grade-level students, exist without the need to evaluate their academic viability or usefulness. This is placed in the context of STEM curriculum, which is intended to provide a more diverse approach to standard science curriculum, giving students new tools to better compete in the world after graduation. With many companies looking to hire more people with autism, or to employ more diverse voices (such as Indigenous peoples), augmented reality is a way of expanding the traditional STEM curriculum into something that is more akin to a well-rounded humanities-based education.

As the author is a special education teacher and teaching artist in Alaska, various enrichment projects based in AR will be discussed, as well as multimedia projects that though they do not fall under the rubric of augmented reality, are quintessential to a well-rounded humanities education that focuses on Indigenous ways of being and knowing, as well as Alaskan specific enrichments that will produce students that have a broader education inside of their general academic careers. Indigenized education is a way of infusing the local Indigenous culture into core curriculum, replacing the given content with more appropriate local cultures. Many educators refer to this as 'decolonizing education', but the term 'Indigenizing education' is a solution-focused approach to replacement curriculum, that will be used here. 'Decolonizing' as a term is problematic, in that it does not always solve any of the issues posed by dominant cultures, it simply works as something akin to a Band-Aid for the horrors of colonization, and does not do well in addressing the actual injustices of colonized thinking. Indigenizing is a philosophical reversal of this trend.

20.2   Molly of Denali Versus Clutch Cargo

With Alaska in the twenty-first century, more aspects of its culture are manifesting in new media formats. The videogame *Never Alone*, being one of the most obvious examples, another visible one being the PBS Kids show *Molly of Denali*. In *Molly of Denali* (Fig. 20.1), we have the first-time that a national Alaska Native children's show has Alaska Native writers and cultural experts on hand. For example, Molly is a Gwich'iin/Koyukon/Dena'ina girl, who lives in Interior Alaska, in the fictional village of Qyah. She uses Athabascan words throughout every episode, and the cultural stuff all around her is from the correct culture, rather than the standard non-specific, stereotypical Alaskana seen elsewhere on TV shows such as *Northern Exposure*. The *Molly of Denali* episode 'Crane Song', written by Princess Daazrhaii Johnson (Neets'aii Gwich'in) tells a story of how Molly helps two white biologists, Nina and Dr. Antigone band baby sandhill cranes for study, while paying respect to the natural world and environment.

Take this in comparison to an episode of *Clutch Cargo* from 1959, entitled 'Arctic Bird Giant', made famous for being in the Quentin Tarantino cult-classic *Pulp Fiction*. In 'Arctic Bird Giant', cultures from all over Alaska are mixed together with a bit of cultural misappropriation. The episode focuses on a totem pole (which are produced by cultural groups in Southeast Alaska, not Arctic peoples) which is misused here as a landmark in an Inuit setting, and a supernatural bird creature stealing cargo from a white ship captain, frozen in place for the winter. The voice of the Inuk man in the episode, Snowshoe Slednick (Fig. 20.2), is the same racist character voice

Fig. 20.1 Molly of Denali (2019). PBS Kids

Fig. 20.2 Snowshoe
Slednick on Clutch Cargo
(Cambria Productions 1959).
First use of syncro-vox
technology to create cheap
animations (early example of
augmented virtuality)

movies and television from that time period would use for Asians, this time applied
to an Inuk man using a bunch of made-up gobbledygook 'Eskimo' words. He is a
simpleton and even ends up hiding in an ice cream truck because it is too hot for him
while he is waiting for the show's heroes to get ready. The show employs a repetitive
make believe phrase, ad nauseum, which the white characters start to use at the end,
after the captain's 'igloo housing complex, with televisions in every igloo' housing
project is constructed.

Fig. 20.3 Molly of Denali (2019). PBS Kids

Clutch Cargo was an animated series from 1959 to 1960 about an adventurer named Clutch Cargo, who traveled the world on insane assignments. There are 52 episodes in the series. The episodes are broken down into five separate four minute-long segments, collectively creating a full story. What is fascinating here, apart from the culturally inappropriate stuff, is that *Clutch Cargo* was the first show to use Syncro-Vox, one of the earliest examples of augmented virtuality. Syncro-Vox was a low-budget way to make animations with synchronized sound. It took video of real human mouths and superimposed it over animated characters, producing a bizarre and unsettlingly ludicrous effect. *Clutch Cargo* employed Syncro-Vox as a time and money saver, to be able to produce more animations at lower costs.

Compare this to the episode of *Molly of Denali* entitled 'New Nivagi' (Fig. 20.3), written by Vera Starbard (Tlingit/Dena'ina) where Molly enters a nivagi contest using her grandfather's recipe. 'Nivagi' is the Dena'ina word for 'Alaska Native ice cream', or 'Indian ice cream', more commonly referred to as 'agutaq' in Alaska. Agutaq is also called 'Eskimo ice cream', and is made from animal fat, berries and dry fish. Nivagi is the appropriate term for the kind of ice cream Molly and her family would make, and the recipe they use is one Southcentral and Interior Alaskans would be familiar with: whipped moose fat, dried moose meat, wild carrots and wild strawberries. In the episode, Molly loses the first batch of nivagi, and has to create her own. It is too late in the season for her to harvest wild strawberries, and she has to remember what her family taught her to collect wild carrots. She improvises by using wild cranberries, and she ends up creating a new recipe for nivagi that her grandfather exclaims is even better than his recipe. These are not little things in terms of cultural values. They illustrate perfectly the resourcefulness and creative problem-solving that is highly regarded in Koyukon and all other Alaskan cultures, and also provides insight to how Alaskan cultures change over time, and are not cultures relegated to history, but rather living cultures.

20.3 The Cannibal Giant

The Cannibal Giant, or the Origin of Mosquitos is a Tlingit story from Klukwan, about a giant who steals salmon from a Tlingit village, then begins eating villagers when the salmon runs out. Eventually the village decides to kill him and they go to his cabin in the mountains and trap him in a bear pit, where they then set him on fire. As he is burning alive, he is screaming curses at the villagers saying he will continue to eat them in perpetuity, at which time the cinders from his flaming body begin falling on the villagers, biting them, while magically turning into mosquitos. This is the Tlingit story of how mosquitos came to be.

In the summer of 2018, the author ran an augmented reality workshop for elementary school children as part of SNEP, the Sitka Native Education Program. In the augmented reality program students explored *The Cannibal Giant* using a combination of target-based augmented reality and sprite editors (Fig. 20.4). Students were told the story and broke it down into a series of sentences, which they illustrated using a sprite editor on iPads (Fig. 20.5), which they augmented with videos of them reciting the sentence they were given to illustrate. Of note here too is that when the students were taught sprite editing, they were taught the math of creating pixel drawings: bitmaps, pixmaps and factors of 2. These were also done in an Indigenized way, through Tlingit culture: at the beginning of the dive into sprite editing, they were only allowed the usage of the traditional Tlingit colors: black, white, blue and red; as those colors are the main colors used in Formline design and totem pole making

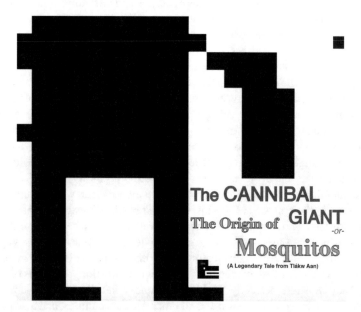

Fig. 20.4 The Cannibal Giant, or the Origin of Mosquitos (Sitka Native Education Program and Shafer 2018). Augmented reality picture book

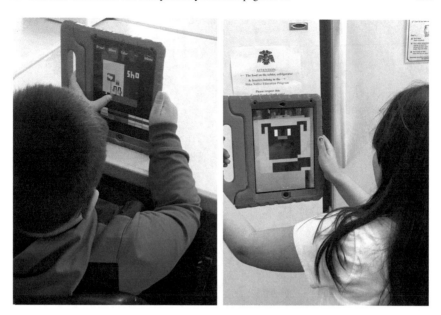

Fig. 20.5 SNEP AR Summer Enrichment (2018)

(Fig. 20.6). As the students got better at designing sprites in traditional Tlingit colors, they began to incorporate the rest of the color spectrum into their work, learning how digital colors work in relationship to physical colors with paint and pencils.

As part of this summer enrichment program Shafer also created a series of educational videos for teachers in the Sitka School District. The district had recently bought the Adobe Suite for all of its teachers, and was interested in having them add more digital media into their classrooms. They were especially interested in augmented reality being used by their teachers. With the collaboration of SNEP, Shafer created *Languages of the Face, an Augmented Portrait* (Fig. 20.7), using Photoshop and HP Reveal; as well as a multipart tutorial on how to build Lego blocks in Sketch-up and then place them in an augmented reality geolayer, using the Layar app. *Languages of the Face* gave teachers a method for incorporating Alaska Native languages into an augmented reality project for kids. Shafer's video used two Alaska Native languages: Deg Xinag, spoken by the Deg Hitan people of western Alaska, and Łingit, the language of the Tlingit people, spoken in southeast Alaska. Deg Xinag translations were provided by George Demintieff Holly, the Łingit translations were provided by Nancy Douglas, of SNEP.

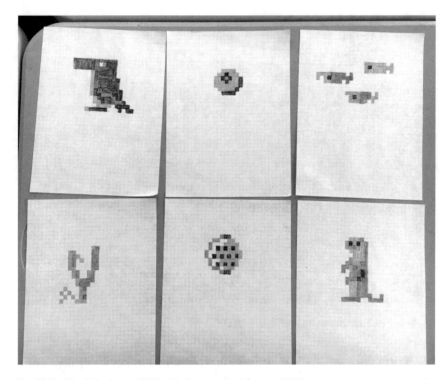

Fig. 20.6 Tlingit Sprites at SNEP AR Summer Enrichment (2018)

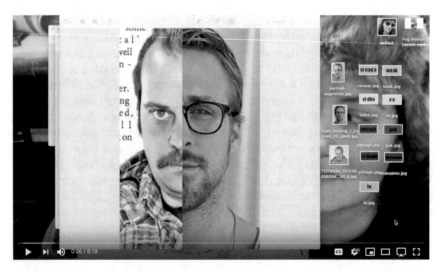

Fig. 20.7 Languages of the Face, and Augmented Portrait (Shafer 2018). Video, augmented reality

20.4 Ya Ne Dah Ah, Dimi Macheras

Dimi Macheras's Ya Ne Dah Ah comic books are sometimes referred to as Ahtna Manga, similar to the nomenclature of Haida illustrator Michael Nicoll Yahgulanaas's Haida Manga books, like *Red* or *War of the Blink*. Macheras's Ahtna Manga stories include three traditional Ahtna Ya Ne Dah Ah (the Ahtna word for legendary tales): *Besiin* (The Owl Story), *Tsaani* (The Grizzly Bear Story) and *C'eyiige' Hwnax* (The Magic House).

Every issue of the Ya Ne Dah Ah opens with some thoughts by Katie Wade, who was a matriarch and leader in the Ahtna Village of Chickaloon, Macheras's grandmother, and author of the memoir *Chickaloon Spirit*, amongst many other things. These openings explain how the stories were told and used by Ahtna, "Since the beginning of time, people were able to communicate with all living things as if they were human beings… Since then these stories were told to the children by their elders… stories were told as a reward to the children… These Ya Ne Dah Ah stories teach children to behave and be respectful… A parent doesn't have to nag and whine to discipline their children. They only have to tell a child, "you are acting like so and so in the stories" and it brings them to attention" (Wade 2005).

Macheras illustrates these three tales in a fantastic and updated manner. The characters employ both modern and Ancestral dress. For example, *C'eyiige' Hwnax* (Fig. 20.8), is a story about Saghani (Raven), Ciił ya (Lynx) and Tsucde (Grandma). Tsucde is in traditional Ahtna clothes, while Lynx is in modern attire and Saghani wears only shoes and a backpack. The combination of all of these together creates a timeless world, where the Ya Ne Dah Ah exist forever. The story itself follows Ciił ya as he comes upon a magic house in the woods one day after he had developed a great hunger from walking. He goes inside and politely greets the spirits of the house, who then offer him food, for which he thanks their hospitality. When Saghani hears of the magic house, he decides to go find it. When he does, he enters without knocking, and this makes the house spirits laugh, which makes Saghani angry and he starts to smash up the house. He then stuffs his backpack full of all the food he can and runs back home, leaving a trail of food. As he is arriving home, a whirlwind of the spirits from the house attack him, and take all of the stolen food back (Fig. 20.9). The story teaches children to be polite, not to enter homes uninvited, or to never take everything, to respect other people's things.

Besiin (Fig. 20.10) is a tale about why one should never spoil their children. It is about a baby who starts crying one night, and is inconsolable. Everyone in the village tries to settle him, but eventually leaves him crying, as they all go to bed. The baby's crying is keeping Besiin awake. An angry Besiin decides to go quiet the child up, so he catches a little fish and ties it to the end of a string, and puts glue on it. Besiin then drops the fish on a string through the top opening of the teepee the baby is in. The baby grabs the fish and is caught by Besiin, who flies him up to his nest. He then begins singing and scratching up the baby's face. The village takes notice the baby is missing and looks for him. They hear Besiin singing his terrible song and notice he has the baby. Besiin refuses to give the baby back, so the baby's uncle

Fig. 20.8 C'eyiige' Hwanx
(The Magic House)
(Macheras 2005). Ya Ne Dah
Ah Comic Book

gets his hatchet and defeats Besiin, saving the baby. The family then disinfects the wounds on the baby's face with urine, which hurts the baby a great deal. The lesson learned is that spoiled children will cry too much for no good reason. Macheras illustrated the comic in black and white with yellow texts, which set a tone of horror. The illustrations of the Uncle, as he transforms into the hatchet-wielding hero, are amazingly out of time, but yet so present in the Ahtna imagination of the past.

Every Ya Ne Dah Ah comic ends with the common Ahtna expression, "Saen kudusaat. Xay kudutdiye." ("Let winter be short. Let summer be long.").

Fig. 20.9 Food is taken back from Saghani from C'eyiige Hwanx (Macheras 2005). Ya Ne Dah Ah Comic Book

20.5   Wintermoot Limited Series

The Wintermoot Series is a limited run, augmented reality comic book series by Nathan Shafer. *Wintermoot Book One: Aqpik and Mars Apple* came out in January of 2019 (Fig. 20.11). It is a cyberpunk story about two Iñupiat superheroes, mother and daughter, Aqpik and Mars Apple. The comic book seeks to accurately depict Iñupiat culture in the context of a science fiction/superhero genre. This includes usage of the Kuawarek dialect of Iñupiatun and cultural norms used in a non-generic way, things like the traditional facial tattoos worn by Iñupiat women. Aqpik's tavlugun (chin tattoos) were designed by Iñupiaq artist Holly Nordlum.

Wintermoot creates a series of Alaskan superheroes that attempt to appropriately reflect Alaskan cultures by collaboratively designing them with other Alaskans. Every installment in the series focuses around a new character, representing different cultures in Alaska. *Wintermoot* is a regional work of genre fiction and employs the same tropes of cape and cowl superhero comics: multiple realities, masks, alien technology, secret societies, and apocalyptic crossover events (Fig. 20.12).

These tropes, when possible are Indigenized, for example, rather than wearing masks, Aqpik and Mars Apple wear traditional snow goggles, as have been worn for thousands of years by the Iñupiat people. In *Book Two: Sourdough and Arête,*

Fig. 20.10 Besiin
(Macheras 2005). Ya Ne Dah
Ah

the cowl is replaced by a sea lion gut hooded parka, worn a mysterious Unangan
character created by David Karabelnikoff and Nathan Shafer (Fig. 20.13).

The augmented reality features inside of *Wintermoot* are literary in nature, they
work to translate the Indigenous languages in the comic, and retell the stories from the
vantage point of another character. Occasionally they expound on the text by offering
vital statistics and information about the characters in the comic book (Fig. 20.14).
In Book One, the augments tell the story from the point of view of Aqpik's daughter,
Mars Apple, as she watches her mother succumb to an extraterrestrial AI, and fall
to Earth, as she is uploading herself into an ancient simulation that exists on Earth
called Cyberingia.

Fig. 20.11 Wintermoot
Book One Aqpik and Mars
Apple (Shafer 2019).
Augmented reality comic
book

20.6   Peer Art Year One: Timeosaurs

In the two sections on the Peer Art class taught by the author, great care has been taken
to keep FERPA information of the participating children confidential. To protect their
anonymity, names have been changed, as well as confidential information related to
who they are. Permission has been given for some of their artwork to be shared, but
for the most part, imagery from the Peer Art class is not included, so that the students
are able to keep their privacy. Most of the information contained herein is anecdotal
in nature, and may not reflect the actual situations as they were.

In the first year of the Peer Art class, at Wendler Middle School in Anchorage, the
class built a videogame together. Due to time constraints and student skill sets, the
class decided on an AR-based videogame that they could continue to work on over
the years, after the initial groundwork was laid out. Each student in the class created
sprites using an on-line sprite editor, and exported these sprites into a 3D modeling
program and game engine.

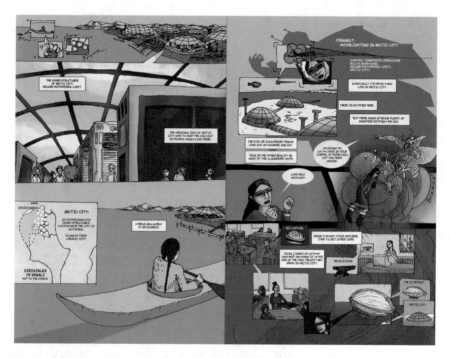

Fig. 20.12 Interior spread from Wintermoot Book One (Shafer 2019). Augmented reality comic book

The game was split up into the three Mesozoic time periods, the ages of dinosaurs: Triassic, Jurassic and Cretaceous (Fig. 20.15). The game was further split up into levels, each having variations based on the Mesozoic ages. The levels were based on the worlds in Nintendo's Mario Bros. franchise: water, air, volcano, etc. Every Mesozoic age was characterized by different eras of videogame history: the Triassic was 8-bit 2D sprites, the Jurassic features 3D characters in 2D environments, and the Cretaceous was an open 3D world, with 3D characters.

The story in the *Timeosaurs* game was that a humanoid dinosaur from the Cretaceous finds a magic mirror and tries to pick it up, where it proceeds to drop and shatter into several pieces. The shards of mirror sink into the fossil layer, throwing the main character into a time-traveling adventure to put all of the pieces back together, and restore the timeline. As this premise for the videogame was more than the middle school students could possibly handle in a class during an academic school year, goals were set for students to produce sprites and texture maps to skin 3D models with.

It is important to note here that to effectively teach an art class to students with autism (and the Peer Art class roster is around 15–20), there are a few things that need to be set in place. Many students with autism spectrum have something called rigid creativity, which is usually locked into their preferred interests, for example, a student may be very artistic, but only wants to trace pictures of dragons, because

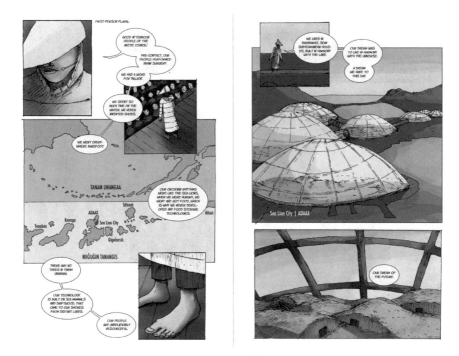

Fig. 20.13 Double page spread of Sngax-Six (Shafer 2019). Augmented reality comic book

dragons are what they like. They may find the notion of tracing a unicorn offensive. He or she may only like dragons from anime, and not want to trace dragons from ancient Chinese sources, or they may get upset by the inclusion of dragons from *Lord of the Rings* or *Game of Thrones*. Then again, they may only like tracing the dragons because they do not want to mess up the way the dragons look online (read in *reality* here), and is completely fine with whatever kinds of dragons there are out there. This rigid creativity comes in a spectrum, and it swings the other way as well. Many students have context blindness or don't understand nonverbal communications, so things like demoing art projects can get tricky. It is inadvisable to have too many examples, to instruct for too long before a hands-on activity, or to go over the same things too much.

To explain, if a teacher in an SLC wants students to make a drawing of their favorite animal, they have to use very specific and controlled language. If the teacher says, "my favorite animal is a dog," and then proceeds to draw a dog in front of the students as an example of what they need to now do, almost all of the students will then go back to their areas and draw a picture of a dog. Many will not process the creative problem solving implied in the instruction, "you need to think of and draw YOUR own favorite animal."

A more effective way to approach this would be to say, "I am going to ask you to think of something, but you can't blurt out your answer. You have to think it quietly.

Fig. 20.14 Augment from Wintermoot Book Two (Shafer 2019). Augmented reality comic book

Fig. 20.15 Brainstorming Session for Timeosaurs (Peer Art Class 2018). Dry erase marker on blackboard

You are going to draw a picture of your favorite animal. I want you to silently think of you favorite animal, and put your head down at your area when you have thought of it. Don't say it out loud. While your head is down I want you to think of how you want to draw it. When you look ready, I will hand out the paper and you can start."

Some students of course will still be caught up in the rigidity of their own thinking here. For example, the notion of having a favorite animal may be completely ridiculous to them, or they may copy someone else's favorite animal because they are trying to fit in. The most important thing is instructing them for a classroom art assignment without giving them a solid example, because they will just copy any specifics that are offered. If you draw a picture of a slice of pizza and then tell them to draw a picture of something they like to eat, they will mostly draw slices of pizza.

To demo new media projects, students with autism need to have the specific behaviors modeled, but not fully completed. To further explain, if one is demoing how to 3D model a home, do not complete the entire model in the demo. Demo the tools that they need to use one at a time to make the home in the 3D modeling program. The students will need processing time between each new tool they are learning, to be able to connect it to their creative problem-solving skills, by physically doing it, learning it kinesthetically. This works for learning simple augmented reality animations. Show the method of placing an animation on top of a static image, after they have already completed their own unique animations. Once they learn the process, they will be able to think creatively with it, rather than replicate the demonstrations, like they would do if the entire process had been done from beginning to end in the demo. This is the same idea as not handing a student with autism a large packet of work to be completed, but rather hand them one-page assignments one by one, as they complete them.

Along with processing time for learning new skills, students on the autism spectrum tend to learn in similar formats to their neurotypical peers. For example, differentiating educational methods can be helpful for both neurotypical students and special education students, simply by approaching curriculum from different ways. Data on the usages of differentiated teaching methods is not very robust (Harvard 2017) and doesn't take several mitigating factors into the equation, but changing up the way information is delivered to students at least breaks up the tedium of lectures.

There is an educational philosophy that looks at basic differentiation of educational materials as a 'pyramid of learning' (based on the notion of different learning styles (auditory, visual and kinesthetic). The fact that the learning pyramid is built upon the neuromyth of different learning styles (A-V-K) should be indicator enough. The biggest issue inherent in the 'pyramid of learning' approach is that it is reliant on retention rates, in the pyramid, lectures produce only a 5% retention rate, while teaching others produces a 90% retention rate. The metrics used to come to these conclusions were produced by the National Training Laboratories and do not add up to effectively show educational growth as retention rates do not necessarily create better educated students. The methods of 'different learning styles' and 'the pyramid of learning' are developed solely to sell third-party curriculum to school districts. This is one of the banes of the American educational system, as third-party curriculum eats a large portion of school budgets and creates an unhealthy administration based-approach to supersede teachers. What is more needed is autonomy on the part of teachers, particularly special educators, to choose the educational methodologies that best fit the needs of their students.

Using differentiated instruction has been part of special education practices for years. In the Peer Art class, differentiation of materials meets several educational services that are built into the IEPs (Individualized Education Programs) for students. For example, students with social communication, or functional language deficits have a need for peer-based instruction to learn social skills. Having students do collaborative art projects does the same thing for students with IEPs as speech/language or occupational therapy services, whether the retention rates are better or not. Arts education as part of a larger humanities-based educational process seeks to create a broader and more diverse brain in a person. Simply put, retention rates are not the same thing as learning, which is the same issue with the inclusion of augmented reality in an educational program. If we view it simply as an enrichment, which seeks to improve the quality of education regardless of results, the anxiety of results-based instruction, such as teaching to the test dissolves, and students are permitted to learn in a way that they can hold on to the things they connect with, and simply experience everything else as *enrichment extras.*

To illustrate, one of the students in the Peer Art class, Gary, who is on the autism spectrum, is obsessed with dinosaurs. It is among the most significant of his preferred interests, and something he would spend a great deal of time talking about and making pictures of. At the beginning of the class, one of the neurotypical peers had noticed Gary's love of dinosaurs and had offered the idea of making the videogame about dinosaurs, as Gary also had impulse control issues and would often very vocally refuse to participate in class.

Once Gary heard the class brainstorming a videogame about dinosaurs, while he was refusing to participate in class by spinning in a swivel chair and telling people they were 'ugly'—became very interested in participating in the brainstorming sessions. With the class, he drew pictures, explained all of the different dinosaurs and Mesozoic time periods, and the extinction event, to all of the other students. Together, they decided to set the dinosaur story in Alaska, and so the dinosaurs that they were going to design were going to be based on the dinosaurs that actually lived in Alaska during the Mesozoic. As an aid to this, they watched and discussed many times over the movie *Walking with Dinosaurs*, from 2013.

In *Walking with Dinosaurs* (Fig. 20.16), the story begins in Kodiak, as a paleontologist is out in the woods and runs into a talking raven. (This is a very Alaskan story at the beginning.) Magically, the talking raven turns into a talking Alexornis (an ancient species not too dissimilar from a raven). The alexornis, called Alex in the movie, then begins to tell the tale of Patchi. Patchi is a pachyrhinosaurus, a species that lived during the Late Cretaceous, around 70 million years ago. The Peer Art students decided to make the main character a humanoid pachyrhinosaurus from the Late Cretaceous.

In keeping with the theme of the Late Cretaceous, in 2019, comic book artist Tadd Galusha produced a wordless graphic novel set in the late Cretaceous, about a young Tyrannosaurus Rex who gets separated from his family, entitled *Cretaceous*

Fig. 20.16 Walking with Dinosaurs (Reliance Entertainment 2013). Feature-length movie

(Fig. 20.17a). The artwork in the graphic novel published by Oni Press is wonderfully illustrated, capable of telling an epic tale without any dialogue or text, save for a few onomatopoeias during action sequences. In terms of special education, the book is substantial in that it can get readers who struggle with reading to go through an entire book, and tell themselves the story they are seeing simply by reading the pictures, such as the sequences of death peppered throughout the book (Fig. 20.17b).

For readers in an SLC setting, it provides pathways for readers struggling with functional language, or communication deficits, to employ their creative problem-solving abilities to understand a story. The fact that the characters are all dinosaurs, only helps with readers who struggle to identify facial expressions, and instead offers them a chance to think about the emotions that the characters of *Cretaceous* are feeling. This may indeed work more effectively with people on the autism spectrum who struggle in this area, as it does not produce 'social fakes' as a result, but rather empathetic responses to emotional expression, regardless of the species involved. The same can be said for robots and the autistic brain: where children with autism are more in tune with the emotional condition of say R2D2 and C-3PO than their human counterparts. Moby, the wily robot sidekick from the BrainPOP series of educational videos, communicates in only beeps and shenanigans, but is an endless vault of non-verbal communication, which is easily read by students on the autism spectrum. In the end, the ability to read and understand non-verbal communication is a major educational goal for students on the autism spectrum.

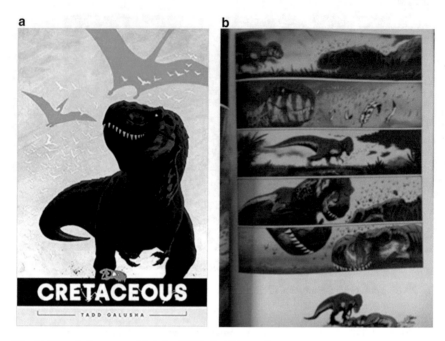

Fig. 20.17 a, **b** Cretaceous (Galusha 2019). Graphic novel

20.7 Peer Art Year Two: Interplanetary Human Spaghetti

At the end of the first year of the Peer Art program, two kids started to hang around the SLC. One was Jean-Louis, a tall, athletic Samoan boy with autism, who had not been receiving the appropriate SPED services, and was slated to start being in the Wendler SLC the following year. The other was Daphne, John-Louis's best friend, an African-American girl, who did not have autism, but was right at home being around the other students in the SLC. Jean-Louis and Daphne are manga-loving metal-heads, which at first was a little scary to the sound-sensitive SLC students, but soon they were getting along with everyone just fine. Daphne and Jean-Louis were also making a comic book together, which they began sharing with all of the other students, regaling them with absurd stories of semi-appropriate characters of whom were battling with the nature of existence.

When it became apparent that both Daphne and Jean-Louis were going to be in the Peer Art program, it was decided that the next year would be a yearlong project in augmented comic books. There would be one big class project, and the kids could do individual pieces. Jobs would be divided and teams made.

The structure of the Peer Art class was developed the way that other Structured Learning classes are. For example, many people on the autism spectrum have context blindness, and need extra supports given to them to help them understand what is being asked of them. Many of them also get stressed out by unpredictability in their daily routines, and require supports that will help them negotiate them. To deal with this, Structured Learning classes create class routines that are predictable, so that students will start feeling comfortable in the predictability of the class and be able to take in the educational content in a more significant way.

What is notable here is the way Indigenous knowledge is integrated in terms of predictability. Anchorage is in Dena'ina Ełnena, the Dena'ina homeland. The Dena'ina are a Dene (Athabascan) group in Alaska. There are many Dene groups in Alaska, each with their own language, and many cultural similarities—one important similarity was noted by cultural anthropologist Dr. Alan Boraas—the definition of 'evil' in northern storytelling traditions.

In the circumpolar north, there are long periods of cold and dark, which are terms usually relegated to a negative metaphorical connotation. Evil characters from more southerly cultures associate coldness and darkness with a negativity and evilness. This is not the way that cultures of the north see the cold, or the dark. In Dena'ina stories, characters are rarely purely good or purely bad, characters like Gujun, a shape-shifter from Dena'ina stories, sometimes does good things, and sometimes bad. Characters that are both good and bad can be frustrating for western audiences, but are reflections of the way humans truly are. Raven from Alaskan stories is another example of a character on the spectrum of good and evil, one who can play many different roles, is a shape-shifter and a trickster.

The few characters that are purely evil in Dena'ina stories tend to not be associated with things like coldness or darkness, but rather unpredictability. Evil characters are chaotic, characters like *Gilyaq* or *Nch'et'eni*. The association of chaos with badness fits perfectly with the notion of building classroom routines that insert predictable structures into daily routines to ease the minds of students with autism.

In the Peer Art classroom Dena'ina culture was blended into the curriculum from the start, beginning with *K'eła Sukdu* (The Mouse Story) as told by Peter Kalifornsky, a Dena'ina storyteller from Yaghanen (Kenai), the homeland of the Kenaitze Dena'ina. *K'eła Sukdu* (Fig. 20.18) is a tale that folds in the Dena'ina character Gujun, who is a benevolent (neutral good) figure in this story. In *K'eła Sukdu*, a lazy young man is not helping with the annual salmon harvesting and begins wandering the forest, where he runs into a mouse trying to get over a windfall. The young man helps the mouse get over it. That winter, the tribe is starving, and the young man returns to the woods to wander around, and runs into a magical woman who invites him into her abode. There, they wait for her husband, who ends up being Gujun. Gujun tells the young man that had shape-shifted into that mouse he helped out in the summer, and that he was grateful to him for his kindness, and then prepares a magical satchel full of food for the young man and his tribe. The young man returns to his people with food and they survive the winter.

Kalifornsky's version of *K'eła Sukdu* (Kalifornsky 1991) was read to Peer Art students on day one and set the tone for the rest of the year. This was followed by an explanation of the Dena'ina worldview of history, which they break down into three eras. The first is the 'time when the animals could talk', when animals existed in their human forms. The second is the 'Coming of the Campfire People' (what the animals call the Dena'ina people), and the third is the era of the 'Under-the-Water People'

Fig. 20.18 K'eła Sukdu
(Peter Kalifornsky)

(what the Dena'ina call white people). This worldview is explained by Boraas, in the book *Dena'ina Huch'ulyeshi: The Dena'ina Way of Living*, in his essay, '"What is Good, What is No Good": The Traditional Dena'ina Worldview' (Boraas 2014).

During the second year of the Peer Art class, Shafer was creating two issues of *Wintermoot* featuring a Dena'ina superhero named Arête, who is also on the autism spectrum (Fig. 20.19). In the third issue of *Wintermoot*, Arête is searching for a villain who has stolen from biotech from secret facility in Whittier, Alaska, named Blood Snow Pioneer. One of the augmented comic projects in the Peer Art class was the backstory of Blood Snow Pioneer. Blood Snow Pioneer is a villain in the traditional Dena'ina fashion. His actions are chaotic and unpredictable. Peer Art students brainstormed what this would like, as he would be a villain specific to Arête. Arête has glacier powers, which were given to her by the Ł i Dnay (the Glacier People from Dena'ina stories), so Blood Snow Pioneer would be a villain with similar ice powers, but his would be chaotic. Students developed him as a French-Canadian vampire who can manipulate microorganisms. He would travel in a vehicle that was based on the structure of an amoeba, called the 'Amoebile' (Fig. 20.20). Blood snow, also called watermelon snow, is a dark red microorganism affecting snow and glaciers, which is right in line with Blood Snow Pioneer's super powers. Blood Snow Pioneer also has an algae laser, which he shoots out of a modified Super-Soaker.

For one of the longer augmented comic projects, students created a storyline for the villain to be interpreted differently by everyone. The storyline was to be basic,

Fig. 20.19 Wintermoot Book Three (Shafer 2019). Augmented reality comic book

Fig. 20.20 Amoebile
Design Concepts (Peer Art
2019)

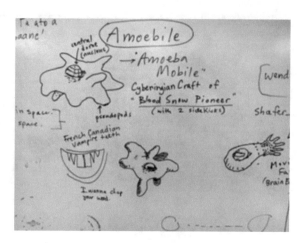

and provide an origin story for Blood Snow Pioneer, though it did not necessarily have to be him. The stories were collectively called *Interplanetary Human Spaghetti*. The structure was set up to only be a few key points that every student had to use.

All *Interplanetary Human Spaghetti* comics must include:

(1) A man is marooned in space from a space ship.
(2) A colony of bacteria begins to grow on the outside of his spacesuit.
(3) The bacteria colony evolves into a miniature civilization.
(4) A Super-Soaker needs to be involved.
(5) The man and bacteria colony are sucked into a black hole.

The collective name of the stories *Interplanetary Human Spaghetti,* is an idiom developed by the class to poetically refer to being pulled into a black hole.

20.8 STEM/Conclusion

Augmented reality as a new media practice is squarely situated in the context of STEM pedagogy (Science Technology Engineering Math), but AR blends in other fields of study/practice that are not necessarily STEM-themed, and tend to fall under the aegis of humanities enrichments. As enrichment strategy for all students, including special education, augmented reality offers a format that can move between the dichotomy of STEM and humanities-based education. Indigenizing curriculum for STEM education through the rubric of augmented reality offers new methods of engaging students in content that may otherwise go unmentioned, as both enrichment and Indigenization are treated as supplemental curriculum to broaden the educational benefits for students who are already performing beyond standards, and are often exempt from standardized testing strictures. As augmented reality begins to blend into pedagogical structures of the twenty-first century, there will be many new methods of helping students who perform poorly on standardized tests, to become better learners, and more empathetic thinkers, without the need for referring to them as enrichments, in much the same way that other computer guided pedagogy is used today.

In Shafer's Peer Art program there is a method at play that seeks to bring together Indigenized curriculum based on regional specificity and new media pedagogy to meet the educational needs of students with exceptionalities. Students with autism populate a unique sub-group of instructional methodologies that require differentiation and individualized learning strategies only moderately different than the way enrichments are used with gifted students. With the increase of the importance of STEM in American educational models, special education has not met these updates in lieu of increasing curriculum to meet special education standards, to met federal guidelines for differentiated education and increase standardized test scores. Special education students should have access the same access to STEM enrichments, including augmented reality.

References

Galusha T (2019) Cretaceous. Oni Press, Portland

Harvard B (2017) The pyramid of myth. https://theeffortfuleducator.com/2017/11/29/the-pyramid-of-myth/. Accessed 15 Sept 2019

Kalifornsky P (1991) A dena'ina legacy k'tl'egh'I sukdu: the collected writings of peter kalifornsky. Alaska Native Language Center, Fairbanks

Macheras D (2005) Ya ne dah ah stories: the magic house, the owl story and the grizzly bear story. Nay'dini'aa Na' Publishing, Chickaloon

Shafer N (2019) Wintermoot limited series, book one: aqpik and mars apple, book two: sourdough and arête, book three: arête and anthrome. Shared Universe, Anchorage

Wade K (2005) Ya ne dah ah stories: the magic house, the owl story and the grizzly bear story. Nay'dini'aa Na' Publishing, Chickaloon

Concluding Remarks

Vladimir Geroimenko

This book has provided the reader with an extensive and detailed research into the educational use of augmented reality, covering a wide range of topics, areas and applications: from mining engineering to foreign language and fine art education, from chemistry to medical and dental training.

Augmented Reality is a relatively new tool in education and training, but it has already positively affected the conventional learning process by providing new ways of teaching and by creating a completely different learning experience. It has facilitated teaching and learning methodologies and open new approaches to education by turning an ordinary class into an engaging experience. Augmented Reality offers solutions for faster and more effective learning, namely active learning with much more fun and with an everlasting 'wow factor'. Also, it adds creativity and interactivity, and simplifies the learning process of complex and abstract subjects.

Augmented Reality technology can be used in the entire range of educational establishments—from pre-school and higher education to corporate and special training, because it offers an almost unlimited amount of practical applications and can be incorporated into nearly any subject. For example, this technology is able to simulate potentially dangerous situations and so to let students and trainees prepare for critical circumstances and, without endangering themselves, to master their actions in such situations. In the same way, students can perform practical experiments without having a dedicated physical lab.

Augmented Reality is changing the conventional learning model. It provides novel approaches and tools for encouraging and motivating students, making learning more engaging and bringing in the elements of interaction and creativity, self-learning and self-exploring, adding gaming elements to support textbook materials, improving learning efficiency. In other words, Augmented Reality is transforming the education industry by making lessons fun learning. Following the widespread use of smartphones and other mobile devices, it has become easily accessible for most young people. Students simply need to employ their own devices and free Augmented Reality apps.

© Springer Nature Switzerland AG 2020
V. Geroimenko (ed.), *Augmented Reality in Education*,
Springer Series on Cultural Computing,
https://doi.org/10.1007/978-3-030-42156-4

In general, however, the use of Augmented Reality is not intended to replace traditional teaching materials, but to augment them by adding a valuable and stimulating layer of digital information in an interactive multimedia format, such as 3D objects, scenes and environments, audio and soundscapes, video and text. In other words, Augmented Reality is the future of education in the sense that traditional textbooks and practical assignments will hardly be acceptable by students if they lack of an interactive and engaging Augmented Reality content. The static two-dimensional world of educational texts and illustrations should definitely be enhanced with three-dimensional multimedia objects, delivered by Augmented Reality technology and discoverable by students' own smartphones and tablet computers. Just as it is impossible to imagine today's textbooks without illustrations, the textbooks of tomorrow will not be imaginable without an extra layer of digital information. The textbooks' traditional structure 'text + illustrations' will be replaced with a more efficient one, namely 'text + illustrations + AR content'. Of course, textbooks and other written teaching materials will remain the main, but not the only one of many areas where educational Augmented Reality can be used. It will go beyond textbooks to classrooms, labs, operating theatres and other physical locations and environments.

The novel technology for teaching and learning, thoroughly considered in this book, will significantly transform the education industry, because this technology allows not only to augment teaching material with interactive and informative digital objects, but also to 'augment' students with motivation and fun.

Printed in the United States
by Baker & Taylor Publisher Services